Great Americana

WITHDRAWN

Sources of the Mississippi
and the Western Louisiana Territory

Zebulon Montgomery Pike

affirmed American rights to the territory and told them that they were "at no time and on no pretence whatever to hoist, or suffer to be hoisted, the English flag."

After his return to St. Louis in 1806, Pike received orders to lead another expedition. This time he was to locate the sources of the Arkansas and Red Rivers and to reconnoiter the Spanish border area. Pike's journey took him across the vast western prairies which, interestingly enough, he believed would provide a beneficial check against over-expansion, "our citizens being so prone to rambling and extending themselves, on the frontiers."

After Pike entered what is today the state of Colorado and after he attempted unsuccessfully to scale the mountain peak which now bears his name, he led his men southward and reached a branch of the Rio Grande River. There he was taken into custody by Spanish troops. Brought first to Santa Fe, and then interviewed by the Spanish general at Chihuahua, Pike and his men were permitted to travel eastward, under Spanish military escort, through Texas, and to cross back into United States territory in 1807. Outspoken in his criticism of the Spanish regimé, Pike was reprimanded by the Spaniards for voicing opinions during the trip which "if generally disseminated, would in a very few years be the occasion of a revolt of those kingdoms." Despite speculation that Pike may have been a party to the Burr-Wilkinson conspiracy to establish an empire in the Southwest, independent of the United States, evidence to support such a charge is lacking.

Pike supplemented his journals with appendices in which he inserted copies of his correspondence with General Wilkinson, his speeches to the Indians, and detailed descriptions of the country through which he passed. In many respects the appendix material possesses a greater value than the journals. A useful study of Pike and his journals is provided by W. Eugene Hollon, *The Lost Pathfinder—Zebulon Montgomery Pike* (Norman, Oklahoma, 1949). Also helpful is the preface of Elliott Coues to his edition of *The Expeditions of Zebulon Montgomery Pike* (New York, 1895), I, v-xviii.

Foreword

When the United States purchased the Louisiana Territory from France in 1803, reliable information about the region was virtually nonexistent. The explorations of Lewis and Clark in 1803-1806 would later provide a clearer picture of what lay beyond the Mississippi, but because of delays in publishing their journals the general public had to wait until 1814 before it could read in detail of their accomplishments. Meanwhile a U.S. army officer, Zebulon Montgomery Pike, led several expeditions into this western territory during the years 1805-1807. In 1810, four years before the publication of the Lewis and Clark journals, Pike, with the blessing of President Jefferson, brought out *An Account Of Expeditions To The Sources of the Mississippi, And Through The Western Parts Of Louisiana,...And A Tour Through The Interior Parts Of New Spain*. Consequently the American public received its first report about the trans-Mississippi territory from Pike's book. The author's description of trade opportunities in the Southwest with New Spain made a particularly strong impression. The keen interest with which Americans read Pike's *Account* was soon shared by many Europeans. An English edition appeared in 1811. French, Dutch, and German translations quickly followed.

General James Wilkinson had ordered Pike, then a young lieutenant, to undertake an expedition in 1805 to find the source of the Mississippi River and to assert American authority over the Indians and over the English traders in the upper Mississippi Valley. Setting out from St. Louis in the summer of that year, Pike went as far north as Leech Lake in Minnesota and mistakenly identified it as the Mississippi's source. In frequent encounters with the Indians and with the English traders he

Sources of the Mississippi and the Western Louisiana Territory

by Zebulon Montgomery Pike

Sources of the Mississippi
and the Western Louisiana Territory

Edwin sc.

Lieut. Z. M. Pike.

AN ACCOUNT OF EXPEDITIONS

TO THE

Sources of the Mississippi,

AND THROUGH THE

WESTERN PARTS OF LOUISIANA,

TO THE SOURCES OF THE

ARKANSAW, KANS, LA PLATTE, AND PIERRE JAUN, RIVERS;

PERFORMED BY ORDER OF THE

GOVERNMENT OF THE UNITED STATES

DURING THE YEARS 1805, 1806, AND 1807.

AND A TOUR THROUGH

THE

INTERIOR PARTS OF NEW SPAIN,

WHEN CONDUCTED THROUGH THESE PROVINCES,

BY ORDER OF

THE CAPTAIN–GENERAL,

IN THE YEAR 1807.

———

BY MAJOR Z. M. PIKE.

———

ILLUSTRATED BY MAPS AND CHARTS.

———

PHILADELPHIA:

PUBLISHED BY C. & A. CONRAD, & Co. No. 30, CHESNUT STREET. SOMER-
VELL & CONRAD, PETERSBURGH. BONSAL, CONRAD, & Co. NORFOLK,
AND FIELDING LUCAS, Jr. BALTIMORE.

———

John Binns, Printer.....1810.

TO THE PUBLIC.

BOOKS of travels, journals and voyages, have become so numerous, and are so frequently impositions on the public, that the writer of the following sheets feels under an obligation to explain, in some measure, the original circumstances that led to the production of this volume. Soon after the purchase of Louisiana, by an enlightened administration, measures were taken to explore the then unknown wilds of our western country, measures founded on principles of scientific pursuits, combined with a view of entering into a chain of philantrophic arrangements for meliorating the condition of the Indians who inhabit those vast plains and deserts. His excellency, *Merriwether Lewis*, then a captain of the first regiment of infantry, was selected by the President of the United States, in conjunction with capt. *C. Clarke*, to explore the then unknown sources of the Missouri, and I was chosen to trace the Mississippi to its source, with the objects in view contemplated by my instructions ; to which I conceived my duty, as a soldier should induce me, to add an investigation into the views of the British traders in that quarter, as to trade, and an enquiry into the limits of the territories of the United States and Great Britain. As a man of humanity and feeling, I made use of the name of my government to stop the savage warfare which had for ages been carried on by two of the most powerful nations of Aborigines in North America. Why I did not execute the power vested in me by the laws of the country, to ruin the British traders and enrich myself, by seizing on the immense property of the North West company, which I found in the acknowledged boundary of the United States, will be explained by my letter to Hugh M'Gillis, Esq. to whom I owe eternal gratitude for his polite and hospitable treatment of myself and party.

In the execution of this voyage I had no gentleman to aid me, and I literally performed the duties (as far as my limited abilities permitted) of astronomer, surveyor, commanding officer, clerk, spy, guide, and hunter ; frequently preceding the party for miles, in order to reconnoitre, and returning in the evening, hungry and fatigued, to sit down in the open air, by fire light, to copy the notes and plot the courses of the day. On my return from the Mississippi voyage, preparations were making for a second, which was to be conducted by another gentleman of the army ; but general Wilkinson solicited as a favor that (which he had a right to command) viz. that I would agree to take charge of the expedition. The late dangers and hardships I had undergone, together with the idea of again leaving my family in a strange country, distant from their connections, made me hesitate; but the ambition of a soldier, and the spirit of enterprize, which was inherent in my breast, induced me to agree to his proposition. The great objects in view by this expedition (as I conceived) in addition to my instructions, were to attach the Indians to our government, and to acquire such geographical knowledge of the south-western boundary of Louisiana as to enable government to enter into a definitive arrangement for a line of demarkation between that territory and North Mexico.

In this expedition I had the assistance of lieutenant *James Wilkinson*, and also of doctor *John H. Robinson*, a young gentleman of science and enterprize, who volunteered his services. I also was fitted out with a complete set of astronomical and mathematical instruments, which enabled me to ascertain the geographical situation of various places to a degree of exactitude, that would have been extremely gratifying to all lovers of science, had I not been so unfortunate as to loose the greater part of my papers by the seizure of the Spanish government.

With respect to the great acquisitions which might have been made to the sciences of botany and zoology, I can only observe, that neither my education nor taste led me to the pursuit, and if they had, my mind was too much engrossed in making the arrangements for our subsistance and safety, to give time to scrutinize the productions of the countries over which we travelled, with the eye of a Linnaeus or Buffon, yet doctor Robinson did make some observations on those subjects which he has not yet communicated. With respect to the Spanish part, it has been suggested to me by some respected friends, that the picture I drew of the manners, morals, &c. of individuals, generally of New Spain, if a good likeness was certainly not making a proper return for the hospitality and kindness with which those people honored me ; those reasons have induced me to omit many transactions, and draw a veil over various habits and customs which might appear in an unfavorable point of view, at the same time that I have dwelt with delight on their virtues.

There has not been wanting, persons of various ranks, who have endeavored to infuse the idea into the minds of the public, that the last voyage was undertaken through some sinister designs of general Wilkinson ; and although this report has been amply refuted by two letters from the secretary of war, published with this work ; yet I cannnot forbear in this public manner, declaring the insinuation to be a *groundless calumny*, arising from the envenomed breasts of persons, who through enmity to the general, would in attempting his ruin, hurl destruction on all those, who either through their official stations or habits of friendship, ever had any connection with that gentleman.

As a military man—as a soldier from the time I was able to bear arms, it cannot be expected that a production of my pen can stand the test of criticism, and I hope by this candid appeal to the justice and indulgence of the learned, to induce them, to spare their censure if they cannot award their praise.

The gentleman who prints this work, knows under what a variety of disadvantages it has gone to the press.*   At a distance during its publication, and engaged in my professional duties, it was impossible to give to it that attention, which in order to reach its proper degree of correctness such a work necessarily would require.

(Signed)   Z. M. PIKE.

---

* THE PUBLISHER owes it to truth, and to colonel Pike, to state that he very much doubts whether any book ever went to press under so many disadvantages as the one now presented to the public.   Some of those disadvantages must be obvious to every man who reads the work ; but there were many others of a nature not sufficiently interesting for publication, yet of sufficient magnitude to retard the work, embarrass the publisher, and impose more anxiety than has fallen to his lot in the various books which he has published.   It is however, confidently believed, that notwithstanding all those circumstances, the JOURNAL and its APPENDIXES will be found particularly interesting and pregnant with important information.

TO THE PRESIDENT

AND MEMBERS OF THE U. S. M. P. S.

—————

FELLOW SOLDIERS AND CITIZENS,

IN presuming to claim your protection and patronage for the following production, I feel less diffidence, knowing, that the very institution of the society will plead in my favor, it being avowedly formed for the promotion of military knowledge.

The work is merely a volume of details, and if it should be found that in the relation, I have delivered myself with perspicuity and exactitude, it is the highest meed of praise that I claim. When I touched on abstract subjects, or presumed to hypothesize, I have merely suggested doubts without conclusions, which, if deemed worthy, may hereafter be analyzed by men of genius and science. It being a work which has arisen from the events of youthful military exertions, the author, perhaps, has the most just and well founded ground for a hope that it may receive the solicited approbation of your honorable institution.

I am, gentlemen, with the greatest respect and high consideration,

Your obedient servant,

Z. M. PIKE, Major,

6th Regt. infantry, M. U. S. M. P. Society.

PIKE'S EXPEDITIONS.

PART I.

JOURNAL OF A VOYAGE, TO THE SOURCES OF THE MISSISSIPPI IN THE YEARS 1805 AND 1806.

SAILED from my encampment, near St. Louis, at 4 o'clock P. M. on Friday, the 9th August 1805: with one sergeant, two corporals, and seventeen privates, in a keel boat, 70 feet long, provisioned for four months: water very rapid: encamped on the east side of the river, at the head of an island.

10*th August; Saturday*—Embarked early; breakfasted opposite to the mouth of the Missouri, near Wood creek. About 5 o'clock P. M. a storm came on from the westward; the boat lay too; having gone out to march with two men behind a cluster of islands, one of my soldiers swam a channel, in the night, to inform me that the boat had stopt during the storm. I remained on the beach all night. Distance 28 1-2 miles.

11*th August; Sunday*—In the morning the boat came up and stopt opposite to the Portage De Sioux. We here spread out our baggage to dry; discharged our guns

at a target, and scaled out our blunderbusses. Dined
at the cave below the Illinois,* at the mouth of which
river, we remained some time. From the course of the
Mississippi, the Illinois might be mistaken for a part of
it. Encamped on the lower point of an island, about 6
miles above the Illinois ; were much detained by passing
the east side of some islands above the Illinois ; and were
obliged to get into the water and haul the boat through.

12th *August ; Monday*—In the morning made several miles to breakfast ; about 3 o'clock P. M. passed Buffaloe, or riviere au Bœuf, above which, about 5 miles,
commences a beautiful cedar cliff, having passed this, the
river expands to nearly two miles in width, and has four
islands, whose lowest points are nearly parallel ; these we
called the four brothers ; encamped on the point of the
E. one. It rained very hard all night ; caught one cat-
fish. Distance 29 3-4 miles.

13th *August ; Tuesday*—Late before we sailed, passed a vast number of islands ; left one of our dogs on
shore ; were much detained by sand bars, and were obliged to haul our boat over several of them ; observed several encampments which had been lately occupied : rained
all day. Distance 27 miles.

14th *August ; Wednesday*—Hard rain in the morning,
but a fine wind springing up, we put off at 1-2 past 6
o'clock ; passed a camp of Sacs, consisting of 3 men,
with their families : they were employed in spearing and
scaffolding a fish, about 3 feet in length, with a long flat
snout ; they pointed out the channel, and prevented us
from taking the wrong one : I gave them a small quantity of whiskey and biscuit ; and they in return, presented me with some fish. Sailed on through a continuation of islands, for nearly twenty miles ; met a young
gentleman, (Mr. Robedoux) by whom I sent a letter to

St. Louis; encamped on an island; caught 1375 small fish; rained all day. Distance 28 miles.

15th *August; Thursday*—Still raining in the morning. From the continued series of wet weather, the men were quite galled and sore. Met a Mr. Kettletas of N. Y. who gave me a line to Mr. Fisher of the Prairie Des Chein; passed a small river, to the W. with a sand bar at its entrance; also, passed Salt river, which, I do not recollect having seen on any chart: it is a considerable stream, and at high water is navigable, for at least 200 miles; left another dog. Distance 26 miles.

16th *August; Friday*—Embarked early, but were so unfortunate, as to get fast on a log; and did not extricate ourselves, until past 11 o'clock, having to saw off a log under the water. At 3 o'clock P. M. arrived at the house of a Frenchman, situate on the W. side of the river, opposite to Hurricane island. His cattle appeared to be in fine order; but his corn in a bad state of cultivation. About one mile above his house, on the W. shore, is a very handsome hill, which he informed me was level on the top, with a gradual descent on either side, and a fountain of fine water. This man likewise told me that two men had been killed on the Big Bay, or Three Brothers; and desired to be informed what measures had been taken in consequence thereof; caught three cat-fish and one perch; encamped 4 miles above the house. Distance 18 miles.

17th *August; Saturday*—Embarked and came on remarkably well; at 10 o'clock stopt for breakfast, and in order to arrange our sail; when the wind served, we put off and continued under easy sail all day. Passed three batteaux. Distance 39 miles.

18th *August; Sunday*—Embarked early; about 11 o'clock passed an Indian camp, on the E. side. They fired several guns; but we passed without stopping. Ve-

ry hard head winds part of the day.   Caught six fish.—
Distance 23 miles.

19th *August*; *Monday*—Embarked early and made
fine way ; but at 9 o'clock in turning the point of a sand
bar, our boat struck a sawyer ; at the moment we did not
know it had injured her ; but in a short time after, discovered her to be sinking, however, by thrusting oakum into
the leak and bailing, we got her to shore on a bar, where,
after entirely unloading, we with great difficulty keeled
her sufficiently to cut out the plank and put in a new one.
This at the time I conceived to be a great misfortune ; but
upon examination we discovered that the injury resulting
from it was greater than we were at first induced to believe ; for upon inspection, we found our provisions and
cloathing considerably damaged.   The day was usefully and
necessarily employed in assorting, suning, and airing those
articles.   One of my hunters (Sparks) having gone on shore
to hunt, swam the river about 7 miles above and killed a
deer ; but finding we did not come on, he returned down
the river, and joined us by swimming.   Whilst we were
at work at our boat on the sand beach, three canoes with
Indians, passed on the opposite shore.   They cried, " How
do you do," wishing us to give them an invitation to come
over ; but receiving no answer they passed on.   We then
put our baggage on board and put off, designing to go
where the young man had killed the deer ; but after dark
we became entangled among the sand bars, and were
obliged to stop and encamp on the point of a beach.
Caught two fish.   Distance 14 miles.

20th *August* ; *Tuesday*—Arrived at the foot of the
rapids De Moyen at 7 o'clock ; and, although no soul
on board had passed them, we commenced ascending them,
immediately.   Our boat, being large and moderately
loaded, we found great difficulty.   The river all the way
through is from 3-4 to a mile wide.   The rapids are 11

miles long, with successive ridges and shoals extending from shore to shore.   The first has the greatest fall and is the most difficult to ascend.   The channel (a bad one) is on the east side in passing the two first bars, then passes under the edge of the third ; crosses to the west, and ascends on that side, all the way to the Sac Village.   The shoals continue the whole distance.   We had passed the first and most difficult shoal, when we were met by Mr. Wm. Ewing, (who I understand is an agent, appointed to reside with the Sacs, to teach them the science of agriculture) with a French interpreter, 4 chiefs and 15 men of the Sac nation, in their canoes ; bearing a flag of the United States.   They came down to assist me up the rapids ; and took out 13 of my heaviest barrels, and put two of their men in the barge to pilot us up.   Arrived at the house of Mr. Ewing, opposite the village, at dusk. The land on both sides of the rapids is hilly, but a rich soil.   Distance 16 miles.

21st *August ; Wednesday*—All the chief men of the village came over to my encampment ; where I spoke to them to the following purport :

" That their great father, the president of the United States, wishing to be more intimately acquainted with the situation, wants, &c. of the different nations of the red people, in our newly acquired territory of Louisiana, had ordered the general to send a number of his young warriors, in different directions, to take them by the hand, and make such enquiries as might afford the satisfaction required.   Also, that I was authorised to choose situations for their trading establishments ; and wished them to inform me if that place would be considered by them as central.

" That I was sorry to hear of the murder, which had been committed on the river below ; but, in consideration of their assurances, that it was none of their nation, and the anxiety exhibited by them on the occasion, I had written to the general and informed him of what they had said on the subject.

" That in their treaty, they engaged to apprehend all traders who came amongst them without license; for that time, I could not examine their traders on this subject; but, that on my return, I would make a particular examination.

" That if they thought proper, they might send a young man in my boat, to inform the other villages of my mission, &c."

I then presented them with some tobacco, knives, and whiskey. They replied to the following purport:

" That they thanked me for the good opinion I had of their nation, and for what I had written the general. That themselves, their young warriors, and the whole nation was glad to see me amongst them.

" That as for the situation of the trading houses, they could not determine, being but a part of the nation. With respect to sending a young man along, that, if I would wait until to-morrow, they would choose one out. And finally, thanked me for my tobacco, knives, and whiskey."

Not wishing to loose any time, after writing to the general* and my friends, I embarked and made six miles above the village. Encamped on a sand bar. One canoe of savages passed.

22d *August; Thursday*—Embarked at 5 o'clock A. M. hard head winds. Passed a great number of islands. The river very wide and full of sand bars. Distance 23 miles.

23d *August; Friday*—Cool morning; came on 5 1-4 miles, where, on the west shore, there is a very

---

* See " appendix to part I," [No. 1] page 1.

handsome situation for a garrison.   The channel of the river passes under the hill, which is about 60 feet perpendicular, and level on the top.   Four hundred yards in the rear, there is a small prairie of 8 or 10 acres, which would be a convenient spot for gardens; and on the east side of the river, there is a beautiful prospect over a large prairie, as far as the eye can extend, now and then interrupted by groves of trees.   Directly under the rock is a limestone spring, which, after an hour's work, would afford water amply sufficient for the consumption of a regiment.   The landing is bold and safe, and at the lower part of the hill, a road may be made for a team in half an hour.   Black and white oak timber in abundance.   The mountain continues about two miles, and has five springs bursting from it in that distance.   Met four Indians and two squaws; landed with them; gave them one quart of *made* whiskey, a few biscuit and some salt.   I requested some venison of them, they pretended they could not understand me; but after we had left them, they held up two hams, and hallooed and laughed at us in derision.   Passed nine horses on shore, and saw many signs of Indians.   Passed a handsome prairie on the east side, and encamped at its head.   Three batteaux from Michilimackinac; stopped at our camp, we were told they were the property of Mr. Myers Michals; we were also informed, that the largest Sac village was about 2 1-2 miles out on the prairie; and that this prairie was called half way to the prairie Des Cheins, from St. Louis.

24th *August ;   Saturday*—In the morning passed a number of islands.   Before dinner, corporal Bradley and myself took our guns and went on shore; we got behind a savannah, by following a stream we conceived to have been a branch of the river, but which led us at least two leagues from it.   My two favorite dogs, having gone out with us, gave out in the prairie, owing to the heat, high grass, and want of water ; but thinking they would come on, we continued our march. We heard the report of a gun, and supposing it to be from our boat, answered it ; shortly after, however, we passed an Indian trail, which appeared as if the persons had been hurried, I presume at the report of our guns ; for with this people, all strangers are enemies. Shortly after we struck the river, and the boat appeared in view ; stayed some time for my dogs ; two of my men volunteered to go in search of them. Encamped on the west shore, nearly opposite to a chalk bank. My two men had not yet returned, and it was extraordinary, as they knew my boat never waited for any person on shore : they endeavored to strike the Mississippi ahead of us. We fired a blunderbuss at three different times, to let them know where we lay. Distance 23 1-2 miles.

25th *August ; Sunday*—Stopt on the sand bank prairie, on the E. side, from which you have a beautiful prospect of at least 40 miles down the river, bearing S. 38° E. Discovered that our boat leaked very fast ; but we secured her inside so completely with oakum and tallow, as nearly to prevent the leak. Fired a blunderbuss every hour, all day, as signals for our men. Passed the river Iowa. Encamped at night on the prairie, marked *Grant's prairie.* The men had not yet arrived. Distance 28 miles.

26th *August ; Monday*—Rain, with a very hard head wind. Towed our boat about nine miles, to where the river Hills joins the Mississippi. Here I expected to find the two men I had lost, but was disappointed. The mercury in Reamur at 13° ; whereas yesterday, it was 26°. Met two peroques full of Indians, who commenced hollowing, " How do you do," &c. they then put to shore and beckoned us to do so likewise, but we continued our course. This day very severe on the men. Distance 28 1-2 miles.

27th August ; Tuesday—Embarked early ; cold N. wind ; mercury 10° ; the wind so hard ahead, that we were obliged to tow the boat all day.   Passed one peroque of Indians, also the Riviere De Roche, late in the day. Some Indians who were encamped there, embarked in their canoes and ascended the river before us.   The wind so very strong, that, although down the stream, they were near sinking.   Encamped about 4 miles above the Riviere De Roche, on the W. shore.   This day passed a pole on a prairie, on which five dogs were hanging.   Distance 22 miles.

28th August ; Wednesday—About an hour after we had embarked, we arrived at the camp of Mr. James Aird, a Scotch gentleman of Michilimackinac. He had encamped, with some goods, on the beach ; and was repairing his boat, which had been injured in crossing the rapids of the Riviere De Roche (at the foot of which we now were.)   He had sent three boats back for the goods left behind.   Breakfasted with him and obtained considerable information.   Commenced ascending the rapids.... Carried away our rudder in the first ; but after getting it repaired, the wind raised, and we hoisted sail ; and, although entire strangers, we sailed through them with a perfect gale blowing all the time ; when, had we struck a rock, in all probability we would have bilged and sunk. But we were so fortunate as to pass without touching.   Met with Mr. Aird's boats (which had pilots) fast on the rocks. Those shoals are a continued chain of rocks, extending in some places from shore to shore, about 18 miles in length.   They afford more water than those of De Moyen, but are much more rapid.

29th August ; Thursday—Breakfasted at the Reynard village, above the rapids ; this is the first village of the Reynards.   I expected to have found my two men here, but was disappointed.   Finding they had not passed, I lay by until 4 o'clock P. M. the wind fair all the time. The chief informed me, by signs, that in four days they could march to Prairie Des Cheins ; and promised to furnish them with mockinsons, and put them on their rout. Set sail and made at least four knots an hour. I was disposed to sail all night, but the wind lulling, we encamped on the point of an island, on the W. shore. Distance 20 miles.

30th August ; Friday—Embarked at 5 o'clock ; wind fair, but not very high. Sailed all day. Passed four peroques of Indians. Distance 43 mil s.

31st August ; Saturday—Embarked early. Passed one peroque of Indians ; also, two encampments ; one on a beautiful eminence, on the W. side, of the river. This place had the appearance of an old town. Sailed almost all day. Distance 31 1-2 miles.

1st Sept. Sunday—Embarked early ; wind fair ; arrived at the lead mines at 12 o'clock. A dys nter with which I had been afflicted several days, was suddenly checked this morning ; which, I believe to have been the occasion of a very violent attack of fever about 11 o'clock. Notwithstanding it was very s vere, I dressed myself, with an intention to execute the orders of the general relative to this place. We were saluted with a field piece, and received with every mark of attention, by Monsieur Dubuque, the proprietor. There were no horses at the house, and it was six miles to where the mines were worked ; it was therefore impossible to make a report by actual inspection. I therefore proposed ten queries, on the answers to which my report was founded.* Dined with Mr. D. who informed me that the Sioux and Sauteurs were as warmly engaged in opposition as ever ; that not long since the former killed 15 Sauteurs, who on the 10th August in re-

---

* See appendix to part I. [No. 2] page 5.

turn killed 10 Sioux, at the entrance of the St. Peters; and that a war party, composed of the Sacs, Reynards, and Puants, of 200 warriors had embarked on an expedition against the Sauteurs, but that they had heard, that the chief having had an unfavorable dream, persuaded the party to return, and that I would meet them on my voyage. At this place I was introduced to a chief, called the Raven of the Reynards. He made a very flowery speech on the occasion, which I answered in a few words, accompanied by a small present.

I had now given up all hopes of my two men, and was about to embark, when a peroque arrived, in which they were, with a Mr. Blondeau, and two Indians, whom that gentleman had engaged above the rapids of Stony river. The two soldiers had been six days without any thing to eat, except muscles: when they met Mr. James Aird, by whose humanity and attention their strength and spirits were in a measure, restored; and they were enabled to reach the Reynard village, where they met with Mr. B. The Indian chief furnished them with corn and shoes, and shewed his friendship, by every possible attention. I immediately discharged the hire of the Indians, and gave Mr. Blondeau a passage to the Prairie Des Cheins. Left the lead mines at 4 o'clock. Distance 25 miles.

2d Sept. Monday—After making two short reaches, we commenced one, which is 30 miles in length, the wind serving, we just made it; and encamped on the E. side opposite to the mouth of Turkey river. In the course of the day, we landed to shoot at pidgeons; the moment a gun was fired, some Indians, who were on the shore above us, ran down and put off in their peroques with great precipitation; upon which Mr. Blondeau informed me, that all the women and children were frightened at the very name of an American boat, and that the men held us in great respect, conceiving us very quarrelsome, and much for war, and also very brave. This information I used as prudence suggested. We stopt at an encampment, about three miles below the town, where they gave us some excellent plums. They despatched a peroque to the village, to give notice, as I supposed, of our arrival. It commenced raining about dusk, and rained all night. Distance 40 miles.

3d Sept. *Tuesday*—Embarked at a pretty early hour. Cloudy. Met two peroques of family Indians; they at first asked Mr. Blondeau, " if we were for war, or if going to war?" I now experienced the good effect, of having some person on board, who could speak their language; for they presented me with three pair of ducks, and a quantity of venison, sufficient for all our crew, one day; in return, I made them some trifling presents. Afterwards met two peroques, carrying some of the warriors spoken of on the 2d inst. They kept at a great distance, until spoken to by Mr. B. when they informed him that their party had proceeded up as high as Lake Pepin, without effecting any thing. It is surprizing what a dread the Indians, in this quarter, have of the Americans: I have often seen them go round islands, to avoid meeting my boat. It appears to me evident, that the traders have taken great pains, to impress upon the minds of the savages, the idea of our being a very vindictive, ferocious, and warlike people. This impression was perhaps made with no good intention; but when they find that our conduct towards them, is guided by magnanimity and justice; instead of operating in an injurious manner, it will have the effect to make them reverence at the same time they fear us. Distance 25 miles.

4th Sept. *Wednesday*—Breakfasted just below the Ouiscousing. Arrived at the Prairie Des Cheins about 11 o'clock; took quarters at capt. Fishers, and were politely received by him and Mr. Frazer.

5th Sept. Thursday——Embarked about half past 10 o'clock in a Schenectady boat, to go to the mouth of the Ouiscousing, in order to take the latitude, and look at the situation of the adjacent hills for a post. Was accompanied by judge Fisher, Mr. Frazer, and Mr. Woods. We ascended the hill on the west side of the Mississippi; and made choice of a spot which I thought most eligible, being level on the top, having a spring in the rear, and commanding a view of the country around. A shower of rain came on which completely wet us; and we returned to the village without having ascended the Ouiscousing as we intended. Marked four trees with A. B. C. D. and squared the sides of one in the centre. Wrote to the general.*

6th Sept. Friday——Had a small council with the Puants, and a chief of the lower band of the Sioux. Visited and laid out a position for a post, on a hill called the *Petit Gris,* on the Ouiscousing, three miles above its mouth. Mr. Fisher who accompanied me, was taken very sick, in consequence of drinking some water out of the Ouiscousing. The Puants never have any white interpreters, nor have the Fols Avoin nation. In my council, I spoke to a Frenchman, he to a Sioux, who interpreted to some of the Puants.

7th Sept. Saturday——My men beat all the villagers jumping and hopping. Began to load my new boats.

8th Sept. Sunday——Embarked at half past 1▸ o'clock in two batteaux. The wind fair and fresh. I found myself very much embarrassed and crampt, in my new boats, with provision and baggage. I embarked two interpreters, one to perform the whole voyage, whose name was

* See appendix to part I. [No. 2.] page 2.

Pierre Rosseau ; and the other named Joseph Reinulle, paid by Mr. Frazer to accompany me as high as the falls of St. Anthony.   Mr. Frazer is a young gentleman, clerk to Mr. Blakely, of Montreal : he was born in Vermont, but has latterly resided in Canada.   To the attention of this gentleman, I am much indebted ; he procured for me every thing in his power that I stood in need of ; despatched his bark canoes, and remained himself to go on with me.   His design was to winter with some of the Sioux bands.   We sailed well, came 18 miles and encamped on the W. bank.   I must not omit here to bear testimony to the politeness of all the principal inhabitants of the village.   There is however a material distinction to be made in the nature of those attentions :   The kindness of Messrs Fisher, Frazer, and Woods, (all Americans) seemed to be the spontaneous effusions of good will : and partiality to their countrymen ; it extended to the accommodation, convenience, exercises, and pastimes of my men ; and whenever they proved superior to the French, openly shewed their pleasure.   But the French Canadians appeared attentive, rather from their natural good manners, than sincere friendship ; however, it produced from them the same effect that natural good will did in the others.

9th Sept. Monday—Embarked early.   Dined at Cape Garlic, or at Garlic river ; after which we came on to an island on the E, side, about 5 miles below the river Iowa, and encamped.   Rained before sun set.   Distance 28 miles.

10th Sept. Tuesday—Rain still continuing, we remained at our camp.   Having shot at some pidgeons, the report was heard at the Sioux lodges ;* when La Fieulle sent down six of his young men to inform me, " that he had

* The same to whom I spoke on the 6th at the Prairie.

" waited three days with meat, &c. but that last night they
" had began to drink, and, that on the next day he would
" receive me with his people sober." I returned him for
answer, " that the season was advanced, that time was
" pressing, and that if the rain ceased, I must go on."
Mr. Frazer and the interpreter went home with the Indians. We embarked about 1 o'clock. Frazer returning, informed me that the chief acquiesced in my reasons for pressing forward, but that he had prepared a pipe
(by way of letter) to present me, to shew to all the Sioux
above; with a message to inform them, that I was a chief
of their new fathers, and that he wished me to be treated
with friendship and respect. On our arrival opposite to
the lodges, the men were paraded on the bank, with their
guns in their hands. They saluted us (with ball) with
what might be termed three rounds; which I returned
with three rounds from each boat with my blunderbusses.
This salute, although nothing to soldiers accustomed to
fire, would not be so agreeable, to many people; as the
Indians had all been drinking, and as some of them, even
tried their dexterity, to see how near the boat they could
strike. They may, indeed, be said, to have struck on
every side of us. When landed, I had my pistols in my
belt, and sword in hand. I was met, on the bank, by
the chief, and invited to his lodge. As soon as my guards
were formed, and sentinels posted, I accompanied him.
Some of my men who were going up with me, I caused
to leave their arms behind, as a mark of confidence. At
the chief's lodge, I found a clean mat and pillow, for me
to sit on, and the before-mentioned pipe, on a pair of
small crutches before me. The chief sat on my right hand,
my interpreter and Mr. Frazer on my left. After smoking, the chief spoke to the following purport: " That,
" notwithstanding he had seen me at the prairie, he was
" happy to take me by the hand amongst his own people,

" and there to shew his young men the respect due to
" their *new father :* That, when at St. Louis in the
" spring, his father had told him, that if he looked down
" the river, he would see one of his young warriors com-
" ing up. He now found it true, and he was happy to see
" me, who knew the Great Spirit was the father of all;
" both the white and the red people; and if one died, the
" other could not live long. That he had never been at
" war with their *new father,* and hoped, always to pre-
" serve, the same good understanding that now existed.
" That he now presented me with a pipe, to shew to the
" upper bands, a token of our good understanding; and
" that they might see his work, and imitate his conduct.
" That he had gone to St. Louis, on a shameful visit, to
" carry a murderer ; but, that we had given the man his
" life, and he thanked us for it. That he had provided
" something to eat, but he supposed I could not eat it,
" and if not, to give it to my young men." I replied :
" that, although I had told him at the prairie, my busi-
" ness up the Mississippi, I would again relate it to him.
" I then mentioned the different objects I had in view;
" with regard to the savages, who had fallen under our
" protection, by our late purchase from the Spaniards.
" The different posts to be established. The objects of
" these posts as related to them'; supplying them with
" necessaries ; having officers and agents of government
" near them, to attend to their business ; and above all,
" to endeavor to make peace with between the Sioux and
" Sauteurs. That it was possible on my return I should
" bring some of the Sauteurs down with me, and take
" with me some of the Sioux chiefs to St. Louis; there
" to settle the long and bloody war, which had existed be-
" tween the two nations. That I accepted his pipe with
" pleasure, as the gift of a great man,* and a brother.

* He is the chief of four bands.

" That it should be used as he desired." I then eat of the
dinner he had provided. It was very grateful. It was
wild rye and venison, of which I sent four bowls to my
men. I afterwards went to a dance, the performance of
which, was attended with many curious manœuvres. Men
and women danced indiscriminately. They were all dressed in the gayest manner; each had in their hand, a small
skin of some description, and would frequently run up,
point their skin, and give a puff with their breath; when
the person blown at, whether man or woman, would fall,
and appear to be almost lifeless, or in great agony; but
would recover slowly, rise, and join in the dance. This
they called their great medicine; or as I understood the
word, dance of religion. The Indians believing, that they
actually puffed something into each others bodies, which
occasioned the falling, &c. It is not every person who
is admitted; persons wishing to join them, must first
make valuable presents to the society, to the amount of
40 or 50 dollars, give a feast, and then are admitted with
great ceremony. Mr. Frazer informed me, that he was
once in the lodge with some young men, who did not belong to the club; when one of the dancers came in, they
immediately threw their blankets over him, and forced
him out of the lodge: he laughed, and the young Indians
called him a fool, and said " he did not know what the
dancer might blow into his body." I returned to my
boat; sent for the chief and presented him with two carrots of tobacco, four knives, half a pound of vermillion,
and one quart of salt. Mr. Frazer asked liberty to present them some rum; we made them up a keg between
us, of 8 gallons.* Mr. Frazer informed the chief, that
he dare not give them any without my permission. The
chief thanked me for all my presents, and said " they

* Two gallons of whiskey.

C

" must come free, as he did not ask for them." I replied,
" that, to those who did not ask for any thing, I gave free-
" ly ; but to those who asked for much, I gave only a little
" or none." We embarked about half past 3 o'clock; came
three miles, and encamped on the W. side. Mr. Frazer
we left behind, but he came up with his two peroques
about dusk. It commenced raining very hard. In the
night a peroque arrived from the lodges at his camp. During our stay at their camp, there were soldiers appointed
to keep the croud from my boats ; who executed their duty with vigilance and rigor; driving men, women, and
children back, whenever they came near my boats. At
my departure, their soldiers said, " As I had shaken hands
" with their chief, they must shake hands with my sol-
" diers." In which request I willingly indulged them.

11th Sept. Wednesday—Embarked at 7 o'clock, although raining. Mr. Frazer's canoes also came on until
nine o'clock. Stopt for breakfast, and made a fire. Mr.
Frazer staid with me, and finding his peroques not quite
able to keep up, he dispatched them. We embarked; came
on until near 6 o'clock, and encamped on the W. side.
Saw nothing of his peroques, after they left us. Supposed to have come 16 miles this day. Rain and cold winds,
all day ahead. The river has never been clear of islands
since I left Prairie Des Chein. I absolutely believe it,
here, to be two miles wide. Hills, or rather prairie knobs
on both sides.

12th Sept. Thursday—It-raining very hard in the
morning, we did not embark until 10 o'clock. Mr. Frazer's peroques then coming up. It was still raining, and
was very cold. Passed the Racine river, also a prairie called Le Cross, from a game of ball played frequently
on it by the Sioux Indians. This prairie is very handsome, it has a small square hill, similar to some mentioned by Carver. It is bounded in the rear, by hills similar

to the Prairie Des Chein. On this prairie Mr. Frazer shewed me some holes, dug by the Sioux, when in expectation of an attack into which they first put their women, and children and then crawl themselves. They were generally round, and about 10 feet in diameter; but some were half moons and quite a breastwork. This I understood was the chief work, which was the principal redoubt. Their modes of constructing them are, the moment they apprehend, or discover, an enemy on a prairie, they commence digging with their knives, tomahawks, and a wooden ladle; and in an incredibly short space of time, they have a hole sufficiently deep to cover themselves and their family, from the balls or arrows of the enemy. They have no idea of taking those subterraneous redoubts by storm, as they would probably loose a great number of men in the attack; and although they might be successful in the event, it would be considered as a very imprudent action. Mr. Frazer finding his canoes not able to keep up, staid at this prairie to organize one of them, intending then, to overtake us. Came on 3 miles further.

13th Sept. Friday—Embarked at 6 o'clock. Came on to a sand bar, and stopt to dry my things. At this place Mr. Frazer overtook me. We remained here three hours; came on to the foot of the hills, at le Montaigne qui Trompe a l'Eau, which is a hill situated on the river. Rain all day, except about two hours at noon. Passed Black river. Distance 21 miles.

14th Sept. Saturday—Embarked early; the fog so thick, we could not distinguish objects twenty yards. When we breakfasted, we saw nothing of Mr. Frazer's canoes. After breakfast, at the head of an island, met Frazer's boats. Wind coming on fair, we hoisted sail, and found that we were more on an equality with our sails than our oars. The birch canoes sailed very well, but we were able to out row them. Met the remainder of the war party (be-

fore noted) of the Sacs and Reynards, returning from
their expedition against the Sauteurs. I directed my interpreter to ask how many scalps they had taken, they replied " none ;" he added they were all squaws, for which
I reprimanded him. Passed the mountain which stands in
the river, or as the French term it, which soaks in the
river. Came on to the Prairie Le Aisle, on the west.
Mr. Frazer, Bradley, Sparks, and myself, went out to
hunt ; we crossed first a dry flat prairie ; when we arrived at the hills, we ascended them, from which we had a
most sublime and beautiful prospect. On the right, we
saw the mountains, which we passed in the morning, and
the prairie in their rear ; and like distant clouds the mountains at the Prairie Le Cross ; on our left and under our
feet, the valley between the two barren hills, through which
the Mississippi wound itself by numerous channels, forming many beautiful islands, as far as the eye could embrace the scene. Our four boats under full sail, their
flags streaming before the wind, was altogether a prospect
so variegated and romantic, that a man may scarcely expect to enjoy such a one but twice or thrice in the course
of his life. I proposed keeping the hills until they led to
the river, encamping and waiting the next day for our
boats ; but Mr. Frazer's anxiety to get to the boats, induced me to yield ; and after crossing a very thick bottom, fording and swimming three branches of the river,
and crossing several morasses, we at 12 o'clock arrived,
opposite our boats, which were encamped on the east side.
We were brought over. Saw great sign of elk, but had
not the good fortune to come across any of them. My
men saw three on the shore. Distance 21 miles.

15th Sept. Sunday—Embarked early ; passed the
riviere Embarrass, and Lean Clare, on the W. which is navigable 135 miles. Encamped opposite to the river Le
Bœuf on the W. shore. At the head of this river, the

Chipeways inhabit, and it is navigable for peroques 40 or
50 leagues. Rained in the afternoon. Mr. Frazer broke
one of his canoes. Came on about 3 miles farther than
him. Distance 25 miles.

16th Sept. Monday—Embarked late, as I wished Mr.
Frazer to overtake me, but came on very well. His canoes overtook us at dinner, at the grand encampment below Lake Pepin. We made the sandy peninsula, on the
east at the entrance of Lake Pepin, by dusk; passed the
Sauteaux river on the east, at the entrance of the lake.
After supper, the wind being fair, we put off, with the
intention to sail across. My interpreter (Rosseau) telling
me, that he had passed the lake twenty times, but never
once in the day; giving as a reason, that the wind frequently rose and detained them by day in the lake—But I
believe the traders true reason, generally is, their fears of
the Sauteurs, as they have made several strokes of war, at
the mouth of this river, never distinguishing between the
Sioux and their traders—However, the wind serving, I
was induced to go on; and accordingly we sailed. My
boat bringing up the rear, for I had put the sail of my
big boat on my batteaux, and a mast of 22 feet. Mr.
Frazer embarked on my boat. At first the breeze was
very gentle, and we sailed with our violins and other music playing; but the sky afterwards became cloudy and
quite a gale arose. My boat ploughed the swells, sometimes almost bow under. When we came to the Traverse, which is opposite to Point De Sable, we thought
it most advisable, the lake being very much disturbed and
the gale increasing, to take harbor in a bay on the east.
One of the canoes, and my boat, came in very well, and
together; but having made a fire on the point to give notice to our boats in the rear, they both ran on the bar
before they doubled it, and were near foundering; but by

jumping into the lake we brought them into a safe harbor. Distance 40 miles.

17th Sept. Tuesday—Although there was every appearance of a very severe storm, we embarked at half past 6 o'clock, the wind fair, but before we had all hoisted sail, those in front had struck theirs. The wind came on hard ahead. The sky became inflamed, and the lightning seemed to roll down the sides of the hills, which bordered the shore of the lake. The storm in all its grandeur, majesty, and horror, burst upon us, in the Traverse, while making to Point De Sable; and it required no moderate exertion, to weather the point and get to the windward side of it. There we found Mr. Cameron, who had sailed from the prairie on the 5th; he had three bark, and one wooden, canoes, with him. He had been laying here two days; his canoes unloaded and turned up for the habitation of his men; his tents pitched, and living in all the ease of an Indian trader. He appeared to be a man of tolerable information, but rather indolent in his habits; a Scotchman by birth, but an Englishman by prejudice. He had with him a very handsome young man, by the name of John Rudsdell, and also his own son, a lad of fifteen. The storm continuing, we remained all day. I was shewn a point of rocks from which a Sioux woman cast herself, and was dashed into a thousand pieces, on the rocks below. She had been informed, that her friends intended matching her to a man she despised; and having refused her the man she had chosen, she ascended the hill, singing her death song; and before they could overtake her, and obviate her purpose, she took the lover's leap! and ended her troubles, with her life. A wonderful display of sentiment in a savage! Distance 3 miles.

18th Sept. Wednesday—Embarked after breakfast. Mr. Cameron, with his boats, came on with me. Crossed the lake, sounded it, and took an observation at the upper end. I embarked in one of his canoes, and we came up to Canoe river, where there was a small band of Sioux, under the command of *Red Wing*, the second war chief in the nation. He made me a speech and presented a pipe, pouch, and buffalo skin. He appeared to be a man of sense, and promised to accompany me to St. Peters; he saluted me, and had it returned. I made him a small present. We encamped on the end of the island, and although not more than 11 o'clock, were obliged to stay all night. Distance 18 miles.

19th Sept. Thursday—Embarked early; dined at St. Croix river. Messrs. Frazer and Cameron, having some business to do with the savages, we left them at the encampment; but they promised to overtake me, though they were obliged to travel until 12 o'clock at night. Fired a blunderbuss for them at Tattoo. The chain of my watch became unhooked, by lending her to my guard; this was a very serious misfortune.

20th Sept. Friday—Embarked after sun rise. Cloudy with hard head winds; a small shower of rain; cleared up in the afternoon, and became pleasant. Encamped on a prairie on the east side, on which is a large painted stone, about 8 miles below the Sioux village. The traders had not yet overtaken me. Distance 26 1-2 miles.

21st Sept. Saturday—Embarked at a seasonable hour, breakfasted at the Sioux village, on the east side. It consists of eleven lodges, and is situated at the head of an island just below a ledge of rocks. The village was evacuated at this time, all the Indians having gone out to the lands to gather fols avoin. About two miles above, saw three bears swimming over the river, but at too great a distance for us to have killed them; they made the shore before I could come up with them. Passed a camp of Sioux, of four lodges, in which I saw only one man, whose name was *Black Soldier*. The garrulity of the women astonished me, for at the other camps they never opened their lips; but here they flocked round us with all their tongues going at the same time; the cause of this freedom must have been the absence of their lords and masters. Passed the encampment of Mr. Ferrebault, who had broken his peroque and had encamped on the west side of the river, about 3 miles below St. Peters. We made our encampment on the N. E. point of the big island, opposite to St. Peters. The Mississippi became so very narrow this day, that I once crossed in my batteaux with forty strokes of my oars. The water of the Mississippi, since we passed Lake Pepin, has been remarkably red; and where it is deep, appears as black as ink. The waters of the St. Croix and St. Peters, appear blue and clear, for a considerable distance below their confluence. I observed a white flag on shore to day, and on landing, discovered it to be white silk; it was suspended over a scaffold, on which were laid four dead bodies, two enclosed in boards, and two in bark. They were wrapped up in blankets, which appeared to be quite new. They were the bodies, I was informed, of two Sioux women (who had lived with two Frenchmen) one of their children and some other relative; two of whom died at St. Peters and two at St. Croix, but were brought here, to be deposited upon this scaffold together. This is the manner of the Sioux burial, when persons die a natural death; but when they are killed, they suffer them to lay unburied. This circumstance brought to my recollection, the bones of a man I found on the hills below the St. Croix; the jaw bone I brought on board. He must have been killed on that spot. Distance 24 miles.

22d Sept. Sunday—Employed in the morning, measuring the river; about 3 o'clock Mr. Frazer and his peroques arrived, and in three hours after, the Petit Corbeau, at the head of his band, arrived with 150 warriors.

They ascended the hill, in the point between the Mississippi and St. Peters, and gave us a salute, *a la mode savage*, with balls; after which we settled the affairs for the council the next day. Mr. Frazer and myself took a bark canoe, and went up to the village, in order to see Mr. Cameron. We ascended the St. Peters to the village, and found his camp. (No current in the river.) He engaged to be at the council the next day, and promised to let me have his barge. The Sioux had marched on a war excursion; but hearing (by express) of my arrival, they returned by land. We were treated very hospitably, and hallooed after to go into every lodge, to eat. Returned to our camp about 11 o'clock and found the Sioux and my men peaceably encamped.

23d Sept. Monday—Prepared for the council, which we commenced about 12 o'clock. I had a bower or shade, made of my sails, on the beach, into which only my gentlemen (the traders) and the chiefs entered. I then addressed them in a speech, which, though long, and touching on many points, its principal object was, the granting of land at this place, falls of St. Anthony and St. Croix, and making peace with the Chipeways. I was replied to by *Le Fils de Pinchow*, *Le Petit Corbeau*, and *l'Original Leve*. They gave me the land required, about 100,000 acres, (equal to 200,000 dollars) and promised me a safe passport, for myself and any chiefs, I might bring down, but spoke doubtfully with respect to the peace. I gave them presents to the amount of about 200 dollars, and as soon as the council was over, I allowed the traders to present them with some liquor, which, with what I myself gave, was equal to 60 gallons. In one half hour they were all embarked for their respective villages.

The chiefs in the council were:

Le Petit Corbeau, signed the grant.

Le Fils de Pinchow, do.

Le Grand Partisan.

Le Original Leve, ⎫ War chief, gave him my father's
Le Demi Douzen, ⎭   tomahawk, &c. &c.

Le Beccasse.

Le Bœuf que Marche.

It was somewhat difficult to get them to sign the grant, as they conceived their word of honor should be taken for the grant without any mark; but I convinced them it was not on their account, but my own, I wished them to sign it.*

24th Sept. Tuesday—In the morning I discovered my flag was missing from off my boat. Being in doubt whether it had been stolen by the Indians, or had fallen overboard and floated away, I sent for my friend, the *Original Leve*, and sufficiently evinced to him, by the vehemence of my action, by the immediate punishment of my guard, (having inflicted on one of them corporeal punishment) and by sending down the shore three miles in search of it; how much I was displeased, that such a thing should have occurred. I sent a flag and two carrots of tobacco, by a Mr. Cameron, to the Sioux, at the head of the St. Peters; made a small draft of the position at this place; sent up the boat I got from Mr. Fisher, to the village, on the St. Peters, and exchanged her for a barge, with Mr. Duncan; my men returned with the barge about sun down. She was a fine light thing, eight men were able to carry her. Employed all day in writing.

25th Sept. Wednesday—I was awakened out of my bed by *Le Petit Corbeau*, (head chief) who came up from his village, to see if we were all killed, or if any accident had happened to us; this was in consequence of their having found my flag floating three miles below their village, (15 miles hence) from which they concluded some affray

See appendix to part I. [No. 3] p. 6, and [No. 4] p. 9.

had taken place, and that it had been thrown overboard. Although I considered this an unfortunate accident for me, I was exceedingly happy at its effect; for it was the occasion of preventing much bloodshed among the savages. A chief called the Outard Blanche, had his lip cut off, and had come to the *Petit Corbeau*, and told him, ", that his face was his looking glass, that it was spoiled, " and that he was determined on revenge." The parties were charging their guns, and preparing for action, when lo! the flag appeared; like a messenger of peace, sent to prevent their bloody purposes. They were all astonished to see it; the staff was broke. When the *Petit Corbeau* arose and spoke to this effect: " That a thing so sacred, " had not been taken from my boat, without violence; " that it would be proper for them, to hush all private " animosities, until they had revenged the cause of their " eldest brother; that he would immediately go up to St. " Peters, to know what dogs had done that thing; in or- " der to take steps to get satisfaction of those, who had " done the mischief." They all listened to this reasoning and he immediately had the flag put out to dry, and em- barked for my camp. I was much concerned to hear of the blood likely to have been shed, and gave him five yards of blue stroud, three yards of calico, one handker- chief, one carrot of tobacco, and one knife, in order to make peace among his people. He promised to send my flag by land to the falls, and make the peace with the *Ou- tard Blanche*. Mr. Frazer went up to the village, and we embarked late, and encamped at the foot of the rapids. In many places, I could scarce throw a stone over the river. Distance 3 miles.

26*th Sept. Thursday*—Embarked at the usual hour, and after much labor in passing through the rapids, ar- rived at the foot of the falls about 3 or 4 o'clock; un- loaded my boat, and had the principal part of her cargo carried over the portage. With the other boat however full loaded, they were not able to get over the last shoot, and encamped about 600 yards below. I pitched my tent and encamped above the shoot. The rapids mentioned in this day's march, might properly be called a continuation of the falls of St. Anthony, for they are equally entitled to this appellation, with the falls of the Delaware and Susquehanna. Killed one deer. Distance 9 miles.

27th Sept. Friday—Brought over the residue of my loading this morning. Two men arrived, from Mr. Frazer, on St. Peters, for my dispatches. This business, closing and sealing, appeared like a last adieu to the civilized world. Sent a large packet to the general, and a letter to Mrs. Pike, with a short note to Mr. Frazer. Two young Indians brought my flag across by land, who arrived yesterday, just as we came in sight of the falls. I made them a present for their punctuality and expedition, and the danger they were exposed to from the journey.— Carried our boats out of the river, as far as the bottom of the hill.

28th Sept. Saturday—Brought my barge over, and put her in the river above the falls—while we were engaged with her 3-4 miles from camp, seven Indians painted black appeared on the heights—We had left our guns at camp, and were entirely defenceless—It occurred to me that they were the small party of Sioux who were obstinate, and would go to war, when the other part of the bands came in ; these they proved to be ; they were better armed than any I had ever seen ; having guns, bows, arrows, clubs, spears, and some of them even a case of pistols. I was at that time giving my men a dram ; and giving the cup of liquor to the first, he drank it off ; but I was more cautious with the remainder. I sent my interpreter to camp with them, to wait my coming ; wishing to purchase one of their war clubs, it being made of elk horn, and decorated with inlaid work.   This and a set of bows and arrows, I wished to get as a curiosity.   But the liquor I had given him, beginning to operate, he came back for me, but refusing to go till I brought my boat, he returned, and (I suppose being offended) borrowed a canoe and crossed the river.   In the afternoon got the other boat near the top of the hill, when the props gave way, and she slid all the way down to the bottom, but fortunately without injuring any person.   It raining very hard, we left her.   Killed one goose and a racoon.

29th Sept. Sunday—I killed a remarkably large racoon.   Got our large boat over the portage, and put her in the river, at the upper landing; this night the men gave sufficient proof of their fatigue, by all throwing themselves down to sleep, preferring rest to supper....
This day I had but 15 men out of 22; the others were sick.   This voyage could have been performed with great convenience, if we had taken our departure in June.   But the proper time would be to leave the Illinois as soon as the ice would permit, when the river would be of a good height.

30th Sept. Monday—Loaded my boat, moved over and encamped on the island.   The large boats loading likewise, we went over and put on board.   In the mean time, I took a survey of the Falls, Portage, &c.   If it be possible to pass the falls in high water, of which I am doubtful, it must be on the east side, about thirty yards from shore; as there are three layer of rocks, one below the other.   The pitch off of either, is not more than five feet; but of this I can say more on my return.*

1st Oct. Tuesday—Embarked late.   The river at first appeared mild, and sufficiently deep; but after about four miles, the shoals commenced, and had very hard water all

* It is never possible, as ascertained on my return.

day; passed three rapids; killed one goose and two ducks. This day the sun shone after I had left the falls; but whilst there, it was always cloudy. Distance 17 miles.

2d Oct. *Wednesday*—Embarked at our usual hour, and shortly after passed some large islands and remarkably hard ripples. Indeed the navigation, to persons not determined to proceed, would have been deemed impracticable. We waded nearly all day, to force the boats off shoals, and draw them through rapids. Killed three geese and two swans. Much appearance of elk and deer. Distance 12 miles.

3d Oct. *Thursday*—Cold in the morning. Mercury at 0°. Came on very well; some ripples. Killed three geese and one racoon, also a *brelaw*, an animal I had never before seen. Water ripply, and shoals. Distance 15 1-2 miles.

4th Oct. *Friday*—Rained in the morning, but the wind serving, we embarked, although extremely raw and cold. Opposite to the mouth of Crow river we found a bark canoe, cut to pieces with tomahawks and the paddles broken on shore; a short distance higher up, we saw five more; and continued to see the wrecks, until we found eight. From the form of the canoes, my interpreter pronounced them to be Sioux; and some broken arrows, to be the Sauteurs. The paddles were also marked with the Indian sign of men and women killed. From all these circumstances, we drew this inference, that the canoes had been the vessels of a party of Sioux, who had been attacked and all killed or taken by the Sauteurs. Time may develope this transaction. My interpreter was much alarmed, assuring me that it was probable that at our first rencounter with the Chipeways, they would take us for Sioux traders, and fire on us before we could come to an explanation; that they had murdered three Frenchmen, whom they found on the shore about this time last spring; but notwithstanding his information, I was on shore, all the afternoon in pursuit of elk. Caught a curious little animal on the prairie, which my Frenchman termed a *prairie mole*, but it is very different from the mole of the States. Killed two geese, one pheasant, and a wolf. Distance 16 miles.

5th Oct. Saturday—Hard water and ripples all day. Passed several old Sioux encampments, all fortified.... Found five litters, in which sick or wounded men had been carried. At this place a hard battle was fought between the Sioux and Sauteurs in the year 1800. Killed one goose. Distance 11 miles.

6th Oct. Sunday—Early in the morning discovered four elk, they swam the river, I pursued them, and wounded one, who made his escape into a marsh; saw two droves of elk. I killed some small game, and joined the boats near night. Found a small *red capot* hung upon a tree; this my interpreter informed me was a sacrifice by some Indians to the *bon Dieu*. I determined to lay by and hunt the next day. Killed three prairie hens, and two pheasants. This day saw the first elk. Distance 12 miles.

7th Oct. Monday—Lay by in order to dry my corn, cloathing, &c. and to have an investigation into the conduct of my sergeant, against whom some charges were exhibited. Sent several of my men out hunting. I went towards evening and killed some prairie hens; the hunters were unsuccessful. Killed three prairie hens and six pheasants.

8th Oct. Tuesday—Embarked early and made a very good day's march; had but three rapids to pass all day. Some woodland on the W. side, oak; but the whole bottom covered with the prickly ash. I made a practice, to oblige every man who complained of indisposition, to march; by which I had some flankers on both sides of the river, who were excellent guards against surprize, they also served as hunters. We had but one racoon killed by all. Distance 20 miles.

9th Oct. *Wednesday*—Embarked early; wind ahead; barrens and prairie. Killed one deer and four pheasants. Distance 3 miles.

10th Oct. *Thursday*—Came to large islands and strong water early in the morning. Passed the place at which Mr. Reinville and Mons. Perlier, wintered in 1797; passed a cluster of islands, more than 20 in the course of four miles; these I called Beaver islands, from the immense sign of those animals, for they have dams on every island and roads from them every two or three rod. I would here attempt a description of this wonderful animal, and its admirable system of architecture, was not the subject already exhausted, by the numerous travellers who have written on this subject. Encamped at the foot of the Grand Rapids. Killed two geese, five ducks, and four pheasants. Distance 16 1-2 miles.

11th Oct. *Friday*—Both boats passed the worst of the rapids, by 11 o'clock, but we were obliged to wade and lift them over rocks, where there was not a foot of water, when at times the next step would be in water over our heads. In consequence of this, our boats were frequently in imminent danger of being bilged on the rocks. About 5 miles above the rapids, our large boat was discovered to leak so fast, as to render it necessary to unload her, which we did. Stopped the leak and reloaded. Near a war encampment, I found a painted buckskin and a piece of scarlet cloth, suspended by the limb of a tree; this I supposed to be a sacrifice to *Matcho Maniton*, to render their enterprize successful; but I took the liberty of invading the rights of his diabolical majesty, by treating them, as the priests of old have often done, that is, converting the sacrifice to my own use.   Killed only two ducks.   Distance eight miles.

12th *October, Saturday.*—Hard ripples in the morning.   Passed a narrow rocky place, after which we had good water.   Our large boat again sprung a leak, and we were obliged again to encamp early and unload.   Killed one deer, one wolf, two geese and two ducks.   Distance 12 1-2 miles.

13th *October, Sunday.*—Embarked early and came on well.   Passed a handsome little river on the east, which we named Clear river; water good.   Killed one deer, one beaver, two minks, two geese, and one duck.   Fair wind.   Discovered the first buffalo sign.   Distance 29 miles.

14th *October, Monday.*—Ripples a considerable way.   My hunters killed three deer, four geese, and two porcupines.   When hunting, discovered a trail, which I supposed to have been made by the savages.   I followed it with much precaution, and at length started a large bear feeding on the carcase of a deer : he soon made his escape.   Yesterday we came to the first timbered land above the falls.   Made the first discovery of bear since we left St. Louis, excepting what we saw three miles below St. Peters.   Distance 17 miles.

15th *October, Tuesday.*—Ripples all day.   In the morning the large boat came up, and I once more got my party together; they had been detained by taking in the game.   Yesterday and this day passed some skirts of good land, well timbered, swamps of hemlock and white pine.   Water very hard.   The river became shallow and full of islands.   We encamped on a beautiful point, on the west, below a fall of the river over a bed of rocks, through which we had two narrow shoots to make our way the next day.   Killed two deer, five ducks, and two geese.   This day's march made me think seriously of our wintering-ground and leaving our large boats, Distance 5 miles.

16*th October, Wednesday.*—When we arose in the morning found that snow had fallen during the night ; the ground was covered and it continued to snow. This indeed was but poor encouragement for attacking the rapids, in which we were certain to wade to our necks. I was determined, however, if possible to make *la riviere de Corbeau*, the highest point ever made by traders in their bark canoes. We embarked, and after four hours work, became so benumbed with cold that our limbs were perfectly useless. We put to shore on the opposite side of the river, about two-thirds of the way up the rapids. Built a large fire ; and then discovered that our boats were nearly half full of water ; both having sprung large leaks so as to oblige me to keep three hands bailing. My sergeant (Kennerman) one of the stoutest men I ever knew, broke a blood-vessel and vomited nearly two quarts of blood. One of my corporals (Bradley) also evacuated nearly a pint of blood, when he attempted to void his urine. These unhappy circumstances, in addition to the inability of four other men, whom we were obliged to leave on shore ; convinced me, that if I had no regard for my own health and constitution, I should have some for those poor fellows, who were killing themselves to obey my orders. After we had breakfasted and refreshed ourselves, we went down to our boats on the rocks, where I was obliged to leave them. I then informed my men that we would return to the camp and there leave some of the party and our large boats. This information was pleasing, and the attempt to reach the camp soon accomplished. My reasons for this step have partly been already stated. The necessity of unloading and refitting my boats, the beauty and convenience of the spot for building huts, the fine pine-trees for peroques, and the quantity of game, were additional inducements. We immediately unloaded our boats and secured their cargoes. In the evening I went out upon a small, but beautiful creek, which empties into the falls, for the purpose of selecting pine-trees to make canoes. Saw five deer, and killed one buck weighing 137 pounds. By my leaving men at this place, and from the great quantities of game in its vicinity, I was ensured plenty of provision for my return voyage. In the party left behind was one hunter, to be continually employed, who would keep our stock of salt provisions good. Distance 233 1-2 miles above the falls of St. Anthony.

17th October, Thursday.—It continued to snow. I walked out in the morning and killed four bears, and my hunter three deers. Felled our trees for canoes and commenced working on them.

18th October, Friday.—Stopped hunting and put every hand to work. Cut 60 logs for huts and worked at the canoes. This, considering we had only two falling-axes and three hatchets, was pretty good work. Cloudy, with little snow.

19th October, Saturday.—Raised one of our houses, and almost completed one canoe. I was employed the principal part of this day in writing letters and making arrangements which I deemed necessary, in case I should never return.

20th October, Sunday.—Continued our labour at the houses and canoes, finished my letters, &c. At night discovered the prairie, on the opposite side of the river, to be on fire; supposed to have been made by the Sauteurs. I wished much to have our situation respectable here, or I would have sent the next day, to discover them.

21st October, Monday.—Went out hunting, but killed nothing, not wishing to shoot at small game. Our labour went on.

22d October, Tuesday.—Went out hunting. About 15 miles up the creek saw a great quantity of deer; but, from the dryness of the woods and the quantity of brush, only shot one through the body, which made its escape. This day my men neglected their work, which convinced me I must leave off hunting and superintend the men. Miller and myself lay out all night, in the pine woods.

23d October, Wednesday.—Raised another block-house, deposited all our property in the one already completed. Killed a number of pheasants and ducks, while visiting my canoe-makers. Sleets and snow.

24th October, Thursday.—The snow having fallen one or two inches thick in the night; I sent out one hunter (Sparks) and went out myself, Bradley, my other hunter, being sick. Each of us killed two deer, one goose, and one pheasant.

25th October, Friday.—Sent out men with Sparks to bring in his game. None of them returned, and I supposed them to be lost in the hemlock swamps, with which the country abounds. My interpreter, however, whom I believe to be a coward, insisted that they were killed by the *Sauteurs*. Made arrangements for my departure.

26th October, Saturday.—Launched my canoes and found them very small. My hunter killed three deer. Took out Miller and remained out all night, but killed nothing.

27th October Sunday.—Employed in preparing our baggage to embark.

28th October, Monday.—My two canoes being finished, launched, and brought to the head of the rapids, I put my provision, ammunition, &c. on board, intending to em-

bark by day.   Left them under the charge of the sentinel, and in an hour one of them sunk, in which was the
ammunition and my baggage : this was occasioned by what
is called a wind-shock.   This misfortune, and the extreme
smallness of my canoes, induced me to build another.   I
had my cartridges spread out on blankets and large fires
made round them.   At that time I was not able to ascertain the extent of the misfortune, the magnitude of which
none can estimate, save only those in the same situation
with ourselves, 1500 miles from civilized society ; and in
danger of losing the very means of defence, nay of existence.

   29th October, Tuesday.——Felled a large pine and commenced another canoe.   I was at work at my cartridges
all day, but did not save five dozen out of 30.   In attempting to dry the powder in pots, blew it up, and it had
nearly blown up a tent and two or three men with it.
Made a dozen new cartridges with the old wrapping-paper.

   30th October, Wednesday.——My men labored as usual.
Nothing extraordinary.

   31st October, Thursday.——Enclosed my little work
completely with pickets.   Hauled up my two boats, and
turned them over on each side of the gate-ways ; by which
means a defence was made to the river, and had it not
been for various political reasons, I would have laughed at
the attack of 800 or 1000 savages, if all my party were
within.   For except accidents, it would only have afforded
amusement, the Indians having no idea of taking a place
by storm.   Found myself powerfully attacked with the
fantastics of the brain, called ennui, at the mention of
which I had hitherto scoffed ; but my books being packed
up, I was like a person entranced, and could easily conceive why so many persons who have been confined to remote places, acquired the habit of drinking to excess and

many other vicious practices, which have been adopted merely to pass time.

1st *November*, *Friday.*—Finding that my canoe would not be finished in two or three days, I concluded to take six men and go down the river about 12 miles, where we had remarked great sign of elk and buffalo. Arrived there about the middle of the afternoon. All turned out to hunt. None of us killed any thing but *Sparks* one doe. A slight snow fell.

2d *November*, *Saturday.*—Left the camp with the fullest determination to kill an elk, if it were possible, before my return. I never had killed one of those animals. Took *Miller*, whose obliging disposition made him agreeable in the woods. I was determined that if we came on the trail of elk, to follow them a day or two in order to kill one. This, to a person acquainted with the nature of those animals, and the extent of the prairies in this country, would appear, what it really was, a very foolish resolution. We soon struck where a herd of 150 had passed. Pursued and came in sight about 8 o'clock, when they appeared, at a distance, like an army of Indians moving along in single file; a large buck, of at least four feet between the horns, leading the van, and one of equal magnitude bringing up the rear. We followed until near night, without once being able to get within point-blank shot. I once made Miller fire at them with his musket, at about 400 yards distance: it had no other effect than to make them leave us about five miles behind on the prairie. Passed several deer in the course of the day, which I think we could have killed, but did not fire for fear of alarming the elk. Finding that it was no easy matter to kill one, I shot a doe through the body, as I perceived by her blood, where she lay down in the snow; yet, not knowing how to track, we lost her. Shortly after saw three elk by themselves near a copse of woods.   Approached near them and broke the shoulder of one ; but he ran off with the other two just as I was about to follow.   Saw a buck deer lying on the grass ; shot him behind the eyes, when he fell over.   I walked up to him, put my foot on his horns, and examined the shot, immediately after which he snorted, bounced up, and fell five steps from me.   This I considered his last effort ; but soon after, to our utter astonishment, he jumped up and ran off. He stopped frequently : we pursued him, expecting him to fall every minute, by which we were led from the pursuit of the wounded elk.   After being wearied out in this unsuccessful chase, we returned in pursuit of the wounded elk, and when we came up to the party, found him missing from the flock.   Shot another in the body ; but my ball being small, he likewise escaped.   Wounded another deer : when hungry, cold, and fatigued, after having wounded three deer and two elk, were obliged to encamp in a point of hemlock woods, on the head of Clear river.   The large herd of elk lay about one mile from us, in the prairie.   Our want of success I ascribe to the smallness of our balls, and to our inexperience in following the track, after wounding them, for it is very seldom a deer drops on the spot you shoot it.

3d November, Sunday.—Rose pretty early and went in pursuit of the elk.   Wounded one buck deer on the way.   We made an attempt to drive them into the woods, but their leader broke past us and it appeared as if the drove would have followed him though they had been obliged to run over us.   We fired at them passing, but without effect.   Pursued them through the swamp till about 10 o'clock, when I determined to attempt to make the river, and for that purpose took a due south course. Passed many droves of elk and buffalo, but being in the middle of an immense prairie, knew it was folly to attempt to shoot them. Wounded several deer, but got none. In fact, I knew I could shoot as many deer as any body; but neither myself nor company could find one in ten, whereas one experienced hunter would get all. Near night struck a lake about five miles long and two miles wide. Saw immense droves of elk on both banks. About sun down saw a herd crossing the prairie towards us. We sat down. Two bucks, more curious than the others, came pretty close. I struck one behind the fore shoulder: he did not go more than 20 yards before he fell and died. This was the cause of much exultation, because it fulfilled my determination, and, as we had been two days and nights without victuals, it was very acceptable. Found some scrub oak. In about one mile made a fire, and with much labor and pains got our meat to it; the wolves feasting on one half while we were carrying away the other. We were now provisioned, but were still in want of water, the snow being all melted. Finding my drought very excessive in the night, I went in search of water, and was much surprised, after having gone about a mile, to strike the Mississippi. Filled my hat and returned to my companion.

4th November, Monday.—Repaired my mockinsons, using a piece of elk's bone as an awl. We both went to the Mississippi and found we were a great distance from the camp. I left Miller to guard the meat and marched for camp. Having strained my ancles in the swamps, they were extremely sore, and the strings of my mockinsons cut them and made them swell considerably. Before I had gone far discovered a herd of 10 elk. Approached within 50 yards and shot one through the body. He fell on the spot; but rose again and ran off. I pursued him at least five miles, expecting every minute to see him drop. I then gave him up. When I arrived at *Clear river*, a deer was standing on the other bank. I killed him on the spot, and while I was taking out the entrails another came up. I shot him also. This was my last ball, and then only could I kill! Left part of my clothes at this place to scare the wolves. Arrived at my camp at dusk, to the great joy of our men, who had been to our little garrison to enquire for me, and receiving no intelligence, had concluded we were killed by the Indians, having heard them fire on the opposite bank. The same night we saw fires on the opposite shore in the prairie; this was likewise seen in the fort, when all the men moved in the works.

5th November, Tuesday.—Sent four of my men with one canoe, loaded with the balance of nine deer, that had been killed, with the other two. Went down the river for my meat. Stopped for the deer, which I found safe. Miller had just started to march home, but returned to camp with us. Found all the meat safe, and brought it to the river, where we pitched our camp.

6th November, Wednesday.—At the earnest entreaties of my men, and with a hope of killing some more game, I agreed to stay and hunt. We went out and found that all the elk and buffalo had gone down the river from those plains the day before, leaving large roads to point out their course. This would not appear extraordinary to persons acquainted with the nature of those animals, as the prairie had unluckily caught fire. After Miller left the camp for home, Sparks killed two deer, about six miles off, and it being near the river, I sent the three men down with the canoe, to return early in the morning. It commenced snowing about midnight, and by morning was six inches deep.

F

7th November, Thursday.—Waited all day with the greatest anxiety for my men. The river became nearly filled with snow, partly congealed into ice. My situation can more easily be imagined than described. Went down the river to where I understood the deer were killed; but discovered nothing of my men. I now became very uneasy on their account, for I was well aware of the hostile disposition of the Indians to all persons on this part of the Mississippi, taking them to be traders—and we had not yet had an opportunity of explaining to them who we were. Snow still continued falling very fast, and was nearly knee-deep. Had great difficulty to procure wood sufficient to keep up a fire all night. Ice in the river thickening.

8th November, Friday.—My men not yet arrived. I determined to depart for the garrison, and when the river had frozen, to come down on the ice with a party, or if the weather became mild, by water, with my other peroques, to search for my poor men. Put up about ten pounds of meat, two blankets, and a bear-skin, with my sword and gun, which made for me a very heavy load. Left the meat in as good a situation as possible. Wrote on the snow my wishes, and put my handkerchief up as a flag. Departed. My anxiety of mind was so great that, notwithstanding my load and the depth of snow, I made into the bottom, above our former hunting camp, a little before night. Passed several deer and one elk, which I might probably have killed; but not knowing whether I should be able to secure the meat, if I killed them, and bearing in mind that they were created for the use, and not the sport of man, I did not fire at them. Whilst I was endeavoring to strike fire I heard voices, and looking round, observed my corporal Meek and three men passing. Called them to me, and we embarked together. They

were on their march down, to see if they could render us
any assistance in ascending the river.   They were much
grieved to hear my report of my other men, corporal
Bradley, Sparks, and Miller.

9th November, Saturday.—Snowed a little.   The
men carried my pack.   I was so sore that it was with difficulty I carried my gun ; fortunately they brought with
them a pair of mockinsons, sent me by one of my soldiers
(Owings), who had rightly calculated that I was bare-foot ;
also a phial of whiskey, sent by the serjeant, which were
both very acceptable to me.   They brought, also, some
tobacco for my lost men.   We experienced difficulty in
crossing the river, owing to the ice.   Moved my command
into the post, who were again encamped out, ready to
march up the river.   Set all hands to making sleds, in
order that, the moment the river closed, I might descend,
with a strong party, in search of my lost men.   Issued provisions, and was obliged to use six venison hams, being
part of a quantity of elegant hams, I had preserved, to take
down, if possible, to the general and some other friends.
Had the two hunters not been found, I must have become
a slave to hunting, in order to support my party.   The ice
still ran very thick.

10th November, Sunday.—Continued making sleds.
No news of my hunters.   Ice in the river very thick and
hard.   Raised my tent with puncheons, and laid a floor
in it.

11th November, Monday.—I went out hunting.   Saw
but two deer. Killed a remarkably large black fox. Bradley and Miller arrived, having understood the writing on
the snow, and left Sparks behind at the camp, to take care
of the meat.   Their detention was owing to their being
lost on the prairie the first night, and not being able to find
their deer.

12*th November, Tuesday.*—Dispatched Miller and Huddleston to the lower hunting-camp, and Bradley and Brown to hunting in the woods. Made my arrangements in camp. Thawing weather.

13*th November, Wednesday.*—Bradley returned with a very large buck, which supplied us for the next four days.

14*th November, Thursday.*—It commenced raining at four o'clock, A. M. lightning and loud thunder. I went down the river in one of my canoes, with five men, in order to bring up the meat from the lower camp; but, after descending about 13 miles, found the river blocked up with ice. Returned about two miles, and encamped in the bottom where I had my hunting camp, on the 1st. inst. Extremely cold towards night.

15*th November, Friday.*—When we meant to embark in the morning, found the river full of ice and hardly moving. Returned to camp and went out to hunt, for we had no provision with us. Killed nothing but five prairie hens, which afforded us this day's subsistence: this bird I took to be the same as grouse. Expecting the ice had become hard, we attempted to cross the river, but could not. In the endeavor one man fell through. Freezing.

16*th November, Saturday.*—Detached Corporal Meek and one private to the garrison, to order the sleds down. No success in hunting except a few fowl. I began to consider the life of a hunter a very slavish life, and extremely precarious as to support; for sometimes I have myself (although no hunter) killed 600 weight of meat in one day; and I have hunted three days successively, without killing any thing but a few small birds, which I was obliged to do to keep my men from starving. Freezing.

17*th November, Sunday.*—One of my men arrived: he had attempted to make the camp before, but lost himself in the prairie, lay out all night, and froze his toes. He informed us that the corporal and the men I sent with him, had their toes frost-bitten, the former very badly; that three men were on their way down by land, the river above not being froze over. They arrived a few hours before night. Freezing.

18*th November, Monday.*—Took our departure down the river on the ice, our baggage on the sled. Ice very rough. Distance 12 miles. Freezing.

19*th November, Tuesday.*—Arrived opposite our hunting camp about noon. Had the meat, &c. moved over. They had a large quantity of meat. I went out and killed a very large buck. Thawing.

20*th November, Wednesday.*—Departed to return to the stockade, part of our meat on the sled and part in the little peroque (the river being open in the middle). Killed four deer. Thawing. Distance 5 miles.

21*st November, Thursday.*—Marched in the morning. Came to a place where the river was very narrow, and the channel blocked up. Were obliged to unload our peroque and haul her over. The river having swelled a good deal, at this place, the ice gave way with myself and two men on it. We seized the sled that stood by us, with some little baggage on it, and by jumping over four cracks, the last two feet wide : providentially made our passage good, without loosing an individual thing. Encamped opposite Clear river. Killed one deer and one otter. Freezing.

22*d November, Friday.*—Were obliged to leave our canoe at Clear river, the river being closed. Made two trips with our sled. Killed one deer. Distance 5 miles.

23*d November, Saturday.*—Having seen a great deal of buffalo sign, I determined to kill one the next day (forgetting the elk chase). Encamped nearly opposite our camp of the 15th and 16th. Thawing. Distance 4 miles.

24th November, Sunday.—Took Miller and Boley and went in pursuit of buffalo. Came up with some about 10 o'clock. In the afternoon wounded one. Pursued them until night, and encamped on the side of a swamp. Thawing.

25th November, Monday.—Commenced again the pursuit of the buffalo, and continued till 11 o'clock, when I gave up the chase. Arrived at the camp about sun down, hungry and weary, having eat nothing since we left it. My rifle was too small a ball to kill buffalo : the balls should not be more than thirty to the pound :—an ounce ball would be still preferable, and the animal should be hunted on horse-back. I think that, in the prairies of this country, the bow and arrow could be used to more advantage than the gun ; for you might ride immediately along side, and strike them where you pleased, leaving them to proceed after others. Thawing.

26th November, Tuesday.—Proceeded up the river. The ice getting very rotten, the men fell through several times. Thawing. Distance 5 miles.

27th November, Wednesday.—Took one man and marched to the post. Found all well. My hunter, Bradley, had killed eleven deer since my departure. Sent all the men down to help the party up. They returned accompanied by two Indians, who informed me they were two men of a band, who resided on Lake Superior, called the Fols Avoins, but spoke the language of the Chipeways. They informed me that Mr. Dickson's, and the other trading houses, were established about 60 miles below ; that there were 70 lodges of Sioux on the Mississippi. All my men arrived at the post. We brought from our camp below the balance of 17 deer and two elks.

28th November, Thursday.—The Indians departed much pleased with their reception. I dispatched corporal

Meek and one private down to Dickson with a letter, which would at least have the effect of attaching the most powerful tribes in this quarter to my interest.

29th November, Friday.——A Sioux (the son of a warrior called the Killeur Rouge, of the *Gens des Feuilles*) and a Fols Avoin came to the post. He said that, having struck our trail below, and finding some to be shoe-tracks, he conceived it to be the establishment of some traders, took it, and came to the post. He informed me that Mr. Dickson had told the Sioux " that they might now hunt where they pleased, as I had gone a head and would cause the Chipeways, wherever I met them, to treat them with friendship; that I had barred up the mouth of the St. Peters, so that no liquor could ascend that river; but that, if they came on the Mississippi, they should have what liquor they wanted :——also, that I was on the river and had a great deal of merchandize to give them in presents." This information of Mr. Dickson to the Indians seemed to have self-interest and envy for its motives; for, by the idea of having prevented liquor from going up the St. Peters, he gave the Indians to understand that it was a regulation of my own, and not a law of the United States; and by assuring them he would sell to them on the Mississippi, he drew all the Indians from the traders on the St. Peters, who had adhered to the restriction of not selling liquor, and should any of them be killed, the blame would all lie on me, as he had (without authority) assured them they might hunt in security. I took care to give the young chief a full explanation of my ideas on the above. He remained all night. Killed two deer.

30th November, Saturday.——I made the two Indians some small presents. They crossed the river and departed. Detached Kennerman with eleven men, to bring up two canoes.

1st December, Sunday.—Snowed a little in the middle of the day. Went out with my gun, but killed nothing.

2d December, Monday.—Sparks arrived from the party below, and informed me they could not kill any game, but had started up with the little peroque :—also, that Mr. Dickson and a Frenchman had passed my detachment about three hours before. He left them on their march to the post. Sparks arrived about 10 o'clock at night.

3d December, Tuesday.—Mr. Dickson, with one engagée and a young Indian, arrived at the fort. I received him with every politeness in my power, and after a serious conversation with him on the subject of the information given me on the 29th ult. was induced to believe it, in part, incorrect. He assured me that no liquor was sold by him, nor by any houses under his direction. He gave me much useful information relative to my future route, which gave me great encouragement as to the certainty of my accomplishing the object of my voyage, to the fullest extent. He seemed to be a gentleman of general commercial knowledge, and possessing much geographical information of the western country, of open, frank, manners. He gave me many assurances of his good wishes for the prosperity of my undertaking.

4th December, Wednesday.—My men arrived with one canoe only. Calculated on returning them two days after.

5th December, Thursday.—Mr. Dickson, with his two men, departed for their station, after having furnished me with a letter for a young man of his house, in Lake de Sable, and a *carte blanche* as to my commands on him. Weather mild.

6th December, Friday.—I dispatched my men down, to bring up the other peroque with a strong sled on which it was intended to put the canoe about one third, and to let

the end drag on the ice.   Three families of the Fols
Avoins arrived and encamped near the fort:—also, one
Sioux, who pretended to have been sent to me, from the
Gens des Feuilles, to inform me that the Yanctongs and Sussitongs (two bands of Sioux from the head of the St.
Peters and the Missouri, and the most savage of them)
had commenced the war-dance and would depart in a few
days, in which case he conceived it would be advisable for
the Fols Avoins to keep close under my protection ; that
making a stroke on the Chipeways would tend to injure
the grand object of my voyage, &c. &c.   Some reasons
induced me to believe he was a self-created envoy ; however, I offered to pay him, or any young Sioux, who would
go to those bands and carry my word.   He promised to
make known my wishes upon his return.   My men returned
in the evening without my canoe, having been so unfortunate as to split her in carrying her over the rough hilly
ice in the ripples below.   So many disappointments almost
wearied out my patience ; but, notwithstanding, I intended
to embark by land and water in a few days.

   7th December, Saturday.—An Indian (by the name
of Chien Blanche) of the Fols Avoin tribe, with his family
and connections, arrived and encamped near the stockade.
He informed me that he had wintered here for ten years
past, that the sugar camp near the stockade was where
he made sugar.   He appeared to be an intelligent man.
I visited his camp in the afternoon, and found him seated
amidst his children and grandchildren, amounting in all to
ten.   His wife, although of an advanced age, was suck-
ling two children, that appeared to be about two years old.
I should have taken them to be twins, had not one been
much fairer than the other.   Upon enquiry, however, I
found that the fairest was the daughter of an Englishman,
by one of the Indian's daughters, lately deceased ; since

whose death the grandmother had taken it to the breast. His lodge was made of rushes plaited into mats, after the manner of the Illinois. I was obliged to give some meat to all the Indians who arrived at the stockade, at the same time explaining our situation. The Chien Blanche assured me it should be repaid with interest in the course of the winter, but that at that time he was without any thing to eat. In fact, our hunters having killed nothing for several days, we were ourselves on short allowance.

8th December, Sunday.—An invalid Sioux arrived with information, that the bands of the Sussitongs and Yanctongs had actually determined to make war on the Chipeways, and that they had formed a party of 150 or 160 men, but that part of the Sussitongs had refused to go to the war, and would be here on a visit to me the next day. This occasioned me to delay crossing the river immediately, on my voyage to Lake Sang Sue, as it was possible that, by having a conference with them, I might still prevent the stroke intended to be made against the Chipeways.

9th December, Monday.—Prepared to embark. Expecting the Sioux, I had two large kettles of soup made for them. Had a shooting-match with four prizes. The Sioux did not arrive, and we eat the soup ourselves. Crossed the river and encamped above the rapids. Wind changed and it grew cold.

10th December, Tuesday.—After arranging our sleds* and peroque commenced our march. The sleds on the prairie and the peroque towed by three men. Found it extremely difficult to get along, the snow being melted off the prairie in spots. The men who had the canoe were

---

* My sleds were such as are frequently seen about farmers' yards, calculated to hold two barrels or 400 weight, in which two men were geared abreast.

obliged to wade and drag her over the rocks in many
places. Shot the only deer I saw. It fell three times, and
after made its escape. This was a great disappointment,
for upon the game we took now we depended for our subsistence. This evening disclosed to my men the real danger they had to encounter. Distance 5 miles.

11*th December, Wednesday.*—It having thawed all
night, the snow had almost melted from the prairie. I
walked on until 10 o'clock, and made a fire. I then went
back to look for the peroque, and at a remarkable rapid in
the river, opposite a high piny island, made a fire and
waited for them to come up, when we partly unloaded. I
returned and met the sleds. When we arrived at the
place pitched on for our camp, sent the men down to
assist the peroque. In the afternoon, from about three
o'clock, we heard the report of not less than 50 guns
a-head, and after dusk much shooting on the prairie. I was
at a loss to know who they could be, unless they were Sauteaux, and what could be their object, in shooting after
dark. Kept a good look out. Distance 5 miles.

12*th December, Thursday.*—The snow having almost
entirely left the prairie, we were obliged to take on but one
sled at a time and treble man it. In the morning my interpreter came to me with quite a martial air, and requested that he might be allowed to go ahead to discover what
Indians we heard fire last evening. I gave him permission
and away he went. Shortly after, I went out with corporal Bradley and a private, and in about an hour overtook my partizan, on a bottom close to the river; he was
hunting racoons, and had caught five. We left him, and
after choosing an encampment, and sending the private
back, to conduct the party to it, anxious to discover the
Indians, the corporal and myself marched on. We
ascended the river about eight miles; saw no Indians;
but discovered that the river was frozen over; which

pleased me more, for we would now be enabled to walk
three times our usual distance in a day. I was much surprized that we saw no Indians. After our return to the
camp, was told that a Fols Avoin Indian had met my party and informed them, that in the rear of the hills, that
bordered the prairie, there were small lakes which by portages communicated with Lake Superior. That in one
days march, on that course, we would find English trading houses. That the Chipeways were there hunting.
That the Sioux who had visited my camp on the 29th ult.
on hearing the firing, had prudently returned, with his
companions, to the west side of the Mississippi, agreeably
to my advice. How persons unacquainted with the searching spirit of trade, and the enterprize of the people of
the north west; would be surprized to find people who
had penetrated from Lake Superior, to lakes little more
than marshes. And it likewise points out the difficulty of
putting a barrier on their trade. All my sleds and peroques
did not get up until half past 10 o'clock. Saw a very
beautiful fox, red back, white tail and breast. My interpreter called them Reynard d'Argent. I had no opportunity of shooting him. Killed six racoons and one porcupine. Fine day. Distance 7 miles.

13th December, Friday.—Made double trips. Embarked at the upper end of the ripples. It commenced
snowing at 3 o'clock. Bradley killed one deer, another
man killed one racoon. Storm continued until next morning. Distance 5 miles.

14th December, Saturday.—We departed from our
encampment at the usual hour, but had not advanced one
mile, when the foremost sled, which happened unfortunately to carry my baggage and ammunition, fell into the
river. We were all in the river up to our middles, in re-
covering the things. Halted and made a fire. Came on
to where the river was frozen over. Stopped and en-

camped on the west shore, in a pine wood.   Upon examining my things, found all my baggage wet and some of
my books materially injured ; but a still greater injury was,
that all my cartridges, and four pounds of double battle
Sussex powder which I had brought for my own use, was
destroyed. Fortunately my kegs of powder were preserved
dry, and some bottles of common glazed powder, which
were so tightly corked, as not to admit water.   Had this
not been the case, my voyage must necessarily have been
terminated, for we could not have subsisted without ammunition.   During the time of our misfortune, two Fols
Avoin Indians came to us, one of whom was at my stockade, on the 29th ult. in company with the Sioux. I signified
to them by signs the place of our intended encampment,
and invited them to come and encamp with us.   They left
me and both arrived at my camp in the evening, having
each a deer which they presented me; I gave them my
canoe, to keep until spring ; and in the morning at part-
ing made them a small present.   Sat up until 3 o'clock
P. M. drying and assorting my ammunition, baggage, &c.
Killed two deer.   Distance 4 miles.

15th December Sunday.——Remained at our camp making sleds.   Killed two deer.   Crossed and recrossed several Indian trails in the woods.

16th December, Monday.——Remained at the same
camp.   Employed as yesterday.   Killed three deer.   I
wounded a buffalo in the shoulder, and by a fair race
overtook him in the prairie and gave him another shot ;
but it being near night left him till morning.

17th December, Tuesday.——Departed from our agreeable encampment at an early hour.   Found our sleds to
be very heavily loaded.   Broke one sled runner, and were
detained by other circumstances.   Bradley, Rosseau (the
interpreter) and myself killed four deer and wounded five
others.   Having eleven on hand already, I found it neces-

sary to leave behind some of my other loading. At night we dug a hole, four feet deep, three feet wide, and six feet long, in which we put one barrel of pork and one barrel of flour, after wrapping them up in seven deer skins, to preserve them from the damp, we then filled up the hole, and built our fire immediately over it.

18th *December, Thursday.*—Did not get off until 8 o'clock, from the delay in bringing in our meat. Ice tolerably good. Began to see the Chipeway's encampments very frequently, but had not entirely left the Sioux country on the western shore. Beautiful pine ridges.

19th *December, Thursday.*—Were obliged to take to the prairie, from the rivers being open ; but the snow was frozen hard and the sleds did not sink deep, so that we made a pretty good days journey. Killed one deer and two otters. River still open. Distance 10 miles.

20th *December, Friday.*—Travelled part of the day on the prairie and on the ice. Killed one deer. Heard three reports of guns just at sun set from the opposite side of the river. Deposited one barrel of flour. Distance 7 miles.

21st *December, Saturday.*—Bradley and myself went on ahead, and overtook my interpreter, who had left camp very early in hopes that he would be able to see the river De Corbeau, where he had twice wintered. He was immediately opposite to a large island, which he supposed to have great resemblance to an island, opposite the mouth of the above river ; but finally he concluded, it was not the island, and returned to camp. But this was actually the river, as we discovered when we got to the head of the island, from which we could see the river's entrance.... This fact exposes the ignorance and inattention of the French and traders, and with the exception of a few intelligent men, what little confidence is to be placed on their information. We ascended the Mississippi, about five miles above the confluence; found it not frozen; but in many places, not more than one hundred yards over; mild and still. Indeed all the appearance of a small river of a low country. Returned and found my party, having broke sleds, &c. had only made good 3 miles, while I had marched 35.

22d December, Sunday.—Killed three deer. Owing to the many difficult places we had to pass, made but 4 1-2 miles.

23d December, Monday.—Never did I undergo more fatigue, in performing the duties of hunter, spy, guide, commanding officer, &c. Sometimes in front; sometimes in the rear; frequently in advance of my party 10 or 15 miles; that at night I was scarcely able to make my notes intelligible. Killed two racoons. From our sleds breaking down, and having to make so many portages on the road, made but 4 miles.

24th December, Tuesday.—Took the latitude of the Isle De Corbeau, and found it to be in 45° 49' 50" N. The Mississippi becomes very narrow above the river De Corbeau, and as if it were the forks, changes its direction from hard W. to N. E. generally. Distance 10 1-2 miles.

25th December, Wednesday.—Marched and encamped at 11 o'clock. Gave out two pounds of extra meat, two pounds of extra flour, one gill of whiskey, and some tobacco per man; this, in order to distinguish Christmas day. Distance 3 miles.

26th December, Thursday.—Broke four sleds; broke into the river four times, and had four carrying places, since we left the river De Corbeau. The timber was all yellow and pitch pine, of which there were scarcely any below. Distance 3 miles.

27th December, Friday.—After two carrying places, we arrived where the river was completely closed with ice; after which we proceeded with some degree of speed and ease. Killed one bear. The country on both sides, presented a dreary and barren prospect of high rocks, with dead pine timber. Snow. Distance 10 miles.

28th December, Saturday.—Two sleds fell through the ice. In the morning passed a very poor country ; bare knobs on each side ; but towards evening the bottoms became larger, and the pine ridges better timbered. Bradley and myself marched 10 miles beyond the sleds. Killed one deer. Distance 12 miles.

29th December, Sunday—Cold windy day. Met with no material interruptions ; passed some rapids. The snow blew from the woods on to the river. The country full of small lakes, some 3 miles in circumference. Distance 21 miles.

30th December, Monday.—The snow having drifted on the ice, retarded the sleds. Numerous small lakes and pine ridges continued. A new species of pine, called the French Sap pine. Killed one otter. Distance 12 miles.

31st December, Tuesday.—Passed Pine river about 11 o'clock. At its mouth there was a Chipeway's encampment of fifteen lodges, this had been occupied in the summer, but is now vacant. By the significations of their marks, we understood, that they had marched a party of 50 warriors against the Sioux ; and had killed four men and four women, which were represented by images carved out of pine or cedar. The four men painted and put in the ground to the middle, leaving above ground those parts which are generally concealed ; by their sides were four painted poles, sharpened at the end to represent the women. Near this were poles with deer skins, plumes, silk handkerchiefs, &c. Also a circular hoop of cedar with something attached, representing a scalp. Near each lodge they had holes dug in the ground, and boughs ready to cover them, as a retreat for their women and children if attacked by the Sioux, &c.

1st Jannary 1806, *Wednesday.*—Passed six very elegant bark canoes, on the bank of the river, which had been laid up by the Chipeways ; also a camp which we conceived to have been evacuated about ten days.   My interpreter came after me in a great hurry, conjuring me not to go so far ahead, and assured me that the Chipeways, encountering me without an interpreter, party, or flag, would certainly kill me.   But, notwithstanding this, I went on several miles farther than usual, in order to make any discoveries that were to be made ; conceiving the savages not so barbarous or ferocious, as to fire on two men, (I had one with me) who were apparently coming into their country, trusting to their generosity ; and knowing, that if we met only two or three we were equal to them, I, having my gun and pistols, and he his buck shot.   Made some extra presents for new years day.

2d January, Thursday—Fine warm day.   Discovered fresh sign of Indians.   Just as we were encamping at night, my sentinel informed us, that some Indians were coming full speed upon our trail or track.   I ordered my men to stand by their guns *carefully.*   They were immediately at my camp, and saluted the flag by a discharge of three pieces ; when four Chipeways, one Englishman, and a Frenchman of the N. W. company presented themselves.   They informed us that some women having discovered our trail gave the alarm, and not knowing, but it was their enemies, they had departed to make a discovery. They had heard of us and revered our flag.   Mr. Grant, the Englishman, had only arrived the day before from Lake De Sable ; from which he marched, in one day and a half.   I presented the Indians with half a deer, which they received thankfully, for they had discovered our fires some days ago, and believing it to be the Sioux, they dared not leave their camp.   They returned, but Mr. Grant remained all night.

3d January, Friday.—My party marched early, but I returned with Mr. Grant to his establishment on the Red Cedar Lake, having one corporal with me. When we came in sight of his house, I observed the flag of Great Britain flying. I felt indignant, and cannot say what my feelings would have excited me to, had he not informed me, that it belonged to the Indians. This was not much more agreeable to me. After explaining to a Chipeway warrior (called *Curly Head*) the object of my voyage, and receiving his answer, that he would remain tranquil, until my return. We eat a good breakfast for the country, departed and overtook my sleds, just at dusk. Killed one porcupine. Distance 16 miles.

4th January, Saturday.—We made twenty eight points in the river; broad, good bottom, and of the usual timber. In the night I was awakened by the cry of the sentinel, calling repeatedly to the men; at length he vociferated, " G—d d—n your souls, will you let the lieutenant be burned to death?" This immediately aroused me, at first I seized my arms, but looking round, I saw my tents in flames. The men flew to my assistance, and we tore them down, but not until they were entirely ruined. This, with the loss of my leggins, mockinsons, socks, &c. which I had hung up to dry, was no trivial misfortune, in such a country, and on such a voyage. But I had reason to thank God that the powder, three small casks of which I had in my tent did not take fire, if it had, I must certainly have lost all my baggage, if not my life.

5th January, Sunday.—Mr. Grant promised to overtake me yesterday, but has not yet arrived. I conceived it would be necessary to attend his motions, with careful observation. Distance 27 miles.

6th January, Monday.—Bradley and myself walked up 31 points, in hopes to discover Lake De Sable; but finding a near cut of 20 yards for ten miles, and being fearful the sleds would miss it, we returned 23 points before we found our camp. They had made only eight points. Met two Frenchmen of the N. W. company with about 180 pounds on each of their backs, with rackets on; they informed me that Mr. Grant had gone on with the Frenchman. Snow fell all day, and was three feet deep. Spent a miserable night.

7th January, Tuesday.—Made but 11 miles, and then were obliged to send a-head and make fires every 3 miles; notwithstanding which, the cold was so intense, that some of the men had their noses, others their fingers, and others their toes frozen, before they felt the cold sensibly. Very severe days march.

8th January, Wednesday.—Conceiving I was at no great distance from Sandy Lake, I left my sleds, and with corporal Bradley, took my departure for that place, intending to send him back the same evening. We walked on very briskly until near night, when we met a young Indian, one of those who had visited my camp near Red Cedar Lake. I endeavored to explain to him, that it was my wish to go to Lake De Sable that evening. He returned with me, until we came to a trail that led across the woods, this he signified was a near course. I went this course with him, and shortly after found myself at a Chipeway encampment, to which I believe the friendly savage had enticed me with an expectation that I would tarry all night, knowing that it was too late for us to make the lake in good season. But upon our refusing to stay, he put us in the right road. We arrived at the place where the track left the Mississippi, at dusk, when we traversed about two leagues of a wilderness, without any very great difficulty, and at length struck the shore of Lake De Sable, over a branch of which our course lay. The snow having covered the trail made by the Frenchmen who had passed before with the rackets, I was fearful of loosing ourselves on the lake ; the consequence of which can only be conceived by those who have been exposed on a lake, or naked plain, a dreary night of January, in latitude 47° and the thermometer below 0.   Thinking that we could observe, the bank of the other shore, we kept a straight course, and sometime after discovered lights, and on our arrival were not a little surprised to find a large stockade.   The gate being open, we entered and proceeded to the quarters of Mr. Grant, where we were treated with the utmost hospitality.

9th January, Thursday.—Marched the corporal early, in order that our men should receive assurances of our safety and success.   He carried with him a small keg of spirits, a present from Mr. Grant.   The establishment of this place was formed twelve years since, by the N. W. company, and was formerly under the charge of a Mr. Charles Brusky. It has attained at present such regularity, as to permit the superintendant to live tolerably comfortable.   They have horses they procured from Red river, of the Indians ; raise plenty of Irish potatoes, catch pike, suckers, pickerel, and white fish in abundance.   They have also beaver, deer, and moose ; but the provision they chiefly depend upon, is wild oats, of which they purchase great quantities from the savages, giving at the rate of about one dollar and a half per bushel.   But flour, pork, and salt, are almost interdicted to persons not principals in the trade.   Flour sells at half a dollar ; salt a dollar ; pork 80 cents ; sugar half a dollar ; coffee ——, and tea 4 dolls. 50 per pound.   The sugar is obtained from the Indians, and is made from the maple tree.

10th January, Friday.—Mr. Grant accompanied me to the Mississippi, to mark the place for my boats, to leave the river.   This was the first time I marched on rackets.   I took the course of the Lake River, from its mouth to the lake.   Mr. Grant fell through the ice with his rackets on, and could not have got out, without assistance.

11*th January, Saturday.*—Remained all day within quarters.

12*th Janury, Sunday.*—Went out and met my men about 16 miles.   A tree had fallen on one of them and hurt him very much, which induced me to dismiss a sled and put the loading on the others.

13*th January, Monday.*—After encountering much difficulty, we arrived at the establishment of the N. W. company, on Lake De Sable, a little before night.   The ice being very bad on the Lake River, owing to the many springs and marshes, one sled fell through.   My men had an excellent room furnished them, and were presented with potatoes and fille.*   Mr. Grant had gone to an Indian lodge to receive his credits.

14*th January, Tuesday.*—Crossed the lake to the north side, that I might take an observation ; found the lat. 46° 9′ 20″ N.   Surveyed that part of the lake.   Mr. Grant returned from the Indian lodges.   They brought a quantity of furs and eleven beaver carcases.

15*th January, Wednesday.*—Mr. Grant and myself made the tour of the lake, with two men, whom I had, for attendants.   Found it to be much larger, than could be imagined at a view.   My men sawed stocks for the sleds, which I found it necessary to construct after the manner of the country.   On our march, met an Indian coming into the fort ; his countenance expressed no little astonishment, when told who I was and from whence I came ; for the people in this country themselves acknowledge, that the savages hold in greater veneration, the Americans, than any other white people.   They say of

---

* A cant term for a dram of spirits.

us. when alluding to warlike atchievements, that " we
" are neither Frenchmen nor Englishmen, but white In-
" dians."

16*th January, Thursday.*—Laid down Lake De Sable,
&c.   A young Indian whom I had engaged, to go as a
guide to Lake Sang Sue, arrived from the woods.

17*th January, Friday.*—Employed in making sleds,*
(or traineau de glace) after the manner of the country.
Two other Indians, arrived from the woods.   Engaged in
writing.

18*th January, Saturday.*—Busy in preparing my baggage, &c. for my departure for Leech Lake, Reading, &c.

19*th January, Sunday.*—Employed as yesterday....
Two men of the N. W. company arrived from the Fond
du Lac Superior with letters; one of which was from
their establishment, in Athapuscow, and had been since last
May, on the route.   While at this post I eat roasted beavers, dressed in every respect, as a pig is usually dressed
with us ; it was excellent.   I could not discern the least
taste of Des Bois.   I also eat boiled moose's head, which
when well boiled, I consider equal to the tail of the beaver ; in taste and substance they are much alike.

20*th January, Monday.*—The men, with the sleds,
took their departure about 2 o'clock.   Shortly after I followed them.   We encamped at the portage between the
Mississippi and Leech Lake River.   Snow fell in the
night.

21*st January, Tuesday.*—Snowed in the morning, but
crossed about 9 o'clock.   I had gone on a few points,
when I was overtaken by Mr. Grant, who informed me
that the sleds could not get along, in consequence of water being on the ice ; he sent his men forward ; we re-

---

* Those sleds are made of a single plank turned up at one end like a fiddle
head, and the baggage is lashed on in bags and sacks.

turned and met the sleds which had scarcely advanced one mile. We unloaded them, sent eight men back to the post, with whatever might be denominated extra-articles; but in the hurry sent my salt and ink. Mr. Grant encamped with me and marched early in the morning.

22d January, Wednesday.—Made a pretty good days journey. My Indian came up about noon. Distance 20 miles.

23d January Thursday.—Marched about 18 miles. Forgot my thermometer, having hung it on a tree. Sent Boley back five miles for it. My young Indian and myself killed eight partridges; took him to live with me.

24th January, Friday.—At our encampment this night, Mr. Grant had encamped on the night of the same day he left me; it was three days march for us. In the evening the father of his girl, came to my camp and staid all night; he appeared very friendly, and was very communicative, but having no interpreter, we made but little progress in conversation. It was late before the men came up.

25th January, Saturday.—Travelled almost all day through the lands, and found them much better than usual. Boley lost the Sioux pipe stem, which I carried along, for the purpose of making peace with the Chipeways; I sent him back for it, he did not return until 11 o'clock at night. It was very warm; thawing all day. Distance 44 points.

26th January, Sunday.—I left my party, in order to proceed to a house (or lodge) of Mr. Grants, on the Mississippi, where he was to tarry until I overtook him. Took with me my Indian, Boley, and some trifling provision; the Indian and myself marched so fast, that we left Boley on the route, about 8 miles from the lodge. Met Mr. Grant's men, on their return to Lake De Sable, having evacuated the house this morning, and Mr. Grant having marched for Leech Lake. The Indian and I arrived before sun down. Passed the night very uncomfortably, having nothing to eat, not much wood, nor any blankets. The Indian slept sound. I cursed his insensibility, being obliged to content myself over a few coals all night. Boley did not arrive. In the night the Indian mentioned something about his son, &c.

27th January, Monday.—My Indian rose early, mended his mockinsons, then expressed by signs something about his son and the Frenchman we met yesterday. Conceiving that he wished to send some message to his family, I suffered him to depart. After his departure I felt the curse of solitude, although he truly was no company. Boley arrived about 10 o'clock. He said that he had followed us until some time in the night, when believing that he could not overtake us, he stopt and made a fire, but having no axe to cut wood, he was near freezing. He met the Indians, who made him signs to go on. I spent the day in putting my gun in order, mending my mockinsons, &c. Provided plenty of wood, still found it cold, with but one blanket. I can only account for the gentlemen of the N. W. company, contenting themselves in this wilderness for 10, 15, and some of them for 20 years, by the attachment they contract for the Indian women. It appears to me, that the wealth of nations would not induce me to remain secluded from the society of civilized mankind, surrounded by a savage and unproductive wilderness, without books or other sources of intellectual enjoyment, or being blessed with the cultivated and feeling mind, of a civilized fair.

28th January, Tuesday.—Left our encampment at a good hour ; unable to find any trail, passed through one of the most dismal cypress swamps I ever saw, and struck the Mississippi at a small lake. Observed Mr. Grant's tracks going through it ; found his mark of a cut off, (agreed on between us) took it, and proceeded very well, until we came to a small lake, where the trail was entirely hid; but after some search on the other side, found it; when we passed through a dismal swamp, on the other side of which, found a large lake; at which I was entirely at a loss; no trail to be seen. Struck for a point about 3 miles, where we found a Chipeway lodge of one man, his wife, and five children, and one old woman. They received us with every mark, that distinguished their barbarity, such as setting their dogs on ours, trying to thrust their hands into our pockets, &c. but we convinced them that we were not afraid, and let them know, we were Chewockomen; (Americans) when they used us more civilly. After we had arranged a camp, as well as possible, I went into the lodge; they presented me with a plate of dried meat. I ordered Miller to bring about two gills of liquor, which made us all good friends. The old squaw gave me more meat, and offered me tobacco, which not using, I did not take. I gave her an order upon my corporal, for one knife and half a carrot of tobacco.... Heaven clothes the lillies and feeds the raven, and the same almighty Providence protects and preserves these creatures. After I had gone out to my fire, the old man came out and proposed to trade beaver skins, for whiskey; meeting with a refusal, he left me; when presently the old woman came out with a beaver skin, she also being refused, he again returned to the charge, with a quantity of dried meat, (this or any other I should have been glad to have had) when I gave him a peremptory refusal; then all further application ceased. It really appeared, that with one quart of whiskey, I might have bought all they were possessed of. Night remarkably cold, was obliged to sit up nearly the whole of it. Suffered much with cold and from want of sleep.

31*st January, Friday.*—Took my clothes into the Indian's lodge to dress, and was received very coolly, but

by giving him a dram (unasked) and his wife a little salt,
I received from them directions for my route.   Passed the
lake or morass, and opened on meadows, (through which
the Mississippi winds its course) of nearly 15 miles long.
Took a straight course through them, to the head; when
I found we had missed the river; made a turn of about
two miles, and regained it.   Passed a fork which I supposed to be Lake Winipie, making the course N. W. the
branch we took was on Leech Lake branch, course S. W.
and W.   Passed a very large meadow or prairie, course
west; the Mississippi only fifteen yards wide.   Encamped
about one mile below the traverse of the meadow.   Saw
a very large animal, which, from its leaps, I supposed to
have been a panther; but if so, it was twice as large as
those on the lower Mississippi.   He evinced some disposition to approach.   I lay down (Miller being in the rear)
in order to entice him to come near, but he would not.
The night remarkably cold.   Some spirits, which I had
in a small keg, congealed to the consistency of honey.

1st *February, Saturday.*—Left our camp pretty early.
Passed a continued train of prairie, and arrived at Lake
La Sang Sue, at half past two o'clock.   I will not attempt
to describe my feelings, on the accomplishment of my
voyage, for this is the main source of the Mississippi.
The Lake Winipie branch is navigable, from thence to
Red Cedar lake, for the distance of five leagues, which is
the extremity of the navigation.   Crossed the lake 12
miles to the establishment of the N. W. company; where
we arrived, about 3 o'clock; found all the gates locked,
but upon knocking were admitted, and received with
marked attention and hospitality by Mr. Hugh M'Gillis.
Had a good dish of coffee, biscuit, butter, and cheese for
supper.

2d *February, Sunday.*—Remained all day within
doors.   In the evening sent an invitation to Mr. Ander-

son, who was an agent of Dickson, and also for some young Indians, at his house, to come over and breakfast in the morning.

3d February, Monday.—Spent the day in reading Volney's Egypt ; proposing some queries to Mr. Anderson, and preparing my young man to return, with a supply of provisions, to my party.

4th February, Tuesday.—Miller departed this morning. Mr. Anderson returned to his quarters. My legs and ancles were so much swelled, that I was not able to wear my own clothes and was obliged to borrow some from Mr. M'Gillis.

5th February, Wednesday.—One of Mr. M'Gillis's clerks had been sent to some Indian lodges, and expected to return in four days, but had now been absent nine. Mr. Grant was despatched, in order to find out what had become of him.

6th February, Thursday.—My men arrived at the fort about four o'clock. Mr. M'Gillis asked, if I had any objections to his hoisting their flag, in compliment to ours. I made none, as I had not yet explained to him my ideas. In making a traverse of the lake, some of my men had their ears, some their noses, and others their chins frozen.

7th February, Friday.—Remained within doors, my limbs being still very much swelled. Addressed a letter to Mr. M'Gillis on the subject of the N. W. company trade in this quarter.*

8th February, Saturday.—Took the latitude and found it to be 47° 16′ 13″. Shot with our rifles.

9th February, Sunday.—Mr. M'Gillis and myself paid a visit to Mr. Anderson, an agent of Mr. Dickson, of the Lower Mississippi, who resided at the west end of the lake. Found him elegibly situated as to trade, but

* See appendix to part I. [No. 5.] page 14.

his houses bad. I rode in a cariole, for one person, constructed in the following manner : Boards plained smooth, turned up in front about two feet, coming to a point ; and about 2 1-2 feet wide behind ; on which is fixed a box covered with dressed skins painted ; this box is open at the top, but covered in front about two thirds of the length. The horse is fastened between the shafts. The rider wraps himself up in a buffalo robe, sits flat down, having a cushion to lean his back against. Thus accoutred with a fur cap, &c. he may bid defiance to the wind and weather. Upon our return, we found that some of the Indians, had already returned from the hunting camps ; also Monsieur Roussand, the gentleman supposed to have been killed by the Indians. His arrival with Mr. Grant, diffused a general satisfaction through the fort.

10*th February*, *Monday.*—Hoisted the American flag in the fort. The English yacht still flying at the top of the flag staff, I directed the Indians and my riflemen to shoot at it, who soon broke the iron pin to which it was fastened, and brought it to the ground. Reading Shenstone, &c.

11*th February*, *Tuesday.*—The Sweet, Buck, Burnt, &c. arrived, all chiefs of note, but the former in particular, a venerable old man. From him I learnt, that the Sioux occupied this ground when (to use his own pharse) " He was a made man, and began to hunt ; that they oc-
" cupied it the year that the French missionaries were kil-
" led, at the river Pacagama." The Indians flocked in.

12*th February*, *Wednesday.*—Bradley and myself with Mr. M'Gillis and two of his men, left Leech Lake at 10 o'clock, and arrived at the house at Red Cedar Lake, at sunset ; a distance of 30 miles. My ancles were very much swelled, and I was very lame. From the entrance of the Mississippi to the streight is called six miles, a south west course. From thence to the south end, South 30,

east 4 miles.   The bay at the entrance, extends nearly E.
and W. six miles.   About two and a half from the north
side to a large point.   This may be called the upper source
of the Mississippi, being 15 miles above Little Lake Winipie ; and the extent of canoe navigation only two
leagues, to some of the Hudson's Bay waters.

13th February, Thursday.—Were favored with a
beautiful day.   Took the latitude, and found it to be 47°
42' 40″ N. At this place it was, Mr. Thompson made
his observations in 1798, from which he determined that
the source of the Mississippi was in 47° 38'.   I walked
about 3 miles back in the country, at two thirds water.
One of our men marched to Lake Winepie and returned
by one o'clock, for the stem of the Sweet's pipe, a matter of more consequence in his affairs, with the Sioux,
than the diploma of many an ambassador.   We feasted
on white fish, roasted on two iron grates fixed horizon-
tally in the back of the chimney ; the entrails left in the
fish.

14th February, Friday.—Left the house at 9 o'clock.
It becomes me here to do justice to the hospitality of our
hosts ; one Roy, a Canadian and his wife, a Chipeway
squaw.   They relinquished for our use, the only thing in
the house, that could be called a bed ; attended us like
servants, nor could either of them be persuaded, to
touch a mouthful, until we had finished our repasts.   We
made the garrison about sundown, having been drawn at
least 10 miles in a sleigh, by two small dogs ; who were
loaded with 200 pounds, and went so fast as to render it
difficult, for the men with snow shoes, to keep up with
them.   The chiefs asked my permission to dance the calumet dance which I granted.

15th February, Saturday.—The Flat Mouth, chief of
the Leech Lake village, and many other Indians arrived.

Received a letter from Mr. M'Gillis.* Noted down the heads of my speech, and had it translated into French, in order that the interpreter should be perfectly master of his subject.

16th *February*, *Sunday*.—Held a council with the chiefs and warriors at this place, and of Red Lake; but it required much patience, coolness, and management to obtain the objects I desired, viz: That they should make peace with the Sioux; deliver up their medals and flags; and that some of their chiefs should follow me to St. Louis.† As a proof of their agreeing to the peace, I directed that they should smoke out of the Wabasha's pipe, which lay on the table; they all smoked, from the head chief to the youngest soldier; they generally delivered up their flags with a good grace; except the Flat Mouth, who said he had left both at his camp, three days march, and promised to deliver them up to Mr. M'Gillis, to be forwarded. With respect to their returning with me; the old Sweet thought it most proper to return, to the Indians of the Red lake, Red river, and Rainy lake river. The Flat Mouth said, it was necessary for him to restrain his young warriors, &c.‡ The other chiefs did not think themselves of consequence sufficient, to offer any reason for not following me to St. Louis, a journey of between two and three thousand miles through hostile tribes of Indians. I then told them, " that I was " sorry to find, that the hearts of the Sauteurs of this " quarter, were so weak, that the other nations would " say—what, are there no soldiers at Leech, Red, and " Rainy Lakes, who had the hearts to carry the calumet " of their chief to their father?" This had the desired effect. The Bucks and Beaux, two of the most celebrat-

---

* See appendix to part I. [No. 6.] page 17.

† See appendix to part I. [No. 7.] page 19.

‡ See appendix to part I. [No. 8.] page 22.

ed young warriors, rose and offered themselves to me, for the embassy; they were accepted; adopted as my children, and I installed their father. Their example animated the others, and it would have been no difficult matter to have taken a company; two however were sufficient. I determined that it should be my care, never to make them regret the noble confidence placed in me; for I would have protected their lives with my own. The Beaux is brother to the Flat Mouth. Gave my new soldiers a dance, and a small dram. They attempted to get more liquor, but a firm and peromptory denial, convinced them, I was not to be trifled with.

17th February, Monday.—The chief of the land brought in his flag, and delivered it up. Made arrangements to march my party the next day. Instructed the Sweet, how to send the parole to the Indians of Red river, &c. Put my men through the manual, and fired their blank rounds, all of which, not a little, astonished the Indians. I was obliged to give my two *new soldiers*, each a blanket, pair of leggins, scissors, and looking glass.

18th February, Tuesday.—We marched for Red Cedar Lake about 11 o'clock, with a guide, provided for me by Mr. M'Gillis; were all provided with snow shoes; marched off, amidst the acclamations and shouts of the Indians, who generally had remained, too see us take our departure. Mr. Anderson promised to come on with letters; he arrived about 12 o'clock, and remained all night. He concluded to go down with me, to see Mr. Dickson.

19th February, Wednesday.—Bradley, Mr. L'Rone, the two young Indians and myself, left Mr. M'Gillis's at 10 o'clock; crossed Leech Lake in a S. E. direction 24 miles. Mr. M'Gillis's hospitality deserves to be particularly noticed; he presented me with his dogs and cariole, valued in this country at two hundred dollars; one of the dogs broke out of his harness, and we were not able during that day to catch him again ; and the other poor fellow, was obliged to pull the whole load, at least 150 pounds.   This days march was from lake to lake.

20*th February, Thursday.*—I allowed my men to march at least three hours before me, notwithstanding which, as it was cold and the road good, my sleigh dogs brought me ahead of all by one o'clock.   Halted for an encampment at half past two o'clock.   Our courses this day, were first S. E. six miles, then S. eighteen miles ; almost all the way over lakes ; some of which were six miles across.   Encamped on the bank of a lake, called Sandy Lake.   Indians were out hunting.

21*st February, Friday.*—Travelled this day, generally south.   Passed but two lakes ; Sandy Lake, which is of an oblong form N. and S. 4 miles, and one other small one.   The Indians, at the instigation of Mr. L'Rone, applied for him to accompany us.   I consented that he should go as far as Red Cedar Lake.   I then wrote a note to M'Gillis upon the occasion.   After Reale had departed with it, L'Rone disclosed to me, that it was his wish, to desert the N. W. company entirely, and accompany me.   To have countenanced for a moment, any thing of this kind, I conceived would have been inconsistent with every principle of honor ; I therefore obliged him to return immediately.   We then had no guide, our Indians not knowing the road.   Our course through woods and bad brush 15 miles.

22*d February, Saturday.*—Our course a little to the south of east, through woods not very thick.   Arrived at White Fish Lake at 11 o'clock, and took an observation. My party crossed the lake and encamped between two lakes.   This may be called the source of Pine river.   At this place has been one of the N. W. company's establishments ; at the N. E. and S. side.   It was a square stockade, of about 50 feet ; but at this time nearly all consumed by fire.   Also one standing over the point on the east side.

23d February, Sunday.—My two Indians, Boley and myself, with my sleigh and dogs left the party, under an idea, that we should make Red Cedar Lake. We marched hard all day, without arriving at the Mississippi. Our course was nearly due east, until near night, when we changed more south. Took no provision nor bedding. My Indians killed fifteen partridges, some nearly black, with a red mark over their eyes, called the Savanna partridge. Were overtaken about noon by two of Mr. Anderson's men, named Brurie and ————, Mr. Anderson himself not being able to come. Distance 30 miles.

24th February, Monday.—We started early, and after passing over one of the worst roads in the world, found ourselves on a lake, about 3 o'clock; took its outlet and struck the Mississippi, about one mile below the canoes mentioned on the first January, by which I knew where we were. Ascended the Mississippi about four miles, and encamped on the west side. Our general course this day, was nearly south, when it should have been S. E. My young warriors were still in good heart; singing and shewing every wish to keep me so. The pressure of my racket strings brought the blood through my socks and mockinsons, from which the pain I marched in may be imagined.

25th February, Tuesday.—We marched and arrived at the Cedar Lake before noon; found Mr. Grant and De Breche (chief of Sandy Lake) at the house. This gave me much pleasure, for I conceive Mr. Grant to be a gentleman of as much candor, as any with whom I had made an acquaintance in this quarter, and the chief (De Breche) is reputed to be a man of better information, than any of the Sauteurs.

26th February, Wednesday.—Sent one of Mr. Grant's men down, with a bag of rice, to meet my people, who found them encamped on the Mississippi. Wrote a letter

K

to Mr. Dickson on the subject of the Fols Avoins,* also some orders to my sergeant. This evening had a long conversation with De Breche, he informed me that a string of Wampum, had been sent among the Chipeways, he thought by the British commanding officer at St. Joseph; he appeared to be a very intelligent man.

27th February, Thursday.—The chief called the White Fisher and seven Indians arrived at the house. My men also arrived about 12 o'clock.

28th February, Friday.—We left Red Cedar Lake, about 11 o'clock, and went to where the canoes were, mentioned in my journal of the 1st January. My young Indians remained behind, under the pretence of waiting for the chief De Breche, who returned to Sandy Lake for his flag and medals, and was to render himself at my post with Mr. Grant, about the 15th of the following month.

1st March, Saturday.—Departed early. Passed our encampment of the 31st December, at 9 o'clock A. M. Passed Pine river at 12 o'clock. Passed our encampment of the 30th December at 3 o'clock. Passed our encampment of the 29th November, just before we came to our present, which we made on the point of the Pine Ridge, below. Distance 43 miles.

2d March, Sunday.—Passed our encampment of the 28th December, at 10 o'clock A. M. that of the 27th December at 1 o'clock P. M. and encamped at that of the 26th December. Found wood nearly sufficient for our use. This morning dispatched Bradley, to the last place we had buried a barrel of flour, to thaw the ground and hunt. This day a party of Indians, struck the river behind Bradley and before us, but left it 10 miles above the Raven river.

* See appendix to part I, [No. 9.] page 23.

3d March, Monday.—Marched early; passed our Christmas encampment, at sunrise. I was ahead of my party, in my cariole. Soon afterwards I observed a smoke on the W. shore. I hallood, and some Indians appeared upon the bank. I waited until my interpreter came up, we then went to the camp. They proved to be a party of Chipeways, who had left the encampment, the same day we left it. They presented me with some roast meat, which I gave my sleigh dogs. They then left their camp and accompanied us down the river. We passed our encampment of the 24th December, at 9 o'clock, of the 23d at 10 o'clock, and of the 22d at eleven o'clock; here the Indians crossed on to the W. shore; arrived at the encampment of the 21st December, at 12 o'clock. Where we had a barrel of flour. I here found corporal Meek and another man, from the post, from whom I heard, that the men were all well; they confirmed the account of a Sioux having fired on a sentinel; and added, that the sentinel had first made him drunk, and then turned him out of the tent, upon which he fired on the sentinel and ran off, but promised to deliver himself up in the spring. The corporal informed me, that the sergeant had used all the elegant hams and saddles of venison, which I had preserved to present to the commander in chief and other friends; that he had made away with all the whiskey, including a keg I had for my own use, having publicly sold it to the men, and a barrel of pork, that he had broken open my trunk and sold some things out of it, traded with the Indians, gave them liquor, &c. and this too contrary to my most pointed and particular directions. Thus, after I had used, in going up the river with my party, the strictest economy, living upon two pounds of frozen venison a day; in order that we might have provision to carry us down in the spring; this fellow was squandering away the flour, pork, and liquor, during the winter, and while we were starving with hunger and cold. I had saved all our corn, bacon, and the meat of six deer, and left it at Sandy Lake, with some tents, my mess boxes, salt, tobacco, &c. all of which we were obliged to sacrifice by not returning the same route we went, and we consoled ourselves, at this loss, by the flattering idea, that we should find at our little post, a handsome stock preserved; how mortifying the disappointment. We raised our barrel of flour, and came down to the mouth of a little river, on the east, which we passed on the 21st December. The ice covered with water.

4th March, Tuesday.—Proceeded early. Passed our encampment of the 20th December at sunrise. Arrived at that of the 19th at 9 o'clock; here we had buried two barrels. Made a large fire to thaw the ground. Went on the prairie and found Sparks, one of my hunters, and brought him to the river at the Pine Camp. Passed on opposite to our encampment, of the 13th of December, and encamped where Sparks and some men had an old hunting camp, and where the Fresaie (a Chipeway chief) surrounded them.

5th March, Wednesday.—Passed all the encampments between Pine creek and the post, at which we arrived about 10 o'clock. I sent a man on ahead, to prevent the salute I had before ordered by letter; this I did from the idea that the Sioux chiefs would accompany me. Found all well. Confined my sergeant. About one o'clock Mr. Dickson arrived, with the Killeur Rouge, his son, and two other Sioux men, with two women; who had come up to be introduced to the Sauteurs, they expected to find with me. Received a letter from Reinville.

6th March Thursday.—Thomas, the Fols Avoin's first chief, arrived with ten others of his nation. I made a serious and authoritative expostulative representation to him of my opinion of the Shawonoe's (another chief

of his nation who had behaved ill) conduct. Had also a
conference with the Killeur Rouge and his people. At
night wrote to Messrs. Grant, M'Gillis, and Anderson.

7th *March, Friday.*—Held conversations with the
Indians. Thomas, the Fols Avoin chief assured me, that
he would interest himself, in obliging the Puants to deliver up the men who had recently committed murders,
on the Ouiscousing and Rock rivers ; and if necessary he
would make it a national quarrel, on the side of the Americans. This Thomas is a fine fellow, of a very mascu-
line figure, noble and animated delivery, and appears to
be very much attached to the Americans. The Sioux
informed me, that they would wait until I had determined
my affairs in this country, and then bear my words to the
river St. Peters.

8th *March, Saturday.*—The Fols Avoin chief presented me with his pipe to give to the Sauteurs on their
arrival, with assurances of their safety on their voyage,
and his wish for them to descend the river. The *Fils de
Killeur Rouge* also presented me with his pipe, to present
to the Sauteur Indians on their arrival, to make them
smoke, and assure them of his friendly disposition, and
that he would wait to see them at Mr. Dicksons. Thomas
made a formal complaint against a Frenchman, (by name
Greignor) who resided in Green bay, who, he said, abused
the Indians, beat them, &c. without provocation. I promised to write to the commanding officer, or Indian agent
at Michilimackinac, upon the occasion. The Indians with
Mr. Dickson, all took their departure. Hitched my dogs
in the sleigh, who drew one of the Indian women down the
ice to the no little amusement of the others. Went some
distance down the river in order to cut a mast. Cut a
pine mast 35 feet long, for my big boat at the prairie.
This day my little boy broke the cock of my gun ; few
trifling misfortunes could have happened, which I should

have regretted more, as the wild fowl just began to return
on the approach of spring.

9th March, Sunday.—I examined into the conduct
of my sergeant, and found that he was guilty and punished him by reduction, &c.   Visited the Fols Avoin lodges
and received a present of some tallow.   One of my men
arrived from the hunting camp with two deer.

10th March, Monday.—Was visited by the Fols
Avoin chief and several others of his nation.   This chief
was an extraordinary hunter; to instance his power, he
killed forty elk and a bear in one day; chasing the former from dawn to eve.   We were all busied in preparing
oars, guns, mast, &c. by the time the ice broke up, which
was opening fast.

11th March, Tuesday.—In a long conversation with
a Reynard, he professed not to believe in an hereafter;
but he believed that the world would all be drowned by
water, at some future period; he asked how it was to be
re-peopled.   In justice to his nation, however, I must observe, that his opinion was singular.

12th March, Wednesday.—Made preparations; had
fine chase with deer on the ice; killed one.   Since our
return I received eight deer from our camp.

13th March, Thursday.—Received two deer from my
hunting camp.   Went out with my gun on the opposite
side of the river.   Ascended the mountain which borders
the prairie.   On the point of it I found a stone, on which
the Indians had sharpened their knives, and a war club
half finished.   From this spot you may extend the eye
over vast prairies without, scarcely any, interruption, but
clumps of trees which at a distance appeared like mountains; from two or three of which the smoke rising in the
air, denoted the habitation of the wandering savage, and
too often marked them out as victims to their enemies;
from whose cruelty, I have had the pleasure in the

course of the winter, and through a wilderness of immense extent to relieve them, as peace has reigned
through my mediation, from the prairie Des Cheins to
the lower Red river.   If a subaltern with but 20 men, at
so great a distance from the seat of his government could
effect so important a change in the minds of those savages,
what might not a great and independent power effect, if
instead of blowing up the flames of discord, they exerted
their influence in the sacred cause of peace?   When I
returned to the fort, I found the Fols Avoin chief who
intended to remain all night.   He told me that near the
conclusion of the revolutionary war, his nation began to
look upon him as a warrior ; that they received a parole
from Michilimackinac, on which he was dispatched with
40 warriors ; that on his arrival he was requested to lead
them against the Americans.   To which he replied, " We
" have considered you and the Americans as one people.
" You are now at war ; how are we to decide who has
" justice on their side ?   Besides you white people are
" like the leaves on the trees for numbers.   Should I
" march with my 40 warriors to the field of battle, they
" with their chief, would be unnoticed in the multitude ;
" and would be swallowed up as the big waters embo-
" som the small rivulets which discharge themselves into
" it.   No, I will return to my nation, where my coun-
" trymen may be of service against our red enemies, and
" their actions renowned in the dance of our nation."

14th *March*, *Friday*.—Took the latitude by an artificial horizon, and measured the river.   Received one
deer and a half from my hunting camp,   Ice thinner.

15th *March*, *Saturday*.—This was the day fixed upon
by Mr. Grant and the Chipeway warriors, for their arrival
at my fort ; and I was all day anxiously expecting them ;
for I knew that should they not accompany me down, the
peace partially effected between them and the Sioux, would

not be on a permanent footing; and upon this I take them to be neither so brave nor generous, as the Sioux, who, in all their transactions, appear to be candid and brave, whereas the Chipeways are *suspicious*, consequently *treacherous*, and of course *cowards*.

16*th March, Sunday.*—Received three deer from our hunting camp.   Examined trees for canoes.

17*th March, Monday.*—Left the fort with my interpreter and Roy, in order to visit Thomas, the Fols Avoin chief, who was encamped, with six lodges of his nation, about 20 miles below us, on a little river which empties into the Mississippi on the W. side, a little above Clear river. On our way down, killed one goose, wounded another, and a deer that the dogs had driven into an air hole; hung our game on the trees.   Arrived at the creek, took out on it; ascended three or four miles on one bank, and descended on the other.   Killed another goose.   Struck the Mississippi below ——.   Encamped at our encampment of the —— of October, when we ascended the river.   Ate our goose for supper.   It snowed all day, and at night a very severe storm arose.   It may be imagined that we spent a very disagreeable night without shelter, and but one blanket each.

18*th March, Tuesday.*—We marched, determined to find the lodges.   Met an Indian, whose track we pursued, through almost impenetrable woods, for about two and a half miles, to the camps; here there was one of the finest sugar camps I almost ever saw, the whole of the timber being sugar tree.   We were conducted to the chief's lodge, who received us in the patriarchal style.   He pulled off my leggins and mockinsons, put me in the best place in his lodge, and offered me dry cloaths.   He then presented us with syrup of the maple to drink, then asked whether I prefered eating beaver, swan, elk or deer; upon my giving the preference to the first, a large kettle was filled by his wife, of which soup was made; this being thickened with flour, we had what I then thought a delicious repast. After we had refreshed ourselves, he asked whether we would visit his people, at the other lodges, which we did; and in each were presented with something to eat; by some with a bowl of sugar; others a beaver's tail, &c. After making this tour, we returned to the chief's lodge, and found a birth provided for each of us, of good soft bear skins nicely spread, and on mine there was a large feather pillow. I must not here omit to mention an anecdote, which serves to characterize, more particularly, their manners. This in the eyes of the contracted moralist, would deform my hospitable host into a monster of libertinism; but by a liberal mind would be considered, as arising from the hearty generosity of the wild savage. In the course of the day observing a ring on one of my fingers, he enquired if it was gold; he was told it was the gift of one, with whom I should be happy to be at that time; he seemed to think seriously, and at night told my interpreter, " That perhaps his father" (as they all called me) " felt much grieved for the want of a wo- " man; if so, he could furnish him with one." He was answered, that with us each man had but one wife, and that I considered it strictly my duty, to remain faithful to her. This he thought strange, (he himself having three) and replied that " He knew some Americans at his nation, " who had half a dozen wives during the winter." The interpreter observed that, they were men without charac- ter; but that all our great men, had each but one wife. The chief acquiesced, but said he liked better to have as many as he pleased. This conversation passing without any appeal to me, as the interpreter knew my mind on those occasions and answered immediately, it did not ap- pear, as an immediate refusal of the woman. Continued snowing very hard all day. Slept very warm.

19th March, Wednesday.—This morning purchased two baskets of sugar, for the amount of which I gave orders on Mr. Dickson. After feasting upon a swan, took our leave for camp; still snowing. Finding my two companions unable to keep up, I pushed on and arrived at the river. When I arrived at the place, I had hung up my first goose, I found that the ravens and eagles had not left a feather, and, feasting upon the deer, was a band sufficient to have carried it away, who had picked its bones nearly clean; what remained I gave my dogs. Stopped at the place where I expected to find the last goose; but could see nothing of it; at length I found it hid under the grass and snow, where some animal had concealed it, after eating off its head and neck. I carried it to the fort, where I arrived about an hour before sundown. Dispatched, immediately, two men with rackets, to meet the interpreter and Le Roy. They arrived about two hours after dark. Some men also arrived at the hunting camp with three deer. The snow ceased falling about one hour after dark; it was nearly two feet deep on a level, the deepest that had fallen so low down this winter.

20th March, Thursday.—Despatched nine men to my hunting camp, from whence received two deer. Cloudy almost all day; but the water rose fast over the ice.

21st March, Friday.—Received a visit from the Fols Avoin chief, called the Shawonoe, and six young men. I informed him without reserve, the news I heard of him at Red Cedar Lake, and the letter I wrote to Mr. Dickson. He denied it in toto, and on the contrary said, that he presented his flag and two medals to the Chipeways, as an inducement for them to descend in the spring; and gave them all the encouragement in his power. His party was much astonished at the language I held with him. But from his firm protestations, we finally parted friends. He informed me that a camp of Sauteurs were on the river, waiting for the chiefs to come down; from which it appeared they were still expected.   At night (after the others had gone) Thomas arrived and staid all night.   We agreed upon a hunting party, also promised to pay the old Shawonoe a visit.   He informed me, that he set out the other day to follow me, but finding the storm so very bad, returned to his wigwam.   The thermometer lower than it has been at any time since I commenced my voyage.

22d March, Saturday.—Ten of my men arrived from the hunting camp, with four deer and a half.   Thomas departed, sent a man with him to his camps, from which he sent me two beavers.

23d March, Sunday.—Agreeably to promise, after breakfast I departed with Miller and my interpreter to pay a visit to the old chief Shawonoe.   We arrived at his camp in about two hours.   On our way we met the Fols Avoin, called the Chein Blanche, who had visited my post, previously to my starting up the river, at whose house we stopped when passing.   We were received by old Shawonoe at his lodge, with the usual Indian hospitality, but very different from the polite reception given us by Thomas.   Charlevoix and others have all borne testimony to the beauty of this nation.   From my own observation, I had sufficient reason to confirm their information as respected the males; for they were all straight and well made, about the middle size; their complexions generally fair for savages, their teeth good, their eyes large and rather languishing; they have a mild but independent expression of countenance, that charms at first sight; in short, they would be considered any where, as handsome men.   But their account of the women, I never before believed to be correct.   In this lodge there were five very handsome women when we arrived; and about sun-down, a married pair arrived, whom my interpreter observed, were the handsomest couple he knew; and in truth they were; the man being about 5 feet 11 inches, and possessing in an eminent manner all the beauties of countenance which distinguish his nation. His companion was 22 years old; having dark brown eyes, jet hair, and an elegantly proportioned neck, and her figure by no means inclining to corpulency, as they generally are after marriage. He appeared to attach himself particularly to me, and informed me his wife was the daughter of an American, who passing through the nation, about twenty three years before, remained a week or two, possessed of her mother, and that she was the fruit of this amour; but his name they were unacquainted with. I had brought six biscuits with me, which I presented her on the score of her being my countrywoman, which raised a loud laugh, and she was called the Bostonian during the rest of my stay. I found them generally extremely hard to deal with; my provision being only a little venison, I wished to procure some bear's oil, for a few gallons of which I was obliged to pay a dollar per gallon, and then they wanted to mix tallow with the oil. They also demanded ten dollars for a bear skin (the most beautiful I ever saw, which I wanted to mount a saddle.) Indeed I was informed that traders in this country, sometimes give as much as sixteen dollars for bear skins; for they are eminently superior to any thing of the kind, on the lower Mississippi; and sell in Europe for double the price. In the evening we were entertained with the calumet and dog dance; also the dance of the ———. Some of the men struck the post and told some of their war exploits, but as they spoke in *Menomene*, my interpreter could not explain it. After the dance, we had the feast of the *dead*, (as it is called) at which each two or three were served with a pan or vessel full of meat, and when all were ready there was a prayer, after which the eating commenced. When it was expected we would eat up our portion entirely, being careful not to drop a bone, but to gather all up and put them in the dish, we were then treated with soup. After the eating was finished the chief again gave an exhortation, which finished the ceremony. I am told they then gather up all the fragments, and throw them in the water, lest the dogs should get them. Burning them is considered as sacrilegeous. In this lodge were collected at one time 41 persons great and small, (17 of whom were capable of bearing arms) besides dogs without number.

24th March, Monday.—Rose early and with my dog-sled arrived at the fort before 10 o'clock. In the afternoon Mr. Grant arrived with De Breche and some of his young men. Saluted him with 14 rounds; found my two young warriors of Leech Lake were brave enough to return to their homes. Mr. Grant and myself sat up late talking.

25th March, Tuesday.—Sent an Indian to Thomas's lodge, and a letter to Mr. Dickson. It snowed and stormed all day. Gave the chief the news.

26th March, Wednesday.—Thomas, the Fols Avoin chief arrived with seven of his men, and the old Shawonoe and six of his party. I had them all to feed as well as my own men. At night I gave them leave to dance in the garrison, which they did until 10 o'clock; but once or twice told me, that if I was tired of them, the dance should cease. The old Shawonoe and the White Dog of the Fols Avoins told their exploits, which we could not understand; but De Breche arose and said, " I once killed " a Sioux and cut off his head with such a spear as I now " present to this Winebago." At the same time presenting one to a Winebago present, with whom the Chipeways were at war; this was considered by the former as a great honor. My hunters went out but killed nothing.

27th March, Thursday.—In the morning the Chipeway chief made a speech and presented his peace pipe to

me to bear to the Sioux, on which were seven strings of wampum, as authority from seven bands of the Chipeways, either to conclude peace or to make war. As he had chosen the former, he sent his pipe to the Sioux and requested me to inform them, that he and his people would encamp at the mouth of the Riviere De Corbeau the ensuing summer, where he would see the United States flag flying. As a proof of his pacific disposition, the Fols Avoin chief then spoke and said, " His nation was ren-
" dered small by its enemies, only a remnant was left,
" but that they could boast of not being slaves ; for that
" always in preference to their women and children being
" taken, they themselves killed them. But that their
" father (as they called me) had travelled far, and had
" taken much pains to prevent the Sioux and Chipeways
" from killing one another ; that he thought none could
" be so ungenerous as to neglect listening to the words of
" their father : that he would report to the Sioux the pa-
" cific disposition of the Sauteurs, and hoped the peace
" would be firm and lasting." I then in a few words informed De Breche, " that I would report to the Sioux all
" he had said, and that I should ever feel pleased and
" grateful that the two nations had laid aside the toma-
" hawk at my request. That I thanked the Fols Avoin
" chief for his good wishes and parole which he had given
" the Sauteurs." After all this, each chief was furnished with a kettle of liquor, to drink each others health ; and De Breche's flag (which I had presented him) was displayed in the fort. The Fols Avoins then departed, at which I was by no means displeased, for they had already consumed all the dry meat, I had laid aside for my voyage, and I was apprehensive that my hunters would not be able to lay up another supply.

28th March, Friday.—Late in the afternoon Mr. Grant and the Sauteurs took their departure, calculating that the Sioux had left the country. Took with me one of my soldiers and accompanied them to the Fols Avoins lodge (called the Shawonese) where we (ten) stayed all night. The Fols Avoins and Sauteurs had a dance, at which I left them and went to sleep. Feasted on elk, sugar, and syrup. Previously to the Indians departing from my post, I demanded the chief's medal and flags; the former he delivered, but with a bad grace, the latter he said were in the lands when I left Lake De Sable; (as instructed by the traders I suppose) and that he could not obtain them. It thundered and lightened.

29th March, Saturday.—We all marched in the morning. Mr. Grant and party for Sandy Lake, and I for my hunting camp. I gave him my spaniel dog. He joined me again after we had seperated about 5 miles. Arrived at my hunting camp about 8 o'clock in the morning, and was informed that my hunters had gone to bring in a deer; they arrived with it, and about 11 o'clock we all went out hunting. Saw but few deer, out of which I had the good fortune to kill two. On our arrival at camp found one of my men at the garrison, with a letter from Mr. Dickson. The soldier informed me that one Sioux had arrived with Mr. Dickson's men. Although much fatigued, soon as I had eat something, I took one of my men and departed for the garrison one hour before sundown. The distance was 21 miles, and the ice very dangerous being rotten, and the water over it nearly a foot deep; we had sticks in our hands, and in many places ran them through the ice. It thundered and lightened with rain. The Sioux not finding the Sauteurs, had returned immediately.

30th March, Sunday.—Wrote to Mr. Dickson and dispatched his man. Considerably stiff from my yesterday's march. Caulked our boats, as the ice had every appearance of breaking up in a few days. Thus whilst on the wing of eager expectation, every day seemed an age.   Received two deers and an half from our hunting camp.

31st March, Monday.—Finished caulking my boats, the difficulty then was with me, what I should get to pitch the seams.   We were all this day and next as anxiously watching the ice, as a lover would the arrival of the priest who was to unite him to his beloved.   Sometimes it moved a little, but soon closed.   An Indian and his woman crossed it when the poles which they held in their hands were forced through in many places.   The provision to which I was obliged to restrict myself and men, viz : two pounds of fresh venison per day, was scarcely sufficient to keep us alive.   Though I had not an extraordinary appetite, yet I was continually hungry.

2d April, Wednesday.—Went out and killed one deer and two partridges.   The ice began to move opposite the fort at the foot of the rapids, but dammed up below.   Received half a dozen bears from my hunting camp.   Launched our canoe and brought her down.

3d April, Thursday.—Sent one man down to see the river, another to the camp, and took two men myself over the hills on the other side of the Mississippi to hunt. In the course of the day I killed a swan and a goose, and we certainly would have killed one or two elk, had it not been for the sleigh dogs; for we lay concealed on the banks of Clear river, when four came and threw themselves into it opposite, and were swimming directly to us, when our dogs bounced into the water, and they turned. We then fired on them, but they carried off all the lead we gave them, and we could not cross the river, unless we rafted (it being bank full) which would have detained us too long a time.   In the evening it became very cold, and we passed rather an uncomfortable night.

4th April, Friday.—Took our course home.   I killed one large buck and wounded another.   We made a

fire and eat breakfast.   Arrived at the fort at 2 o'clock P.
M. was informed that the river was still shut below, at the
cluster of islands.   Received some bear meat, and one
deer from the camp.

5th April, Saturday.—In the morning dispatched two
men down the river in order to see if it was open.   My
hunters arrived from the camps.   Tallowed my boats with
our candles and launched them, they made considerable
water.   The young Shawonoe arrived in my canoe from
above, with about 1000 lbs. of fur, which he deposited
in the fort.   The men returned and informed me that the
river was still shut about 10 miles below.

6th April, Sunday.—Sailed my peroque with sergeant
Bradley and two men, to descend the river and see if it
was yet open below.   They returned in the afternoon and
reported all clear.   I had previously determined to load
and embark the next day, and hoped to find it free by the
time I arrived.   The Fols Avoin, called the Shawonoe,
arrived and encamped near the stockade.   He informed
me that his nation had determined to send his son down in
his place, as he declined the voyage to St. Louis.   All
hearts and hands were employed in preparing for our departure.   In the evening the men cleared out their room
and danced to the violin, and sang songs until 11 o'clock.
So rejoiced was every heart at leaving this savage wilderness.

7th April, Monday.—Loaded our boats and departed
forty minutes past ten o'clock.   At one o'clock arrived at
Clear river, where we found my canoe and men.   Although
I had partly promised the Fols Avoin chief to remain one
night, yet time was too precious, and we put off; passed
the Grand Rapids, and arrived at Mr. Dickson's just before sun-down; we were saluted with three rounds.   At
night he treated all my men with a supper and dram.

M

Mr. Dickson, Mr. Paulier and myself, sat up until four o'clock in the morning.

8th April, Tuesday.—Were obliged to remain this day on account of some information to be obtained here. I spent the day in making a rough chart of St. Peters, making notes on the Sioux, &c. settling the affairs of the Indian department with Mr. Dickson, for whose communications, and those of Mr. Paulier, I am infinitely indebted. Made every necessary preparation for an early embarkation.

9th April, Wednesday.—Rose early in the morning and commenced my arrangements. Having observed two Indians drunk, during the night, and finding upon enquiry, that the liquor had been furnished them by a Mr. Greignor or Jennesse, I sent my interpreter to them to request they would not sell any strong liquor to the Indians, upon which Mr. Jennesse demanded the restrictions in writing, which were given to him.* On demanding his licence it amounted to no more, than merely a certificate that he had paid the tax required by a law of the Indiana territory, on all retailers of merchandize ; but it was by no means an Indian licence ; however, I did not think proper to go into a more close investigation. Last night was so cold that the water was covered with floating cakes of ice, of a strong consistence. After receiving every mark of attention from Messrs. Dickson and Paulier, I took my departure at 8 o'clock. At 4 P. M. arrived at the house of Mr. Paulier, 25 leagues, to whose brother I had a letter. Was received with politeness by him and a Mr. Veau, who wintered along side of him, on the very island, at which we had encamped on the night of the —— of Oct. in ascending. After having left this place some time, we discovered a bark canoe a-head, we gained on it for some time.

* See appendix to part I. [No. 10.] page 24.

when it turned a point about 300 yards before; and on our turning it also, it had entirely disappeared. This excited my curiosity, I stood up in the barge, and at last discovered it turned up in the grass of the prairie, but after we had passed a good gun shot, three savages made their appearance from under it, launched her in the river, and followed, not knowing of my other boats which had just turned the point immediately upon them. They then came on; and, on my stopping for the night at a vacant trading house also stopped, and addressed me " *Saggo commandant*, or " *your servant captain*." I directed my interpreter to enquire their motives for concealing themselves. They replied, that their canoe leaked, and that they had turned her up to discharge the water. This I did not believe, as their conduct was equivocal, I received them rather sternly; I gave them however a small dram and piece of bread. They then re-embarked, and continued down the river. Their conduct brought to mind the visit of the Fils de Pinchow to Mr. Dickson, during the winter; one principal cause of which was, that he wished to inform me that the seven men, whom I mentioned to have met when crossing the portage of St. Anthony, had since declared that they would kill him for agreeing to the peace between the Sioux and Sauteurs : *me* for being instrumental in preventing them from taking their revenge for relations killed by the Sauteurs in August 1805; and *Thomas*, the Fols Avoin chief, for the support he seemed disposed to give me. This information had not made the impression it ought to have made, coming from so respectable a source, as the first chief of the village; but the conduct of those fellows put me to the consideration of it. And I appeal to God and my country, if self preservation would not have justified me, in cutting those scoundrels to pieces wherever I found them? This my men would have done, if ordered, amidst a thousand of them, and I should have been supported, by the chiefs of the St. Peters, at the mouth of which were 300 warriors, attending my arrival; also the rascal who fired on my sentinel last winter. I dreaded the consequences of the meeting not for the present; but for fear the impetuosity of my conduct might not be approved of by my government; who did not so intimately know the nature of those savages. This day, for the first time, we saw the commencement of vegetation, yet the snow was a foot deep in some places.

10*th April, Thursday*.—Sailed at half past 5 o'clock; about 7 passed Rum river, and at 8 were saluted by 6 or 7 lodges of Fols Avoins, amongst whom was a Mr. ——, a clerk of Mr. Dickson's. Those people had wintered on Rum river, and were waiting for their chiefs and traders to descend in order to accompany them to the Prairie Des Chiens. Arrived at the Falls of St. Anthony at 10 o'clock. Carried over all our loading and the canoe to the lower end of the portage, and hauled our boats up on the bank. I pitched my tents at the lower end of the encampment where all the men encamped except the guard, whose quarters were above. The appearance of the Falls was much more tremendous than when we ascended; the increase of water occasioned the spray to raise much higher, and the mist appeared like clouds. How different my sensations now, from what they were when at this place before; at that time not having accomplished more than half my route, winter fast approaching; war existing between the most savage nations in the course of my route; my provisions greatly diminished, and but a poor prospect of an additional supply. Many of my men sick, and the others not a little disheartened; and our success in this arduous undertaking, very doubtful; just upon the borders of the haunts of civilized men, about to launch into an unknown wilderness; for ours was the first canoe

that had ever crossed this portage, were sufficient to dis-
possess my breast of contentment and ease.   But now we
have accomplished every wish, peace reigns throughout
the vast extent ; we have returned thus far on our voyage, without the loss of a single man, and hoping soon
to be blessed with the society of our relations and friends.
The river this morning covered with ice, which continued
floating all day.   The shores still barricaded with it.

11*th April, Friday.*—Although it snowed very hard,
we brought over both boats and descended the river to the
island at the entrance of the St. Peters.   I sent to the
chiefs and informed them I had something to communicate
to them.   The Fils de Pinchow immediately waited on
me, and informed me that he would provide a place for
the purpose.   About sun-down I was sent for and introduced into the council house, where I found a great many
chiefs of the Sussitongs, Gens des Feuilles, and the
Gens du Lac.   The Yanctongs had not yet come down.
They were all waiting for my arrival.   There were about
100 lodges or 600 people ; we were saluted on our crossing the river with ball as usual.   The council house was
two large lodges, capable of containing 300 men.   In the
upper were 40 chiefs, and as many pipes, set against the
poles ; along side of which I had the Sauteurs' pipes arranged.   I then informed them in short detail, of my
transactions with the Sauteurs ; but my interpreters were
not capable of making themselves understood.   I was
therefore obliged to omit mentioning every particular relative to the rascal who fired on my sentinel, and of the
scoundrel who broke the Fols Avoins' canoes, and threatened my life ; the interpreters however informed them that
I wanted some of their principal chiefs to go to St. Louis ;
and that those who thought proper might descend to the
prairie where we would give them more explicit information.   They all smoked out of the Sauteurs' pipes, ex-

cepting three, who were painted black, and were some of those who lost their relations last winter. I invited the Fils de Pinchow, and the son of the Killeur Rouge, to come over and sup with me ; when Mr. Dickson and my-self endeavored to explain what I intended to have said to them, could I have made myself understood ; that at the prairie we would have all things explained ; that I was desi-rous of making a better report of them than capt. Lewis could do from their treatment of him. The former of those savages was the person who remained around my post all last winter, and treated my men so well ; they endeavored to excuse their people, &c.

12th *April, Saturday*.—Embarked early. Although my interpreter had been frequently up the river, he could not tell me where the cave (spoken of by Carver) could be found ; we carefully sought for it, but in vain. At the Indian village, a few miles above St. Peters, we were about to pass a few lodges, but on receiving a very parti-cular invitation to come on shore, we landed, and were received in a lodge kindly ; they presented us sugar, &c. I gave the proprietor a dram, and was about to depart, when he demanded a kettle of liquor ; on being refused, and after I had left the shore, he told me, that he did not like the arrangements, and that he would go to war this summer. I directed the interpreter to tell him, that if I returned to the St. Peters with the troops, I would settle that affair with him. On our arrival at the St. Croix, I found the Petit Corbeau with his people, and Messrs. Fra-zer and Wood. We had a conference, when the Petit Corbeau made many apologies for the misconduct of his people ; he represented to us the different manners in which his young warriors had been inducing him to go to war ; that he had been much blamed for dismissing his party last fall ; but that he was determined to adhere as far as lay in his power to our instructions ; that he thought it most prudent to remain here and restrain the warriors. He then presented me with a beaver robe and pipe, and his message to the general. That he was determined to preserve peace, and make the road clear ; also a remembrance of his promised medal. I made him a reply, calculated to confirm him in his good intentions, and assured him that he should not be the less remembered by his father, although not present. I was informed, that, notwithstanding the instruction of his licence, and my particular request, Murdoch Cameron had taken liquor and sold it to the Indians on the river St. Peters ; and that his partner below had been equally imprudent. I pledged myself to prosecute them according to law ; for they have been the occasion of great confusion, and of much injury to the other traders. This day met a canoe of Mr. Dickson's, loaded with provision, under the charge of Mr. Anderson, brother of the Mr. Anderson, at Leech Lake. He politely offered me any provision he had on board, (for which Mr. Dickson had given me an order) but not now being in want, I did not accept of any. This day, for the first time, I observed the trees beginning to bud, and indeed the climate seemed to have changed very materially since we passed the Falls of St. Anthony.

13th April, Sunday.—We embarked after breakfast. Messrs. Frazer and Wood accompanied me. Wind strong a-head. They outrowed us ; the first boat or canoe we met with on the voyage able to do it, but then they were double manned and light. Arrived at the band of the Aile Rouge at 2 o'clock, where we were saluted as usual. We had a council, when he spoke with more detestation of the conduct of the rascals at the mouth of the St. Peters, than any man I had yet heard. He assured me, speaking of the fellow who had fired on my sentinel, and threatened to kill me, that if I thought it requisite, he should be killed ; but that as there were many chiefs above, with whom he wished to speak, he hoped I would remain one day, when all the Sioux would be down, and I might have the command of a thousand men of them, that I would probably think it no honor ; but that the British used to flatter them they were proud of having them for soldiers. I replied in general terms, and assured him that it was not for the conduct of two or three rascals that I meant to pass over all the good treatment I had received from the Sioux nation ; but, that in general council I would explain myself. That as to the scoundrel who fired at my sentinel, had I been at home, the Sioux nation would never have been troubled with him, for I would have killed him on the spot. But that my young men did not do it, apprehensive that I would be displeased. I then gave him the news of the Sauteurs, &c. that as to remaining one day, it would be of no service ; that I was much pressed to arrive below ; as my general expected me, my duty called me, and that the state of my provision demanded the utmost expedition ; that I would be happy to oblige him, but that my men must eat. He replied, that Lake Pepin being yet shut with ice, if I went on and encamped on the ice, it would not get me provision. That he would send out all his young men the next day ; and, that if the other bands did not arrive he would depart the day after with me. In short, after much talk, I agreed to remain one day, knowing that the lake was closed and that we could proceed, only nine miles if we went ; this appeared to give general satisfaction. I was invited to different feasts, and entertained at one by a person whose father was enacted a chief by the Spaniards. At this feast I saw a man (called by the French the Roman nose, and by the Indians the Wind that Walks) who was formerly the second chief of the Sioux, but being the cause of the death of one of the traders, seven years since, he voluntarily relinquished the dignity, and has frequently requested to be given up to the whites. But he was now determined to go to St. Louis and deliver himself up where he said they might put him to death. His long repentance, the great confidence of the nation in him, would perhaps protect him from a punishment which the crime merited. But as the crime was committed long before the United States assumed its authority, and as no law of theirs could affect it, unless it was ex post facto, and had a retrospective effect, I conceive it would certainly be dispunishable now. I did not think proper, however, to inform him so. I here received a letter from Mr. Rollet, partner of Mr. Cameron, with a present of some brandy, coffee and sugar. I hesitated about receiving those articles from the partner of the man I intended to prosecute; their amount being trifling, however I accepted of them, offering him pay. I assured him that the prosecution arose from a sense of duty, and not from any personal prejudice. My canoe did not come up, in consequence of the head wind. Sent out two men in a canoe to set fishing lines; the canoe overset, and had it not been for the timely assistance of the savages, who carried them into their lodges, undressed them and treated them with the greatest humanity and kindness, they must inevitably have perished. At this place I was informed, that the rascal spoken of as having threatened my life, had actually cocked his gun to shoot me from behind the hills, but was prevented by the others.

14th *April, Monday.*—Was invited to a feast by the *Roman Nose.* His conversation was interesting, and shall be detailed hereafter. The other Indians not yet arrived. Messrs. Wood, Frazer, and myself, ascended a high hill called the Barn, from which we had a view of Lake Pepin. The valley through which the Mississippi by numerous channels wound itself to the St. Croix; the Cannon river and the lofty hills on each side.

N

15*th April, Tuesday.*—Arose very early and embarked about sunrise, much to the astonishment of the Indians, who were entirely prepared for the council, when they heard I had put off ; however after some conversation with Mr. Frazer, they acknowledged that it was agreeably to what I had said, that I would sail early, and that they could not blame me. I was very positive in my word, for I found it by far the best way to treat the Indians. The *Aile Rouge* had a beaver robe and pipe prepared to present, but was obliged for the present to retain it. Passed through Lake Pepin with my barges, the canoe being obliged to lay by, did not come on. Stopt at a prairie on the right bank descending, about nine miles below Lake Pepin. Went out to view some hills which had the appearance of the old fortifications spoken of ; but I will speak more fully of them hereafter. In these hollows I discovered a flock of elk, took out fifteen men, but we were not able to kill any. Mr. Frazer came up and passed on about two miles. We encamped together. Neither Mr. Wood's nor my canoe arrived. Snowed considerably.

16*th April, Wednesday.*—Mr. Frazer's canoes and my boats sailed about one hour by sun. We waited some time expecting Mr. Wood's barges, and my canoe, but hearing a gun fired first just above our encampment, we were induced to make sail. Passed the Aile Prairie, also La Montagne qui Trompe a L'eau, the prairie De Cross, and encamped on the W. shore, a few hundred yards below, where I had encamped on the   day of September, in ascending. Killed a goose flying. Shot at some pidgeons at our camp, and was answered from behind an island with two guns ; we returned them, and were replied to by two more. This day the trees appeared in bloom. Snow might still be seen on the sides of the hills. Distance 75 miles.

17*th April, Thursday.*—Put off pretty early and arrived at Wabasha's band at 11 o'clock, where I detained all day for him; but he alone of all the hunters remained out all night. Left some powder and tobacco for him. The Sioux presented me with a kettle of boiled meat and a deer. I here received information that the Puants had killed some white men below. Mr. Wood's and my canoe arrived.

18*th April, Friday.*—Departed from our encampment very early. Stopped to breakfast at the Painted Rock. Arrived at the Prairie Des Cheins at two o'clock; and were received by crouds on the bank. Took up my quarters at Mr. Fisher's. My men received a present of one barrel of pork from Mr. Campbell, a bag of biscuit, 20 loaves of bread, and some meat from Mr. Fisher. A Mr. Jearreau, from Cahokia, is here, who embarks tomorrow for St. Louis. I wrote to general Wilkinson by him.* I was called on by a number of chiefs, Reynards, Sioux of the Des Moyan, &c. The Winebagos were here intending, as I was informed, to deliver some of the murderers to me. Received a great deal of news from the States and Europe, both civil and military.

19*th April, Saturday.*—Dined at Mr. Campbell's in company with Messrs. Wilmot, Blakely, Wood, Rollet, Fisher, Frazer, and Jearreau. Six canoes arrived from the upper part of the St. Peters with the Yanctong chiefs from the head of that river. Their appearance was indeed savage, much more so than any nation I have yet seen. Prepared my boat for sail. Gave notice to the Puants that I had business to do with them the next day. A band of the Gens Du Lac arrived. Took into my pay as interpreter Mr. Y. Reinville.

20*th April, Sunday.*—Held a council with the Puant chiefs, and demanded of them the murderers of their na-

* See appendix to part I. [No. 11] page 25.

tion ;† they required till to-morrow to consider of it ; this afternoon they had a great game of the cross on the prairie, between the Sioux on the one side, and the Puants and Reynards on the other. The ball is made of some hard substance and covered with leather, the cross sticks are round and net work, with handles of three feet long. The parties being ready, and bets agreed upon, (sometimes to the amount of some thousand dollars) the goals are set up on the prairie at the distance of half a mile. The ball is thrown up in the middle, and each party strives to drive it to the opposite goal ; and when either party gains the first rubber, which is driving it quick round the post, the ball is again taken to the centre, the ground changed, and the contest renewed ; and this is continued until one side gains four times, which decides the bet. It is an interesting sight to see two or three hundred naked savages contending on the plain who shall bear off the palm of victory ; as he who drives the ball round the goal is much shouted at by his companions. It sometimes happens that one catches the ball in his racket, and depending on his speed endeavors to carry it to the goal, and when he finds himself too closely pursued, he hurls it with great force and dexterity to an amazing distance, where there are always flankers of both parties ready to receive it ; it seldom touches the ground, but is sometimes kept in the air for hours before either party can gain the victory. In the game which I witnessed, the Sioux were victorious, more I believe, from the superiority of their skill in throwing the ball, than by their swiftness, for I thought the Puants and Reynards the swiftest runners. I made a written demand of the magistrates to take depositions concerning the late murders.‡ Had a private conversation with Wabasha.

---

† See appendix to part I. [No. 12] page 26.
‡ See appendix to part I. [No. 13] page 29.

21*st April, Monday.*—Was sent for by La Feuille, and had a long and interesting conversation with him, in which he spoke of the general jealousy of his nation towards their chiefs ; and that although he knew it might occasion some of the Sioux displeasure, he did not hesitate to declare that he looked on the Nez Corbeau, as the man of most sense in their nation ; and that he believed it would be generally acceptable if he was reinstated in his rank.   Upon my return I was sent for by the *Red Thunder*, chief of the Yanctongs, the most savage band of the Sioux.   He was prepared with the most elegant pipes and robes I ever saw ; and shortly he declared, " That white " blood had never been shed in the village of the Yanc- " tongs, even when rum was permitted ; that Mr. Mur- " doch Cameron arrived at his village last autumn ; that " he invited him to eat, gave him corn as a bird ; that he " (Cameron) informed him of the prohibition of rum, " and was the only person who afterwards sold it in the " village."   After this I had a council with the Puants. Spent the evening with Mr. Wilmot, one of the best informed and most gentlemanly man in the place.

22*d April, Tuesday.*—Held a council with the Sioux and Puants, the latter of whom delivered up their medals and flags.   Prepared to depart tomorrow.

23*d April, Wednesday.*—After closing my accounts, &c. at half past 12 o'clock left the prairie, at the lower end of it was saluted by 17 lodges of the Puants.   Met a barge, by which I received a letter from my lady.   Further on, met one batteaux and one canoe of traders.   Passed one trader's camp.   Arrived at Mr. Dubuque's at 10 o'clock at night, found some traders encamped at the entrance with 40 or 50 Indians, obtained some information from Mr. D. and requested him to write me on certain points.   After we had boiled our victuals, I divided my men into four watches and put off, wind a-head.   Observed for the first time the half formed leaves on the trees.

24th April, Thursday.—In the morning used our oars until 10 o'clock, and then floated while breakfasting.   At this time two barges, one bark, and two wooden, canoes passed us under full sail ; by one of which I sent back a letter to Mr. Dubuque, that I had forgotten to deliver. Stopped at dark to cook supper, after which, rowed under the windward shore expecting we could make head way with four oars ; but were blown on the lee shore in a few moments, when all hands were summoned, and we again with difficulty made to windward, came too, placed one sentry on my bow, and all hands beside went to sleep. It rained, and before morning, the water overflowed my bed in the bottom of the boat, having no cover, or any extra accommodations, as it might have retarded my voyage. The wind very hard a-head.

25th April, Friday.—Obliged to unship our mast to prevent its rolling overboard with the swell.   Passed the first Reynard village at 12 o'clock, counted 18 lodges. Stopped at the prairie in descending on the left, about the middle of the rapids, where there is a beautiful cove or harbor.   There were three lodges of Indians here, but none of them came near us.   Shortly after we had left this, observed a barge under sail, with the United States flag, which upon our being seen put to shore on the Big Island, about three miles above Stony river, where I also landed ; it proved to be capt. Many of the artillerists, who was in search of some Osage prisoners amongst the Sacs and Reynards.   He informed me that at the village of Stony Point, the Indians evinced a strong disposition to commit hostilities ; that he was met at the mouth of the river by an old Indian, who said that all the inhabitants of the village were in a state of intoxication, and advised him to go up alone.   This advice however he had reject-

ed. That when they arrived there, they were saluted by
the appellation of the bloody Americans who had killed
such a person's father, and such a person's mother, brother, &c. The women carried off the guns and other
arms, and concealed them. That he then crossed the
river opposite to the village, and was followed by a number of Indians, with pistols under their blankets. That
they would listen to no conference whatever, relating to
the delivery of the prisoners ; but demanded insolently
why he wore a plume in his hat ; and declared that they
looked on it as a mark of war, and immediately decorated themselves with their raven's feathers, worn only in
cases of hostility. We regretted that our orders would
not permit of our punishing the scoundrels, as by a *coup
de main* we might easily have carried the village. Gave
capt. Many a note of introduction to Messrs. Campbell,
Fisher, Wilmot, and Dubuque, and every information in
my power. We sat up late conversing.

26*th April, Saturday.*—Capt. Many and myself took
breakfast and embarked ; wind directly a-head, and a
most tremendous swell to combat, which has existed ever
since we left the prairie. Capt. Many under full sail :
descended by all the sinuosity of the shore to avoid the
strength of the wind and force of the waves. Indeed I
was confident I could sail much faster up than we could
possibly make down. Encamped on Grant's prairie, where
we had encamped on the 25th August when ascending.
There was one Indian and family present, to whom I gave
some corn.

27*th April, Sunday.*—It cleared off during the night.
We embarked early and came from eight or ten leagues
above the river Iowa, to the establishment at the lower
Sac village, by sundown, a distance of nearly 48 leagues.
Here I met with Messrs. Maxwell and Blondeau ; took
the deposition of the former, on the subject of the In-

dian's intoxication at this place, for they were all drunk.
They had stolen a horse from the establishment, and offered to bring him back for liquor, but laughed at them
when offered a blanket and powder. Passed two canoes
and two barges. At the establishment received two letters from Mrs. Pike, took with us corporal Eddy and the
other soldier whom capt. Many had left. Rowed with
four oars all night. A citizen took passage with me.

28th April, Monday.—In the morning passed a wintering ground, where from appearance, there must have
been at least seven or eight different establishments. At
12 o'clock arrived at the French house, mentioned in our
voyage up, about the 16th of August. Here we landed
our citizen, his name was ————, and he belonged to
the settlement on Copper river. He informed me there
were about 25 families in the settlement. Stopped at
some islands about 10 miles above Salt river, where there
were pidgeon roosts, and in about fifteen minutes my men
had knocked on the head and brought on board 298. I
had frequently heard of the fecundity of this bird, but
never gave credit to what I then thought inclined to the
marvellous; but really the most fervid imagination cannot
conceive their numbers. Their noise in the woods was
like the continued roaring of the wind, and the ground
may be said to have been absolutely covered with their
excrement. The young ones which we killed were nearly
as large as the old, they could fly about ten steps, and
were one mass of fat; their craws were filled with acorns
and the wild pea. They were still reposing on their nests,
which were merely small bunches of sticks joined, with
which all the small trees were covered. Met four canoes
of the Sacs, with wicker baskets filled with young pidgeons.
They made motions to exchange them for liquor, to which
I returned the back of my hand. Indeed those scoundrels had become so insolent through the instigation of

the traders, that nothing but the lenity of our government and humanity for the poor devils, could have restrained me on my descent from carrying some of their towns by surprize, which I was determined to have done had the information of their firing on capt. Many proved to have been correct. Put into the mouth of Salt river to cook supper, after which although raining, we put off and set our watches, but so violent a gale and thunder storm came on about 12 o'clock, that we put ashore ; discovered that one of my sleigh dogs was missing.

29th April, Tuesday.—In the morning still raining, and wind up the river, hoisted sail, and returned to the mouth of the river; but neither here nor on the shore could we find my dog; this was no little mortification, as it broke the match, whose important services I had already experienced, after having brought them so near home. We continued on until 12 o'clock, when it ceased raining for a little time, and we put ashore for breakfast. Rowed till sun-down, when I set the watch. Night fine and mild.

30th April, Wednesday.—By day light found ourselves at the Portage de Sioux. I here landed captain Many's two men, and ordered them across by land to the cantonment. As I had never seen the village, I walked up and through it ; there are not more than twenty-one houses, at furthest, which are built of square logs. Met lieut. Hughes, about four miles above St. Louis with more than twenty Osage prisoners, conveying them to the cantonment on the Missouri ; he informed me my friends were all well. Arrived about 12 o'clock at the town, after an absence of eight months and twenty two days.

(Signed)   Z. M. Pike, Lieut.

Meteorological Observations made by lieutenant Pike, in his voyage up the Mississippi river, in the years 1805 and 1806.

Time of observat.		Thermometer			Sky.	Wind.		Latitude.	Longitude.	Variation.	Barometer.	Remarks.
days	mon.	sun-rise	3 P. M.	sun-set		Course.	Force.					
		deg.	deg.									
6	AUGUST.	-	90	-	clear	S S E	fresh	N 39 1	W 15 20 Ph.	7 54	28 5	
7		-	90	-	thunder storm	N W	very hard	-	-	-	28	
8		-	75	-	rain	N W	do.	-	-	-	28 6	
9		-	83	-	cloudy	S by E	light	-	-	-	28 8	
10		-	97	-	flying, clouds.	W	squally	-	-	-	28	
11		-	108 1-2	-	do.	W by S		-	-	-	20	
12		-	101 3-4	-	some rain	S by W	fresh	-	-	-	29 2	
13		-	83 3-4	-	hard rain	N W	do.	-	-	-	-	
14		-	81 1-2	-	do.	S by E	do.	-	-	-	28 5	
15		-	88 1-4	-	rainy	N W	do.	-	16 41	-	29	
16		-	90 1-2	-	clear	N W	gentle, light	40 31	-	-	30	
17		-	88 1-4	-	do.	S E	do.	-	-	-	28 2	
18		-	81 1-2	-	cloudy	N W	strong	-	-	-	28 5	
19		-	99 1-2	-	clear	N W	gentle	-	-	-	30	
20		-	90 1-2	-	do.	E	do.	-	-	-	30	
21		-	88 1-4	-	cloudy	S E	fresh	40 32 12	-	-	29	
22		-	90 1-2	-	clear	N by W	strong	-	-	-	29 5	
23		-	106 1-4	-	do.	-	-	-	-	-	30	
24		-	82 3-4	-	clear	-	-	-	-	-	30	
25		-	81 1-4	-	cloudy	N by W	strong	-	-	-	29	
26		61 1-4	72 1-2	-	rain	N by W	gale, head wind	-	-	-	-	
27		54 1-2	63 1-4	-	do.	N by W	do.	-	-	-	-	
28		52 1-4	61 1-4	-	do.	S by E	hard	-	-	-	-	
29		52 1-4	72 1-2	-	cloudy	S by W	fresh	-	-	-	28 5	
30		61 1-4	88 1-4	-	clear	S by W	do.	-	-	-	28 5	
31			92 3-4	-	do.	S by W	gentle	-	-	-	28 5	

Meteorological Observations made by lieutenant Pike, in his voyage up the Mississippi river, in the years 1805 and 1806.

Time of observat.		Thermometer			Sky.	Wind		Latitude.	Longitude.	Variation.	Barometer.	Remarks.
mon.	days.	sun-rise. deg.	3 P. M.	sun-set.		Course.	Force.					
SEPTEMBER	1	-	88 1-4	-	clear	S E	fresh	-	-	-	30	At the mines.
	2	-	95	-	do.	S	gentle	-	-	-	29 3	
	3	-	79 1-4	-	cloudy	N W	do.	-	-	-	28 8	
	4	-	77	-	do.	S W	do.	N 43 44 8	-	-	29	At Prairie De Chien.
	5	-	88 1-4	-	rain	S W	fresh	-	-	-	27	
	6	-	95	-	clear	S by E	do.	-	-	-	27	
	7	-	86	-	cloudy	S by E	do.	-	-	-	28 5	
	8	-	99 1-2	-	do.	S by E	do.	-	-	-	29 8	
	9	-	92 3-4	-	do.	S	gentle	-	-	-	28	
	10	-	72 1-2	-	rain	N by W	fresh	-	-	-	-	Below 24.
	11	-	59	-	do.	N by E	hard	-	-	-	-	
	12	-	52 1-4	-	do.	N by E	do.	-	-	-	-	
	13	-	50	-	do.	N	gentle	-	-	-	-	
	14	-	43 1-4	-	clear	S E	do.	-	-	-	28 5	
	15	-	65 3-4	-	rain	S E	do.	-	-	-	28	
	16	-	77	-	rising clouds	S E	fresh	45 44 8	-	-	-	Lake Pepin.
	17	-	65 3-4	-	rain	N W	hard	-	-	-	-	
	18	-	77	-	cloudy	S E	gentle	-	-	-	28 5	
	19	-	65 3-4	-	do.	N W	fresh	-	-	-	28	
	20	-	73 1-2	-	clear	S E	do.	-	-	-	29	
	21	41	77	-	do.	N W	gentle	-	-	-	-	River St. Peter's.
	22	-	81 1-2	-	do.	N W	fresh	-	-	-	28 5	
	23	-	86	-	cloudy	N W	do.	-	-	-	-	
	24	-	77	-	do.	N W	do.	-	-	-	-	
	25	-		-	flying clouds	S E	do.	-	-	-	-	
	26	-	65 3-4	-	cloudy	S E	-	-	-	-	-	Falls of St. Anthony.
	27	-	65 3-4	-	do.	S by E	hard.	-	-	-	28	
	28	-	65 3-4	-	rain	S by E	fresh and hard	-	-	-	-	
	29	-	72 1-2	-	cloudy	N E	-	-	-	-	-	
	30	-	65 3-4	-	do.			-	-	-	-	

Meteorological observations made by lieutenant Pike, in his voyage up the Mississippi river, in the years 1805 and 1806.

Time of observat.		Thermometer			Sky	Wind		Latitude	Longitude	Variation	Barometer	Remarks
days	mon.	sun-rise	3 P. M.	sun-set		Course	Force					
1		50 deg.	65 3-4	— deg.	cloudy	N W	fresh	N 45	-	-	28 5	
2		50	72 1-2	—	rain	N W		-	-	-	28	
3		32	50	—	clear	N W		-	-	-	28 4	
4		32	50	—	cloudy, hail	N W		-	-	-	29	
5		32	23	—	clear	N W	hard	-	-	-	29 5	
6		23	23	—	do.	N W	do.	-	-	-	29 5	
7		36 1-2	23	—	do.	N W	do.	-	-	-	29	
8		26	50	—	do.	S E	fresh	-	-	-	29 5	
9		41	50	—	do.	W by N		-	-	-	29 5	
10		54 1-2	88 1-4	65 3-4	do.	S by W	do.	-	-	-	29	
11		50	65 3-4	54 1-2	do.	N by W	do.	-	-	-	29 5	
12		36 1-2	65 3-4	36 1-2	do.	N by W	hard	-	-	-	29 5	
13		36	72 1-2	59	do.	S by W	fresh	-	-	-	36 2	
14		36	65 3-4	50	do.	N W	gentle	-	-	-	29	
15		36	54 1-2	41	cloudy and rain	N by W	fresh	-	-	-	28 5	
16		43 1-4	54 1-2	54 1-2	snow	do.	do.	45 33 3	-	-	28 5	Pine Creek Rapids.
17		50	65 3-4	52	do.	do.	do.	-	-	-	28	
18		41	50	50	cloudy	S by W	do.	-	-	-	29 5	
19		43 1-4	59	54 1-2	clear & cloudy	do.	gentle	-	-	-	29 8	
20		45 1-2	54	43 1-4	do.	do.	do.	-	-	-	29 5	
21		23	54	20	clear	do.	do.	-	-	-	29	
22		29	45	32	cloudy & snow	N by W	do.	-	-	-	28 5	
23		20	27	23	do. do.	N W	do.	-	-	-	29 3	
24		20	27	23	do. do.	N W	do.	r	-	-	29	
25		16	23	43	cloudy	—	do.	-	-	9 10	29 5	
26		11	20	32	clear	W	do.	-	-	-	30	
27		20	32	43 1-4	do.	W	do.	-	-	-	29 5	
28		20	43	47	do.	N E	do.	45 33 3	-	9 10 S	29	Pine Creek.
29		27	50	43	cloudy & rain	N E	do.	-	-	-	29 5	
30		50	52 1-2	50	do.	N E	do.	-	-	-	28 5	
31		32	43	47	cloudy	N	do.	-	-	9 10 S	28	

OCTOBER.

Meteorological Observations made by lieutenant Pike, in his voyage up the Mississippi river, in the years 1805 and 1806.

Time of observat. days	mon.	Thermometer sun-rise	3 P. M.	sun-set	Sky	Wind Course	Force	Latitude	Longitude	Variation	Barometer	Remarks
1	NOVEMBER	36 deg.	-	-	rain	-	-	N 45 33 3	.	.	28	Absent from camp.
2		-	-	-	snow	-	-	.	.	.	.	
3		-	warm	-	fair	-	-	.	.	.	.	
4		-	fresh	-	do.	N E	gentle	.	.	.	.	
5		-	warm	-	do.	-	-	.	.	.	.	
6		-	cool	-	snow	-	-	.	.	.	.	Thunder and lightning.
7		-	warm	-	hail and rain	N W	-	.	.	.	.	
8		-	do.	-	light snow	do.	-	.	.	.	.	
9		-	cold	27 deg.	do.	do.	-	.	.	.	28	Return.
10		14	20 deg.	20	clear	N W	gentle	.	.	.	.	Thaws.
11		20	25	25	do.	S E	do.	.	.	.	.	Ditto.
12		27	23	27	cloudy	S W	do.	.	.	.	8 5	Smoky.
13		38	35	38	do.	-	do.	.	.	.	8 5	Thunder and lightning.
14		41	-	1	rain	-	-	.	.	.	.	
15		47	38	47	cloudy	-	-	.	.	.	.	
16		54	36	47	do.	-	-	.	.	.	.	Freezing.
17		47	36	32	de.	-	-	.	.	.	.	Ditto.
18		30	34	32	clear	-	-	.	.	.	.	Ditto.
19		38	36	23	do.	-	-	.	.	.	.	Ditto.
20		38	36	41	do.	-	-	.	.	.	.	Thaws.
21		41	36	45	-	-	-	.	.	.	.	Ditto.
22		41	36	38	-	-	-	.	.	.	.	Freezing.
23		41	32	27	-	-	-	.	.	.	.	Thaws.
24		38	34	32	-	-	-	.	.	.	.	Ditto.
25		41	38	38	-	-	-	.	.	.	.	Ditto.
26		38	32	34	-	-	-	.	.	.	.	Ditto.
27		38	38	34	clear	-	-	.	.	.	.	
28		29	43	41	do.	N W	fresh	.	.	.	.	
29		23	32	35	do.	N	gentle	.	.	.	.	
30		16	27	25		N by W	do.	.	.	.	.	

(Remarks for days 16–26 are bracketed together as "Absent.")

Meteorological Observations, made by lieutenant Pike in his voyage up the Mississippi river, in the years 1805 and 1806.

Time of observat. days, mon.	Thermometer sun-rise	Thermometer 3 P.M.	Thermometer sun-set	Sky.	Wind. Course.	Wind. Force.	Latitude.	Longitude.	Variation.	Barometer.	Remarks.
DECEMBER											
1	25 deg.	32 deg.	32 deg.	snow	S W	gentle	N 45 33 9				
2	7	27	16	clear	S E	do.					
3	16	32	20	do.	S E	do.					
4	20	32	27	do.	S E	do.					
5	23	32	32	cloudy	S E	do.					
6	25	32	32	clear	S E	do.					
7	20	27	25	do.	S E	do.					
8	16	25	27	do.	S E	do.					
9	20	25	23	do.	N E	fresh					
10	23	27	29	cloudy	S E	do.					Thawing.
11	27	—	43	do.	S E	gentle					Slight snow.
12	29	—	32	do.	N W	fresh					Storm.
13	38	—	32	snow	N W	hard					Stormy.
14	29	—	7	-	N W	do.					
15	7	—	11	cloudy	N W	do.					
16	9	—	43	clear	S	gentle					
17	20	—	32	do.	S E	do.					Thaws.
18	36	—	36	do.	S E	do.					Thaws.
19	36	—	25	cloudy	S E and N W	fresh					Freezes.
20	25	—	39	do.	N E	gentle	50				Ditto.
21	18	—	27	clear	N E	do.					Ditto.
22	2	—	5	do.	N E	do.	45 49				Ditto.
23	5	—	32	do.	N E	do.					Ditto.
24	27	—	27	cloudy	N E	do.					Ditto.
25	23	—	27	do.	N W	do.					Ditto.
26	23	—	29	snow	E	do.					
27	23	—	32	cloudy	S W	do.					
28	20	—	11	clear	N W	hard					Very cold.
29	9	—	11	do.	W	do.					
30	9	—	20	do.	W	do.					Very cold.

Meteorological Observations made by lieutenant Pike, in his voyage up the Mississippi river, in the years 1805 and 1806.

Time of observ'at. days/mon	Thermometer sun-rise	Thermometer 3 P.M.	Thermometer sun-set	Sky	Wind Course	Wind Force	Latitude	Longitude	Variation	Barometer	Remarks
JANUARY											
1	17 4-10	—	11 deg.	cloudy and snow	N E	fresh					
2	2	—	20	clear	E	do.					
3	20	—	25	do.	W						
4	23	—	25	do.	W						
5	33 5-10	—	20	do.	E						
6	20	—	9	snow	W	hard					
7	15 2-10	—	1	clear			N 46 9 20				
8		—									Lake Sable.
9		—									Absent for six days.
10		—		do.	S E						
11		—	2	do.							
12	28 8-10	—	6	do.	N		46 9 20	22 13	3 41 W		
13	24	—	1	do.			46 9 20				
14	19 8-10	—	6								
15	5-10	—	5								
16		23	20								
17	6	25	20								
18	9	—	—								
19	—	—	—								
20			23	do.	N W						
21	14	—	27	do.							
22	27	—	27	cloudy	S by E						
23	27	29	32								
24		27	—								
25	—	5	—								
26	—	6	—								
27	4	2	5								
28	5	14	11								
29	1	14	—								
30	8	14	—								

Meteorological Observations, made by lieutenant Pike in his voyage up the Mississippi river, *in the years* 1805 *and* 1806.

Time of observat.		Thermometer.			Sky.	Wind.		Latitude.	Longitude.	Variation.	Barometer.	Remarks.
days.	mon.	sun-rise.	3 P. M.	sun-set.		Course.	Force.					
1	FEBRUARY.	10 deg.	7 deg.	5 deg.	Clear	-	-	N 47 16 13	-	-	-	Leech Lake.
2		5	9	14	do.	-	-	-	-	-	-	
3		7	27	23	do.	-	-	-	-	-	-	
4		1	9	1	do.	-	-	-	-	-	-	
5		10	14	7	do.	-	-	-	-	-	-	
6		5	27	11	do.	W	Fresh	-	-	-	-	
7		2	23	20	do.	W	hard	-	-	-	-	
8		8	1	9	snow	-	-	-	-	-	-	
9		17 5-10	1	8	do.	N E	gentle	-	-	-	-	
10		17 5-10	1	5	clear	S E	-	-	-	-	-	
11		1	7	1	do.	N E	-	-	-	-	-	
12		5	16	1	hail and clouds	S by E	fresh	-	-	-	-	
13		23	36	32	clear	N W	-	-	-	-	-	
14		11	36	32	do.	N W	-	-	-	-	-	
15		5	20	16	do.	S W	-	-	-	-	-	
16		2	23	16	sleets of snow	-	-	-	-	-	-	
17		5	32	32	clear	-	-	-	-	-	-	
18		14	32	-	do.	-	-	-	-	-	-	
19		-	-	20	do.	-	-	-	-	-	-	
20		1	-	27	do.	-	-	-	-	-	-	
21		14	-	27	do.	-	-	-	-	-	-	
22		16	-	27	do.	-	-	46 32 32	-	-	-	White Fish Lake.
23		14	-	23	do.	-	-	-	-	-	-	
24		16	-	20	do.	-	-	-	-	-	-	
25		11	-	25	do.	do.	-	-	-	-	-	
26		23	-	36	do.	N W	-	-	-	-	-	
27		16	-	11	-	N W	-	-	-	-	-	
28		16	-	-	-	-	-	-	-	-	-	

Meteorological Observations, made by Lieutenant Pike in his voyage up the Mississippi river, in the years 1805 and 1806.

Time of observat. days	Thermometer sun-rise	Thermometer 3 P. M.	Thermometer sun-set	Sky	Wind Course	Wind Force	Latitude	Longitude	Variation	Barometer	Remarks
1	16 deg.	—	16 deg.	Clear	S E	-	-	.	.	.	Lower Red Cedar Lake.
2	16	—	20	cloudy	S E	-	-	.	.	.	
3	20	—	43	clear	E	-		.	.	.	
4	20	—	27	do.	E	-		.	.	.	
5	25	—	29	do.	-	-		.	.	.	
6	36	—	27	clear and snow at night.			N 45 33 3	.	.	.	Pine Creek.
7	29	41 deg.	27	do. and warm			-	.	.	.	
8	29	26	23	cloudy	S E	hard	-	.	.	.	
9	36	43	41	clear	S E	-	-	.	.	.	Very warm—ice melting fast.
10	25	25	27	do.	N E	-	-	.	.	.	
11	32	36	88	cloudy	S E	fresh	-	.	.	.	Raw and disagreeable.
12	34	47	38	clear	N W	do.	-	.	.	.	Ice melting fast.
13	33	43	27	do.	N W	-	45 14 8	.	.	.	
14	38	43	34	do.	N W	do.	-	.	.	.	
15	50	41	36	do.	N	do.	-	.	.	.	Small snow in the night.
16	38	43	36	do.	E	do.	-	.	.	.	
17	32	32	32	snow	N W	do.	43 44 8	.	.	.	Sleet and snow.
18	32	32	32	do.	N	do.	-	.	.	.	Heavy snow.
19	32	32	29	do.	N E	do.	-	.	.	.	Do. do.
20	29	38	29	cloudy	N by E	do.	-	.	.	.	Thawing in the middle of the day—water rising.
21	9	32	20	clear	N W	do.	-	.	.	.	Cold.
22	1	9	14	do.	N E	do.	-	.	.	.	Extraordinary cold.
23	7	32	32	do.	E	do.	-	.	.	.	
24	5	32	32	cloudy	N E	do.	-	.	.	.	Sauteurs.
25	25	25	32	snow	S E	-	-	.	.	.	Very stormy.
26	11	25	27	clear	E	do.	-	.	.	.	Moderate.
27	38	54	43	do.	S E	do.	-	.	.	.	Warm.
28	36	41	43	do.	S W	do.	-	.	.	.	Do. thunder and lightning.
29	29	70	54	do.	S E	do.	-	.	.	.	Do. do. do. and rain.
30	52	56	43	cloudy	N E	do.	-	.	.	.	
31	32	61	43	clear	N E	-	-	.	.	.	

MARCH.

Meteorological Observations made by lieutenant Pike, in his voyage up the Mississippi river, in the years 1805 and 1806.

Time of observat.		Thermometer.			Sky.	Wind.		Latitude.	Longitude.	Variation.	Barometer.	Remarks.
days.	mon.	sun-rise.	3 P. M.	sun-set.		Course.	Force,					
1	APRIL.	29 deg.	61 deg.	43 deg.	clear	N E	fresh	·	·	·	·	Ice breaking up by degrees.
2		34	74	63	do.	S	hard	·	·	·	·	Ice commenced running.
3		45	70	43	do.	N E	do.	·	·	·	·	Ditto.
4		20	45	'1	do.	N E	do.	·	·	·	·	
5		29	45	38	cloudy	N E	do.	·	·	·	·	Snow.
6		27	43	36	do.	N E	do.	·	·	·	·	River entirely breaks up.
7		23	—	33	snow	N E	-	·	·	·	·	
8		41	—	34	cloudy	N	snow with hail	·	·	·	·	
9		5	18	32	clear	N E	-	·	·	·	·	Remarkably cold.
10		54	54	25	do.	N E	-	·	·	·	·	
11		18	32	32	snow	S E	-	·	·	·	·	Snow falls three inches.
12		16	54	43	clear	S E	-	·	·	·	·	
13		32	50	45	do.	S E	hard	·	·	·	·	
14		38	50	45	cloudy and rain	do.	-	·	·	·	·	
15		34	52	32	snow	S E	-	·	·	·	·	
16		34	50	41	do.	N W	fresh	·	·	·	·	
17		34	70	43	clear	N W	do.	·	·	·	·	
18		45	93	63	do.	N W	do.	·	·	·	·	
19		50	99	81	do.	S E	do.	·	·	·	·	
20		59	95	79	do.	N W	-	·	·	·	·	
21		54	92	63	cloudy	N W	do.	·	·	·	·	
22		43	63	52	clear	N W	-	·	·	·	·	
23		36	72	63	do.	S E	hard	·	·	·	·	
24		43	70	61	cloudy	S E	do.	·	·	·	·	
25		43	54	47	cloudy & rain	S E	do.	·	·	·	·	
26		43	—	—	do.	& E	gentle	·	·	·	·	
27		43	95	77	clear	N E	do.	·	·	·	·	
28		43	81	72	cloudy	S E	-	·	·	·	·	
29		38	59	—	rain	N W	-	·	·	·	·	

These observations are very imperfect, my mode of travelling being such as to prevent my making regular references to the thermometer; and during the intense cold which prevailed some part of the winter, the mercury of the barometer sunk into the bulb. Those different circumstances occasioned the omissions which appear in the table. The instrument employed was Reaumer's, but the observations made have been adapted to the scale of Fahrenheit. Z. M. PIKE, 1st lieutenant.

I was also frequently obliged to be absent from my party, when it was impossible for me to carry instruments.

PIKE'S EXPEDITION.

PART II.

_____

INSTRUCTIONS TO LIEUTENANT PIKE.

St. Louis, June 24th, 1806.

Sir,

YOU are to proceed without delay to the cantonment on the Missouri, where you are to embark the late Osage captives, and the deputation recently returned from Washington, with their presents and baggage, and are to transport the whole up the Missouri and Osage rivers to the town of the Grand Osage.

The safe delivery of this charge at the point of destination, constitutes the primary object of your expedition, and therefore you are to move with such caution as may prevent surprise from any hostile band, and are to repel with your utmost force any outrage which may be attempted.

Having safely deposited your passengers and their property, you are to turn your attention to the accomplishment of a permanent peace between the Kanses and Osage nations, for which purpose you must effect a meeting between the head chiefs of those nations, and are to employ such arguments, deduced from their own obvious interests, as well as the inclinations, desires, and commands of the president of the United States, as may facilitate your purpose and accomplish the end.

A third object of considerable magnitude will then claim your consideration. It is to effect an interview and establish a good understanding with the Yanctons, Tetaus, or Camanches.

For this purpose you must interest White Hair, of the Grand Osage, with whom and a suitable deputation you will visit the Panis republic, where you may find interpreters, and inform yourself of the most feasible plan, by which to bring the Camanches to a conference.—Should you succeed in this attempt (and no pains must be spared to effect it), you will endeavor to make peace between that distant powerful nation, and the nations which inhabit the country between us and them, particularly the Osage; and finally you will endeavor to induce eight or ten of their distinguished chiefs, to make a visit to the seat of government next September, and you may attach to this deputation four or five Panis, and the same number of Kanses chiefs. As your interview with the Camanches will probably lead you to the head branches of the Arkansaw and Red rivers, you may find yourself approximated to the settlements of New Mexico, and there it will be necessary you should move with great circumspection, to keep clear of any hunting or reconnoitring parties from that province, and to prevent alarm or offence; because the affairs of Spain and the United States, appear to be on the point of amicable adjustment, and moreover it is the desire of the president, to cultivate the friendship and harmonious intercourse of all the nations of the earth, and particularly our near neighbours the Spaniards.

In the course of your tour, you are to remark particularly upon the geographical structure, the natural history and population of the country through which you may pass, taking particular care to collect and preserve specimens of every thing curious in the mineral or botanical worlds, which can be preserved and are portable. Let your courses be regulated by your compass, and your distances by your watch, to be noted in a field-book, and I would advise you when circumstances permit, to protract and lay down in a separate book the march of the day at every evening's halt.

The instruments, which I have furnished you, will enable you to ascertain the variation of the magnetic needle and the latitude with exactitude; and at every remarkable point, I wish you to employ your telescope in observing the eclipses of Jupiter's satelites, having previously regulated and adjusted your watch by your quadrant, taking care to note with great nicety the periods of immersions and emersions of the eclipsed satelites. These observations may enable us after your return, by application to the appropriate tables, which I cannot now furnish you, to ascertain the longitude.

It is an object of much interest with the executive, to ascertain the direction, extent, and navigation of the Arkansaw and Red river:

as far, therefore, as may be compatible with these instructions and practicable to the means you may command, I wish you to carry your views to those subjects, and should circumstances conspire to favor the enterprise, that you may detach a party with a few Osage to descend the Arkansaw under the orders of lieutenant Wilkinson, or sergeant Ballinger, properly instructed and equipped to take the courses and distances, to remark on the soil, timber, &c. &c. and to note the tributary streams. This party will, after reaching our post on the Arkansaw, descend to fort Adams and there wait further orders; and you yourself may descend the Red river accompanied by a party of the most respectable Camanches to the post of Nachitoches, and there receive further orders.

To disburse your necessary expences and to aid your negotiations, you are herewith furnished six hundred dollars worth of goods, for the appropriation of which you are to render a strict account, vouched by documents to be attested by one of your party.

Wishing you a safe and successful expedition,
I am, sir,
With much respect and esteem,
Your obedient servant,

(Signed)   JAMES WILKINSON.
Lieutenant Z. M. Pike.

ADDITIONAL INSTRUCTIONS TO LIEUTENANT PIKE.

Cantonment, Missouri, July 12th, 1806.

SIR,

THE health of the Osages being now generally restored, and all hopes of the speedy recovery of their prisoners, from the hands of the Potowatomies, being at an end, they have become desirous to commence their journey for their villages, you are therefore to proceed to-morrow.

In addition to the instructions given you on the 24th ultimo, I must request you to have the talks under cover delivered to White Hair and the Grand Peste, the chief of the Osage band, which is settled on the waters of the Arkansaw, together with the belts which accompany them. You will also receive herewith a small belt for the Panis and a large one for the Tetaus or Camanches.

Should you find it necessary, you are to give orders to Maugraine the resident interpreter at the Grand Osage to attend you.

I beg you to take measures for the security and safe return of your boats from the Grand Osage to this place.

Doctor Robinson will accompany you as a volunteer. He will be furnished medicines, and for the accommodations which you give him, he is bound to attend your sick.

Should you discover any unlicensed traders in your route, or any person from this territory, or from the United States, without a proper licence or passport, you are to arrest such person or persons and dispose of their property as the law directs.

My confidence in your caution and discretion, has prevented my urging you to be vigilant in guarding against the stratagems and treachery of the Indians, holding yourself above alarm or surprise, the composition of your party, though it be small, will secure to you the respect of an host of untutored savages.

You are to communicate from the Grand Osage and from every other practicable point, directly to the secretary of war, transmitting your letters to this place under cover, to the commanding officer, or by any more convenient route.

I wish you health and a successful and honorable enterprise, and am,

Yours with friendship,

(Signed)   JAMES WILKINSON.

Lieutenant Z M. Pike.

PIKE'S EXPEDITION.

PART II.

DIARY OF AN EXPEDITION MADE UNDER THE ORDERS
OF THE WAR DEPARTMENT, BY CAPTAIN Z. M. PIKE,
IN THE YEARS 1806 AND 1807, TO EXPLORE THE
INTERNAL PARTS OF LOUISIANA.

15th July, 1806, *Tuesday.*—We sailed from the
landing at Belle Fontaine, about 3 o'clock P. M. in two
boats. Our party consisted of two lieutenants, one sur-
geon, one serjeant, two corporals, sixteen privates, and
one interpreter. We had also under our charge, chiefs
of the Osage and Pawnees, who, with a number of women and children, had been to Washington. These Indians had been redeemed from captivity among the Potowatomies, and were now to be returned to their friends,
at the Osage towns. The whole number of Indians
amounted to fifty one.

We ascended the river about six miles, and encamped on the south side behind an island. This day my boat
swung round twice ; once when we had a tow rope on
shore, which it snaped off in an instant. The Indians
did not encamp with us at night. Distance 6 miles.

16th July, Wednesday.—We rejoined our red brethren at breakfast, after which we again seperated, and with
very severe labor arrived late in the evening opposite to
the village of St. Charles, where the Indians joined us.
Distance 15 miles.

17th *July, Thursday.*—We crossed the river to learn if any communications had arrived from St. Louis, and if there was any news of other Indian enemies of the Osages. Called at Mr. James Morrison's and was introduced to a Mr. Henry (of New Jersey), about eight and twenty years of age: he spoke a little Spanish, and French tolerably well: he wished to go with me as a volunteer. From this place I wrote letters back to Belle Fontaine, whilst the Indians were crossing the river.* A man by the name of Ramsay reported to the Indians that 500 Sacs, Ioways, and Reynards, were at the mouth of Big Maniton. This gave them considerable uneasiness and it took me some time to do away the impression it made upon them; for I by no means believed it. We were about sailing when my interpreter was arrested by the sheriff, at the suit of Manuel de Liza, for a debt between three and four hundred dollars, and was obliged to return to St. Louis. This made it necessary for me to write another letter to the general. We encamped about three-fourths of a mile above the village.

18th *July, Friday.*—Lieutenant Wilkinson and Dr. Robinson went with the Indians across the country to the village La Charette. Mr. George Henry engaged, under oath, to accompany me on my tour. Wrote to the general, and enclosed him one of Henry's engagements.† After we had made our little arrangements we marched by land joined the boats (which had sailed early) at twelve o'clock. Two of the men being sick, I steered one boat and Mr. Henry the other, by which means we were enabled to keep employed our full complement of oars, although we put the sick men on shore. Encamped on the north side. About eleven o'clock at night a tremendous thunder

* See appendix to part II. [No. 3.] page 32.
† See appendix to part II. [No. 4.] page 33.

storm arose, and it continued to blow and rain, with thunder and lightning, until day.   Distance 15 miles.

19*th July, Saturday.*—In consequence of the rain, we did not put off until past nine o'clock ; my sick men marched.   I had some reason to suspect, that one of them intended never joining us again.   At dinner time the sick man of my own boat came on board ; I then went on board the other, and we continued to run races all day, and although this boat had hitherto kept behind ; yet I arrived at the encamping ground with her, nearly half an hour before the other.   The current not generally so strong as below. Distance 14 miles.

20*th July, Sunday.*—Embarked about sun-rise. Wishing to ascertain the temperature of the water, I discovered my large thermometer to be missing, which probably had fallen into the river.   Passed one settlement on the north side, and, after turning the point to the south, saw two more houses on the south side.   We encamped in a long reach, which bore north and west.   The absentees had not yet joined us.   Distance 15 miles.

21*st July, Monday.*—It commenced raining near day, and continued until 4 o'clock in the afternoon : the rain was immensely heavy, with thunder and lightning remarkably severe.   This obliged me to lay by ; for, if we proceeded with our boats, it necessarily exposed our baggage much more than when at rest ; for the tarpauling could then cover all.   We set sail at a quarter past four o'clock, and arrived at the village La Charette a little after the dusk of the evening, here we found lieutenant Wilkinson and Dr. Robinson with the Indians—also, Baroney (our interpreter) with letters from the general and our friends.   The weather still continued cloudy, with rain.   We were received into the house of a Mr. Chartron, and every accommodation in his power offered us.   Distance 6 miles.

P

22d July, Tuesday.—We arranged our boats, dried our loading, and wrote letters for Belle Fontaine.

23d July, Wednesday.—I dispatched an express to the general, with advertisements relative to Kennerman, the soldier who had deserted.*   We embarked after breakfast, and made good progress : lieutenant Wilkinson steered one boat and I the other, in order to detach all the men on shore, with the Indians, that we could spare.   We crossed to the south side, a little below Shepherd river. Dr. Robinson killed a deer, which was the first killed by the party.   Distance 13 miles.

24th July, Thursday.—We embarked at half past 6 o'clock.   Very foggy.   The Indians accompanied by only three of my people.   Lieutenant Wilkinson being a little indisposed, I was obliged to let Baroney steer his boat. We made an excellent day's journey, and encamped five miles from the Gasconade river.   Killed three deer, one bear, and three turkies.   But three or four of the Indians arrived ; the others encamped a small distance below. Distance 18 miles.

25th July, Friday.—We embarked at half past 6 o'clock, and arrived at the entrance of the Gasconade river half past eight o'clock, at which place I determined to remain the day, as my Indians and foot people were yet in the rear, and they had complained to me of being without shoes, leggins, &c.   One of our Pawnees did not arrive until late ; the other had communicated his suspicion to me that the Oto, who was in company, had killed him : he acknowledged that he proposed to him to take out their baggage, and return to St. Louis.   The real occasion of his absence, however, was his having followed a large fresh trace up the Gasconade a considerable distance ; but finding it led from the Missouri, he examined it and discovered

* See appendix to part II. [No. 5.] page 33. and [No. 6.] p ge 36.

horses to have been on it, he then left it, joined our's, and came in. This being generally the route taken by the Poto-watomies, when they go to war against the Osage, it occasioned some alarm. Every morning we were awoke by the mourning of the savages, who commenced crying about daylight, and continued for the space of an hour. I made enquiry of my interpreter with respect to this, who informed me that this was a custom not only with those who had recently lost their relatives, but also with others who recalled to mind the loss of some friend, dead long since, and joined the other mourners purely from sympathy. They appeared extremely affected, tears ran down their cheeks, and they sobbed bitterly; but in a moment they dry their cheeks and they cease their cries. Their songs of grief generally run thus: " My dear father exists no longer : have pity on me, O Great Spirit ! you see I cry forever; dry my tears and give me comfort." The warriors songs are thus: " Our enemies have slain my father (or mother); he is lost to me and his family ; I pray to you, O Master of Life ! to preserve me until I revenge his death, and then do with me as thou pleaseth." Distance 5 miles.

26th July, Saturday.—We commenced at 5 o'clock to ferry the Indians over the Gasconade, and left the entrance of this river half past 6 o'clock in the afternoon. Met five Frenchmen, who informed us that they had just left the Osage river, and that it was so low they could not ascend it with their canoe. We wrote letters, and sent them back by them.* Dr. Robinson, Baroney, Sparks, and all the Indians encamped about one league above us. Killed one bear, two deer, one otter, three turkies, and one racoon. Distance 15 miles.

* See appendix to part II. [No. 7.] page 36.

27*th July, Sunday.*—We embarked at half past five
o'clock, and arrived at the Indians' camp at 7 o'clock.
They had been alarmed the day before, and in the evening sent men back in the trace, and some of the chiefs sat
up all night. Breakfasted with them. About half past
three o'clock encamped in sight of the Osage river. There
being every appearance of rain, we halted thus early in
order to give the Indians time to prepare temporary camps
and to secure our baggage. I went out to hunt, and firing
at a deer, near two of the Indians who were in the woods,
they knew the difference of the report of my rifle from
their guns, were alarmed, and immediately retired to camp.
Distance 13 miles.

28*th July, Monday.*—Embarked at half past 5
o'clock, and at half past 10 arrived in the Osage river,
where we stopped, discharged our guns, bathed, &c. We
then proceeded on about six miles, where we waited for
and crossed the Indians to the west shore, and then proceeded on to the first island and encamped on the west
side. Sans Oreille, and four or five young men only,
coming up, the rest encamping some distance behind.
Killed one deer and one turkey. Distance 19 miles.

29*th July, Tuesday.*—All the Indians arrived very
early and the Big Soldier, whom I had appointed the officer to regulate the march, was much displeased that Sans
Oreille and the others had left him, and said for that reason he would not suffer any woman to go in the boat, and
by that means separate the party; but in truth it was from
jealousy of the men whose women went in the boats. He
began by flogging one of the young men and was about to
strike Sans Oreille's wife, but was stopped by him and
told that he knew he had done wrong, but that the women
were innocent. We then crossed them and embarked at
half past eight o'clock. About twelve o'clock we found

the Indians rafting the river, when the first chief of the Little Osage, called Tuttasuggy (or the Wind), told me that the man whom the Big Soldier struck had not yet arrived with his wife, " but that he would throw them away." As I knew he was extremely mortified at the dissensions which appeared to reign amongst them, I told him by no means,—that one of my boats should wait for the woman and her child, but that the man might go to the devil, as a punishment for his insubordination.

I then left Baroney with one boat, and proceeded with the other. We were called ashore by three young Indians, who had killed some deer, and, on putting them on board, gave them about one or two gills of whiskey, which intoxicated all of them. It commenced raining about one o'clock, and continued incessantly for three hours, which obliged us to stop and encamp. One of our men (Miller) lost himself, and did not arrive until after dark. Killed five deer, one turkey, and one racoon. Distance 14 miles.

30*th July, Wednesday.*—After the fog dispersed I left lieutenant Wilkinson with the party to dry the baggage, and I went with Dr. Robinson and Bradley. About two o'clock we returned, set sail, and having passed the first rapid about three miles, encamped on the eastern shore. Killed three deer. Distance 5 miles.

31*st July, Thursday.*—We embarked early, and passed several rapids pretty well. Dined with the Indians. Two of them left us in the morning for the village, and they all had an idea of doing the same, but finally concluded otherwise. One of the Osage, who had left the party for the village, returned and reported that he had seen and heard strange Indians in the woods. This we considered as merely a pretext to come back. I this day lost my dog, and the misfortune was the greater, as we had no other dog who would bring any thing out of the water : this was the dog Fisher presented to me at Prairie des Chiens. Killed three deer and one turkey. Distance 18 miles.

1st August, Friday.—It having rained all night, the river appeared to have risen about six inches. We spread out our baggage to dry, but it continuing to rain, by intervals, all day, the things were wetter at sun-down than in the morning. We rolled them up, and left them on the beach. We sent out two hunters in the morning, one of whom killed three deer ; all the Indians killed three more —Total, six.

2d August, Saturday.—The weather cleared up. The loading being spread out to dry, Dr. Robinson, myself, Bradley, Sparks, and Brown went out to hunt. We killed four deer ; the Indians two. Having reloaded the boats, we embarked at five o'clock, and came about two miles. The river rose, in the last twenty-four hours, four inches.

3d August, Sunday.—Embarked early, and wishing to save the fresh, I pushed hard all day. Sparks was lost, and did not arrive until night. We encamped about 25 paces from the river, on a sand-bar. Near day I heard the sentry observe that the boats had better be brought in, when I got up and found the water within a rod of our tent, and before we could get all our things out it had reached the tent. Killed nine deer, one wild cat, one goose, and one turkey. Distance 18 miles.

4th August, Monday.—We embarked early and continued on for some time, not being able to find a suitable place to dry our things, but at length stopped on the east shore. Here we had to ferry the Indians over a small channel which we did not before observe ; all of them, however, not arriving, we put off and continued our route.

Finding our progress much impeded by our mast I unshipped it and stripped it of its iron, and, after lieutenant Wilkinson had carved our names on it, set it adrift, followed by the yards. This mast had been cut and made at Pine creek, Upper Mississippi. After proceeding some miles, we found the Indians on the west shore, they having rafted the river. We stopped for them to cook, after which we proceeded on. The navigation had become very difficult from the rapidity of the current, occasioned by the rise of the water, which rose one foot in an hour. Killed two deer. Distance 10 miles. Rainy.

5th August, Tuesday.—We lay by this day, in order to give the Indians an opportunity to dry their baggage. Dr. Robinson and myself, accompanied by Mr. Henry, went out to hunt; we lost the latter about two miles from camp. After hunting some time on the west shore, we concluded to raft the river, which we effected with difficulty and danger, and hunted for some time, but without success. We then returned to the party and found Mr. Henry, who had been lost, had arrived one hour before us: he had met one of the soldiers, who brought him in. To-day in our tour I passed over a remarkably large rattlesnake, as he lay curled up, and trod so near him as to touch him with my foot, he drawing himself up to make room for my heel.

Dr. Robinson, who followed me, was on the point of treading on him, but by a spring avoided it. I then turned round and touched him with my ram-rod, but he shewed no disposition to bite, and appeared quite peaceable. The gratitude which I felt towards him for not having bit me induced me to save his life. Killed four deer. River rises thirteen inches. Rain continues.

6th August, Wednesday.—We embarked at half past eight o'clock, it having cleared off and had the appear-

ance of a fine day. Passed Gravel river on the west.
About three miles above this river the Indians left us and
informed me, by keeping a little to the south and west,
they would make in 15 miles what would be at least 35
miles for us. Dr. Robinson, Mr. Henry, and serjeant
Ballenger accompanied them. Killed two deer. Distance
13 miles.

7th August, Thursday.—Not being detained by the
Indians, we are *for once* enabled to embark at a quarter past
five o'clock. The river having fell, since yesterday morning, about four feet, we wish to improve every moment of
time previous to its entire fall. We proceeded extremely
well, passed the Saline river on the east, and encamped
opposite *La Belle Roche* on the west shore. This day we
passed many beautiful cliffs on both sides of the river, saw
a bear and wolf swimming the river. I employed myself
part of the day in translating into French a talk of general Wilkinson to the Cheveux Blanche. Distance 21.
miles.

8th August, Friday.—We embarked 20 minutes past
five o'clock. Found the river had fallen about two feet
during the night. At the confluence of the Youngar with
the Osage river we breakfasted. Encamped at night on a
bar. Distance 21 miles.

9th August, Saturday.—We embarked at five o'clock,
and at half past six o'clock met the Indians and our gentlemen. They had met with nothing extraordinary. They
had killed in their excursion seven deer and three bear.
We proceeded to an old wintering ground, where there
were eight houses, which were occupied last winter by
——————, who had not been able to proceed any higher
for want of water. Passed the Old Man's Rapids, below
which, on the west shore, are some beautiful cliffs. Dined
with the Indians, after which we passed Upper Gravel

river on the west, Pottoe river on the east. Sparks went out to hunt, and did not arrive at our encampment, nor did the Indians. Distance 25 miles.

10*th August, Sunday.*—Embarked a quarter past five o'clock, when the sun shone out very clearly; but in fifteen minutes it began to rain, and continued to rain very hard until one o'clock. Passed the Indians, who were encamped on the west shore, about half a mile, and halted for them. They all forded the river but Sans Oreille, who brought his wife up to the boats, and informed me that Sparks had encamped with them, but left them early to return in search of us. We proceeded after breakfast. Sparks arrived just at the moment we were embarking. The Indians traversing the country on the east had sent Sparks with Sans Oreille. About two o'clock A. M. split a plank in the bottom of the batteaux. Unloaded and turned her up, repaired the breach, and continued on the route : by four o'clock found the Indians behind a large island : we made no stop, and they followed us. We encamped together on a bar, where we proposed halting to dry our corn, &c. on Monday. Killed four deer. Distance 18 1-2 miles.

11*th August, Monday.*—We continued here to dry our corn and baggage. This morning we had a match at shooting : the prize offered to the successful person was a jacket and a twist of tobacco, which I myself was so fortunate as to win ; I made the articles, however, a present to the young fellow who waited on me. After this, taking Huddleson with me, I went out to hunt : after travelling about twelve miles we arrived at the river, almost exhausted with thirst. I here indulged myself by drinking plentifully of the water, and was rendered so extremely unwell by it, that I was scarce capable of pursuing my route to the camp. On arriving opposite it, I swam the

Q

river, from which I experienced considerable relief. The party informed me they had found the heat very oppressive, and the mercury, at sun-down, was at 25° Reaumer. This day, for the first time, I saw trout west of the Allegheny mountains. Reloaded our boats, and finished two new oars, which were requisite.

12th *August, Tuesday.*—Previously to our embarkation, which took place at half past five o'clock, I was obliged to convince my red brethren that, if I protected them, I would not suffer them to plunder my men with impunity, for the chief had got one of my lads' tin cups attached to his baggage, and notwithstanding it was marked with the initials of the soldier's name, he refused to give it up. On which I requested the interpreter to tell him, "that I had no idea that he had purloined the cup, but supposed some other person had attached it to his baggage ; but that, knowing it to be my soldier's, I requested him to deliver it up, or I should be obliged to take other measures to obtain it." This had the desired effect ; for I certainly should have put my threats into execution from this principle, formed from my experience during my incourse with Indians, *that if you have justice on your side, and do not enforce it, they universally despise you.* When we stopped for dinner, one of my men took his gun and went out ; not having returned when we were ready to re embark, I left him. Passed the Indians twice when they were crossing the river. Passed some very beautiful cliffs on the west shore ; also Vermillion and Grand rivers, the latter of which is a large stream, and encamped at the ———.

Immediately after our encampment a thunder storm came on, which blew overboard my flag-staff and a number of articles of my clothing, which were on top of the cabbin, and sunk them immediately. Being much fatigued, and the bank difficult of ascent, lay down in the cabin, without supper and slept all night.   It continued to rain.   The man I left on shore arrived on the opposite bank in the night, having killed two deer; but was obliged to leave the largest behind.   Finding he was not to be sent for, he concealed his gun and deer, and swam the river. Distance 24 miles.

13th August, Wednesday.—It continued to rain.   In the morning sent a boat over for Sparks's gun and deer. Embarked at half past 9 o'clock.   Stopped to dine at two o'clock.   During the time we halted, the river rose over the flat bar, on which we were: this, if we had no other proof, would convince us we were near the head of the river, as the rain must have reached it.   We made almost a perfect circle, so that I do not believe we were, at night, three miles from where we encamped last night.   This day, for the first time, we have prairie hills.   Distance 13 miles.

14th August, Thursday.—Embarked at half past five o'clock.   Passed the *Park*, which is ten miles round, and not more than three quarters of a mile across, bearing from S. 5° E. to due N.   At its head we breakfasted, and just as we were about to put off we saw and brought to a canoe manned with three engagees of Mr. ————, who informed us that the Little Osage had marched a war party against the Kans, and the Grand Osage a party against our citizens on the Arkansaw river.   Wrote by them to the general* and all friends.   Gave the poor fellows some whiskey and eight quarts of corn, they having had only two turkies for four days.   We left them and proceeded, passing on our east some of the largest cedars I ever saw. Came on very well in the afternoon, and encamped on an island above Turkey island.   Distance 28 miles.

* See appendix to part II. [No. 8.] page 37.

15th August, Friday.—We embarked at five o'clock, and at eight o'clock met the Indians and the gentlemen who accompanied them. Found all well. They had been joined by their friends and relatives from the village, with horses to transport their baggage. Lieutenant Wilkinson informed me that their meeting was very tender and affectionate—" Wives throwing themselves into the arms of their husbands, parents embracing their children, and children their parents, brothers and sisters meeting, one from captivity, the others from the towns—they, at the same time, returning thanks to the *Good God* for having brought them once more together;" in short, the *toute ensemble* was such as to make polished society blush, when compared with those savages, in whom the passions of the mind, either joy, grief, fear, anger, or revenge, have their full scope: why can we not correct the baneful passions, without weakening the good ? Sans Oreille made them a speech, in which he remarked, " Osage, you now see your wives, your brothers, your daughters, your sons, redeemed from captivity. Who did this? was it the Spaniards? No. The French ? No. Had either of those people been governors of the country, your relatives might have rotted in captivity, and you never would have seen them ; but the Americans stretched forth their hands, and they are returned to you ! ! What can you do in return for all this goodness ? Nothing : all your lives would not suffice to repay their goodness." This man had children in captivity, not one of whom were we able to obtain for him.

The chief then requested that lieutenant Wilkinson and Dr. Robinson might be permitted to accompany them by land, which I consented to. Wrote a letter to the Cheveux Blanche, by lieutenant Wilkinson. When we parted (after delivering the Indians their baggage) Sans Oreille put an Indian on board, to hunt, or obey any other commands I might have for him. We stopped at eleven o'clock to dry our baggage. Found our biscuit and crackers almost all ruined. Put off at half past four o'clock, and encamped at three quarters past five o'clock. Distance 15 1-2 miles.

16th *August, Saturday.*—We embarked at five o'clock and came on extremely well in the barge to a French hunting camp (evacuated), twelve miles to breakfast, the batteaux coming up late: we exchanged hands. About twelve o'clock passed the grand fork, which is equal in size to the one on which we pursued our route. Waited to dine at the rocks called the Swallow's Nest, on the west shore above the forks. The batteaux having gained nearly half an hour, the crews are convinced that it is not the boat, but men who make the difference: each take their own boat, after which we proceeded very well, the water being good and men in spirits. Saw an elk on the shore, also met an old man alone hunting, from whom we obtained no information of consequence. Encamped on the west shore at Mine river. Passed the place where the chief, called the Belle Oiseau, and others were killed.* Distance 37 miles.

17th *August, Sunday.*—We embarked at five o'clock and came twelve miles to breakfast. At four o'clock arrived at ten French houses on the east shore, where was then residing a Sac, who was married to an Osage femme and spoke French *only*. We afterwards passed the posi-

---

* The *Belle Oiseau* was killed by the Sacs in the year 1804, in a boat of Manuel de Liza, when on his way down to St. Louis, in order to join the first deputation of his nation, who were forwarded to the seat of government by governor Lewis. A particular relation of the event, no doubt, has been given by that gentleman. This chief had a son who accompanied me to the Pawnee nation, who, for his honorable deportment, attachment to our government, amiableness of disposition, and the respect and esteem in which he was held by his compeers, entitle him to the attention of our agents to his nation.

tion where Mr. Chouteau formerly had his fort, not a ves-
tige of which was remaining, the spot being only marked
by the superior growth of vegetation. Here the river bank
is one solid bed of stone-coal, just below which is a very
shoal and rapid ripple; from whence to the village of the
Grand Osage is nine miles across a large prairie. We came
about two miles above, and encamped on the west shore.
This day the river has been generally bounded by prairies
on both sides.   Distance 41 1-2 miles.

18*th August, Monday.*—We put off at half past five
o'clock.   Stopped at nine o'clock to breakfast.   Passed
the second fork of the river at twelve o'clock, the right
hand fork bearing N. about 30 yards wide, the left (the
one we pursued) N. 60° W. and not more than 50 or 60
feet in width, very full of old trees, &c. but plenty of
water. Observed the road where the chiefs and lieutenant
Wilkinson crossed.   We proceeded until one o'clock,
when we were halted by a large drift quite across the river.
Dispatched Baroney to the village of the Grand Osage,
to procure horses to take our baggage nearer to the towns;
unloaded our boats, and in about two hours lieutenant
Wilkinson, with Tuttasuggy, arrived at our camp, the former of whom presented me an express from the general,[*]
and letters from my friends.   The chiefs remained at our
camp all night.   I was attacked by a violent head-ache.
It commenced raining, and continued with great force
until day.   Distance 19 1-4 miles.

19*th August, Tuesday.*—We commenced very early
to arrange our baggage, but had not finished at one o'clock,
when the chief of the Grand Osage, and 40 or 50 men
of his village, arrived with horses.   We loaded and took
our departure for the place where Manuel de Liza had his

---

[*] See appendix to part II. [No. 9.] page 38.

establishment, at which we arrived about four o'clock, and commenced pitching our encampment near the edge of the prairie, when I was informed that three men had arrived from St. Louis, sent by Manuel de Liza. I dispatched lieutenant Wilkinson to the village, with Baroney, who brought to camp the man who had charge of the others from St. Louis : he having no passport, I detained him until further consideration.   Our reception by the Osage was flattering, and particularly by the *White Hair* and our fellow-travellers.   This evening there arrived in the village of the Grand Osage an express from the Arkansaw, who brought the news that a boat, ascending that river, had been fired on, and had two white men killed and two wounded, and that the brother-in-law of the Cheveux Blanche, who happened to be on board, was also killed. This put the whole village in mourning.

20*th August*, *Wednesday.*—About twelve o'clock I dispatched Baroney for the chiefs of the Grand village, in order to give the general's parole to the Cheveux Blanche, also a young man to the village of the Little Osage.   The Cheveux Blanche and his people arrived about three o'clock, and after waiting some time for the *Wind* and his people, I just informed the chiefs that I had merely assembled them to deliver the parole of the general, and present the marks of distinction intended for the Cheveux Blanche and his son, hanging a grand medal round the neck of the latter. The packets committed to my charge for the relations of the deceased Osages, were then delivered to them, the widow making the distribution.   It must be remarked that I had merely requested the Cheveux Blanche to come with his son, and receive the general's message ; but instead of coming with a few chiefs, he was accompanied by 186 men, to all of whom we were obliged to give something to drink.   When the council was over we mounted our horses and rode to the village, and halted at the quarters of the chief, where we were regaled with boiled pumpkins : 'then we went to two different houses, and were invited to many others, but declined, promising that I would pay them a visit, previous to my departure, and spend the whole day. We then returned to camp. After enquiring of White Hair if the men of Manuel de Liza had any ostensible object in view, he informed me that they had only said to him that they expected Manuel would be up to trade in the autumn. I concluded to take the deposition of Babtiste Larme as to the manner in which he was employed by Manuel de Liza, and forward the same to Dr. Brown and the attorney-general of Louisiana, and permit the men to return to St. Louis, as it was impossible for me to detach a party with them as prisoners.

21st August, Thursday.—In the morning White Hair paid us a visit, and brought us a present of corn, meat, and grease, and we invited him, his son, and son-in-law to breakfast with us, and gave his companions something to eat. I then wrote a number of letters to send by express, and enclosed the deposition of Larme. In the afternoon we rode to the village of the Little Osage, and were received by our fellow-travellers with true hospitality. Returned in the evening, when a tremendous storm of rain, thunder and lightning commenced, and continued with extraordinary violence until half past nine o'clock. It was with great difficulty we were enabled to keep our tents from blowing down. The place prepared for an observatory was carried away.

22d August, Friday.—Preparing in the morning for the council, and committing to paper the heads of the subject on which I intended to speak. The chiefs of the Little Osage arrived about one o'clock, also the interpreter of the Grand Osage, who pretended to say that the Grand Osage had expected us at their village with the Little Osage. The Cheveux Blanche arrives with his chiefs. The ceremony of the council being arranged, I delivered them the general's *parole* forwarded by express. My reason for not delivering it until this time was, in order to have the two villages together, as it was equally interesting to both. After this I explained at large the will, wishes, and advice of their *Great Father*, and the mode which I conceived most applicable to carry them into effect. The Cheveux Blanche replied in a few words, and promised to give me a full reply to-morrow. The Wind replied to the same amount; after which the Cheveux Blanche addressed himself to the Wind as follows ;—" I am shocked at your conduct, Tuttasuggy, you who have lately come from the States, and should have been wise; but you led the redeemed captives, with an officer of the United States, to your village, instead of bringing them through my town in the first instance." To this the *Wind* made no reply, but left his seat shortly after under pretence of giving some orders to his young men. I conceived this reprimand intended barely to shew us the superiority of the one and inferiority of the other, and originated, in my opinion, from an altercation of lieutenant Wilkinson and the Cheveux Blanche, in which allusions were made by the former, on the friendly conduct of the *Little Chief*, (alias the Wind) when compared to that of the latter. I must here observe that when the chiefs and prisoners left me, accompanied by lieutenant Wilkinson, I did not know the geographical situation of the two villages, but conceived that, in going to the *Little Village*, they would pass by the *Grand Village*, and of course that lieutenant Wilkinson and the chief would arrange the affair properly.

R

23d August, Saturday.—I expected to have received from the chiefs their answers to my demands; but received an express from both villages, informing that they wished to put them off until to-morrow. I then adjusted my instruments. Took equal altitudes and a meridional altitude of the sun, but, owing to flying clouds, missed the immersions of Jupiter's satellites.*

24th August, Sunday.—Was nearly half the day in adjusting the line of collimation in the telescopic sights of my theodolite. It began to cloud before evening, and although the sky was not entirely covered, I was so unfortunate as to miss the time of an immersion and (although clear in the intermediate period) an emersion also. I was informed by Baroney that the Little Village had made up eleven horses for us. In the evening, however, the interpreter, accompanied by the Son-in-law and son of the Cheveux Blanche, came to camp, and informed me that there were no horses to be got in the village of the Big Osage.†

---

* See Meteorological Tables, latter end of Appendix to part II.

† On the 24th August the son, son-in-law, and interpreter of the Cheveux Blanche came to camp, when the son-in-law spoke as follows:—viz. " I am come to give you the news of our village, which is unfortunate for us, our chief having assembled his young men and warriors and proposed to them to furnish horses, &c. they have generally refused him; but I, who am the principal man after the Cheveux Blanche, will accompany you."

The son.—" Our young men and warriors will not take pity on my father, nor on me, nor on you, and have refused to comply with your request; but I will accompany you with two horses to carry provision for your voyage."

The interpreter.—" The Cheveux Blanche was ashamed to bring you this answer, but will again assemble his village and to-morrow come and give you the answer."

I replied—" That I had made the demand without explanation, merely to let the Osage act agreeably to their inclination, in order that we might see what disposition they would exhibit towards us: but why do I ask of their chiefs to follow me to the Pawnees? Is it for our good, or their own? Is it not to make peace with the Kans? To put their wives and children out of danger! As to their horses which they may furnish us with, I will pay them for their hire; but it is uncertain

25th August, Monday.—In the morning we were visited by the Cheveux Blanche and three or four of his chiefs, who were pleased to accord to my demands. He found much difficulty in informing me that, in all his village, he could only raise four horses, but that we should be accompanied by his son and son-in-law. I then expressed to him the difference of our expectations from the reality. He remained until after twelve o'clock, when I went to the Little Osage village, and was received with great friendship by the chief. Remained all night at the house of Tuttasuggy. Took the census.*

26th August, Tuesday.—Rose early and found my friends in council, which was merely relative to our horses. The chief then declared their determination to me, and that he himself gave me one horse, and lent me eight more to carry our baggage to the Pawnees. Sold the old batteaux for 100 dollars, in merchandise, which I conceived infinitely preferable to leaving her to the uncertain safe-guard of the Indians. About this time we received the news that the party of Potowatomies were discovered to be near the towns. I gave them the best advice I was capable of giving, and then returned to our camp.

27th August, Wednesday.—Spent in arranging our baggage for the horses. Received four horses from the Little Village and two from the Big Village. In the evening lieutenant Wilkinson rode to the Grand Village. I observed two immersions of Jupiter's satellites.

28th August, Thursday.—Writing to the secretary at

---

whether I can pay them here, or give them an order on the superintendant of Indian affairs at St. Louis: but this I do not now wish them to be made acquainted with.

* See Statistical Tables, Appendix to part II. page 53, and opposite page 53.

war and the general, and making arrangements for our departure. Visited by the Wind and Sans Oreille.

29th August, Friday.—Forenoon writing letters. In the afternoon Dr. Robinson and myself went to the Grand Village, at which we saw the great medicine dance. Remained at the village all night.

30th August, Saturday.—Returned to the camp after settling all my affairs at the town. Sealed up our dispatches and sent off the general's express.* In the afternoon we were visited by the principal men of the Little Village and the chief, to whom I presented a flag, and made the donations which I conceived requisite to the different Indians, on account of horses, &c.

31st August, Sunday.—Arranging our packs and loading our horses, in order to fit our loads, as we expected to march on the morrow. Up late writing letters.

1st September, Monday.—Struck our tents early in the morning, and commenced loading our horses. We now discovered that an Indian had stolen a large black horse, which the Cheveux Blanche had presented to lieutenant Wilkinson. I mounted a horse to pursue him; but the interpreter sent to town, and the chief's wife sent another in its place. We left the place about twelve o'clock with fifteen loaded horses, our party consisting of two lieutenants, one doctor, two sergeants, one corporal, fifteen privates, two interpreters, three Pawnees, and four chiefs of the Grand Osage, amounting in all to 30 warriors and one woman. We crossed the Grand Osage fork and a prairie N. 80° W. five miles to the fork of the Little Osage. Joined by Sans Oreille and seven Little Osage, all of whom I equipped for the march. Distance 8 miles.

2d September, Thursday.—Marched at six o'clock. Halted at ten o'clock, and two o'clock on the side of the

---

* See Appendix to part II. [No. 10.] page 40; [Nos. 11 and 12.] page 43.

creek, our route having been all the time on its borders. Whilst there I was informed by a young Indian that Mr. C. Chouteau had arrived at the towns. I conceived it proper for me to return, which I did, accompanied by Baroney, first to the Little Village; from whence we were accompanied by the *Wind* to the Big Village, where we remained all night at the lodge of the Cheveux Blanche. Mr. Chouteau gave us all the news; after which I scrawled a letter to the general and my friends.

3d September, Wednesday.—Rose early, and went to the Little Village to breakfast. After giving my letters to Mr. Henry, and arranging my affairs, we proceeded, and overtook our party at two o'clock. They had left their first camp about four miles. Our horses being much fatigued, we concluded to remain all night. Sent out our red and white hunters, all of whom only killed two turkies. Distance 4 miles.

4th September, Thursday.—When about to march in the morning, one of our horses was missing, and we left Sans Oreille, with the two Pawnees, to search for him, and proceeded till about nine o'clock; then stopped until twelve o'clock, and then marched. In about half an hour was overtaken and informed that Sans Oreille had not been able to find our horse; on which we encamped, and sent two horses back for the load. One of the Indians, being jealous of his wife, sent her back to the village. After making the necessary notes, Dr. Robinson and myself took our horses and followed the course of the little stream, until we arrived at the Grand river, which was distant about six miles. We here found a most delightful bason of clear water, of 25 paces diameter and about 100 in circumference, in which we bathed; found it deep and delightfully pleasant. Nature scarcely ever formed a more beautiful place for a farm. We returned to camp about dusk, when I was informed that some of the Indians had been *dreaming* and wished to return. Killed one deer, one turkey, one racoon. Distance 13 miles.

5th September, Friday.—In the morning our Little Osage all came to a determination to return, and, much to my surprise, Sans Oreille amongst the rest! I had given an order on the chiefs for the lost horse to be delivered to Sans Oreille's wife, previously to my knowing that he was going back, but took from him his gun, and the guns from all the others also. In about five miles we struck a beautiful hill, which bears south on the prairie: its elevation I suppose to be 100 feet. From its summit the view is sublime to the east and south-east. We waited on this hill to breakfast, and had to send two miles for water. Killed a deer on the rise, which was soon roasting before the fire. Here another Indian wished to return and take his horse with him, which, as we had so few, I could not allow, for he had already received a gun for the use of his horse. I told him he might return, but his horse would go to the Pawnees. We marched, leaving the Osage trace, which we had hitherto followed, and crossed the hills to a creek which was almost dry. Descended it to the main river, where we dined. The discontented Indian came up, and put on an air of satisfaction and content. We again marched about six miles further, and encamped at the head of a small creek, about half a mile from water. Distance 19 miles.

6th September, Saturday.—We marched at half past six o'clock, and arrived at a large fork of the little Osage river, where we breakfasted. In the holes in the creek we discovered many fish, which, from the stripes on their bellies, and their spots, I supposed to be trout and bass: they were twelve inches long. This brought to mind the necessity of a net, which would have frequently afforded subsistence to the whole party. We halted at one o'clock and remained until four o'clock. Being told that we could not arrive at any water, we here filled our vessels. At five o'clock arrived at the dividing ridge, between the waters of the Osage and Arkansaw (alias White river), the dry branches of which interlock within 20 yards of each other. The prospect from the dividing ridge to the east and south-east is sublime. The prairie rising and falling in regular swells, as far as the sight can extend, produces a very beautiful appearance. We left our course, and struck down to the south-west on a small creek, or rather a puddle of water. Killed one deer. Distance 20 miles.

7th September, Sunday.—We left this at half past six o'clock, before which we had a difficulty with the son of the chief, which was accommodated. At nine o'clock we came on a large fork and stopped for breakfast. Proceeded on and encamped on a fine stream, where we swam our horses and bathed ourselves. Killed four deer. Distance 15 miles.

8th September, Monday.—Marched early, and arrived at a grand fork of the White river. The Indians were all discontented: we had taken the wrong ford; but, as they were dispersed through the woods, we could not be governed by their movements. Previously to our leaving the camp, the son of the Cheveux Blanche proposed returning, and offered no other reason than that he felt too lazy to perform the route. The reason I offered to prevent his going was ineffectual, and he departed with his hunter, who deprived us of one horse. His return left us without any chief or man of consideration, except the son of the Belle Oiseau, who was but a lad. The former appeared to be a discontented young fellow, and filled with self pride : he certainly should have considered it as an honor to be sent on so respectable an embassy as he was. Another Indian, who owned one of our horses, wished to return with him, which was positively refused him; but fearing he might steal him, I contented him with a present. We marched, and made the second branch, crossing one prairie twelve miles, in which we suffered much with drought. Distance 22 miles.

9th September, Tuesday.—Marched at seven o'clock, and struck a large creek at eleven miles distance. On holding a council, it was determined to ascend this creek to the highest point of water, and then strike across to a large river of the Arkansaw. We ascended four miles and a half, and encamped. Killed one cabrie, two deer, two turkies. Distance 12 miles.

10th September, Wednesday.—Marched early. Struck and passed the divide between the *Grand* river and the Verdegris river. Stopped to breakfast on a small stream of the latter; after which we marched and encamped on the fourth small stream. Killed one elk, one deer. Distance 21 miles.

11th September, Thursday.—Passed four branches and over high hilly prairies. Encamped at night on a large branch of Grand river. Killed one cabrie, one deer. Distance 17 miles.

12th September, Friday.—Commenced our march at seven o'clock. Passed very ruff flint hills. My feet blistered and very sore. I stood on a hill, and in one view below me saw buffalo, elk, deer, cabrie, and panthers. Encamped on the main branch of Grand river, which had very steep banks and was deep. Dr. Robinson, Bradley, and Baroney arrived after dusk, having killed three buffalo, which, with one I killed, and two by the Indians, made six; the Indians alledging it was the Kans' hunting-ground, therefore they would destroy all the game they possibly could. Distance 18 miles.

13*th September, Saturday.*—Late in marching, it having every appearance of rain. Halted to dine on a branch of Grand river. Marched again at half past two o'clock, and halted at five, intending to dispatch Dr. Robinson and one of our Pawnees to the village to-morrow. Killed six buffalo, one elk, and three deer. Distance 9 miles.

14*th September, Sunday.*—The doctor and Frank (a young Pawnee) marched for the village at day-light; we at half past six o'clock. Halted at one o'clock. On the march we were continually passing through large herds of buffalo, elk, and cabrie; and I have no doubt but one hunter could support 200 men. I prevented the men shooting at the game, not merely because of the scarcity of ammunition, but, as I conceived, the laws of morality forbid it also. Encamped at sun-set on the main branch of White river hitherto called Grand river. Killed one buffalo and one cabrie. Distance 21 miles.

15*th September, Monday.*—Marched at seven o'clock passed a very large Kans encampment, evacuated, which had been occupied last summer. Proceeded on to the dividing ridge, between the waters of the White river and the Kans. This ridge was covered with a layer of stone, which was strongly impregnated with iron ore, and on the west side of said ridge we found spa springs. Halted at one o'clock, very much against the inclination of the Osage, who, from the running of the buffalo, conceived a party of the Kans to be near. Killed two buffalo. Distance 18 miles.

16*th September, Tuesday.*—Marched late, and in about four miles and a half distance, came to a very handsome branch of water, at which we stopped and remained until after two o'clock, when we marched and crossed two

branches.   Encamped on the third.   At the second creek
a horse was discovered on the prairie, when Baroney went
in pursuit of him on a horse of lieutenant Wilkinson, but
arrived at our camp without success.   Distance 13 miles.

17th September, Wednesday.—Marched early and
struck the main south-east branch of the Kans river : at
nine o'clock it appeared to be 25 or 30 yards wide, and is
navigable in the flood seasons. We passed it six miles to a
small branch to breakfast.   Game getting scarce, our provision began to run low.   Marched about two o'clock, and
encamped at sun-down on a large branch. Killed one buffalo.   Distance 21 miles.

18th September, Thursday.—Marched at our usual
hour, and at twelve o'clock halted at a large branch of the
Kans, which was strongly impregnated with salt.   This
day we expected the people of the village to meet us. We
marched again at four o'clock.   Our route being over a
continued series of hills and hollows, we were until eight
at night before we arrived at a small dry branch.   It was
nearly ten o'clock before we found any water.   Commenced raining a little before day.   Distance 25 miles.

19th September, Friday.—It having commenced raining early, we secured our baggage and pitched our tents.
The rain continued without any intermission the whole
day, during which we employed ourselves in reading
the Bible, Pope's Essays, and in pricking on our arms
with India ink some characters, which will frequently bring
to mind our forlorn and dreary situation, as well as the
happiest days of our life.   In the rear of our encampment
was a hill, on which there was a large rock, where the
Indians kept a continual sentinel, as I imagine, to apprise
them of the approach of any party, friends or foes, as
well as to see if they could discover any game on the
prairies.

20th September, Saturday.—It appearing as if we possibly might have a clear day, I ordered our baggage spread
abroad to dry; but it shortly after clouded up and commenced raining. The Osage sentinel discovered a buffalo
on the prairies; upon which we dispatched a hunter on
horseback in pursuit of him, also some hunters out on
foot, and before night they killed three buffalo, some of the
best of which we brought in and jerked or dried by the
fire. It continued showery until afternoon, when we put
our baggage again in a position to dry, and remained encamped. The detention of the doctor and our Pawnee
ambassador began to be a serious matter of consideration.

21st September, Sunday.—We marched at eight
o'clook, although every appearance of rain, and at eleven
o'clock passed a large creek remarkably salt. Stopped at
one o'clock on a fresh branch of the salt creek. Our interpreter having killed an elk, we sent out for some meat,
which detained us so late that I concluded it best to encamp where we were, in preference to running the risk
of finding no water. Lieutenant Wilkinson was attacked
with a severe head head-ache and slight fever. One of
my men had been attacked with a touch of the pleurisy
on the 18th, and was still ill. We were informed by an
Osage woman that two of the Indians were conspiring to
desert us in the night and steal some of our horses, one
of whom was her husband. We engaged her as our spy.
Thus were we obliged to keep ourselves on our guard
against our own companions and fellow-travellers, men of
a nation highly favored by the United States, but whom I
believe to be a faithless set of poltrons, incapable of a
great and generous action. Among them, indeed, there
may be some exceptions.

In the evening, finding that the two Indians above
mentioned had made all preparations to depart, I sent for

one of them, who owned a horse and had received a gun and other property for his hire, and told him, " I knew his plans, and that if he was disposed to desert, I should take care to retain his horse; that as for himself, he might leave me if he pleased, as I *only* wanted *men* with us." He replied, " that he was a *man*, that he always performed his promises, that he had never said he would return, but that he would follow me to the Pawnee village, which he intended to do." He then brought his baggage and put it under charge of the sentinel, and slept by my fire; but notwithstanding I had him well watched. Killed one elk. Distance 10 miles.

22d *September*, *Monday*.—We did not march until eight o'clock, owing to the indisposition of lieutenant Wilkinson. At eleven waited to dine. Light mists of rain, with flying clouds. We marched again at three o'clock, and continued our route twelve miles to the first branch of the republican fork. Met a Pawnee hunter, who informed us that the chief had left the village the day after the doctor arrived, with 50 or 60 horses and many people, and had taken his course to the north of our route; consequently we had missed each other. He likewise informed that the Tetaus had recently killed six Pawnees, the Kans had stolen some horses, and that a party of 300 Spaniards had lately been as far as the Sabine; but for what purpose unknown. Distance 11 miles.

23d *September*, *Tuesday*.—Marched early and passed a large fork of the Kans river, which I suppose to be the one generally called Solomon's. One of our horses fell into the water and wet his load. Halted at ten o'clock on a branch of this fork. We marched at half past one o'clock, and encamped at sun-down, on a stream where we had a great difficulty to find water. We were overtaken by a Pawnee, who encamped with us. He offered his horse for our use. Distance 21 miles.

24th *September, Wednesday.*—We could not find our horses until late, when we marched. Before noon met Frank (who had accompanied Dr. Robinson to the village) and three other Pawnees, who informed us that the chief and his party had only arrived at the village yesterday, and had dispatched them out in search of us. Before three o'clock we were joined by several Pawnees: one of them wore a scarlet coat, with a small medal of general Washington, and a Spanish medal also. We encamped at sun-set on a middle sized branch, and were joined by several Pawnees in the evening, who brought us some buffalo meat. Here we saw some mules, horses, bridles and blankets, which they obtained of the Spaniards. Few only had *breech cloths*, most being wrapped in buffalo robes, otherwise quite naked. Distance 18 miles.

25th *September, Thursday,*—We marched at a good hour, and in about eight miles struck a very large road on which the Spanish troops returned and on which we could yet discover the grass beaten down in the direction which they went.

When we arrived within about three miles of the village, we were requested to remain, as the ceremony of receiving the Osage into the towns was to be performed here. There was a small circular spot, clear of grass, before which the Osage sat down. We were a small distance in advance of the Indians. The Pawnees then advanced to within a mile of us, and halted, divided into two troops, and came on each flank at full charge, making all the gestures and performing the manœuvres of a real war charge. They then encircled us around, and the chief advanced in the centre and gave us his hand: his name was *Caracterish.* He was accompanied by his two sons

and a chief by the name of *Iskatappe*.   The Osage were
still seated ; but the Belle Oiseau then rose and came forward with a pipe, and presented it to the chief, who took a
whiff or two from it.   We then proceeded on : the chief,
lieutenant Wilkinson and myself in front ; my serjeant,
on a white horse, next with the colors ; then our horses
and baggage, escorted by our men, with the Pawnees on
each side, running races, &c.   When we arrived on the
hill over the town we were again halted, and the Osage
seated in a row, when each Pawnee who intended so to do
presented them with a horse, gave a pipe to smoke to the
Osage to whom he had made the present.   In this manner
were eight horses given.   Lieutenant Wilkinson then proceeded on with the party to the river above the town, and
encamped.   As the chief had invited us to his lodge to
eat, we thought it proper for one to go.   At the lodge he
gave me many particulars which were interesting to us, relative to the late visit of the Spaniards.*   I went up to our

---

* I will here attempt to give some memoranda of this expedition, which was
the most important ever carried on from the province of New Mexico, and in fact
the only one directed north-east, except that mentioned by the abbe Raynal (in his
history of the Indies) to the Pawnees—of which see a more particular account
hereafter.   In the year 1806 our affairs with Spain began to wear a very serious
aspect, and the troops of the two governments almost came to actual hostilities on
the frontiers of Texas and the Orleans territory.   At this time, when matters
bore every appearance of coming to a crisis, I was fitting out for my expedition
from St Louis, where some of the Spanish emissaries in that country transmitted
the information to Majar. Merior and the Spanish council at that place, who immediately forwarded on the information to the then commandant of Nacogdoches
(captain Sebastian Rodreriques), who forwarded it to colonel Cordero, by whom
it was transmitted to the seat of government.   This information was personally
communicated to me, as an instance of the rapid means they possessed of transmitting the information relative to the occurrences transacting on our frontiers.
The expedition was then determined on, and had three objects in view : viz.—

1st.   To descend the Red river, in order, if he met our expedition, to intercept
and turn us back, or should major Sparks and Mr. Freeman have missed the party
from Nacogdoches, under the command of captain Viana, to oblige them to return
and not penetrate further into the country, or make them prisoners of war.

camp in the evening, having a young Pawnee with me loaded with corn for my men.   Distance twelve miles.

2d. To explore and examine all the internal parts of the country from the frontiers of the province of New Mexico to the Missouri, between the La Platte

3d. To visit the Tetaus, Pawnees republic, Grand Pawnees; Pawnee Mahaws and Kans. To the head chief of each of those nations: the commanding officer bore flags, a commission; grand medal, and four mules; and with all of whom he had to renew the chains of ancient amity, which was said to have existed between their father, his most Catholic majesty, and his children the red people.

The commanding officers also bore positive orders to oblige all parties or persons in the above specified countries, either to retire from them into the acknowledged territories of the United States, or to make prisoners of them and conduct them into the province of N. Mexico. Lieut. Don Facundo Malgares, the officer selected from the five internal provinces, to command this expedition, was an European, (his uncle, was one of the royal judges of the kingdom of New Spain) and had distinguished himself in several long expeditions against the Appaches and other Indian nations, with whom the Spaniards were at war: added to these circumstances, he was a man of immense fortune, and generous in its disposal, almost to profusion: possessed a liberal education, high sense of honor, and a disposition formed for military enterprize. This officer marched from the province of Biscay with 100 dragoons of the regular service, and at Santa Fe, (the place where the expedition was fitted out from) he was joined by 500 of the mounted militia of that province, armed after the manner described by my notes on that subject, and compleatly equipt with ammunition, &c. for six months; each man leading with them (by order) two horses and one mule, the whole number of their beasts were two thousand and seventy five. They descended the Red river 233 leagues, met the grand bands of the Tetaus; held councils with them, then struck off N. E. and crossed the country to the Arkansaw, where lieut. Malgares left 240 of his men, with the lame and tired horses, whilst he proceeded on with the rest to the Pawnee republic; here he was met by the chiefs and warriors of the Grand Pawnees; held councils with the two nations, and presented them the flags, medals, &c. which were destined for them. He did not proceed on to the execution of his mission with the Pawnee Mahaws and Kans, as he represented to me, from the poverty of their horses, and the discontent of his own men, but as I conceive, from the suspicion and discontent which began to arise between the Spaniards and the Indians. The former wishing to revenge the death of *Villineuve* and party, whilst the latter possessed all the suspicions of conscious villainy deserving punishment. Malgares took with him all the traders he found there from our country, some of whom having been sent to Natchitoches, were in abject poverty at that place, on my arrival, and applied to me for means to return to St. Louis. Lieut. Malgares returned to Santa Fe the   of October, when his militia was disbanded, but he remained in the vicinity of that place, until we were brought in, when he, with dragoons, became our escort to the seat of government.

26th September, Friday.—Finding our encampment not eligible as to situation, we moved down on to the prairie hill, about three-fourths of a mile nearer the village. We sent our interpreter to town to trade for provision. About three o'clock in the afternoon twelve Kans arrived at the village, and informed Baroney that they had come to meet us, hearing we were to be at the Pawnees village. We pitched our camp upon a beautiful eminence, from whence we had a view of the town, and all that was transacting. In the evening Baroney, with the chief, came to camp to give us the news, and returned together.

27th September, Saturday.—Baroney arrived from the village about one o'clock, with Characterish* and three other chiefs, to all of whom we gave a dinner. I then made an appropriate present to each, after which lieutenant Wilkinson and myself accompanied them to town, where we remained a few hours, and returned. Appointed to-morrow for the interview with the Kans and Osage.

28th September, Sunday.—Held a council of the Kans and Osage, and made them smoke of the pipe of peace. Two of the Kans agreed to accompany us. We received a visit from the chief of the village. Made an observation on an emersion of one of Jupiter's satellites.

29th September, Monday.—Held our grand council with the Pawnees, at which were present not less than 400 warriors, the circumstances of which were extremely interesting. The notes I took on my grand council held with the Pawnee nation were seized by the Spanish government, together with all my speeches to the different nations. But it may be interesting to observe here (in case they should never be returned) that the Spaniards

* Characterish's commission from the governor of New Mexico was dated Santa Fe, 15th June, 1806.

had left several of the their flags in this village; one of
which was unfurled at the chief's door the day of the grand
council, and that amongst various *demands* and *charges*
I gave them, was, that the said flag should be delivered to
me, and one of the United States' flags be received and
hoisted in its place.   This probably was carrying the
pride of nations a little too far, as there had so lately been
a large force of Spanish cavalry at the village, which had
made a great impression on the minds of the young men,
as to their power, consequence, &c. which my appearance
with 20 infantry was by no means calculated to remove.
After the chiefs had replied to various parts of my dis-
course, but were silent as to the flag, I again reiterated the
demand for the flag, "adding that it was impossible for
" the nation to have two fathers; that they must either be
" the children of the Spaniards or acknowledge their
" American father."   After a silence of some time, an
old man rose, went to the door, and took down the Spanish flag, and brought it and laid it at my feet, and then
received the American flag and elevated it on the staff,
which had lately borne the standard of his Catholic majesty. This gave great satisfaction to the Osage and Kans,
both of whom, decidedly avow themselves to be under
the American protection.   Perceiving that every face in
the council was clouded with sorrow, as if some great national calamity was about to befal them, I took up the contested colors, and told them " that as they had now shewn
" themselves dutiful children in acknowledging their great
" American father, I did not wish to embarrass them
" with the Spaniards, for it was the wish of the Americans
" that their red brethren should remain peaceably round
" their own fires, and not embroil themselves in any dis-
" putes between the white people: and that for fear the
" Spaniards might return there in force again, I returned

T

" them their flag, but with an injunction that it should
" never be hoisted during our stay." At this there was
a general shout of applause and the charge particularly attended to.

30th September, Tuesday.—Remained all day at the
camp but sent Baroney to town, who informed me on his
return that the chief appeared to wish to throw great obstacles in our way. A great disturbance had taken place
in the village, owing to one of the young Pawnees who
lately came from the United States, (Frank) having taken
the wife of an Osage and ran away with her. The chief,
in whose lodge the Osage put up, was extremely enraged, considering it a breach of hospitality to a person
under his roof, and threatened to kill Frank if he caught
him.

1st October, Wednesday.—Paid a visit to town, and had
a very long conversation with the chief, who urged every
thing in his power to induce us to turn back. Finally, he
very candidly told us that the Spaniards wished to have
gone further into our country, but he induced them to
give up the idea—that they had listened to him and he
wished us to do the same—that he had promised the Spaniards to act as he now did, and that we must proceed no
further, or he must stop us by force of arms. My reply
was, " that I had been sent out by our *great father* to ex-
" plore the western country, to visit all his red children,
" to make peace between them, and turn them from shed-
" ding blood; that he might see how I had caused the
" Osage and Kans to meet to smoke the pipe of peace
" together, and take each other by the hands like bro-
" thers ; that as yet my road had been smooth, and a blue
" sky over our heads. I had not seen any blood in our
" paths ; but he must know that the young warriors of
" his *great American father were not women* to be turned

" back by *words*, that I should therefore proceed, and if
" he thought proper to stop me, he could attempt it; but
" we were *men*, well armed, and would *sell our lives* at a
" dear rate to his nation—that we knew our *great father*
" would send our young warriors there to gather our
" bones and revenge our *deaths* on his people—when our
" spirits would rejoice in hearing our exploits sung in the
" war songs of our chiefs." I then left his lodge and returned to camp in considerable perturbation of mind.

2d October, Thursday.—We received advice from our
Kans that the chief had given publicity to his idea of stopping us by force of arms, which gave serious reflections to
me, and was productive of many singular expressions from
my brave lads, which called for my esteem at the same
time that they excited my laughter. Attempted to trade
for horses but could not succeed. In the night we were
alarmed by some savages coming near our camp in full
speed, but they retreated equally rapid, on being hailed
with fierceness by our sentinels. This created some degree of indignation in my little band, as we had noticed
that all the day had passed without any traders presenting
themselves, which appeared as if all intercourse was interdicted!! Writing to the secretary at war, the general,
&c.

3d October, Friday.—The intercourse again commenced. Traded for some horses. Writing for my express.

4th October, Saturday.—Two French traders arrived at
the village in order to procure horses to transport their
goods from the Missouri to the village. They gave us
information that *captains Lewis and Clark*, with all their
people, had descended the river to St. Louis: this diffused
general joy through our party. Our trade for horses advanced none this day.

5th October, Sunday.—Buying horses. Preparing to march, and finishing my letters.

6th October, Monday.—Marched my express.* Purchasing horses and preparing to march on the morrow.

7th October, Tuesday.—In the morning found two of our newly purchased horses missing. Sent in search of them: the Indians brought in one pretty early. Struck our tents and commenced loading our horses. Finding there was no probability of our obtaining the other lost one, we marched at two P. M. and as the chief had threatened to stop us by force of arms, we had made every arrangement to make him pay as dear for the attempt as possible. The party was kept compact, and marched on by a road round the village, in order that if attacked the savages would not have their houses to fly to for cover. I had given orders not to fire until within five or six paces, and then to charge with the bayonet and sabre, when I believe it would have cost them at least 100 men to have exterminated us (which would have been necessary) the village appeared all to be in motion. I galloped up to the lodge of the chief, attended by my interpreter and one soldier, but soon saw there was no serious attempt to be made, although many young men were walking about with their bows, arows, guns and lances. After speaking to the chief with apparent indifference, I told him that I calculated on his justice in obtaining the horse, and that I should leave a man until the next day at 12 o'clock to bring him out. We then joined the party and pursued our route: when I was once on the summit of the hill which overlooks the village, I felt my mind as if relieved from a heavy burthen; yet all the evil I wished the *Pawnees* was that I might be the instrument in the hands

* See Appendix to part II. [No. 13.] page 45. [No. 14.] page 47.

of our government, to open their *ears* and *eyes* with a *strong hand*, to convince them of our power. Our party now consisted of two officers, one doctor, 18 soldiers, one interpreter, three Osage men and one woman, making 25 warriors. We marched out and encamped on a small branch, distant seven miles, on the same route we came in. Rain in the night.

8th October, Wednesday.—I conceived it best to send Baroney back to the village with a present, to be offered for our horse, the chief having suggested the propriety of the measure; he met his son and the horse with Sparks. Marched at ten o'clock, and at four o'clock came to the place where the Spanish troops encamped the first night they left the Pawnee village. Their encampment was circular, and having only small fires round the circle to cook by. We counted 59 fires; now if we allowed six men to each fire, they must have been 354 in number..... We encamped on a large branch of the second fork of the Kans river. Distance 18 miles.

9th October, Thursday.—Marched at eight o'clock, being detained until that time by our horses being at a great distance. At eleven o'clock we found the forks of the Spanish and Pawnee roads, and when we halted at twelve o'clock, we were overtaken by the second chief (or Iskatappe) and the American chief with one-third of the village. They presented us with a piece of bear meat. When we were about to march, we discovered that the dirk of the doctor had been stolen from behind his saddle; after marching the men the doctor and myself, with the inter- preter, went to the chief and " demanded that he should " cause a search to be made ;" it was done, but when the dirk was found, the possessor asserted that he had found it on the road; I told him " that he did not speak the " truth," and informed the chief that we never suffered a

thing of ever so little value to be taken without liberty.
At this time the prairie was covered with his men, who
began to encircle us around, and lieutenant Wilkinson
with the troops had gained half a mile on the road.   The
Indian demanded a knife before he would give it up ; but
as we refused to give any, the chief took one from his belt
and gave him, took the dirk and presented it to the doctor, who immediately returned it to the chief as a present,
and desired Baroney to inform him he now saw it was not
the value of the *article* but the *act* we despise, and then
galloped off.   In about a mile we discovered a herd of elk
which we pursued ; they took back in sight of the Pawnees, who immediately mounted 50 or 60 young men and
joined in the pursuit ; then for the first time in my life, I
saw animals slaughtered by the true savages, with their
original weapons, bows and arrows ; they buried the arrow
up to the plume in the animal.   We took a piece of meat
and pursued our party : we overtook them and encamped
within the Grand or Solomon Fork, which we crossed on
the 23d September, (lower down) on our route to the
Pawnees.   This was the Spanish encamping ground.   In
the evening two Pawnees came to our camp, who had not
eaten for three days ; two of which they had carried a
sick companion whom they had left that day ; we gave
them supper, some meat and corn, and they immediately
departed in order to carry their sick companion this seasonable supply.   When they were coming into camp, the
centinel challenged, it being dark ; they immediately (on
seeing him bring his piece to the charge) supposing he was
about to fire on them, advanced to give him their hands,
he, however, not well discerning their motions, was on
the point of firing, but being a cool collected little fellow,
called out that there were two Indians advancing on him,
and if he should fire ; this brought out the guard, when

the poor affrighted savages were brought into camp, very much alarmed, for they had not heard of a white man's being within their country, and thought they were entering one of the camps of their own people. Distance 18 miles.

10*th October, Friday.*—Marched at seven o'clock and halted at twelve o'clock to dine. Were overtaken by the Pawnee chiefs, whose party we left the day before; who informed us the hunting party had taken another road, and that he had come to bid us good by. We left a large ridge on our left, and at sun down crossed it.... From this place we had an extensive view of the south-west: we observed a creek at a distance, for which I meant to proceed. The doctor, interpreter, and myself, arrived at eight o'clock at night; found water and wood, but had nothing to eat. Kindled a fire in order to guide the party, but they not being able to find the route, and not knowing the distance, encamped on the prairie without wood or water.

11*th October, Saturday.*—Ordered Baroney to return to find the party and conduct them to our camp. The doctor and myself went out to hunt, and on our return found all our people had arrived, except the rear guard, which was in sight. Whilst we halted five Pawnees came to our camp and brought some bones of a *horse* which the Spanish troops had been obliged to eat, at their encampment on this creek; we took up our line of march at twelve o'clock, and at sun-down the party halted on the saline. I was in pursuit of buffalo and did not make the camp until near ten o'clock at night. Killed one buffalo. Distance 12 miles.

12*th October, Sunday.*—Here the Belle Oiseau and one Osage left us, and there remained only one man and woman of that nation—their reason for leaving us was that

our course bore too much west, and they desired to bear
more for the hunting ground of the Osage. In the morning sent out to obtain the buffalo meat, and laid by until
after breakfast. Proceeded at eleven o'clock, and crossing the river two or three times, we passed two camps
where the Spanish troops had halted. Here they appeared to
have remained some days, their roads being so much
blended with the traces of the buffalo that we lost them entirely. This was a mortifying stroke, as we had reason to
calculate, that they had good guides, and were on the best
route for wood and water. We took a south-west direction, and before night, were fortunate enough to strike
their roads on the left, and at dusk, much to our surprise,
struck the east fork of the Kans or La Touche de la Cote
Bucanieus. Killed one buffalo. Distance 18 miles.

13th October, Monday.—The day being rainy, we did
not march until two o'clock, when it having an appearance
of clearing off, we raised our camp, after which we marched seven miles and encamped on the head of a branch of
the river we left. Had to go two miles for water. Killed
one cabrie.

14th October, Tuesday.—It having drizzled rain all
night, and the atmosphere being entirely obscured, we did
not march until a quarter past nine o'clock, and commenced crossing the dividing ridge between the Kans and
Arkansaw rivers. Arrived on a branch of the latter at
one o'clock; continued down it in search of water, until
after dusk, when we found a pond on the prarie, which
induced us to halt. Sparks did not come up, being
scarcely able to walk with rheumatic pains. Wounded
several buffalo, but could get none of them. Distance
24 miles.

15th October, Wednesday.—In the morning road out
in search of the south trace, and crossed the low prairie,

which was nearly all covered with ponds, but could not discover it. Finding Sparks did not arrive, sent two men in search of him, who arrived with him about eleven o'clock. At twelve o'clock we commenced our line of march, and at five o'clock, Dr. Robinson and myself left the party at a large creek (having pointed out a distant wood to lieutenant Wilkinson for our encampment) in order to search some distance up it for the Spanish trace. Killed two buffalo and left part of our clothing with them, to scare away the wolves. Went in pursuit of the party. On our arrival at the creek appointed for the encampment, did not find them. Proceeded down it for some miles, and not finding them, encamped, struck fire, and then supped on one of our buffalo tongues.

16th October, *Thursday.*—Early on horseback; proceeded up the creek some distance in search of our party, but at twelve o'clock crossed to our two buffaloes; found a great many wolves at them, notwithstanding the precaution taken to keep them off. Cooked some marrow bones and again mounted our horses, and proceeded down the creek to their junction. Finding nothing of the party, I began to be seriously alarmed for their safety. Killed two more buffalo, made our encampment and feasted sumptuously on the marrow-bones. Rain in the night.

17th October, *Friday.*—Rose early, determining to search the creek to its source. Very hard rain, accompanied by a cold north-west all day. Encamped near night without being able to discover any signs of the party. Our sensations now became excruciating, not only for their personal safety, but the fear of the failure of the national objects intended to be accomplished by the expedition; and our own situation was not the most agreeable, not having more than four rounds of ammunition each, and 400 miles in the nearest direction from the first civilized inhabitant;

we, however, concluded to search for them on the morrow, and if we did not succeed in finding them, to strike the Arkansaw, where we were in hopes to discover some traces, if not cut off by the savages.

18th October, Saturday.—Commenced our route at a good time, and about ten o'clock, discovered two men on horse-back in search of us, (one my waiter ;) they informed us the party was encamped on the Arkansaw, about three miles south of where we then were: this surprised us very much as we had no conception of that river being so near. On our arrival were met by lieutenant Wilkinson, who with all the party was greatly concerned for our safety. The Arkansaw, on the party's arrival, had not water in it six inches deep, and the stream was not more than 20 feet wide, but the rain of the two days covered all the bottom of the river, which in this place is 450 yards from bank to bank, which are not more than four feet in height, bordered by a few cotton-wood trees on the north side by a low swampy prairie, on the south by a sandy sterile desert at a small distance. In the afternoon the doctor and myself took our horses and crossed the Arkansaw, in order to search for some trees which might answer the purpose to make canoes; found but one and returned at dusk. It commenced raining at 12 o'clock at night.

19th October, Sunday.—Finding the river rising rapidly, I thought it best to secure our passage over, we consequently made it good by ten o'clock, A. M. Rain all day. Preparing our tools and arms for labor and the chase on the morrow.

20th October, Monday.—Commenced our labor at two trees for canoes, but one proved too much doated.... Killed two buffalo and one cabrie. Discharged our guns at a mark, the best shot a prize of one tent and a pair of shoes. Our only dog, was standing at the root of the tree, in the grass, and one of the balls, struck him on the head and killed him. Ceased raining about 12 o'clock.

21st October, Tuesday.—Doctor Robinson and myself mounted our horses, in order to go down the river to the entrance of the three last creeks, we had crossed on our rout, but meeting with buffalo, we killed four; also, one cabrie. Returned to camp and sent for the meat.

22d October, Wednesday.—Having sat up very late last evening, expecting the sergeant, and party (who did not arrive) we were very anxious for them, but about 10 o'clock Bradley arrived and informed us, that they could not find the buffalo, which we had killed on the prairie, they all arrived before noon, and in the afternoon we scaffolded some meat and nearly compleated the frame of a skin Canoe, which we concluded to build; overhauled my instruments and made some rectifications preparatory to taking an observation &c.

23d October, Thursday.—Dr. Robinson and myself, accompanied by one man, ascended the river with an intention of searching the Spanish trace; at the same time, we dispatched *Baroney* and our two hunters to kill some buffalo, to obtain the skins for canoes. We ascended the river, about 20 miles to a large branch on the right; just at dusk gave chase to a buffalo and was obliged to shoot nineteen balls into him, before we killed him. Encamped in the fork.

24 October, Friday.—We assended the right branch about five miles, but could not see any sign of the Spanish trace; this is not surprizing, as the river bears south west, and they no doubt kept more to the west from the head of one branch to another. We returned and on our way, killed some prairie squirrels, or wishtonwishes,

and nine large rattle snakes, which frequent their villages.*
On our arrival, found the hunters had come in a boat,
one hour, with two buffalo and one elk skin.

---

* The Wishtonwish of the Indians, prairie dogs of some travellers; or squirrels as I should be inclined to denominate them; reside on the prairies of Louisiana
in towns or villages, having an evident police established in their communities.
The sites of their towns are generally on the brow of a hill, near some creek or
pond, in order to be convenient to water, and that the high ground which they
inhabit, may not be subject to inundation Their residence, being under ground,
is burrowed out, and the earth which answers the double purpose of keeping out
the water, and affording an elevated place in wet seasons to repose on, and to give
them a further and more distinct view of the country. Their holes descend in a
spiral form, therefore I could never ascertain their depth; but I once had 140 kettles of water pored into one of them in order to drive out the occupant, but without effect. In the circuit of the villages, they clear off all the grass, and leave the
earth bare of vegetation ; but whether it is from an instinct they possess inducing
them to keep the ground thus cleared, or whether they make use of the herbage,
as food, I cannot pretend to determine. The latter opinion, I think entitled to a
preference, as their teeth designates them to be of the granivorous species, and I
know of no other substance which is produced in the vicinity of their positions,
on which they could subsist ; and they never extend their excursions more than
half a mile from the burrows. They are of a dark brown color, except their bel
lies, which are white. Their tails are not so long as those of our grey squirrels,
but are shaped precisely like theirs ; their teeth, head, nails, and body, are the
perfect squirrel, except that they are generally fatter than that animal. Their
villages sometimes extend over two and three miles square, in which there must be
innumerable hosts of them, as there is generally a burrow every ten steps in
which there are two or more, and you see new ones partly excavated on all the
borders of the town. We killed great numbers of them with our rifles and found
them excellent meat, after they were exposed a night or two to the frost, by
which means the rankness acquired by their subterranneous dwelling is corrected.
As you approach their towns, you are saluted on all sides by the cry of Wishtonwish,
from which they derive their name with the Indians, uttered in a shrill and
piercing manner. You then observe them all retreating to the entrance of their
burrows, where they post themselves, and regard every, even the slightest, movement that you make. It requires a very nice shot with a rifle to kill them, as they
must be killed dead, for as long as life exists, they continue to work into their cells.
It is extremely dangerous to pass through their towns, as they abound with rattle snakes, both of the yellow and black species ; and strange as it may appear, I
have seen the Wishtonwish, the rattle snake, the horn frog, of which the prairie
abounds, (termed by the Spaniards the cammellion, from their taking no visible
sustenance) and a land tortoise all take refuge in the same hole. I do not pretend
to assert, that it was their common place of resort, but I have witnessed the above
facts more than in one instance.

25th October, Saturday.—Took an observation, passed the day in writing, and preparing for the departure of Lt. Wilkinson.

26th October, Sunday.—Delivered out a ration of corn by way of distinction of the Sabbath. Preparing for our departure.

27th October, Monday.—Delivered to lieutenant Wilkinson, letters for the general and our friends,* with other papers, consisting of his instructions, traverse tables of our voyage and a draught of our route, to that place complete; in order that if we were lost, and he arrived in safety; we might not have made the tour, without some benefit to our country. He took with him in corn and meat, 21 days provisions and all the necessary tools, to build canoes or cabbins. Launched his canoes. We concluded, we would separate in the morning. He to descend and we to ascend to the mountains.

28th October, Tuesday.—As soon as possible, all was in motion, my party crossing the river to the north side, and lieutenant Wilkinson, launching his canoes of skins and wood. We breakfasted together, and then filed off; but I suffered my party to march, and I remained to see lieutenant Wilkinson sail, which he did at ten o'clock, having one skin canoe, made of four buffalo skins and two elk skins; this held three men besides himself and one Osage. In his wooden canoe, were, one soldier, one Osage and their baggage; one other soldier marched on shore. We parted with " God bless you" from both parties; they appeared to sail very well. In the pursuit of our party, Doctor Robinson, Baroney, one soldier and myself, killed a brelau and a buffalo, of the latter we took only his marrow bones and liver. Arrived where our men had encamped, about dusk. Distance 14 miles.

* See Appendix to part II. [No. 15.] page 50.

29th October, Wednesday.—Marched after breakfast and in the first hours march, passed two fires, where twenty one Indians had recently encamped, in which party (by their paintings on the rocks,) there were seven guns. Killed a buffalo, halted, made fire and feasted on the choice pieces of meat. About noon discovered two horses feeding with a herd of buffalo; we attempted to surround them, but they soon cleared our fleetest coursers. One appeared to be an elegant horse; these were the first wild horses we had seen. Two or three hours before night, struck the Spanish road; and, as it was snowing, halted and encamped the party, at the first woods on the bank of the river. The doctor and myself then forded it (the ice running very thick) in order to discover the course the Spaniards took, but owing to the many buffalo roads, could not ascertain it; but it evidently appeared that they had halted here some time, as the ground was covered with horse dung, for miles around. Returned to camp. The snow fell about two inches deep and then it cleared up. Distance 12 miles.

30th October, Thursday.—In the morning sent out to kill a buffalo, to have his marrow bones for breakfast, which was accomplished; after breakfast the party marched upon the north side, and the doctor and myself crossed with considerable difficulty (on account of the ice) to the Spanish camp, where we took a large circuit in order to discover the Spanish trace and came in at a point of woods; south of the river, where we found our party encamped. We discovered also that the Spanish troops had marked the river up, and that a party of savages had been there not more than three days before. Killed two buffalo. Distance 4 miles.

31st October, Friday.—Fine day—marched at three quarters past nine o'clock, on the Spanish road. Encamped,

sun an hour high, after having made sixteen miles. We observed this day a species of chrystilization on the road (when
the sun was high) in low places where there had been
water settled, on tasting it found it to be salt; this gave
in my mind some authenticity to the report of the prairie
being covered for leagues.   Discovered the trace of about
twenty savages who had followed our road; and horses
going down the river.   Killed one buffalo, one elk, one
deer.

1*st November, Saturday.*—Marched early, just after
commencing our line, heard a gun on our left; the doctor,
Baroney and myself being in advance, and laying on the
ground waiting for the party; a band of Cabrie came up,
amongst our horses, to satisfy their curiosity; we could
not resist the temptation of killing two, although we had
plenty of meat.   At the report of the gun they appeared
astonished, and stood still until we hallowed at them to
drive them away.   Encamped in the evening on an island,
upon using my glass to observe the adjacent country, I
observed on the prairie a herd of horses; doctor Robinson and Baroney, accompanied me to go and view them;
when within a quarter of a mile, they discovered us, and
came immediately up near us, making the earth tremble
under them (this brought to my recollection a charge of
cavalry).   They stopt and gave us an opportunity to view
them, among them there were some very beautiful bays,
blacks and greys, and indeed of all colours.   We fired at a
black horse, with an idea of creasing him, but did not succeed; they flourished round and returned again to see us,
when we returned to camp.

2*d November, Sunday.*—In the morning for the purpose of trying the experiment, we equipped six of our
fleetest coursers with riders and ropes, to noose the wild
horses if in our power, to come among the band.   They

stood until they came within forty yards of them, neighing and whinnowing, when the chase began, which we continued about two miles, without success. Two of our horses ran up with them; we could not take them. Returned to camp. I have since laughed at our folly, for taking the wild horses, in that manner, is scarcely ever attempted, even with the fleetest horses, and most expert ropers, (see my account of wild horses, and the manner of taking them in my dissertations on the province of Texas). Marched late. River turned to north by west. Hills change to the north side. Distance 13 1-2 miles. Killed one buffalo.

3d November, Monday.—Marched at ten o'clock passed numerous herds of buffalo, elk, some horses &c. all travelling south. The river bottoms, full of salt ponds; grass similar to our salt meadows. Killed one buffalo. Distance 25 1-2 miles.

4th November, Tuesday.—This day brought to our recollection, the fate of our countrymen at Recovery; when defeated by the indians, in the year '91. In the afternoon discovered the north side of the river to be covered with animals; which, when we came to them proved to be buffalo cows and calves. I do not think it an exaggeration to say there were 3,000 in one view. It is worthy of remark, that in all the extent of country yet crossed, we never saw one cow, and that now the face of the earth appeared to be covered with them. Killed one buffalo. Distance 24 1-2 miles.

5th November, Wednesday.—Marched at our usual hour; at the end of two miles, shot a buffalo and two deer and halted, which detained us so long that we foolishly concluded to halt the day and kill some cows and calves, which lay on the opposite side of the river. I took post on a hill, and sent some horsemen over, when a scene took place which gave a lively representation of an engagement. The herd of buffalo being divided into separate bands covered the prairie with dust, and first charged on the one side then to the other, as the pursuit of the horsemen impelled them : the report and smoke from the guns, added to the pleasure of the scene, which in part compensated for our detention.

6th *November, Thursday*.—Marched early, but was detained two or three hours by the cows, which we killed. The cow buffalo, was equal to any meat I ever saw, and we feasted sumptuously on the choice morsels. I will not attempt to describe the droves of animals we now saw on our route ; suffice it to say, that the face of the prairie was covered with them, on each side of the river ; their numbers exceeded imagination. Distance 16 miles.

7th *November, Friday*.—Marched early. The herbage being very poor, concluded to lay by on the morrow, in order to recruit our horses, killed three cow buffalo, one calf, two wolves, one brelaw. Distance 18 miles.

8th *November, Saturday*.—Our horses being very much jaded and our situation very eligible, we halted all day, jerked meat, mended mockinsons &c.

9th *November, Sunday*.—Marched early. At twelve o'clock, struck the Spanish road, (which had been on the outside of us) which appeared to be considerably augmented, and on our arrival, at the camp, found it to consist of 96 fires, from which a reasonable conclusion might be drawn. that there were from 6 to 700 men. We this day found the face of the country considerably changed ; being hilly, with springs: passed numerous herds of buffalo and some horses. Distance 27 miles.

10th *November, Monday*.—The hills increased, the banks of the river, covered with groves of young cotton wood ; the river itself much narrower and crooked. Our

x

horses growing weak, two gave out, being then along empty, cut down trees at night, for them to browze on. Killed one buffalo.   Distance 20 miles.

11th November, Tuesday.—Marched at the usual hour. Passed two old, and one last summer, camps which had belonged to the savages, and we suppose Tetaus. Passed a Spanish camp where it appeared they remained some days as we conjectured to lay up meat, previously to entering the Tetau country, as the buffalo evidently began to grow much less numerous.   Finding the impossibility of performing the voyage in the time proposed, I determined to spare no pains to accomplish every object even should it oblige me to spend another winter, in the desert.   Killed one buffalo, one brelaw.   Distance 24 miles.

12th November, Wednesday.—Was obliged to leave two horses, which entirely gave out.   Missed the Spanish road.   Killed one buffalo.   Distance 20 miles.

13th November, Thursday.—We marched at the usual hour.   The river banks begin to be entirely covered with woods on both sides, but no other specie than cotton wood.   Discovered very fresh signs of indians, and one of our hunters informed me, he saw a man on horseback, ascending a ravine on our left.   Discovered signs of war parties ascending the river.   Wounded several buffalo. Killed one turkey, the first we have seen since we left the Pawnees.

14th November, Friday.—In the morning, doctor Robinson, one man and myself, went up the ravine, on which the man was supposed to have been seen, but could make no important discovery.   Marched at two o'clock; passed a point of red rocks and one large creek.   Distance 10 miles.

15th November, Saturday.—Marched early.   Passed two deep creeks and many high points of the rocks; also, large herds of buffalo. At two o'clock in the afternoon I thought I could distinguish a mountain to our right, which appeared like a small blue cloud; viewed it with the spy glass, and was still more confirmed in my conjecture, yet only communicated it to doctor Robinson, who was in front with me, but in half an hour, they appeared in full view before us. When our small party arrived on the hill they with one accord gave three *cheers* to the *Mexican mountains.* Their appearance can easily be imagined by those who have crossed the Alleghany; but their sides were whiter as if covered with snow, or a white stone. Those were a *spur* of the grand western chain of mountains, which divide the waters of the Pacific from those of the Atlantic oceans, and it divided the waters which empty into the bay of the Holy Spirit, from those of the Mississippi; as the Alleghany does, those which discharge themselves into the latter river and the Atlantic. They appear to present a natural boundary between the province of Lousiana and New Mexico and would be a defined and natural boundary. Before evening we discovered a fork on the south side bearing S. 25° W. and as the Spanish troops, appeared to have borne up it, we encamped on its banks, about one mile from its confluence, that we might make further discoveries on the morrow. Killed three buffalo. Distance 24 miles.

16*th November, Sunday.*—After asserting that the Spanish troops had ascended the right branch or main river; we marched at two o'clock P. M. The Arkansaw appeared at this place to be much more navigable, than below, where we first struck it; and for any impediment I have yet discovered in the river, I would not hesitate to embark in February at its mouth and ascend to the Mexican mountains, with crafts properly constructed. Distance 11 1-2 miles.

17*th November, Monday.*—Marched at our usual hour, pushed with an idea of arriving at the mountains, but found at night, no visible difference in their appearance, from what we did yesterday: one of our horses gave out and was left in a ravine, not being able to ascend the hill: but I sent back for him and had him brought to the camp. Distance 23 1-2 miles.

18*th November, Tuesday.*—As we discovered fresh signs of the savages, we concluded it best to stop and kill some meat, for fear we should get into a country where we could not kill game. Sent out the hunters; I walked myself, to an eminence from whence I took the courses to the different mountains, and a small sketch of their appearance. In the evening, found the hunters had killed without mercy, having slain 17 buffalo and wounded at least 20 more.

19*th November, Wednesday.*—Having several buffalo brought in, gave out sufficient to last this month; I found it expedient to remain and dry the meat, as our horses were getting very weak, and the one died which was brought up on the 18th. Had a general feast of marrow bones; 136 of them, furnishing the repast.

20*th November, Thursday.*—Marched at our usual hour; but as our horses's loads were considerably augmented by the death of one horse and the addition of 900 lbs. of meat, we moved slowly, and made only 18 miles. Killed two buffalo and took some choice pieces.

21*st November, Friday.*—Marched at our usual hour, passed two Spanish camps, within three miles of each other. We again discovered the tracks of two men, who had ascended the river yesterday. This caused us to move with caution; but at the same time, increased our anxiety to discover them. The river was certainly as navigable here (and I think much more so,) than some hundred miles below, which I suppose arises from its flowing through a long course of sandy soil, which must absorb much of the water, and render it shoaler below than above, near the mountains. Distance 21 miles.

22d November, Saturday.—Marched at our usual hour, and with rather more caution than usual. After having marched about five miles on the prairie, we descended into the bottom, the *front only ;* when Baroney cried out *Voila un Savage*, when we observed a number running from the woods towards us, we advanced to them and on turning my head to the left, I observed several running on the hill, as it were to surround us ; one with a stand of colors. This caused a momentary halt ; but perceiving those in front, reaching out their hands, and without arms we again advanced, they met us with open arms, crouding round, to touch and embrace us. They appeared so anxious that I dismounted my horse, and in a moment, a fellow had mounted him and was off. I then observed the doctor and Baroney, were in the same predicament. The indians were embracing the soldiers ; after some time tranquility was so far restored, (they having returned our horses all safe) as to enable us to learn they were a war party, from the grand Pawnees, who had been in search of the Tetaus ; but not finding them were now on their return. An unsuccessful war party on their return home, are always ready to embrace an opportunity, of gratifying their disappointed vengeance, on the first persons whom they meet. Made for the woods and unloaded our horses ; when the two partizans endeavored to arrange the party; it was with great difficulty that they got them tranquil, and not until there had been a bow or two, bent on the occasion. When in some order, we found them to be sixty warriors, half with fire arms, and half with bows, arrows, and lances. Our party was sixteen total. In a short time they were arranged in a ring and I took my seat be-

tween the two partizans; our colors were placed opposite
each other, the utensils for smoking &c. were paraded
on a small seat before us; thus far all was well. I then
ordered half a carrot of tobacco, one dozen knives, 60 fire
steels and 60 flints to be presented them. They demanded
ammunition, corn, blankets, kettles &c. all of which they
were refused, notwithstanding the pressing instances of
my interpreter, to accord to some points. The pipes yet
lay unmoved, as if they were undetermined whether to
treat us as friends or enemies; but after some time we
were presented with a kettle of water, drank, smoked, and
eat together. During this time doctor Robinson was
standing up, to observe their actions, in order that we
might be ready to commence hostilities as soon as them.
They now took their presents and commenced distributing
them, but some malcontents, threw them away, by way of
contempt. We began to load our horses, when they encircled us and commenced stealing every thing they could.
Finding it was difficult to preserve my pistols; I mounted
my horse when I found myself frequently surrounded
during which some were endeavoring to steal the pistols.
The doctor was equally engaged in another quarter, and all
the soldiers in their positions; in taking things from them
one having stolen my tomahawk, I informed the chief, but
he paid no respect, except to reply that " *they were pitiful*;"
finding this I determined to protect ourselves, as far as was
in my power, and the affair began to take a serious aspect.
I ordering my men to take their arms, and separate themselves from the savages; at the same time declaring to
them, I would *kill* the first man who touched our baggage.
On which they commenced filing off immediately; we
marched about the same time and found, they had made
out to steal one sword, tomahawk, broad axe, five can-
teens, and sundry other small articles. After our leaving

them; when I reflected on the subject, I felt myself sincerely mortified, that the smallness of my number obliged me thus to submit to the insults of a lawless banditti, it being the first time ever a savage took any thing from me, with the least appearance of force. After encamping at night the doctor and myself went about one mile back, and way laid the road, determined in case we discovered any of the rascals pursuing us to steal our horses, to kill two at least; but after waiting behind some logs until some time in the night, and discovering no person, we returned to camp. Distance 17 miles, killed two buffalo and one deer.

23d November, Sunday.—Marched at ten o'clock; at one o'clock came to the third fork on the south side and encamped at night in the point of the grand forks. As the river appeared to be dividing itself into many small branches and of course must be near its extreme source, I concluded to put the party in a defensible situation; and ascend the north fork, to the high point of the blue mountain, which we conceived would be one days march, in order to be enabled from its pinical, to lay down the various branches and positions of the country. Distance 19 miles. Killed five buffalo.

24th November, Monday.—Early in the morning cut down 14 logs, and put up a breast work, five feet high on three sides and the other was thrown on the river. After giving the necessary orders for their government, during my absence, in case of our not returning. We marched at one o'clock with an idea of arriving at the foot of the mountain; but found ourselves obliged to take up our nights lodging under a single cedar, which we found in the prairie, without water and extremely cold. Our party besides myself consisted of doctor Robinson, privates Miller and Brown. Distance 12 miles.

25th November, Tuesday.—Marched early, with an expectation of ascending the mountain, but was only able to encamp at its base, after passing over many small hills covered with cedars and pitch pines. Our encampment was on a creek where we found no water for several miles from the mountain, but near its base, found springs sufficient. Took a meridional observation, and the altitude of the mountain. Killed two buffalo. Distance 22 miles.

26th November, Wednesday.—Expecting to return to our camp that evening, we left all our blankets and provisions, at the foot of the mountain. Killed a deer of a new species, and hung his skin on a tree with some meat. We commenced ascending, found it very difficult, being obliged to climb up rocks, sometimes almost perpendicular; and after marching all day, we encamped in a cave, without blankets, victuals or water. We had a fine clear sky, whilst it was snowing at the bottom. On the side of the mountain, we found only yellow and pitch pine. Some distance up we found buffalo, higher still the new species of deer and pheasants.

27th November, Thursday.—Arose hungry, dry, and extremely sore, from the inequality of the rocks, on which we had lain all night, but were amply compensated for toil by the sublimity of the prospects below. The unbounded prairie was overhung with clouds, which appeared like the ocean in a storm; wave piled on wave and foaming, whilst the sky was perfectly clear where we were. Commenced our march up the mountain, and in about one hour arrived at the summit of this chain: here we found the snow middle deep; no sign of beast or bird inhabiting this region. The thermometer which stood at 9° above 0 at the foot of the mountain, here fell to 4° below 0. The summit of the Grand Peak, which was entirely bare of vegetation and covered with snow, now appeared at the distance of 15 or 16 miles from us, and as high again as what we had ascended, and would have taken a whole day's march to have arrived at its base, when I believe no human being could have ascended to its pinical. This with the condition of my soldiers who had only light overalls on, and no stockings, and every way ill provided to endure the inclemency of the region; the bad prospect of killing any thing to subsist on, with the further detention of two or three days, which it must occasion, determined us to return. The clouds from below had now ascended the mountain and entirely enveloped the summit on which rests eternal snows. We descended by a long deep ravine with much less difficuly than contemplated. Found all our baggage safe, but the provisions all destroyed. It began to snow, and we sought shelter under the side of a projecting rock, were we, all four, made a meal on one partridge, and a piece of deer's ribs, the ravens had left us, being the first we had eaten in that 48 hours.

28th November, Friday.—Marched at nine o'clock. Kept straight down the creek to avoid the hills. At half past one o'clock shot two buffalo, when we made the first full meal we had made in three days. Encamped in a valley under a shelving rock. The land here very rich, and covered with old Tetau camps,

29th November, Saturday.—Marched after a short repast, and arrived at our camp before night; found all well.

30th November, Sunday.—Marched at eleven o'clock, it snowing very fast, but my impatience to be moving would not permit my lying still at that camp. The doctor, Baroney and myself, went to view a Tetau encampment, which appeared to be about two years old;

and from their having cut down so large a quantity of trees
to support their horses, conclude there must have been at
least one thousand souls : passed several more in the course
of the day ; also one Spanish camp. Distance 15 miles.
Killed two deer. This day came to the first cedar and
pine.

　　　1st December, Monday.—The storm still continuing
with violence, we remained encamped ; the snow by night
one foot deep ; our horses being obliged to scrape it away,
to obtain their miserable pittance, and to increase their
misfortunes, the poor animals were attacked by the mag-
pies, who attracted by the scent of their sore backs, alight-
ed on them, and in defiance of their wincing and kicking,
picked many places quite raw ; the difficulty of procuring
food rendered those birds so bold as to light on our mens
arms and eat meat out of their hands. One of our hunter's
out but killed nothing.

　　　2d December, Tuesday.—It cleared off in the night,
and in the morning the thermometer stood at 17 below 0,
(Reaumer) being three times as cold as any morning
we had yet experienced. We killed an old buffalo on
the opposite side of the river, which here was so deep as
to swim horses. Marched and found it necessary to cross
to the north side, about two miles up, as the ridge joined
the river. The ford was a good one, but the ice ran very
bad, and two of the men got their feet froze before we
could get accommodated with fire &c. Secured some of
our old buffalo and continued our march. The country
being very rugged and hilly, one of our horses took a freak
in his head and turned back, which occasioned three of our
rear guard to lay out all night ; I was very apprehensive
they might perish on the open prairie. Distance 18
miles.

3d December, Wednesday.—The weather moderating to 3 below 0, our absentees joined, one with his feet frozen, but were not able to bring up the horse; sent two men back on horseback. The hardships of last voyage had now began, and had the climate only been as severe as the climate then was, some of the men must have perished, for they had no winter clothing; I wore myself cotton overalls, for I had not calculated on being out in that inclement season of the year. Dr. Robinson and myself, with assistants, went out and took the altitude of the north mountain, on the base of a mile;* after which, together with Sparks, we endeavoured to kill a *cow* but without effect. Killed two bulls, that the men might use pieces of their hides for mockinsons. Left Sparks out. On our return to camp found the men had got back with the strayed horse, but too late to march.

4th December, Thursday.—Marched about five; took up Sparks who had succeeded in killing a cow. Killed two buffalo and six turkies. Distance 20 miles.

5th December, Friday.—Marched at our usual hour. Passed one very bad place of *falling rocks*; had to carry our loads. Encamped on the main branch of the river, near the entrance of the south mountain. In the evening walked up to the mountain. Heard 14 guns at camp during my absence, which alarmed me considerably; returned as quickly as possible, and found that the cause of my

---

* The perpendicular height of the mountain from the level of the prairie, was 10,581 feet, and admitting that the prairie was 8000 feet from the level of the sea, it would make the elevation of this peak 18,581 feet, equal to some, and surpassing the calculated height of others, for the peak of Teneriffe and falling short of that of Chimborazo only 1,701 feet. Indeed it was so remarkable as to be known to all the savage nation for hundreds of miles around, and to be spoken of with admiration by the Spaniards of N. Mexico, and was the bounds of their travels N. W. Indeed in our wandering in the mountains, it was never out of our sight, (except when in a valley) from the 14th November to the 27th January.

alarm was their shooting turkies. Killed two buffalo and nine turkies. Distance 18 miles.

6th *December, Saturday.*—Sent out three different parties to hunt the Spanish trace, but without success. The doctor and myself followed the river into the mountain, which was bounded on each side by the rocks of the mountain, 200 feet high, leaving a small valley of 50 or 60 feet. Killed two buffalo, two deer, one turkey.

7th *December, Sunday.*—We again dispatched parties in search of the trace ; one party discovered it on the other side of the river, and followed it into the valley of the river at the entrance of the mountain, where they met two parties who were returning from exploring the two branches of the river, in the mountains : of which they reported, to have ascended until the river was merely a brook, bounded on both sides with perpendicular rocks, impracticable for horses ever to pass them ; they then recrossed the river to the north side, and discovered (as they supposed) that the Spanish troops had ascended a dry valley to the right—on their return they found some rock salt, samples of which were brought me. We determined to march the morrow to the entrance of the valley ; there to examine the salt, and the road. Killed one wild cat.

8th *December, Monday.*—On examining the trace found yesterday, conceived it to have been only a reconnoitering party, dispatched from the main body, and on analysing the rock salt, found it to be strongly impregnated with sulphur. There were some very strong sulphurated springs at its foot. Returned to camp ; took with me Dr. Robinson and Miller, and descended the river, in order to discover certainly, if the whole party had came by this route. Descended about seven miles on the south side. Saw great quantities of turkies and deer. Killed one deer.

9th *December, Tuesday.*—Before we marched, killed a fine buck at our camp as he was passing. Found the Spanish camp about four miles below, and from every observation we could make, conceived they had all ascended the river. Returned to camp, where we arrived about two o'clock. Found all well; would have moved immediately, but four men were out reconnoitering. Killed three deer.

10th *December, Wednesday.*—Marched and found the road over the mountain to be excellent. Encamped on a dry ravine. Obliged to melt snow for ourselves and horses; and as their was nothing else for the latter to eat, gave them one pint of corn each. Killed one buffalo.

11th *December, Thursday.*—Marched at ten o'clock, and in one mile struck a branch of the Arkansaw, on which the *supposed* Spaniards had encamped, where there was both water and grass. Kept up this branch, but was frequently embarrassed as to the trace; at three o'clock P. M. having no sign of it, halted and encamped, and went out to search it; found it about one mile to the right. Distance 15 miles.

12th *December, Friday.*—Marched at 9 o'clock. Continued up the same branch as yesterday. The ridges on our right and left, appeared to grow lower, but mountains appeared on our flanks, though the intervals covered with snow. Owing to the weakness of our horses, made only 12 miles.

13th *December, Saturday.*—Marched at the usual hour and passed large springs, and the (supposed) Spanish camp; and at twelve o'clock, a dividing ridge, and immediately fell on a small branch running N. 20° W. There being no appearance of wood, we left it, and the *Spanish Trace* to our right, and made for the hills to encamp. After the halt I took my gun and went out to see what discovery I could make, and after marching about two miles north, fell on a river 40 yards wide, frozen over; which after some investigation, I found run north east, this was the occasion of much surprise, as we were taught to expect to have met with the branches of the Red river, which should run south east. Quere. Must it not be the head waters of the river Platte? If so the Missouri must run much more west, than is generally represented; for the Platte is a small river by no means presenting an expectation of so extensive a course. Distance 18 miles. One horse gave out and was left.

14th December, Sunday.—Marched. Struck the river, ascended it four miles, and encamped on the north side. The prairie being about two miles wide, was covered at least six miles (on the banks of the river) with horse dung and the marks of indian camps, which had been since the cold weather, as was evident by the fires which were in the centre of the lodges; the sign made by their horses was astonishing, and would have taken a thousand horses some months. As it was impossible to say which course the Spaniards pursued, amongst this multiplicity of signs, we halted early, and discovered that they or the savages had ascended the river. We determined to persue them, as to the geography of the country, had turned out to be so different from our expectation; we were somewhat at a loss which course to pursue, unless we attempted to cross the snow cap'd mountains, to the south east of us which was almost impossible. Bursted one of our rifles, which was a great loss, as it made three guns which had bursted, and the five which had been broken on the march, and one of my men was now armed with my sword and pistols. Killed two buffalo.

15th December, Monday.—After repairing our guns, we marched, but were obliged to leave another horse.

Ascended the river, both sides of which were covered with old Indian camps, at which we found corn cobs; this induced us to believe that those savages although erratic, must remain long enough in one position to cultivate this grain, or obtain it of the Spaniards; from their sign they must have been extremely numerous, and possessed vast numbers of horses.   My poor fellows suffered extremely with cold, being almost naked.   Distance 10 miles.

16th December, *Tuesday.*—Marched up the river about two miles and killed a buffalo.   When finding no road up the stream, we halted and dispatched parties different courses; the doctor and myself ascending high enough to enable me to lay down the course of the river into the mountains.   From a high ridge we reconnoitered the adjacent country, and concluded putting the *Spanish trace* out of the question, and to bear our course south west, for the head of Red river.   One of our party found a large camp, which had been occupied by at least 3000 Indians, with a large cross in the middle.   Quere. Are those people catholics?

17th December, *Wednesday.*—Marched, and on striking a left hand fork of the river we had left, found it to be the main branch; ascended it some distance, but finding it to bear too much to the north, we encamped about two miles from it, for the purpose of benefitting by its water.   Distance 15 miles.

18th December, *Thursday.*—Marched and crossed the mountain which lay south-west of us, in a distance of seven miles, arrived at a small spring; some of our lads observed, they supposed it to be Red river, to which I then gave very little credit.   On entering a gap in the next mountain, came past an excellent spring which formed a fine creek, which we followed through narrows in the mountains for about six miles; found many evacuated camps of indians the latest yet seen, after pointing out the ground for the encampment, the doctor and myself went on to make discoveries (as was our usual custom,) and in about four miles march we struck (what we supposed to be Red river) which here was about 25 yards wide, ran with great rapidity and was full of rocks. We returned to the party with the news, which gave general pleasure. Determined to remain a day or two in order to examine the source. Distance 18 miles. Snowing.

19*th December, Friday.*—Marched down the creek near the opening of the prairie, and encamped, sent out parties hunting, &c. but had no success. Still snowing and stormy, making preparations to take an observation.

20*th December, Saturday.*—Having found a fine place for pasture on the river sent our horses down to it with a guard, also three parties out a hunting, all of whom returned without success. Took an observation. As there was no prospect of killing any game, it was necessary that the party should leave that place, I therefore determined that the doctor and Baroney should descend the river in the morning ; that myself and two men would ascend and the rest of the party descend after the doctor until they obtained provision and could wait for me.

21*st December, Sunday.*—The doctor and Baroney marched ; the party remained for me to take a meridional observation ; after which we separated. Myself and the two men who accompanied me (Mountjoy and Miller) ascended 12 miles and encamped on the north side, the river continuing close to the north mountain and running through a narrow rocky channel and in some places not more than 20 feet wide and at least 10 feet deep. Its banks bordered by yellow pine, cedars, &c.

22*d December, Monday.*—Marched up thirteen miles, to a large point of the mountain from whence we had a view at least 35 miles, to where the river entered the mountains, it being at that place not more than ten or fifteen feet wide, and properly speaking, only a *brook*; from this place after taking the course, and estimating the distance we returned to our camp of last evening. Killed one turkey and a hare.

23d December, Tuesday.—Marched early, and at two o'clock, P. M. discovered the trace of the party on the opposite side of the river; forded it, although extremely cold and marched until some time in the night, when we arrived at the second nights encampment of the party. Our cloathing was frozen stiff, and we ourselves were considerably benumbed.

24th December, Wednesday.—The party's provision extending only to the 23d, and their orders being not to halt until they killed some game, and then wait for us: consequently they might have been considerably advanced. About 11 o'clock, met doctor Robinson on a prairie, who informed me that he and Baroney had been absent from the party two days without killing any thing, (also without eating,) but that over night, they had killed four buffalo, and that he was in search of the men; and suffered the two lads with me to go to the camp where the meat was, as we had also been nearly two days without eating. The doctor and myself pursued the trace and found them encamped on the river bottom. Sent out horses for the meat, shortly after Sparks arrived and informed us he had killed four cows. Thus from being in a starving condition we had 8 beeves in our camp. We now again found ourselves all assembled together on Christmas Eve, and appeared generally to be content, although all the refreshment we had to celebrate that day with, was buffalo meat, without salt, or any other thing whatever. My little excursion up the river was in order to establish the geography of the sources of the (supposed) Red River, as I well knew the indefatigable researches of doctor Hunter, Dunbar and Freeman, had left nothing unnoticed in the extent of their voyage up said river, I determined that its upper branches should be equally well explored; as in this voyage I had already ascertained the sources of the Osage, and White Rivers, (been round the head of the Kans River) and on the head waters of the Platte.

25th December, Thursday.—It being stormy weather and having meat to dry; I concluded to lie by this day. Here I must take the liberty of observing that in this situation, the hardships and privations we underwent, were on this day brought more fully to our mind. Having been accustomed to some degree of relaxation, and extra enjoyments; but here 800 miles from the frontiers of our country, in the most inclement season of the year; not one person clothed for the winter, many without blankets, (having been obliged to cut them up for socks, &c.) and now laying down at night on the snow or wet ground; one side burning whilst the other was pierced with the cold wind: this was in part the situation of the party whilst some were endeavoring to make a miserable substitute of raw buffalo hide for shoes &c. I will not speak of diet, as I conceive that to be beneath the serious consideration of a man on a voyage of such nature. We spent the day as agreeably as could be expected from men in our situation. Caught a bird of a new species, having made a trap for him.*

*This bird was of a green color, almost the size of a quail, and had a small tuft on its head like a pheasant, and was of the carnivorous species; it differed from any bird we ever saw in the United States. We kept him with us in a small wicker cage, feeding him on meal, until I left the interpreter on the Arkansaw, with whom left it. We at one time took a companion of the same species, and put them in the same cage, when the first resident never ceased attacking the stranger until he killed him.

26th December, Friday.—Marched at two o'clock and made 7 1-2 miles to the entrance of the mountains.   On this piece of prairie the river spread considerably, and formed several small Islands, a large stream enters from the south.   As my boy and some others were sick, I omitted pitching our tent in order that they might have it ; in consequence of which we were completely covered with snow on top, as well as that part on which we lay.

27th December. Saturday.—Marched over an extreme rough road, our horses received frequent falls and cut themselves considerably on the rocks.   From there being no roads of buffalo, or sign of horses, I am convinced that neither those animals, nor the aborigines of the country, ever take this route, to go from the source of the river out of the mountains, but that they must cross one of the chains to the right or left, and find a smoother tract to the lower country.   Was obliged to unload our horses and carry the baggage at several places.   Distance 12 1-2 miles.

28th December, Sunday.—Marched over an open space and from the appearance before us, concluded we were going out of the mountains, but at night encamped at the entrance of the most perpendicular precipices on both sides, through which the river ran and our course lay. Distance 16 miles.

29th December, Monday.—Marched but owing to the extreme ruggedness of the road, made but five miles. Saw one of a new species of animals on the mountains ; ascended it to kill him, but did not succeed.   Finding the impossibility of getting along with the horses, made one sled, which with the men of three horses, carries their load.

30th December, Tuesday.—Marched : but at half past one o'clock; were obliged to halt and send back for the sled loads, as they had broken it and could not proceed owing to the waters running over the ice.   Distance 8 miles.   Crossed our horses twice on the ice.

31st December, Wednesday.—Marched ; had frequently to cross the river on the ice, horses falling down, we were obliged to pull them over on the ice.   The river turned so much to the north, as almost induced us to believe it was the Arkansaw.   Distance 10 3-4 miles.

1st January 1807, *Thursday.*—The doctor and one man marched early, in order to precede the party until they should kill a supply of provision.   We had great difficulty in getting our horses along, some of the poor animals having nearly killed themselves falling on the ice.   Found on the way one of the mountain rams which the doctor and Brown had killed and left in the road.   Skinned it with horns &c.   At night ascended a mountain, and discovered a prairie ahead about eight miles, the news of which gave great joy to the party.

2d January, Friday.—Laboured all day, but made only one mile, many of our horses much wounded in falling on the rocks.   Provision growing short, left Stoute and Miller with two loads, to come on with a sled on the ice, which was on the water in some of the coves.   Finding it almost impossible to proceed any further with the horses by the bed of the river, ascended the mountain and immediately after were again obliged to descend an almost perpendicular side of the mountain ; in effecting which, one horse fell down the precipice, and bruised himself so miserably, that I conceived it mercy to cause the poor animal to be shot.   Many others were nearly killed with falls received : left two more men with loads and tools to make sleds.   The two men we had left in the morning had passed us.

3d January, Saturday.—Left two more men to make sleds and come on.   We pursued the river, and with great difficulty made six miles by frequently cutting roads on the ice, and covering it with earth, in order to go round precipices, &c. The men left in the morning encamped with us at night, but those of the day before, we saw nothing off. This day two of the horses became senseless, from the bruises received on the rocks, and were obliged to be left.

4th January, Sunday.—We made the prairie about three o'clock, when I detached Mr. Baroney and two soldiers with the horses, in order to find some practicable way for them to get out of the mountains light; I then divided the others into two parties of two men each, to make sleds and bring on the baggage. I determined to continue down the river alone, until I could kill some sustenance, and find the two men who left us on the 2d inst. or the doctor and his companion, for we had no provision, and every one had then to depend on his own exertion for safety and subsistance. Thus we were divided into eight different parties, viz. 1st. The doctor and his companion ; 2d. The two men with the first sled ; 3d. The interpreter and the two men with the horses ; 4th. Myself ; 5th. 6th. 7th. and 8th. two men each with sleds at different distances ; all of whom except the last, had orders, if they killed any game, to secure some part in a conspicuous place, for their companions in the rear. I marched on about five miles on the river, which was one continued fall through a narrow channel and immense cliffs on both sides. Near night I came to a place where the rocks were perpendicular on both sides, and no ice (except a narrow border) on the water. I began to look about, in order to discover which way the doctor and his companion had managed, and to find what had become of the two lads with the first sled, when I discovered one of the latter climbing up the side of the rocks ; I called to him; he and his companion immediately joined me; they said they had not known whether we were before or in the rear; that they had eaten nothing for the last two days, and that this night they had intended to have boiled a deer skin to subsist on. We at length discovered a narrow ravine, where was the trace of the doctor and his companion; as the water had ran down it and frozen hard, it was one continued sheet of ice; we ascended it with the utmost difficulty and danger, loaded with the baggage. On the summit of the first ridge we found an encampment of the doctor, and where they had killed a deer, but they had now no meat. He afterwards informed me that they had left the greatest part of it hanging on a tree, but supposed the birds had destroyed it. I left the boys to bring up the remainder of the baggage, and went out in order to kill some subsistence: wounded a deer, but the darkness of the night approaching, could not find him, when I returned hungry, weary and dry, and had only snow to supply the calls of nature. Distance 8 miles.

5th January, Monday.—I went out in the morning to hunt, whilst the two lads were bringing up some of their loads still left at the foot of the mountain. Wounded several deer, but was surprised to find I killed none, and on examining my gun, discovered her bent, owing as I suppose, to some fall on the ice, or rocks; shortly after received a fall, on the side of a hill, which broke her off by the breach; this put me into *desespoir*, as I calculated on it, as my grandest resource for great part of my party; returned to my companions sorely fatigued and hungry; I then took a double barrelled gun and left them, with assurances that the first animal I killed, I would return with part for their relief. About ten o'clock rose the highest summit of the mountain, when the unbounded space of the prairies again presented themselves to my view, and from some distant peaks, I immediately recognized it to be the outlet of the Arkansaw, which we had left nearly one month since! This was a great mortification, but at the same time I consoled myself with the knowledge I had acquired of the source of the La Platte and Arkansaw rivers, with the river to the north west, supposed to be the Pierre Jaun, which scarcely any person but a madman would ever purposely attempt to trace any further than the entrance of those mountains, which had hitherto secured their sources from the scrutinizing eye of civilized man.

I arrived at the foot of the mountain, and bank of the river, in the afternoon, and at the same time discovered on the other shore, Baroney with the horses; they had found quite an eligible pass, and had killed one buffalo and some deer. We proceeded to our old camp, which we had left the 10th of December, and re-occupied it. Saw the traces of the doctor and his companion, but could not discover their retreat.

This was my birth-day, and most fervently did I hope never to pass another so miserably. Distance 7 miles. Fired a gun off as a signal for the doctor.

6th January, Tuesday.—Dispatched the two soldiers back with some provision to meet the first lads, and assist them on, and the interpreter a hunting. About eight o'clock the doctor came in, having seen some of the men. He had been confined to the camp for one or two days, by a vertigo which proceeded from some berries he had eaten on the mountains. His companion brought down six deer, which they had at their camp; thus we again began to be out of danger of starving. In the afternoon, some of the men arrived, and part were immediately returned with provisions, &c. Killed three deer.

7th January, Wednesday.—Sent more men back to

assist in the rear, and to carry the poor fellows provisions; at the same time kept Baroney and one man hunting..... Killed three deer.

8th January, Thursday.—Some of the different parties arrived. Put one man to stocking my rifle; others sent back to assist up the rear. Killed two deer.

9th January, Friday.—The whole party was once more joined together, when we felt comparatively happy, notwithstanding the great mortifications I experienced at having been so egregiously deceived as to the Red river. I now felt at considerable loss how to proceed, as any idea of services at that time from my horses were entirely preposterous; thus after various plans formed and rejected, and the most mature deliberation, I determined to build a small place for defence and deposit, and leave part of the baggage, horses, my interpreter and one man, and with the balance, our packs of Indian presents, ammunition, tools, &c. on our backs, cross the mountains on foot, find the Red river, and then send back a party to conduct their horses and baggage by the most eligible route we could discover, by which time the horses would be so recovered as to be able to endure the fatigues of the march. In consequence of this determination, some were put to constructing the block houses, some to hunting, some to taking care of horses, &c. &c. I, myself, made preparations to pursue a course of observations, which would enable me to ascertain the latitude and longitude of that situation, which I conceived to be an important one. Killed three deer.

10th January, Saturday.—Killed five deer; took equal altitudes; angular distances of two stars, &c. but do not now recollect which. Killed three deer.

11th January, Sunday.—Ascertained the latitude and took the angular distances of some stars. Killed four deer.

12th January, Monday.—Preparing the baggage for a march by separating it, &c. Observations continued.

13th January, Tuesday.—Weighed out each man's pack. This day I obtained the angle between sun and moon, which I conceived the most correct way I possessed of ascertaining the longitude, as an immersion and emersion of Jupiter's satellites could not now be obtained. Killed four deer.

14th January, Wednesday.—We marched our party, consisting of 18 soldiers, the doctor and myself, each of us carrying 45lb. and as much provision as he thought proper, which, with arms, &c. made on an average, 70lbs. leaving Baroney and one man, Patrick Smith.

We crossed the first ridge (leaving the main branch of the river to the north of us,) and struck on the south fork, on which we encamped, intending to pursue it thro' the mountains, as its course was more southerly.

The doctor killed one deer. Distance 13 miles.

15th January, Thursday.—Followed up this branch and passed the main ridge, of what I term the Blue Mountains. Halted early. The doctor, myself, and one hunter, went out with our guns, each killed a deer, and brought them into camp. Distance 19 miles.

16th January, Friday.—Marched up the creek all day. Encamped early as it was snowing. I went out to hunt, but killed nothing. Deer on the hill; the mountains lessening. Distance 18 miles.

17th January, Saturday.—Marched about four miles, when the great White Mountain presented itself before us, in sight of which we had been for more than one month, and through which we supposed lay the long sought Red river. We now left the creek on the north of us, and bore away more east, to a low place in the mountains. About sun-set we came to the edge of a prairie, which bounded the foot of the mountain, and as there was no wood or water where we were, and the woods from the skirts of the mountains appeared to be at no great distance, I thought proper to march for it; in the middle of said prairie, crossed the creek, which now bore east. Here we all got our feet wet. The night commenced extremely cold. When we halted at the woods, at eight o'clock, for encampment; after getting fires made, we discovered that the feet of nine of our men were frozen, and to add to the misfortune, of both of those whom we called hunters among the number. This night we had no provision. Reaumer's thermometer stood at 18 1-2° below 0. Distance 28 miles.

18th January, Sunday.—We started two of the men least injured; (the doctor and myself, who fortunately were untouched by the frost) also went out to hunt something to preserve existence, near evening we wounded a buffalo with three balls, but had the mortification to see him run off notwithstanding. We concluded it was useless to go home to add to the general gloom, and went amongst some rocks where we encamped and sat up all night; from the intense cold it was impossible to sleep. Hungry and without cover.

19th January, Monday.—We again took the field and after crawling about one mile in the snow, got to shoot eight times among a gang of buffalo, and could plainly perceive two or three to be badly wounded, but by accident they took the wind of us, and to our great mortification all were able to run off. By this time I had become extremely weak and faint, being the fourth day, since we had received sustenance; all of which we were marching hard and the last night had scarcely closed our eyes to sleep. We were inclining our course to a point of woods determined to remain absent and die by ourselves rather than to return to our camp and behold the misery of our poor lads, when we discovered a gang of buffalo coming along at some distance. With great exertions I made out to run and place myself behind some cedars and by the greatest of good luck, the first shot stopped one, which we killed in three more shots; and by the dusk had cut each of us a heavy load with which we determined immediately to proceed to the camp in order to relieve the anxiety of our men, and carry the poor fellows some food. We arrived there about 12 o'clock, and when I threw my load down, it was with difficulty I prevented myself from falling; I was attacked with a giddiness of the head, which lasted for some minutes. On the countenances of the men was not a frown, nor a desponding eye; but all seemed happy to hail their officer and companions, yet not a mouthful had they eat for four days. On demanding what was their thoughts, the sergeant replied, on the morrow the most robust had determined to set out in search of us; and not return unless they found us, or killed something to preserve the life of their starving companions.

20*th January, Tuesday.*—The doctor and all the men able to march, returned to the buffalo to bring in the balance of the meat.

On examining the feet of those who were frozen we found it impossible for two of them to proceed, and two others only without loads by the help of a stick. One of the former was my waiter, a promising young lad of twenty whose feet were so badly frozen, as to present every probability of loosing them.

The doctor and party returned towards evening loaded with the buffalo meat.

21*st January, Wednesday.*—This day, separated the four loads, we intended to leave and took them at some distance from the camp, where we secured them. I went up to the foot of the mountain to see what prospect there was of being able to cross it, but had not more than fairly arrived at its base, when I found the snow four or five feet deep ; this obliged me to determine to proceed and cotoyer the mountain to the south, where it appeared lower, and until we found a place where we could cross.

22d January, Thursday.—I furnished the two poor lads who were to remain with ammunition and made use of every argument in my power to encourage them to have fortitude to resist their fate ; and gave them assurance of my sending relief as soon as possible.

We parted, but not without tears. We pursued our march, taking merely sufficient provisions for one meal in order to leave as much as possible for the two poor fellows, who remained (who were John Sparks and Thomas Dougherty.) We went on eight miles and encamped on a little creek, which came down from the mountains; at three o'clock went out to hunt, but killed nothing. Little snow.

23d January, Friday.—After shewing the sergeant a point to steer for, the doctor and myself proceeded on ahead in hopes to kill something, as we were again without victuals. About one o'clock it commenced snowing very hard, we retreated to a small copse of pine where we constructed a camp to shelter us, and as it was time the party should arrive, we sallied forth to search them. We separated and had not marched more than one or two miles, when I found it impossible to keep any course without the compass, continually in my hand, and then not being able to see more than 10 yards. I began to perceive the difficulty even of finding the way back to our camp and I can scarcely conceive a more dreadful idea than remaining on the wild, where inevitable death must have ensued. It was with great pleasure I again reached the camp.

where I found the doctor had arrived before me. We lay down and strove to dissipate the idea of hunger, and our misery by the thoughts of our far distant homes and relatives. Distance 8 miles.

24th January, Saturday.—We sallied out in the morning and shortly after perceived our little band, marching through the snow (about two and a half feet deep,) silent and with downcast countenances. We joined them and learnt that they finding the snow to fall so thickly that it was impossible to proceed; had encamped about one o'clock the preceeding day. As I found all the buffalo had quit the plains, I determined to attempt the traverse of the mountain, in which we persevered, until the snow became so deep, it was impossible to proceed ; when I again turned my face to the plain and for the first time in the voyage found myself discouraged ; and the first time I heard a man express himself in a seditious manner ; he exclaimed, " that it was more than human nature could bear, to " march three days without sustenance, through snows " three feet deep, and carry burthens only fit for hor- " ses" &c. &c.

As I knew very well the fidelity and attachment of the majority of the men, and even of this poor fellow, (only he could not endure fasting) and that it was in my power to chastise him, when I thought proper, I passed it unnoticed for the moment, determined to notice it at a more auspicious time. We dragged our weary and emaciated limbs along, until about 10 o'clock. The doctor and myself who were in advance discovered some buffalo on the plain, when we left our loads, and orders on the snow, to proceed to the nearest woods to encamp. We went in pursuit of the buffalo, which were on the move.

The doctor who was then less reduced than myself, ran and got behind a hill and shot one down, which stop-

ped the remainder. We crawled up to the dead one and shot from him as many as twelve or fourteen times among the gang; when they removed out of sight. We then proceeded to butcher the one we had shot; and after procuring each of us a load of the meat, we marched for the camp, the smoke of which was in view. We arrived at the camp to the great joy of our brave lads, who immediately feasted sumptuously, after our repast I sent for the lad who had presumed to speak discontentedly in the course of the day, and addressed him to the following effect : " *Brown*, you this day presumed to make use of lan-
" guage which was seditious and mutinous ; I then pass-
" ed it over, pitying your situation and attributing it to
" your distress, rather than your inclination, to sow dis-
" content amongst the party. Had I reserved provisions
" for ourselves, whilst you were starving; had we been
" marching along light and at our ease, whilst you were
" weighed down with your burden ; then you would have
" had some pretext for your observations ; but when we
" were equally hungry, weary, emaciated and charged
" with burden, which I believe my natural strength is less
" able to bear, than any man's in the party ; when we are
" always foremost in breaking the road, reconnoitering and
" the fatigues of the chace; it was the height of ingratitude
" in you, to let an expression escape which was indica-
" tive of discontent ; your ready compliance and firm per-
" severance, I had reason to expect, as the leader of men
" and my companions, in miseries and dangers. But your
" duty as a soldier called on your obedience to your officer,
" and a prohibition of such language, which for this time,
" I will pardon, but assure you, should it ever be repeated,
" by instant *death*, I will revenge your ingratitude and
" punish your disobedience. I take this opportunity like-
" wise to assure you, soldiers generally of my thanks for

" obedience, perseverance and ready contempt of every
" danger, which you have generally evinced; I assure you
" nothing shall be wanting on my part, to procure you
" the rewards of our government and gratitude of your
" countrymen."

They all appeared very much affected, and retired with
assurances of perseverance in duty &c. Distance 9 miles.

25th January, Sunday.—I determined never again
to march with so little provision on hand; as had the
storm continued one day longer, the animals would have
continued in the mountains, and we should have became
so weak as not to be able to hunt, and of course have
perished.

The doctor went out with the boys, and they secured
three of the buffalo; we commenced bringing in the meat,
at which we continued all day.

26th January, Monday.—Got in all the meat and dried
it on a scaffold, intending to take as much as possible along
and leave one of my frozen lads with the balance, as a
deposit for the parties who might return for their baggage &c. on their way to Baroney's camp.

27th January, Tuesday.—We marched, determining
to cross the mountains, leaving Menaugh encamped with
our deposit, after a bad days march, through snows, some
places three feet deep; we struck on a brook which led
west, which I followed down, and shortly came to a small
run, running west; which we hailed with fervency as the
waters of the Red river. Saw some sign of elk. Distance
14 miles.

28th January, Wednesday.—Followed down the ravine
and discovered after some time that there had been a road
cut out, and on many trees were various hieroglyphicks
painted; after marching some miles, we discovered through
the lengthy vista at a distance, another chain of mountains

and nearer by at the foot of the White mountains, which
we were then descending, sandy hills.   We marched on
the outlet of the mountains, and left the sandy desert to
our right; kept down between it and the mountain.....
When we encamped, I ascended one of the largest hills
of sand, and with my glass could discover a large river,
flowing nearly north by west, and south by east, through
the plain which came out of the third chain of mountains,
about N. 75° W. the prairie between the two mountains bore nearly north and south.   I returned to camp
with the news of my discovery.   The sand hills extended
up and down at the foot of the White mountains, about
15 miles, and appeared to be about five miles in width.

Their appearance was exactly that of the sea in a
storm, (except as to color) not the least sign of vegetation
existing thereon.   Distance 15 miles.

29th January, Thursday.—Finding the distance too
great to attempt crossing immediately to the river, in a direct line, we marched obliquely to a copse of woods,
which made down a considerable distance from the mountains.   Distance 17 miles.   Saw sign of horses.

30th January, Friday.—We marched hard, and arrived in the evening on the banks (then supposed Red
river) of the Rio del Norte.   Distance 24 miles.

31st January, Saturday—As there was no timber
here we determined on descending until we found timber,
in order to make transports to descend the river with,
where we might establish a position that four or five might
defend against the insolence, cupidity and barbarity of the
savages, whilst the others returned to assist on the poor
fellows who were left behind, at different points.   We
descended 18 miles, when we met a large west branch,
emptying into the main stream, up which about five miles,

we took up our station. Killed one deer. Distance 18 miles.

1st February, Sunday.—Laid out the place for our works, and went out hunting.

2d February, Monday.—The doctor and myself went out to hunt, and with great difficulty, by night, killed one deer, at the distance of seven or eight miles from camp, which we carried in.

3d February, Tuesday.—Spent in reading, &c.

4th February, Wednesday.—Went out hunting, but could not kill any thing. One of my men killed a deer.

5th February, Thursday.—The doctor and myself went out to hunt, and after chasing some deer for several hours, without success, we ascended a high hill, which lay south of our camp, from whence we had a view of all the prairie and rivers to the north of us ; it was at the same time one of the most sublime and beautiful inland prospects ever presented to the eyes of man. The prairie lying nearly north and south, was probably 60 miles by 45.

The main river bursting out of the western mountain, and meeting from the north-east, a large branch, which divides the chain of mountains, proceeds down the prairie, making many large and beautiful islands, one of which I judge contains 100,000 acres of land, all meadow ground, covered with innumerable herds of deer ; about six miles from the mountains which cross the prairie, at the south end, a branch of 12 steps wide, pays its tribute to the main stream from the west course. Due W. 12°. N. 75°. W. 6°. Four miles below is a stream of the same size, which enters on the east ; its general course is N. 65°. E. up which was a large road ; from the entrance of this down, was about three miles, to the junction of the west fork, which waters the foot of the hill on the north, whilst the main river wound along in meanders on the east. In short,

this view combined the sublime and beautiful; the great
and lofty mountains covered with eternal snows, seemed
to surround the luxuriant vale, crowned with perennial
flowers, like a terrestrial paradise, shut out from the view
of man.

    6th February, Friday.—The doctor having some pe-
cuniary demands in the province of New Mexico, conceived this to be the most eligible point for him to go in,
and return previous to all my party having joined me
from the Arkansaw, and that I was prepared to descend to
Natchitoches: he therefore this day made his preparations
for marching to-morrow. I went out hunting, and killed
a deer at three miles distance, which, with great difficulty
I brought in whole.

    We continued to go on with the works of our stock-
ade or breast work, which was situated on the north bank
of the west branch, about five miles from its junction with
the main river, and was on a strong plan.*

---

* The stockade was situated in a small prairie on the west fork of the Rio del
Norte. The south flank joining the edge of the river (which at that place was
not fordable), the east and west curtains were flanked by bastions in the north-east
and north-west angles, which likewise flanked the curtain of the north side of the
work. The stockade from the centre of the angle of the bastions was 36 feet
square. There were heavy cotton-wood logs, about two feet diameter, laid up
all round about six feet, after which lighter ones, until we made it twelve feet in
height: those logs were joined together by a lap of about two feet at each end.
We then dug a small ditch on the inside all round, making it perpendicular on the
internal side and sloping next the work. In this ditch we planted small stakes, of
about six inches diameter, sharpened at the upper end to a nice point, slanted them
over the top of the work, giving them about two feet and a half projection. We
then secured them below and above in that position, which formed a small pointed
frise, which must have been removed before the works could have been scaled.
Lastly, we had dug a ditch round the whole four feet wide, and let the water in
all round, the earth taken out being thrown against the work formed an excellent
rampart against small arms three or four feet high. Our mode of getting in was
to crawl over the ditch on a plank, and into a small hole sunk below the level of
the work near the river for that purpose. Our port-holes were pierced about eight
feet from the ground, and a platform prepared to shoot from.

7th February, Saturday.—The doctor marched alone for Santa Fe,* and as it was uncertain whether this gentleman would ever join me again, I at that time, committed the following testimonial of respect for his good qualities to paper, which I do not, at this time, feel any disposition to efface. He has had the benefit of a liberal education, without having spent his time as too many of our gentlemen do in colleges, viz. in skimming on the surfaces of sciences, without ever endeavouring to make themselves masters of the solid foundations, but Robinson studied and reasoned ; with these qualifications he possessed a liberality of mind too great ever to reject an hypothesis, because it was not agreeable to the dogmas of the schools ; or adopt it, because it had all the eclat of novelty—his soul could conceive great actions, and his hand was ready to atchieve them ; in short, it may truly be said that nothing was

Thus fortified, I should not have had the least hesitation of putting the 100 Spanish horse at defiance until the first or second night, and then to have made our escape under cover of the darkness—or made a sally and dispersed them, when resting under a full confidence of our being panic struck by their numbers and force.

* The demands which Dr. Robinson had on persons in New Mexico, although legitimate, were in some degree spurious *in his hands :* the circumstances were as follow : viz.—In the year 1804 William Morrison Esq. an enterprising merchant, of Kaskaskias, sent a man by the name of Babtiste La Lande, a Creole of the country up the Missouri and La Platte, directing him if possible to push into Santa Fe. He sent in Indians, and the Spaniards came out with horses and carried him and his goods into the province. Finding that he sold the goods high, had land offered him and the woman kind : he concluded to expatriate himself and convert the property of Morrison to his own benefit. When I was about to sail. Morrison, conceiving that it was possible that I might meet some Spanish factors on the Red river, intrusted me with the claim, in order, if they were acquainted with La Lande, I might negotiate the thing with some of them. When on the frontiers, the idea suggested itself to us of making this claim a pretext for Robinson to visit Santa Fe. We therefore gave it the proper appearance, and he marched for that place. Our views were to gain a knowledge of the country, the prospect of trade, force, &c. whilst, at the same time, our treaties with Spain guaranteed to him, as a citizen of the United States, the right of seeking the recovery of all just debts or demands before the legal and authorised tribunals of the country, as a franchised inhabitant of the same, as specified in the 22d article of said treaty.

above his genius, nor any thing so minute that he conceived it entirely unworthy of consideration. As a gentleman and companion in dangers, difficulties and hardships, I in particular, and the expedition, generally, owe much to his exertions. In the evening I dispatched corporal Jackson, with four men, to re-cross the mountains, in order to bring in the baggage left with the frozen lads, and to see if they were yet able to come on. This detachment left me with four men only ; two of which had their feet frozen : they were employed in finishing the stockade, and myself to support them by the chase.

8th February, Sunday.—Refreshing my memory as to the French grammar, and overseeing the works.

9th February, Monday.—Hunting, &c.

10th February, Tuesday.—Read and labored at our works.

11th February, Wednesday.—Hunting. Killed three deer.

12th February, Thursday.—Studying.

13th February, Friday.—Hunting. Killed two deer.

14th February, Saturday.—Crossed the river and examined the numerous springs, which issued from the foot of the hill, opposite to our camp, which were so strongly impregnated with mineral qualities, as not only to keep clear of ice previous to their joining the main branch, but to keep open the west fork until its junction with the main river, and for a few miles afterwards, whilst all the other branches in the neighbourhood were bound in the adamantine chains of winter.

15th February, Sunday.—Reading, &c. Works going on.

16th February, Monday.—I took one man and went out hunting, about six miles from the post, shot and wounded a deer. Immediately afterwards, discovered two horsemen rising the summit of a hill, about half a mile to our right. As my orders were to avoid giving alarm or offence to the Spanish government of New Mexico, I endeavoured to avoid them at first, but when we attempted to retreat, they persued us at full charge, flourishing their lances, and when we advanced, they would retire as fast as their horses could carry them; seeing this we got in a small ravine, in hopes to decoy them near enough to oblige them to come to a parley, which happened agreeably to our desires, as they came on hunting us with great caution; we suffered them to get within 40 yards, where we had allured them, but were about running off again, when I ordered the soldier to lay down his arms and walk towards them; at the same time standing ready with my rifle to kill either, who should lift an arm in an hostile manner; I then hollowed to them, that we were Americans, and friends, which were almost the only two words I knew in the Spanish language; when with great signs of fear they came up, and proved to be a Spanish dragoon and a civilized Indian, armed after their manner, of which we see a description in the *Essai Militaire*. We were jealous of our arms on both sides, and acted with great precaution. They informed me that was the fourth day since they had left Santa Fe; that Robinson had arrived there, and was received with great kindness by the governor. As I knew them to be spies, I thought proper to inform them merely, that I was about to descend the river to Natchitoches. We sat here on the ground a long time, and finding they were determined not to leave me, we rose and bid them adieu, but they demanded where our camp was; and finding they were not about to leave us, I thought it most proper to take them with me, thinking we were on Red river, and of course in the territory claimed by the United States.

We took the road to my fort, and as they were on horseback, they travelled rather faster than myself; they were halted by the sentinel, and immediately retreated much surprised. When I came up, I took them in, and then explained to them, as well as possible, my intentions of descending the river to Natchitoches, but at the same time told them that if governor Allencaster would send out an officer with an interpreter, who spoke French or English, I would do myself the pleasure to give his excellency every reasonable satisfaction as to my intentions in coming on his frontiers. They informed me that on the second day they would be in Santa Fe, but were careful never to suggest an idea of my being on the Rio del Norte. As they concluded, I did not think as I spoke; they were very anxious to ascertain our numbers, &c.; seeing only five men here, they could not believe we came without horses, &c. To this I did not think proper to give them any satisfaction, giving them to understand we were in many parties, &c.

17th February, Tuesday.—In the morning, our two Spanish visitors departed, after I had made them some trifling presents, with which they seemed highly delighted. After their departure, we commenced working at our little work, as I thought it probable the governor might dispute my right to descend the Red river, and send out Indians, or some light party to attack us; I therefore determined to be as much prepared to receive them as possible. This evening the corporal and three of the men arrived, who had been sent back to the camp of the frozen lads. They informed me that two men would arrive the next day; one of which was Menaugh, who had been left alone on the 27th January, but that the other two, Dougherty and

Sparks, were unable to come. They said that they had hailed them with tears of joy, and were in despair when they again left them, with the chance of never seeing them more. They sent on to me some of the bones taken out of their feet, and conjured me by all that was sacred, not to leave them to perish far from the civilized world. Ah! little did they know my heart, if they could suspect me of conduct so ungenerous. No! before they should be left, I would for months have carried the end of a litter, in order to secure them, the happiness of once more seeing their native homes; and being received in the bosom of a grateful country.

Thus those poor lads are to be invalids for life, made infirm at the commencement of manhood and in the prime of their course, doomed to pass the remainder of their days in misery and want; for what is the pension? not sufficient to buy a man his victuals! what man would even lose the smallest of his joints for such a trifling pittance.

18th February, Wednesday.—The other two boys arrived; in the evening I ordered the sergeant and one man to prepare to march to-morrow for the Arkansaw, where we had left our interpreter, horses, &c. to conduct them on, and on his return to bring the two lads who were still in the mountains.

19th February, Thursday.—Sergeant William E. Meek, marched with one man, whose name was Theodore Miller, and I took three other men to accompany him out some distance, in order to point out to him a pass in the mountain, which I conceived more eligible for horses than the one we had come. I must here remark the effect of habit, discipline and example in two soldiers soliciting a command of more than 180 miles over two great ridges of mountains covered with snow, inhabited by lands of unknown savages, in the interest of a nation, with whom

we were not on the best understanding ; and to perform
this journey, each had about ten pounds of venison ; only
let me ask what would our soldiers generally think, on
being ordered on such a tour, thus equipped? yet those
men volunteered it, with others and were chosen ; for
which they thought themselves highly honored ; we accompanied them about six miles, pointed out the pass
alluded to, in a particular manner, but the corporal reported that the new one which I obliged him to take was
impassable, having been three days in snows nearly middle
deep.

We then separated and having killed a deer, sent one
of the men back to the fort with it.   With the other two, I
kept on my exploring trip down the river on the east side,
at some leagues from its banks, intending to return up it ;
at nine o'clock at night, encamped on a small creek which
emptied into the river by nearly a due east course.

20th February, Friday.—We marched down the river
for a few hours, but seeing no fresh sign of persons, or any
other object to attract our attention took up our route for
the fort ; discovered the sign of horses and men on the
shore.   We arrived after night and found all well.

21st February, Saturday.—As I was suspicious that
possibly some party of indians might be harboring round,
I gave particular orders to my men, if they discovered any
people to endeavor to retreat undiscovered but if not,
never to run, and not to suffer themselves to be disarmed
or taken prisoners but conduct whatever party discovered them, if they could not escape to the fort.

22d February, Sunday.—As I began to think it was
time we received a visit from the Spaniards or their emisa-
ries, I established a look out guard on the top of a hill all
day and at night a sentinel in a bastion on the land side ;

studying, reading &c.   Working at our ditch to bring the river round the works.

23d February, Monday.—Reading, writing &c. the men at their usual work, &c.

24th February, Tuesday.—Took one man with me and went out on the Spanish road hunting; killed one deer and wounded several others; and as we were a great distance from the fort, we encamped near the road all night. Saw several signs of horses.

25th February, Wednesday.—Killed two more deer when we marched for our post.   Took all three of the deer with us, and arrived about 9 o'clock at night, as much fatigued &c. as ever I was in my life.   Our arrival dissipated the anxiety of the men, who began to be apprehensive we were taken or killed by some of the savages.

26th February, Thursday.—In the morning was apprized by the report of a gun, from my lookout guard; of the approach of strangers.   Immediately after two Frenchmen arrived.

My sentinel halted them and ordered them to be admitted after some questions; they informed me that his excellency governor Allencaster had heard it was the intention of the Utah Indians, to attack me; had detached an officer with 50 dragoons to come out and protect me, and that they would be here in two days.   To this I made no reply; but shortly after the party came in sight to the number of, I afterwards learnt 50 dragoons and 50 mounted militia of the province, armed in the same manner, viz : Lances, escopates and pistols.   My sentinel halted them at the distance of about 50 yards.   I had the works manned.   I thought it most proper to send out the two Frenchmen to inform the commanding officer that it was my request he should leave his party in a small copse of woods where he halted, and that I would meet him myself in the prairie, in which our work was situated. This I did, with my sword on me only. When I was introduced to Don Ignatio Saltelo and Don Bartholemew Fernandez, two lieutenants, the former the commandant of the party. I gave them an invitation to enter the works, but requested the troops might remain where they were; this was complied with, but when they came round and discovered that to enter, they were obliged to crawl on their bellies over a small draw-bridge, they appeared astonished but entered without further hesitation.

We first breakfasted on some deer, meal, goose and some biscuit (which the civilized indian who came out as a spy) had brought me, After breakfast the commanding officer addressed me as follows: " Sir, the governor of " New Mexico, being informed you had missed your route, " ordered me to offer you, in his name, mules, horses, " money, or whatever you may stand in need of to con- " duct you to the head of Red river; as from Santa Fe to " where it is sometimes navigable, is eight days journey " and we have guides and the routes of the traders to " conduct us." " What, said I, (interrupting him) is not " this the Red river," " No sir! the Rio del Norte." I immediately ordered my flag to be taken down and rolled up, feeling how sensibly I had committed myself, in entering their territory, and was conscious that they must have positive orders to take me in.

" He now" added " that he had provided one hun- " dred mules and horses, to take in my party and baggage " and how anxious his excellency was to see me at Santa " Fe." I stated to him, the absence of my sergeant, the situation of the balance of the party and that my orders would not justify my entering into the Spanish territory. He urged still further until I began to feel myself a little heated in the argument and told him in a peremptory style, I

would not go until the arrival of my sergeant with the balance of the party. He replied that there was not the least restraint to be used, only that it was necessary his excellency should receive an explanation of my business on his frontier, but that I could go now, or on the arrival of my party; but that if none went in at present he should be obliged to send in for provisions, but that if I would now march, he would leave an Indian interpreter and an escort of dragoons to conduct the sergeant into Santa Fe. His mildness induced me to tell him that I would march, but must leave two men, in order to meet the sergeant and party, to instruct him as to coming in, as he never would come without a fight, if not ordered.

I was induced to consent to the measure, by conviction, that the officer had positive orders to bring me in, and as I had no orders to commit hostilities, and indeed had committed myself, although innocently, by violating their territory, I conceived it would appear better to shew a will to come to an explanation than to be any way constrained; yet my situation was so eligible, and I could so easily have put them at defiance, that it was with great reluctance I suffered all our labor to be lost without once trying the efficacy of it.

My compliance seemed to spread general joy through their party as soon as it was communicated, but it appeared to be different with my men, who wished to have a little *dust* (as they expressed themselves) and were likewise fearful of treachery.

My determination being once taken, I gave permission for the Spanish lieutenant's men to come to the outside of the works, and some of mine to go out and see them; when the hospitality and goodness of the Creoles and Metifs began to manifest itself by their producing

their provision and giving it to my men, covering them with their blankets, &c.

After writing orders to my sergeant, and leaving them with my corporal and one private, who was to remain, we sallied forth, mounted our horses, and went up the river about 12 miles, to a place where the Spanish officers had made a camp deposit, from whence we sent down mules for our baggage, &c.

Z. M. PIKE, Captain,
1st United States Battalion Infantry.

Washington City, January, 1808.

PIKE'S EXPEDITION.

PART III.

———————

DIARY OF A TOUR, MADE THROUGH THE INTERIOR
PROVINCES OF NEW SPAIN, IN THE YEAR 1807,
BY CAPTAIN Z. M. PIKE, OF THE ARMY OF THE
UNITED STATES, WHEN UNDER AN ESCORT OF
SPANISH DRAGOONS.

27th February, Friday.—In the morning I discovered the Spanish lieutenant, was writing letters addressed to the governor and others; on which I demanded
if he was not going on with me to Santa Fe. He appeared
confused and said no: that his orders were so positive as
to the safe conduct and protection of my men, that he dare
not go and leave any behind; that his companion would
accompany me to Santa Fe with 50 men, whilst he with
the others would wait for the sergeant and his party. I
replied that he had deceived me and had not acted with
candor; but that it was now too late for me to remedy the
evil.

We marched about 11 o'clock, ascending the Rio del
Norte, five miles more S. 60° W. when we went round
through a chain of hills and bore off to the south. We
proceeded on nine miles further, when we crossed the

main branch of that stream, which was now bearing nearly west towards the main chain of the third chain of mountains. We encamped on the opposite side. Distance 15 miles. Intensely cold, obliged to stop frequently and make fires. Snow deep.

28th February, Saturday.—We marched late. One of the Frenchmen informed me, that the expedition which had been at the Pawnees, had descended the Red river 233 leagues and from thence crossed to the Pawnees expressly in search of my party (this was afterwards confirmed by the gentleman who commanded the troops.) He then expressed great regret at my misfortunes, as he termed them in being taken, and offered his services in secreting papers &c. I took him at his word, and for my amusement I thought I would try him and give him, a leaf or two of my journal (copied) which mentioned the time of my sailing from Belle Fontaine, and our force. This I charged him to guard very carefully and give to me after the investigation of my papers at Santa Fe. This day we saw a herd of wild horses. The Spaniards pursued them and caught two colts, one of which the indians killed and eat; the other was let go. We pursued our journey over some hills, where the snow was very deep, and encamped at last on the top of a pretty high hill, among some pines. Distance 36 miles. We left the river which in general ran about 6, 8, and 10 miles to the left or east of us. Saw great sign of elk.

1st March, Sunday.—We marched early and although we rode very hard we only got to the village of L'eau Chaud or Warm Spring, sometime in the afternoon, which was about 45 miles. The difference of climate was astonishing, after we left the hills and deep snows, we found ourselves on plains where there was no snow, and where vegetation was sprouting.

The village of the Warm Springs or Aqua caliente (in their language) is situated on the eastern branch of a creek of that name, and at a distance, presents to the eye a square enclosure of mud walls, the houses forming the wall. They are flat on top, or with extremely little ascent on one side, where there are spouts to carry off the water of the melting snow and rain when it falls, which we were informed, had been but once in two years, previous to our entering the country.

Inside of the enclosure were the different streets of houses of the same fashion, all of one story; the doors were narrow, the windows small, and in one or two houses there were talc lights. This village had a mill near it, situated on the little creek, which made very good flour.

The population consisted of civilized Indians, but much mixed blood.

Here we had a dance which is called the *Fandango*, but there was one which was copied from the Mexicans, and is now danced in the first societies of New Spain, and has even been introduced at the court of Madrid.*

This village may contain 500 souls. The greatest natural curiosity is the warm springs, which are two in number, about 10 yards apart, and each afford sufficient water for a mill seat. They appeared to be impregnated with copper, and were more than 33° above blood heat. From this village the Tetaus drove off 2000 horses at one time, when at war with the Spaniards.

2d March, Monday.—We marched late, and passed several little mud walled villages and settlements, all of which had round mud towers of the ancient shape and construction, to defend the inhabitants from the intrusions of the savages. I was this day shewn the ruins of several

* See description and dissertation on morals, manners, &c. in Appendix to Part III. p. 36.

old villages, which had been taken and destroyed by the Tetaus. We were frequently stopped by the women, who invited us into their houses to eat; and in every place where we halted a moment, there was a contest who should be our hosts. My poor lads who had been frozen, were conducted home by old men, who would cause their daughters to dress their feet; provide their victuals and drink, and at night, gave them the best bed in the house. In short, all their conduct brought to my recollection the hospitality of the ancient patriarchs, and caused me to sigh with regret at the corruption of that noble principle, by the polish of modern ages.

We descended the creek of Aqua Caliente, about 12 miles, where it joined the river of Conejos from the west. This river was about 30 yards wide, and was settled, above its junction with the Aqua Caliente, 12 miles, as the latter was its whole course from the village of that name. From where they form a junction, it was about 15 miles to the Rio del Norte, on the eastern branch of which was situated the village of St. John's, which was the residence of the president priest of the province, who had resided in it 40 years.

The house tops of the village of St. John's, were crowded, as well as the streets, when we entered, and at the door of the public quarters, we were met by the president priest. When my companion who commanded the escort, received him in a street and embraced him, all the poor creatures who stood round, strove to kiss the ring or hand of the holy father; for myself, I saluted him in the usual style. My men were conducted into the quarters, and I went to the house of the priest, where we were treated with politeness: he offered us coffee, chocolate, or whatever we thought proper, and desired me to consider myself at home in his house.

As I was going some time after, to the quarters of my men, I was addressed at the door by a man in broken English :—" My friend, I am very sorry to see you here : " we are all prisoners in this country and can never re- " turn : I have been a prisoner for nearly three years, and " cannot get out." I replied, " that as for his being a pri- " soner, it must be for some crime, that with respect to " myself, I felt no apprehension, and requested him to " speak French, as I could hardly understand his Eng- " lish." When he began to demand of me so many different questions on the mode of my getting into the country, my intention, &c.; that by the time I arrived in the room of my men, I was perfectly satisfied of his hav- ing been ordered by some person to endeavor to obtain some confession or acknowledgment of sinister designs in my having appeared on the frontiers, and some confidential communications which might implicate me. As he had been rather insolent in his enquiries, I ordered my men to shut and fasten the door ; I then told him that I believed him to be an emissary sent on purpose by the governor, or some person, to endeavour to betray me, that all men of that description were scoundrels, and never should escape pun- ishment, whilst I possessed the power to chastise them, immediately ordering my men to seize him, and cautioning him at the same time, that if he cried out, or made the least resistance, I would be obliged to make use of the sa- bre, which I had in my hand ; on which he was so much alarmed, that he begged me for God's sake not to injure him; that he had been ordered by the government to meet me, and endeavour to trace out, what, and who I was, and what were my designs, by endeavoring to pro- duce a confidence in him, by his exclaiming against the Spaniards, and complaining of the tyranny which they had exercised towards him. After this confession, I ordered my men to release him, and told him, that I looked upon him as too contemptible for further notice, but that he might tell the governor, the next time he employed emissaries, to choose those of more abilities and sense, and that I questioned if his excellency would find the sifting of us an easy task.

This man's name was Baptiste Lalande, he had come from the Illinois to the Pawnees, to trade with goods furnished him by William Morrison, a gentleman of the Illinois, and from thence to New Mexico with the goods, which he had procured and established himself, and was the same man on whom Robinson had a claim. He returned into the priest's house with me, and instead of making any complaint, he in reply to their enquiries of who I was, &c. informed them, that when he left Louisiana, I was governor of the Illinois. This I presume he took for granted from my having commanded for some time the post of Kaskaskias, the first military post the United States had established in that country since the peace; however the report served but to add to the respect with which my companion and host treated me. Having had at this place the first good meal, wine, &c. with the heat of the house, and perhaps rather an immoderate use of the refreshments allowed me, produced an attack of something like the cholera morbus, which alarmed me considerably, and made me determine to be more abstemious in future. This father was a great naturalist, or rather florist: he had large collections of flowers, plants, &c. and several works on his favorite studies, the margin and bottoms of which were filled with his notes in the Castilian language. As I had neither a natural turn for botany, sufficient to induce me to puzzle my head much with the Latin, and did not understand the Castilian, I enjoyed but little of his lectures, which he continued to give me nearly for two hours on those subjects, but by the exercise of a small degree of patience, I entirely acquired the esteem of this worthy father, he calling me his son, and lamenting extremely that my fate had not made me one of the holy catholic church.*

St. John's was enclosed with a mud wall, and probably contained 1000 souls; its population consisted principally of civilized Indians, as indeed does all the villages of New Mexico, the whites not forming the one twentieth part of the inhabitants.

3d March, Tuesday.—We marched after breakfast, B. Lalande accompanying us, and in about six miles came to a village, where I suppose there were more than 2000 souls. Here we halted at the house of the priest, who understanding that I would not kiss his hand, would not present it to me.

The conduct and behaviour of a young priest who came in, was such as in our country would have been amply sufficient forever to have banished him from the clerical association, strutting about with a dirk in his boot, a cane in his hand, whispering to one girl, chucking another under the chin, and going out with a third, &c. From this village to another small village of 500 inhabitants, is seven miles. At each of those villages is a small stream, sufficient for the purpose of watering their fields. At the father's house we took coffee. From this village, it was 17 miles to another of 400 civilized Indians. Here we changed horses and prepared for entering the capital, which we came in sight of in the evening. It is situated along the banks of a small creek, which comes down from the mountains, and runs west to the Rio del Norte. The length of the capital on the creek may be estimated at one mile; it is but three streets in width.

* See Appendix to Part III. [No. 7.] page 69.

Its appearance from a distance, struck my mind with the same effect as a fleet of the flat bottomed boats, which are seen in the spring and fall seasons, descending the Ohio river. There are two churches, the magnificence of whose steeples form a striking contrast to the miserable appearance of the houses. On the north side of the town is the square of soldiers houses, equal to 120 or 140 on each flank. The public square is in the centre of the town ; on the north side of which is situated the *palace* (as the term it) or government house, with the quarters for guards, &c. The other side of the square is occupied by the clergy and public officers. In general the houses have a shed before the front, some of which have a flooring of brick ; the consequence is, that the streets are very narrow, say in general 25 feet. The supposed population is 4,500 souls. On our entering the town, the crowd was great, and followed us to the government house. When we dismounted, we were ushered in through various rooms, the floors of which were covered with skins of buffalo, bear, or some other animal. We waited in a chamber for some time, until his excellency appeared, when we rose, and the following conversation took place in French.

Governor. Do you speak French ?

Pike. Yes sir.

Governor. You come to reconnoitre our country, do you ?

Pike. I marched to reconnoitre our own.

Governor. In what character are you ?

Pike. In my proper character, an officer of the United States army ?

Governor. And this Robinson, is he attached to your party ?

Pike. No.

Governor. Do you know him?

Pike. Yes, he is from St. Louis. [I had under-stood the doctor was sent 45 leagues from Santa Fe, un-der a strong guard, and the haughty and unfriendly recep-tion of the governor induced me to believe war must have been declared, and that if it was known Dr. Robinson accompanied me, he would be treated with great severity. I was correct in saying he was not attached to my party, for he was only a volunteer, he could not properly be said to be one of my command.]

Governor. How many men have you?

Pike. Fifteen.

Governor. And this Robinson makes sixteen.

Pike. I have already told your excellency that he does not belong to my party, and shall answer no more in-terrogatories on that subject.

Governor. When did you leave St. Louis?

Pike. 15th July.

Governor. I think you marched in June.

Pike. No, sir!

Governor. Well! return with Mr. Bartholemew to his house, and come here again at seven o'clock, and bring your papers ; on which we returned to the house of my friend Bartholemew, who seemed much hurt at the in-terview.

At the door of the government house, I met the old Frenchman, to whom I had given the scrap of paper on the 27th February. He had left us in the morning, and as I suppose, hurried in to make his report, and I presume had presented this paper to his excellency. I demanded with a look of contempt, if he had made his report? to which he made reply in an humble tone, and began to excuse himself, but I did not wait to hear his excuses. At the hour appointed we returned, when the governor demanded my papers ; I told him, I understood my trunk was taken possession of by his guard : he expressed surprise, and immediately ordered it in, and also sent for one Solomon Colly, formerly a serjeant in our army, and one of the unfortunate company of Nolan. We were seated, when he ordered Colly to demand my name, to which I replied ; he then demanded in what province I was born; I answered in English, and then addressed his excellency in French, and told him that I did not think it necessary to enter into such a catechising ; that if he would be at the pain of reading my commission from the United States, and my orders from my general, it would be all that I presumed would be necessary to convince his excellency that I came with no hostile intentions towards the Spanish government, on the contrary, that I had express instructions to guard against giving them offence or alarm, and that his excellency would be convinced that myself and party were rather to be considered objects, on which the so-much-celebrated generosity of the Spanish nation might be exercised, than proper subjects to occasion the opposite sentiments.

He then requested to see my commission and orders, which I read to him in French ; on which he got up and gave me his hand, for the first time, and said he was happy to be acquainted with me as a man of honor and a gentleman ; that I could retire this evening, and take my trunk with me ; that on the morrow he would make further arrangements.

4th March, Wednesday.—Was desired by the governor to bring up my trunk, in order that he might make some observations on my route, &c. When he ordered me to take my trunk over night, I had conceived the examination of papers was over, and as many of my documents were entrusted to the care of my men, and I found that the inhabitants were treating the men with liquor ; I was fearful they would become intoxicated, (and through inadvertancy) betray or discover the papers ; I had therefore obtained several of them and had put them in the trunk, when an officer arrived for myself and it, and I had no opportunity of taking them out again before I was taken up to the palace.   I discovered instantly that I was deceived, but it was too late to remedy the evil.

After examining the contents of my trunk, he informed me, I must (with my troops) go to Chihuahua, province of Biscay, to appear before the commandant-general; he added, you have the key of your trunk in your own possession ; the trunk will be put under charge of the officer who commands your escort.   The following conversation then took place.

Pike.   If we go to Chihuahua we must be considered as prisoners of war ?

Governor.   By no means.

Pike.   You have already disarmed my men without my knowledge, are their arms to be returned or not ?

Governor.   They can receive them any moment.

Pike.   But sir, I cannot consent to be led three or four hundred leagues out of my route, without its being by force of arms.

Governor.   I know you do not go voluntarily, but I will give you a certificate from under my hand of my having obliged you to march.*

Pike.   I will address you a letter on the subject.†

Governor.   You will dine with me to day, and march afterwards to a village about six miles distant, escorted by captain Anthony D'Almansa, with a detachment of dragoons, who will accompany you to where the remainder

* See Appendix to Part III. [No. 9.] page 70.
† See Appendix to Part III. [No. 8.] page 69.

of your escort is now waiting for you, under the command of the officer who commanded the expedition to the Pawnees.

Pike. I would not wish to be impertinent in my observations to your excellency, but pray sir! do you not think it was a greater infringement of our territory to send 600 miles in the Pawnees, than for me with our small party to come on the frontiers of yours with an intent to descend Red river?

Governor. I do not understand you.

Pike. No Sir! any further explanation is unnecessary. I then returned to the house of my friend Bartholemew and wrote my letter to his excellency, which I had not finished before we were hurried to dinner.

In the morning I had received from the governor by the hands of his private secretary twenty one dollars, notifying to me that it was the amount of the king's allowance for my party to Chihuahua and that it would be charged to me on account of my subsistence; from this I clearly understood that it was calculated that the expences of the party to Chihuahua would be defrayed by the United States. I also received by the same hands from his excellency a shirt and neck cloth, with his compliments, wishing me to accept of them " as they were made in " Spain by his sister and never had been worn by any per- " son;" for which I returned him my sincere acknowledgments, and it may not be deemed irrelevant if I explain at this period the miserable appearance we made and situation we were in; with the causes of it. When we left our interpreter and one man on the Arkansaw, we were obliged to carry all our baggage on our backs, consequently that which was the most *useful* was preferred to the few ornamental parts of dress we possessed. The ammunition claimed our first care, tools secondary, leather, leg-

gins, boots and mockinsons were the next in consideration ;
consequently, I left all my uniform, clothing, trunks, &c. as
did the men, except what they had on their backs ; conceiving that which would secure the feet and legs from the
cold, as preferable to any less indispensable portion of our
dress. Thus, when we presented ourselves at Santa Fe ;
I was dressed in a pair of blue trowsers, mockinsons,
blanket coat and a cap made of scarlet cloth, lined with
fox skins and my poor fellows in leggings, breech cloths and
leather coats and not a hat in the whole party. This
appearance was extremely mortifying to us all, especially
as soldiers, and although some of the officers used frequently to observe to me, that " worth made the man," &c.
with a variety of adages to the same amount. Yet the
first impression made on the ignorant is hard to eradicate ;
and a greater proof cannot be given of the ignorance of the
common people, than their asking if we lived in houses or
camps like the indians, or if we wore hats in our country ;
those observations are sufficient to shew the impression
our uncouth appearance made amongst them.

The dinner at the governor's was rather splendid,
having a variety of dishes and wines of the southern provinces, and when his excellency was a little warmed with
the influence of cheering liquor, he became very sociable.
He informed me that there existed a serious difficulty between the commandant general of the internal provinces and the marquis Caso Calvo, who had given permission to Mr. Dunbar, to explore the Ouchata contrary to
the general principles of their government ; and in consequence of which, the former had made representations
against the latter to the court of Madrid. After dinner
his excellency ordered his coach ; captain D'Almansa,
Bartholemew and myself entered with him, and he drove
out 3 miles. He was drawn by six mules and attended by

E e

a guard of cavalry.　When we parted his adieu was " remember Allencaster, in peace or war."

Left a note for my sergeant, with instructions to keep up good discipline and not be alarmed or discouraged. As I was about leaving the public square, poor Colly (the American prisoner,) came up with tears in his eyes and hoped I would not forget him, when I arrived in the United States.

After we left the governor we rode on about three miles to a defile where we halted for the troops and I soon found that the old soldier who accompanied us and commanded our escort was fond of a drop of the cheering liquor, as his boy carried a bottle in his cochmelies (a small leather case attached to the saddle for the purpose of carrying small articles.)　We were accompanied by my friend Bartholemew.　We ascended a hill and galloped on until about ten o'clock ; snowing hard all the time, when we came to a precipice which we descended, meeting with great difficulty (from the obscurity of the night) to the small village where we put up in the quarters of the priest, he being absent.

After supper, captain D'Almansa related to me that he had served his catholic majesty, 40 years to arrive at the rank he then held, which was a first lieutenant in the line, and a captain by brevet, whilst he had seen various young Europeans promoted over his head ; after the old man had taken his *quantum sufficit* and gone to sleep, my friend and myself sat up for some hours, he explaining to me their situation, the great desire they felt for a change of affairs, and an open trade with the United States.　I pointed out to him with chalk on the floor the geographical connection and route, from North Mexico and Louisiana, and finally gave him a certificate addressed to the citizens of the United States, stating his friendly disposition and his being a man of influence. This paper he seemed to estimate as a very valuable acquisition, as he was decidedly of opinion we would invade that country the ensuing spring and not all my assurances to the contrary, could eradicate that idea.

5th March, Friday.—It snowing very bad in the morning we did not march until 11 o'clock. In the mean time Bartholemew and myself paid a visit to an old invalid Spaniard, who received us in the most hospitable manner, giving us chocolate &c. He made many enquiries as to our government and religion, and of ********** who did not fail to give them the brightest colouring; he being enthusiastic in their favor from his many conversations with me, and drawing comparisons with his own country. What appeared to the old veteran, most extraordinary, was, that we ever changed our president; I was obliged to draw his powers on a nearer affinity with those of a monarch, than they really are, in order that they might comprehend his station and that there was a perfect freedom of consience permitted in our country. He however expressed his warm approbation of the measure. In the priests house in which we put up, were two orphan girls, who were adopted by him in their infancy and at this time constituted his whole family.

I bid adieu to my friend Bartholemew and could not avoid shedding tears: he embraced me, and all my men.

We arrived at the village of St. Domingo at two o'clock. It is as I supposed, nine miles on the east side of the Rio del Norte, and is a large village, the population being about 1000 natives, generally governed by its own chief. The chiefs of the villages were distinguished by a cane with a silver head and black tassell and on our arrival at the public house; captain D Almansa was waited on by the governor, cap in hand, to receive his orders as to the furnish-

ing of our quarters and ourselves with wood, water, provisions &c. for the house itself contained nothing but bare
walls and small grated windows, and brought to my recollection the representation of the Spanish inhabitants, as
given by Dr. Moore in his travels through Spain, Italy,
&c. This village as well as that of St. Philip's and St.
Bartholemew, are of the nation of Keres, many of whom
do not yet speak good Spanish.

After we had refreshed ourselves a little, the captain
sent for the keys of the church: when we entered it, and
I was much astonished to find enclosed in mud-brick
walls, many rich paintings, and the Saint (Domingo) as
large as life, elegantly ornamented with gold and silver:
the captain made a slight inclination of the head, and intimated to me, that this was the patron of the village. We
then ascended into the gallery, where the choir are generally placed. In an outside hall was placed another image
of the saint, less richly ornamented, where the populace
repaired daily, and knelt to return thanks for benefactions
received, or to ask new favors. Many young girls, indeed, chose the time of our visit to be on their knees before the holy patron. From the flat roof of the church
we had a delightful view of the village; the Rio del Norte
on our west; the mountains of St. Dies to the south, and
the valley round the town, on which were numerous herds
of goats, sheep, and asses; and upon the whole, this was
one of the handsomest views in New Mexico.

6th March, Friday.——Marched down the Rio del
Norte on the east side. Snow one foot deep. Passed
large flocks of goats. At the village of St. Philip's, crossed a bridge of eight arches, constructed as follows, viz.
the pillars made of neat wood work, something similar to
a crate, and in the form of a keel boat, the sharp end, or
bow, to the current; this crate or butment was filled with

stone, in which the river lodged sand, clay, &c. until it had become of a tolerable firm consistency. On the top of the pillars were laid pine logs, length ways, squared on two sides, and being joined pretty close, made a tolerable bridge for horses, but would not have been very safe for carriages, as there were no hand rails.

On our arrival at the house of the father, we were received in a very polite and friendly manner, and before my departure, we seemed to have been friends for years past.

During our dinner, at which we had a variety of wines, and were entertained with music, composed of bass drums, French horns, violins and cymbals; we likewise entered into a long and candid conversation as to the creoles, wherein he neither spared the government nor its administrators. As to government and religion, Father Rubi displayed a liberality of opinion and a fund of knowledge, which astonished me. He shewed me a statistical table, on which he had in a regular manner, taken the whole province of New Mexico, by villages, beginning at Tous, on the north-west, and ending with Valencia on the south, and giving their latitude, longitude, and population, whether natives or Spaniards, civilized or barbarous, Christians or Pagans, numbers, name of the nation, when converted, how governed, military force, clergy, salary, &c. &c.; in short, a complete geographical, statistical and historical sketch of the province. Of this I wished to obtain a copy, but perceived that the captain was somewhat surprised at its having been shewn to me. When we parted, we promised to write to each other, which I performed from Chihuahua.

Here was an old Indian who was extremely inquisitive to know if we were Spaniards, to which an old gentleman, called Don Francisco, who appeared to be an inmate of father Rubi, replied in the affirmative ; but says the Indian, " they do not speak Castillian," true replied the other, but you are an Indian of the nation of Keres, are you not ? Yes.   Well the Utahs are Indians also ? Yes. But still you do not understand them, they speaking a different language.   True replied the Indian ; well, said the old gentleman, those strangers are likewise Spaniards, but do not speak the same language with us.   This reasoning seemed to satisfy the poor savage, and I could not but smile at the ingenuity displayed to make him believe there was no other nation of whites but the Spaniards.

Whilst at dinner, father Rubi was informed one of his parishioners was at the point of death, and wished his attendance to receive his confession.

We took our departure, but were shortly after overtaken by our friend, who after giving me another hearty shake of the hand, left us.   Crossed the river and passed two small hamlets and houses on the road to the village of St. Dies, opposite the mountain of the same name, where we were received in a house of father Rubi, this making part of his domains.

7th March, Saturday.—Marched at nine o'clock through a country better cultivated and inhabited than any I had yet seen.   Arrived at Albuquerque, a village on the east side of the Rio del Norte.   We were received by father Ambrosio Guerra in a very flattering manner, and led into his hall.   From thence, after taking some refreshment, into an inner appartment, where he ordered his adopted children of the female sex, to appear, when they came in by turns, Indians of various nations, Spanish, French, and finally, two young girls, who from their complexion I conceived to be English : on perceiving I noticed them, he ordered the rest to retire, many of whom were beautiful, and directed those to sit down on the sofa beside me; thus situated, he told me that they had been taken to the east by the Tetaus; passed from one nation to another, until he purchased them, at that time infants, but they could recollect neither their names nor language, but concluding they were my country-women, he ordered them to embrace me as a mark of their friendship, to which they appeared nothing loth; we then sat down to dinner, which consisted of various dishes, excellent wines, and to crown all, we were waited on by half a dozen of those beautiful girls, who like Hebe at the feast of the gods, converted our wine to nectar, and with their ambrosial breath shed incense on our cups. After the cloth was removed some time, the priest beckoned me to follow him, and led me into his " sanctum sanctorum," where he had the rich and majestic images of various saints, and in the midst the crucified Jesus, crowned with thorns, with rich rays of golden glory surrounding his head; in short, the room being hung with black silk curtains, served but to augment the gloom and majesty of the scene. When he conceived my imagination sufficiently wrought up, he put on a black gown and mitre, kneeled before the cross, and took hold of my hand and endeavoured gently to pull me down beside him; on my refusal, he prayed fervently for a few minutes and then rose, laid his hands on my shoulders, and as I conceived, blessed me. He then said to me, " You will not be a Christian; Oh! what a pity! oh! " what a pity!" He then threw off his robes, took me by the hand and led me out of the company smiling; but the scene I had gone through had made too serious an impression on my mind to be eradicated, until we took our departure, which was in an hour after, having received great marks of friendship from the father.

Both above and below Albuquerque, the citizens were beginning to open the canals, to let in the water of the river to fertilize the plains and fields which border its banks on both sides; where we saw men, women and children of all ages and sexes at the joyful labor which was to crown with rich abundance their future harvest and ensure them plenty for the ensuing year. Those scenes brought to my recollection the bright descriptions given by Savary of the opening of the canals of Egypt. The cultivation of the fields was now commencing and every thing appeared to give life and gaiety to the surrounding scenery. We crossed the Rio del Norte, a little below the village of Albuquerque where it was 400 yards wide, but not more than three feet deep and excellent fording. At father Ambrosio's, was the only chart we saw in the province, that gave the near connection of the sources of the Rio del·Norte and the Rio Coloredo of California, with their ramifications. On our arriving at the next village a dependency of father Ambrosio, we were invited into the house of the commandant; when I entered, I saw a man sitting by the fire reading a book, with blooming cheeks, fine complexion and a genius speaking eye, he arose from his seat. It was Robinson! not that Robinson who left my camp, on the head waters of the Rio del Norte, pale, emaciated, with uncombed locks and beard of eight months growth, but with fire, unsubdued enterprise and fortitude. The change was indeed surprising. I started back and exclaimed " Robinson!" " Yes;" " but I do not know you;" I replied; " but I know you," he exclaimed " I would not be unknown to you here, in this land of tyranny and oppression; to avoid all the pains they dare to inflict. Yet, my friend I grieve to see you here and thus, for I presume you are a prisoner." " I replied no? I wear my sword you see, and all my men have their arms, and the moment they dare to ill treat us we will surprise their guards in the night, carry off some horses and make our way to Appaches and then set them at defiance." At this moment captain D'Almansa entered and 1 introduced Robinson to him, as *Companion de Voyage* and friend, he having before seen him at Santa Fe. He did not appear much surprised and received him with a significant smile, as much as to say, I knew this. We then marched out to the place were the soldiers were encamped, not one of whom would recognize him (agreeably to orders,) until I gave them the sign. Then it was a joyful meeting, as the whole party was enthusiastically fond of him. He gave me the following relation of his adventures after he left me.

" I marched the first day up the branch on which we
" were situated, as you know we had concluded it would
" be the most proper to follow it to its source, and then
" cross the mountains west, where we had conceived we
" should find the Spanish settlements, and at night en-
" camped on its banks; the second day I left it a little and
" bore more south, and was getting up the side of the
" mountain, when I discovered two indians, for whom I
" made; they were armed with bows and arrows, and
" were extremely shy of my approach, but after some time,
" confidence being somewhat restored; I signified a wish
" to go to Santa Fe, when they pointed due south, down
" the river, I left you on. As I could not believe them
" I reiterated the enquiry and received the same reply. I
" then concluded that we had been deceived, and that you
" were on the Rio del Norte, instead of Red river, and
" was embarrassed whether I should not immediately re-
" turn to apprise you of it, but concluded it to be too late,
" as I was discovered by the indians, whom if I had not
" met or some others I should have continued on and
" crossed the mountain on the waters of the Coloredo,
" and descended them, until from their course I should
" have discovered my mistake. I therefore offered them

F f

" some presents to conduct me in; they agreed, con-
" ducted me to their camp where their women were,
" and in about five minutes we were on our march. That
" night we encamped in the woods, and I slept very little,
" owing to my distrust of my companions. The next day
" at three o'clock, P. M. We arrived at the village of
" Aqua Caliente, where I was immediately taken into the
" house of the commandant, and expresses dispatched to
" Santa Fe. That night I was put to sleep on a matrass on
" the floor. The next day we departed early, leaving my
" arms and baggage at the commandants, he promising to
" have them forwarded to me at the city. On our arrival
" at Santa Fe, the governor received me with great austeri-
" ty at first, and entered into an examination of my busi-
" ness and took possession of all my papers. After all
" this was explained, he ordered me to a room where the
" officers were confined when under an arrest and a non-
" commissioned officer to attend me, when I walked out
" into the city, which I had free permission to do. I was
" supplied with provisions from the governor's table, who
" had promised he would write to Babtiste Lalande to come
" down and answer to the claim I had against him; whose
" circumstance I had apprized myself of. The second day
" the governor sent for me, and informed me, that he had
" made enquiry as to the abilities of Lalande, to discharge
" the debt, and found that he possessed no property, but
" that at some future period, he would secure the money
" for me. To this I made a spirited remonstrance, as an
" infringement of our treaties and a protection of a refugee
" citizen of the United States against his creditors, which
" had no other effect than to obtain me an invitation to
" dinner, and rather more respectful treatment than I had
" hitherto received from his excellency, who being slightly
" afflicted with the dropsy, requested my advice as to his

" case ; on which I prescribed a regimen and mode of
" treatment which happened to differ from the one adopt-
" ed by a monk and practising physician of the place,
" brought on me his enmity and ill offices. The ensuing
" day I was ordered by the governor to hold myself in rea-
" diness to proceed to the internal parts of the country, to
" which I agreed ; determining not to leave the country in
" a clandestine manner, unless they attempted to treat me
" with indignity or hardship ; and conceiving it in my
" power to join you on your retreat, or find Red river
" and descend it ; should you not be brought in, but in
" that case to share your destiny : added to this I feel a
" desire to see more of the country for which purpose I was
" willing to run the risk of future consequences. We
" marched the ensuing day, I having been equipped by my
" friend, with some small articles of which I stood in
" need of, such as I would receive out of the numerous
" offers of his country. The fourth day I arrived at the
" village of St. Fernandez, where I was received, and taken
" charge of by Lt. Don Faciendo Malgares who command-
" ed the expedition to the Pawnees, and whom you will
" find a gentleman, a soldier and one of the most gallant
" men you ever knew ; with him I could no longer keep
" the disguise and when he informed me, (two days since)
" that you were on the way in, I confessed to him my be-
" longing to your party, and we have ever since been anti-
" cipating the pleasure we three will enjoy, in our journey
" to Chihuahua ; for he is to command the escort, his
" dragoons being now encamped in the field, waiting your
" arrival. Since I have been with him I have practiced phy-
" sic in the country in order to have an opportunity of ex-
" amining the manners, customs, &c. of the people, and to
" endeavor to ascertain the political and religious feelings
" and to gain every other species of information which

" would be necessary to our country or ourselves. I am
" now here, on a visit to this man's wife; attended by a
" corporal of dragoons as a guard, who answers very well
" as a waiter guide, &c. in my excursions through the coun-
" try; but I will immediately return with you to Malgares."
Thus ended Robinson's relation, and I in return related
what had occurred to the party and myself. We agreed
upon our future line of conduct and then joined my old captain in the house; who had been persuaded to tarry all
night, provided it was agreeable to me, as our host wished
Robinson to remain until the next day; with this proposition, I complied in order that Robinson and myself might
have a further discussion before we joined Malgares, who
I suspected would watch us close. The troops proceeded on
to the village of Tousac, that evening.

8th March, Sunday.—Marched after taking breakfast
and halted at a little village, three miles distance, called
Tousac, situated on the west side of the Rio del Norte.
The men informed me that on their arrival over night,
they had all been furnished with an excellent supper, and
after supper, wine, and a violin, with a collection of the
young people to a dance. When we left this village the
priest sent a cart down to carry us over, as the river was
nearly four feet deep. When we approached the village
of St. Fernandez, we were met by lieutenant Malgares, accompanied by two or three other officers; he received me
with the most manly frankness and the politeness of a man
of the world. Yet my feelings were such as almost overpowered me and obliged me to ride by myself for a short
period in order to recover myself: those sensations arose
from my knowledge, that he had now been absent from
Chihuahua ten months, and it had cost the king of Spain
more than 10,000 dollars, to effect that which a mere accident and the deception of the governor had effected.

Malgares finding I did not feel myself at ease took every means in his power to banish my reserve, which made it impossible on my part not to endeavor to appear chearful ; we conversed as *well as we could* and in two hours were as well acquainted as some people would be in the same number of months.   Malgares possessing none of the haughty Castillian pride, but much of the urbanity of a Frenchman; and I will add my feeble testimony to his loyalty, by declaring that he was one of the few officers or citizens whom I found, who was loyal to their king, felt indignant at the degraded state of the Spanish monarchy ; who deprecated a revolution or separation of Spanish America, from the mother country ; unless France should usurp the government of Spain. These are the men who possess the heads to plan, the hearts to feel and the hands to carry this great and important work into execution. In the afternoon our friend wrote the following notification to the Alcaldes of several small villages around us.   " Send this evening " six or eight of your handsomest young girls, to the vil- " lage of St. Fernandez, where I propose giving a fan- " dango, for the entertainment of the American officers " arrived this day."

(Signed)   Don Faciendo.

This order was punctually obeyed, and pourtrays more clearly than a chapter of observations, the degraded state of the common people. In the evening when the company arrived, the ball began after their usual manner, and there was really a handsome display of beauty.

It will be proper to mention here, that when my small paper trunk was brought in, Lt. Malgares struck his foot against it, and said : " the governor informs me this is a " prisoner of war, or that I have charge of it, but, sir, only " assure me, that you will hold the papers therein contain-

" ed sacred, I will have nothing to do with it." I bowed assent, and I will only add, that the condition was scrupulously adhered to; as I was bound by every tie of military and national honor; and let me add gratitude not to abuse his high confidence in the honor of a soldier. He further added that " Robinson being now acknowledged " as one of your party, I shall withdraw his guard and " consider him, as under your parole of honor." Those various marks of politeness and friendship, caused me to endeavor to evince to my brother soldier, that we were capable of appreciating his honorable conduct towards us.

9th March, Monday.—The troops marched about ten o'clock. Lt. Malgares and myself accompanied captain D'Almansa, about three miles back on his rout to Santa Fe, to the house of a citizen, where we dined; after which we separated. I wrote by the captain to the governor, in French and to father Rubi in English. D'Almansa presented me with his cap and whip, and gave me a letter of recommendation to an officer at Chihuahua. We returned to our old quarters and being joined by our waiters, commenced our route. Passed a village called St. Thomas one mile distant from the camp. The camp was formed in an ellipsis, the two long sides presenting a breast work formed of the saddles and heads of the mules, each end of the ellipsis having a small opening to pass and repass at; in the centre was the commandant's tent. Thus in case of an attack on the camp there were ready formed works to fight from. Malgares' mode of living, was superior to any thing we have an idea of in our army; having eight mules loaded with his common camp equipage, wines, confectionary, &c. But this only served to evince the corruption of the Spanish discipline, for if a subaltern indulged himself with such a quantity of baggage, what would be the cavalcade attending on an army? Doctor Robinson had been called over the river to a small village to see a sick woman and did not return that night. Distance 12 miles.

10*th March, Tuesday.*—Marched at eight o'clock and arrived at the village of Sibilleta, passed on the way the village of Sabinez on the west side, and Xaxales, on the same side. Sibilleta is situated on the east side and is a regular square, appearing like a large mud wall on the outside, the doors, windows, &c. facing the square, and is the neatest and most regular village I have yet seen; it is governed by a sergeant at whose quarters I put up.

11*th March, Wednesday.*—Marched at eleven o'clock came 12 miles and encamped, the troops having preceeded us. Lieutenant Malgares not being well, took medicine. The village we staid at last night, being the last, we now entered the wilderness and the road became rough, small hills running into the river, making vallies; but the bottoms appear richer than those more to the north.

12*th March, Thursday.*—Marched at seven o'clock, and passed on the west side of the river, the mountains of Magdalen, the black mountains on the east. Passed the encampment of the caravan, going out with about 15,000 sheep for the other provinces from which they bring back merchandize. This expedition consisted of about 300 men, chiefly citizens escorted by an officer and 35 or 40 troops; they are collected at Sibilleta and separate there on their return. They go out in February and return in March; a similar expedition goes out in the autumn, during the other parts of the year no citizen travels the road, the couriers excepted. At the pass of the Rio del Norte, they meet and exchange packets, when each return to their own province. Met a caravan of 50 men and probably 200 horses, loaded with goods for New-Mexico. Halted at twelve o'clock and marched at three. Lt. Malgares shewed me the place where he had been in two affairs with the

Appaches ; one he commanded himself, and the other was commanded by captain D'Almansa; in the former there was one Spaniard killed and eight wounded and ten Appaches made prisoners, in the latter 52 Appaches were wounded and 17 killed ; they being surprised in the night. Malgares killed two himself, and had two horses killed under him.

13th, March, Friday.——Marched at seven o'clock, saw many deer. Halted at eleven o'clock and marched at four o'clock. This day one of our horses threw a youg woman and ran off, (as was the habit of all the Spanish horses, if by chance they throw their rider) when many of the dragoons and Malgares pursued him. I being mounted on an elegant horse of Malgares, joined in the chase, and notwithstanding their superior horsemanship overtook the horse, caught his bridle and stopped him, when both of the horses were nearly at full speed. This act procured me the applause of the Spanish dragoons, and it is astonishing how much it operated on their good will.

14th March, Saturday.——Marched at ten o'clock, and halted at a mountain, distance ten miles, this is the point from which the road leaves the river for two days journey bearing due south, the river taking a turn south west, by the river, five days to where the roads meet. We marched at four o'clock and eight miles below, crossed the river to the west side, two mules fell in the water, and unfortunately they carried the stores of lieutenant Malgares, by which means we lost all our bread, an elegant assortment of buiscuit, &c. Distance 18 miles.

15th, March, Sunday.——Marched at half past ten o'clock. Made 28 miles, the route rough and stony ; course S. 20° W.

16th March, Monday.——Marched at 7 o'clock, and halted at twelve. Passed on the east side the horse mountain, and the mountain of the dead. Came on a trail of appearance of 200 horses, supposed to be the trail of an expedition from the province of Biscay, against the indians.

17th March, Tuesday.—Marched at ten o'clock, and at four in the afternoon, crossed the river to the east side; saw several fresh indian tracks, also the trail of a large party of horses, supposed to be Spanish troops in pursuit of the indians. Marched down the river 26 miles, fresh sign of indians, also of a party of horses; country mountainous on both sides of the river.

18th March, Wednesday.—Marched down the river 26 miles; fresh sign of indians, also a party of horses; country mountainous on both sides of the river.

19th March, Thursday.—Struck out east about three miles and fell in with the main road, (or a large flat prairie) which we left at the mountain of the friar Christopher.

20th March, Friday.—Halted at ten o'clock, at a salt lake. Marched until two o'clock, halted for the day; vegetation began to be discoverable on the 17th and this day the weeds and grass were quite high.

21st March, Saturday.—Marched in the morning and arrived at the passo del Norte at 11 o'clock, the road leading through a hilly and mountainous country. We put up at the house of Don Francisco Garcia who was a merchant and a planter; he possessed in the vicinity of the town 20,000 sheep and 1000 cows; we were received in a most hospitable manner, by Don Pedro Roderique Rey, the lieutenant governor, and father Joseph Prado, the vicar of the place. This was by far the most flourishing place we had been in; for a more particular account of its situation, population, &c.*

22d March, Sunday.—Remained at the Passo.

23d March, Monday.—Mass performed, leave the Passo at three o'clock, to fort Elisiaira, accompanied by the

* See Appendix to part III. [No. 1] page 7.

lieutenant governor, the Vicar and Allencaster a brother
of the governor.   Malgares, myself and the doctor took up
our quarters at the house of capt. ————--, who was then
at Chihuahua ; but his lady and sister entertained us in a
very elegant and hospitable manner.   They began playing
cards and continued until late the third day. Malgares who
won considerably, would send frequently 15 or 20 dollars
from the table to the lady of the house, her sister and
others ; and beg their acceptance, in order that the goddess
of fortune, might still continue propitious, in this manner
he distributed 500 dollars ; around this fort were a great
number of Appaches, who were on a treaty with the Spaniards.   These people appeared to be perfectly independent
in their manners, and were the only savages I saw in the
Spanish dominions, whose spirit was not humbled, whose
necks were not bowed to the yoke of their invaders. With
those people Malgares was extremely popular and I believe
he sought popularity with them, and all the common people, for there was no man so poor or so humble, under
whose roof he would not enter ; and when he walked
out, I have seen him put a handful of dollars in his pocket
give them all to the old men, women and children before he
returned to his quarters ; but to equals he was haughty and
overbearing.   This conduct he pursued through the whole
province of New Mexico and Biscay, when at a distance
from the seat of government, but I could plainly perceive
that he was cautious of his conduct, as he approached the
capital.   I here left a letter for my sergeant.

24th March. Tuesday.—Very bad weather.

25th March, Wednesday.—The troops marched, but
Lt. Malgares and my men remained.

26th March, Thursday.—Divine service was performed in the morning, in the garrison, at which all the
troops attended under arms ; at one part of their mass,

they present arms, at another, sink on one knee and rest the muzzle of the gun on the ground, in signification of their submission to their divine master. At one o'clock, we bid adieu to our friendly hostess, who was one of the finest women I had seen in New Spain. At dusk arrived at a small pond made by a spring, which arose in the centre, called the *Ogo mall a Ukap*, and seemed formed by providence to enable the human race, to pass that route as it was the only water within 60 miles, on the route ; here we overtook sergeant Belardie with the party of dragoons from Senora and Biscay, who had left us at fort Elisiaira, where we had received a new escort.   Distance 20 miles.

27th *March, Friday.*—Arrived at Carracal, at twelve o'clock.   Distance 28 miles ; the road well watered and the situation pleasant. The father-in-law of our friend, commanded six or seven years here; when we arrived at the fort, the commandant, Don Pedro Rues Saramende received Robinson and myself, with a cold bow and informed Malgares, that we could repair to the public quarters.   To this Malgares indignantly replied, that he should accompany us and turned to go when the commandant took him by the arm, made many apologies to him and us, and we at length reluctantly entered his quarters ; here for the first time, I saw the Gazettes of Mexico, which gave rumors of colonel Burr's conspiracies, the movements of our troops, &c. &c. but which were stated in so vague and undefined a manner, as only to create our anxiety without throwing any light on the subject.

28th *March, Saturday.*—Marched at half past three o'clock and arrived at the Warm Springs at sun down ; crossed one little fosse on the route.

29th *March, Sunday.*—Marched at ten o'clock and continued our route, with but a short halt, until sun down ; when we encamped without water.   Distance 30 miles.

30th March, Monday.—Marched before seven o'clock, the front arrived at water, at eleven o'clock; the mules at twelve. The spring on the side of the mountain to the east of the road, a beautiful situation, I here saw the first ash timber, I observed in the country. This water is 52 miles from the Warm Springs. Yesterday and to-day, saw Cabrie, marched fifteen miles further and encamped, without wood or water; passed two other small springs to the east of the road.

31st March, Tuesday.—Marched early and arrived at an excellent spring at ten o'clock. The roads from Senora, Tanos and Buenaventura, &c. joins about 400 yards, before you arrive at the spring.

Arrived at the village of ———— at night, a large and elegant house, for the country; here were various labors carried on by criminals in irons.

We here met with a Catalonian, who was but a short time from Spain, and whose dialect was such that he could scarcely be understood by Malgares, and whose manners were much more like those of a citizen of our western frontiers, than of a subject of a despotic prince.

1st April, Wednesday.—In the morning Malgares dispatched a courier, with a letter to the commandant general Salcedo to inform him of our approach and also one to his father in law.

2d April, Thursday.—When we arrived at Chihuahua, we pursued our course through the town to the house of the general. I was much astonished to see with what anxiety Malgares anticipated the meeting with his military chief; after having been on the most arduous and enterprizing expedition, ever undertaken by any of his majesty's officers from these provinces and having executed it with equal spirit and judgment, yet was he fearful of his meeting him, with an eye of displeasure; and appeared to be much more agitated than ourselves, although we may be supposed to have also had our sensations; as on the will of this man depended our future destiny, at least until our country could interfere in our behalf. On our arrival at the general's, we were halted in the hall of the guard, until word was sent to the general of our arrival, when Malgares was first introduced, who remained some time, during which a Frenchman came up and endeavored to enter into conversation with us, but was soon frowned into silence as we conceived he was only some authorised spy. Malgares at last came out and asked me to walk in. I found the general sitting at his desk; he was a middle sized man, apparently about fifty-five years of age, with a stern countenance, but he received me graciously and beckoned to a seat: he then observed " you have given us and yourself " a great deal of trouble."

Captain Pike. " On my part entirely unsought, and " on that of the Spanish government voluntary."

General. " Where are your papers ?"

Captain Pike. "Under charge of lieutenant Malgares," who was then ordered to have my small trunk brought in; which being done, a lieutenant Walker came in, who is a native of New Orleans, his father an Englishman, his mother a French woman, and spoke both those languages equally well, also the Spanish. He was a lieutenant of dragoons in the Spanish service, and master of the military school at Chihuahua. This same young gentleman was employed by Mr. Andrew Ellicott, as a deputy surveyor on the Florida line between the United States and Spain, in the years '97 and '98. General Salcedo then desired him to assist me in taking out my papers, and requested me to explain the nature of each, and such as he conceived was relevant to the expedition, he caused to be laid on one side, and those which were not of a public nature on the other ; the whole either passing through the hands of the general or Walker, except a few letters from my lady, which on my taking up and saying they were letters from a lady, the general gave a proof, that if the ancient Spanish bravery had degenerated in the nation generally, their gallantry still existed, by bowing, and I put them in my pocket.   He then informed me that he would examine the papers, but that in the mean while he wished me to make out and present to him a short sketch of my voyage,* which might probably be satisfactory. This I would have positively refused, had I had an idea that it was his determination to keep the papers, which I could not at that time conceive, from the urbanity and satisfaction which he appeared to exhibit on the event of our interview.   He then told me that I would take up my quarters with Walker, in order (as he said) to be better accommodated by having a person with me who spoke the English language ; but the object as I suspected, was for him to be a spy on our actions, and on those who visited us.   Robinson all this time had been standing in the guard room, boiling with indignation at being so long detained *there*, subject to the observations of the soldiery and gaping curiosity of the vulgar.   He was now introduced by some mistake of one of the aid-de-camps.   He appeared and made a slight bow to the general, who demanded of Malgares who he was ? He replied a doctor who accompanied the expedition.   " Let him re-" tire," said the governor, and he went out.   The general then invited me to return and dine with him, and we went to the quarters of Walker, where we received several different invitations to take quarters at houses where we might be better accommodated, but understanding that the general had designated our quarters we were silent.

We returned to dine at the palace, where we met Malgares, who, with ourselves, was the only guest.   He

* See Appendix to Part III. [No. 13.] page 73.

had at the table the treasurer *Truxillio*, and a priest called father Rocus.

3d April, Friday.—Employed in giving a sketch of our voyage for the general and commandant of those provinces. Introduced to Don Bernardo Villamil, Don Alberto Mayner, lieutenant colonel and father-in-law to Malgares, and Don Manuel Zuloaga, a member of the secretary's office, to whom I am under obligations of gratitude and shall remember with esteem. Visited his house in the evening.

4th April, Saturday.—Visited the hospital where were two officers, who were fine looking men, and I was informed had been the gayest young men of the province, who were mouldering away by disease, and there was not a physician in his majesty's hospitals who was able to cure them ; but after repeated attempts had given them up to perish. This shews the deplorable state of the medical science in the provinces. I endeavored to get Robinson to undertake the cure of these poor fellows, but the jealousy and envy of the Spanish doctors made it impracticable.

5th April, Sunday.—Visited by lieutenant Malgares, with a very polite message from his excellency, and delivered in the most impressive terms, with offers of assistance, money, &c. for which I returned my respectful thanks to the general. Accompanied Malgares to the public walk, where we found the secretary, captain Villamil, Zuloaga and other officers of distinction. We here likewise met the wife of my friend Malgares, to whom he introduced us. She was like all the other *ladies* of New Spain, a little *en bon point*, but possessed the national beauty of eye in a superior degree. There were a large collection of ladies, amongst whom were two of the most celebrated, in the capital—Senora Maria Con. Caberairi, and Senora Margeurite Vallois, the only two ladies who had spirit sufficent, and their husbands generosity enough to allow them to think themselves rational beings, to be treated on an equality, to receive the visits of their friends, and give way to the hospitality of their dispositions without constraint: they were consequently the envy of the ladies, and the subject of scandal to prudes; their houses were the rendezvous of all the fashionable male society; and every man who was conspicuous for science, arts or arms, was sure to meet a welcome. We, as unfortunate strangers, were consequently not forgotten. I returned with Malgares to the house of his father-in-law, lieutenant colonel Mayner, who was originally from Cadiz, a man of good information.

6th April, Monday.—Dined with the general. Writing, &c. In the evening visited Malgares and the secretary.

After dinner wine was set on the table, and we were entertained with songs in the French, Italian, Spanish and English languages. Accustomed as I was to sitting some time after dinner I forgot their *siesta*, (or repose after dinner) until Walker suggested the thing to me, when we retired.

7th April, Tuesday.—Dined at Don Antonio Caberairi's, in company with Villamil, Zuloaga, Walker, &c..... Sent in a sketch of my voyage to the general. Spent the evening at colonel Mayner's with Malgares.

8th April, Wednesday.—Visited the treasurer, who showed me the double-barrel gun given by governor Claiborne, and another formerly the property of Nolan.

9th April, Thursday.—In the evening was informed that David Fero was in town and wished to speak to me. This man had formerly been my father's ensign, and was taken with Nolan's party at the time the latter was killed. He possessed a brave soul, and had withstood every oppression since his being made prisoner, with astonishing fortitude. Although his leaving the place of his confinement (the village of St. Jeronimie) without the knowledge of the general, was in some measure clandestine, yet, a countryman, an acquaintance, and formerly a brother soldier, in a strange land, in distress, had ventured much to see me—could I deny him the interview from any motives of delicacy ? No ; forbid it humanity ! forbid it every sentiment of my soul !

Our meeting was affecting, tears standing in his eyes. He informed me the particulars of their being taken, and many other circumstances since their being in the country. I promised to do all I could for him consistent with my character and honor, and their having entered the country without the authority of the United States. As he was obliged to leave the town before day, he called on me at my quarters, when I bid him adieu, and gave him what my *purse* afforded, not what my *heart* dictated.

10*th April, Friday.*—In the evening at colonel Maynor's. Captain Rodiriques arrived from the province of Texas, who had been under arrest one year, for going to Natchitoches with the marquis Cassa Calvo.

11*th April, Saturday.*—Rode out in the coach with Malgares ; was hospitably entertained at the house of one of the Vallois : here we drank London Porter. Visited the secretary Villamil.

12*th April, Sunday.*—Dined (with the doctor) at Don Antonio Caberarie's with our usual guests. In the evening at the public walks.

13*th April, Monday.*—Nothing extraordinary.

14*th April, Tuesday.*—Spent the forenoon in writing ; the afternoon at Don Antonio Caberarie's.

15*th April. Wednesday.*—Spent the evening at colonel

H h

Maynor's with our friend Malgares. Wrote a letter to governor Salcedo on the subject of my papers.*

16*th April, Thursday.*—Spent the evening at the secretary's Don Villamil's.

17*th April, Friday.*—Sent my letter to his excellency.
Spent the evening with my friend Malgares.

18*th April, Saturday.*—Spent the evening at Caberarie's, &c. Wrote to governor Allencaster.

19*th April, Sunday.*—In the evening at a Fandango.

20*th April, Monday.*—We this day learned that an
American officer had gone on to the city of Mexico. This
was an enigma to us inexplicable, as we conceived that the
jealousy of the Spanish government would have prevented
any foreign officer from penetrating the country; and
what the United States could send an authorised agent to
the vice royalty, when the Spanish government had at the
seat of our government a charge des affairs, served but to
darken the conjectures. The person alluded to was Mr.
Burling, a citizen of Mississippi Territory, whose mission
is now well known to the government. We likewise received an account of a commercial treaty having been entered into between Great Britain and the United States,
which by the Dons was only considered as the preliminary
step to an alliance offensive and defensive between the two
nations.

21*st, April, Tuesday.*—Presented the commanding
general with a letter for general Wilkinson, which he promised to have forwarded to the governor of Texas.

22*d April, Wednesday.*—Spent the day in reading and
studying Spanish; the evening at captain Villamil's.

23*d April, Thursday.*—Dined at Don Pedro Vallois; the evening with colonel Maynor; bid him adieu as

* See Appendix to Part III. [No. 14.] page 78.

he was to march the next day.   In the evening received a
letter from the commandant general, informing me my papers were to be detained, giving a certificate of their numbers, contents, &c. &c.*

    24th April, Friday.—Spent the evening at Zulo-
aga's with his relations. About sun down an officer of the
government called upon me, and " told me that the go-
" vernment had been informed, that in conversations in all
" societies, Robinson and myself had held forth political
" maxims and principles, which if *just*, I must be con-
" scious if generally disseminated, would in a very few
" years be the occasion of a revolt of *those* kingdoms;
" that those impressions had taken such effect as that it
" was no uncommon thing (in the circles in which we as-
" sociated) to hear the comparative principles of a republi-
" can and monarchical government discussed; and even
" the allegiance due (*in case of certain events*) to the court
" called in question; that various characters of considera-
" tion had indulged themselves in those conversations, *all*
" *of whom were noted and would be taken care of;* but, that,
" as it respected myself and companion, it was the desire
" of his excellency, that whilst in the dominions of Spain we
" would not hold forth any conversations whatsoever, ei-
" ther on the subject of religion or politics." I replied, that
" it was true I had held various and free conversations on
" the subjects complained of, but only with men high in
" office, who might be supposed to be firmly attached to
" the king, and partial to the government of their country.
" That I had never gone amongt the poor and illiterate,
" preaching up republicanism or a free government. That
" as to the catholic religion, I had only combatted some of
" what I conceived to be its illiberal dogmas; but that I

* See appendix to part III. [No. 15 & 16.] page 80, 81.

" had spoken of it in all instances as a respectable branch
" of the Christian religion, which as well as all others,
" was tolerated in the United States ; but that, had I came
" to that kingdom in a diplomatic character, delicacy to-
" wards the government would have sealed my lips. Had
" I been a prisoner of war, personal safety might have
" had the same effect ; but being there in the capacity
" which I was ; not voluntarily, but by coercion of the
" Spanish government, but, who, at the same time had of-
" ficially notified me that they did not consider me under
" *any restraint whatever*—therefore, when called on,
" should always give my opinions freely, either as to poli-
" tics or religion ; but at the same time with urbanity, and
" a proper respect to the legitimate authorities of the coun-
" try where I was."

He replied, " Well you may then rest assured your
" conduct will be represented in no very favorable point
" of view to your government."

I replied, " To my government I am certainly re-
" sponsible, and to no other." He then left me, and I
immediately waited on some of my *friends* and notified
them of the threat, at which they appeared much *alarmed*,
and we went immediately to consult ———— who, to great
attachment to his friends, joined the most incorruptible
loyalty and the confidence of the government. Our consultation ended in a determination only to be silent and
watch events.

We suspected ———— to be the informant, but whether just in our suspicion or not, I will not pretend to determine, for Robinson and myself frequently used to hold
conversations in his presence purposely to have them communicated ; but he at last discovered our intentions, and
told us, that if we calculated on making him a carrier of
news, we were mistaken ; that he despised it.

25th April, Saturday.—At eleven o'clock called on his excellency, but was informed he was engaged: about three o'clock received a message from him by lieutenant Walker, informing me that he was surprized I had not returned, and to call without ceremony in the evening, which I did, and presented him with a letter.* He then also candidly informed me my party would not join me in the territory of the king of Spain, but that they should be attended to punctually, and forwarded on immediately after me; but requested that I should give orders to my sergeant to deliver up all his ammunition, and dispose in some manner of the horses of which he had charge. I stated in reply, " that with respect to the ammunition, I would give " orders to my sergeant to deliver (if demanded) all they " possessed, more than was necessary to fill their horns; " but that as to the horses, I considered their loss was a " charge which must be adjusted between the two govern- " ments, therefore should not give any directions respect- " ing them, except as to bringing them on as far and as " long as they were able to travel." He then gave me an invitation to dine with him on the morrow.

26th April, Sunday.—Dined at the general's. In the evening went to Malgares, Zuloaga's and others. Wrote to my sergeant and Fero; to the latter of whom I sent ten dollars, and to the other 161 dollars 84 cents, to purchase clothes for the party. We had been for some time suspicious that the doctor was to be detained, but this evening he likewise obtained permission to pursue his journey with me, which diffused general joy through all the party.

27 April, Monday.—Spent the day in making arrangments for our departure; writing to the sergeant, &c. I will here mention some few anecdotes relative to ————, with

* See appendix to part III. [No. 17.] page 82.

whom we boarded during our stay in Chihuahua. When
we came to the city we went to his quarters, (by order of
the general) and considered ourselves as guests, having not
the least idea that we should be charged with board, knowing with what pleasure any American officer would receive
and entertain a foreign brother soldier situated as we were,
and that we should conceive it a great insult to be offered
pay under similar circumstances. But one day after we had
been there about a week, he presented to me an account
for Robinson's and my board, *receipted*, and begged if the
general enquired of me, that I would say I had paid it.
This naturally led me to demand how the thing originated;
he with considerable embarrassment observed, that he had
taken the liberty to remark to the general, that he thought
he should be allowed an extra allowance, in order to be enabled to treat us with some little distinction. The general flew
into a most violent passion, and demanded if I had not paid
him for our board? to which the other replied no, he did not
expect pay of us. He ordered him immediately to demand
pay, to receive it, sign a receipt and lodge it in his hands;
and added, he would consult me if the thing was done, but
which he never did, yet I took care every Sunday after that,
to deposit in the hands of Walker, a sum which was considered the proportion for Robinson and myself. Malgares and several other of the Spanish officers having heard
of the thing, waited on us much mortified—saying, with
what pleasure they would have entertained us had not the
designation of the general pointed out his will on the subject———had living with him an old negro, (the only one I
saw on that side of St. Antonio) who was the property of
some person who resided near Natchez, who had been
taken with Nolan. Having been acquainted with him in
the Mississippi country, solicited and obtained permission

for old Cæsar to live with him. I found him very communicative and extremely useful. The day I arrived,
when we were left alone he came in, and looked around at
the walls of the room and exclaimed, " What ! all gone."
I demanded an explanation, and he informed me that the
maps of the different provinces as taken by ———— and
other surveyors, had been hung up against the walls, but
the day we arrived they had all been taken down and deposited in a closet which he designated. W— gave various
reasons for his having left the United States and joined the
Spanish service ; one of which was, his father having been
ill-treated as he conceived by G. at Natchez. At Chihuahua he had charge of the military school, which consisted of about 15 young men of the first families of the
provinces ; also of the public water-works of the city, on
a plan devised by the royal engineer of Mexico ; of the
building of a new church ; of the casting of small artillery,
fabrication of arms, &c. &c. Thus, though he had ten-
dered his resignation, they knew his value too well to part
with him, and would not accept of it, but still kept him in
a subordinate station, in order that he might be the more
dependant and the more *useful*. And although he candidly confessed his disgust to their service, manners, morals,
and political establishments, yet, he never made a communication to us which he was bound in honor to conceal ;
but on the contrary fulfilled the station of informer,
which in that country is considered no disgrace, with
great punctuality and fidelity. In this city the pro-
verb was literally true, that " the walls had ears," for
there was scarcely any thing could pass that his excellency
did not know in a few hours after. In the evening I was
notified to be ready to march the next day at three
o'clock.

28th April, Tuesday.—In the morning Malgares waited on us, and informed us he was to accompany us some distance on the route. After bidding adieu to all our friends, marched at a quarter past three o'clock, and encamped at nine o'clock at night at a spring—stony—passed near Chihuahua a small ridge of mountains, and there encamped in a hollow.

This day as we were riding along, Malgares rode up to me and informed me that the general had given orders that I should not be permitted to make any astronomical observations. To this I replied, that he well knew I never had attempted making any since I was conducted into the Spanish dominions.

29th April, Wednesday.—Arrived at a settlement at eight o'clock—plenty of milk, &c. When about to make my journal, Malgares changed color, and informed me it was his orders I should not take notes, but added, you have a good memory, and when you get to Cogquilla you can bring it all up. At first I felt considerably indignant, and was on the point of refusing to comply; but thinking for a moment of the many politenesses I had received from his hands, induced me merely to bow assent with a smile, and we proceeded on our route, but had not proceeded far before I made a pretext to halt—established my boy as a vedet, and sat down peaceably under a bush and made my notes, &c. This course I pursued ever after, not without some very considerable degree of trouble to separate myself from the party.

Arrived at the fort of St. Paul at eleven o'clock, situated on a small river of the same name, the course of which is north-east by south-west. At the time we were there the river was not wider than a mill stream, but sometimes it is three hundred yards wide and impassable. Distance 30 miles.

30th April, Thursday.—Marched at six o'clock, and at eleven arrived at the river Conchos 24 miles—beautiful green trees on its banks. I was taken very sick at half past ten o'clock.

Arrived at night at a small station on the river Conchos, garrisoned by a sergeant and ten men from the fort Conchos, fifteen leagues up said river. Distance 43 miles.

1st May, Friday.—Marched up the Conchos to its confluence with the river Florada, 15 leagues from where we left the former river, and took up the latter, which bears from the Conchos S. 80° and 50° E. On its banks, are some very flourishing settlements, and they are well timbered. A poor miserable village at the confluence..... Came ten miles up the Florada to dinner, and at night stopt at a private house. This property or plantation was valued formerly at 300,000 dollars, extending on the Florada from the small place we slept at on the last of April, 30 leagues up said river. Distance 45 miles.

Finding that a new species of discipline had taken place, and that the suspicions of my friend Malgares were much more acute than ever, I conceived it necessary to take some steps to secure the notes I had taken, which were clandestinely acquired. In the night I arose, and after making my men charge all their pieces well, I took my small books and rolled them up in small rolls, and tore a fine shirt to pieces, and wrapt it round the papers and put them down in the barrels of the guns, until we just left room for the tompoins, which were then carefully put in ; the remainder we secured about our bodies under our shirts. This occupied about two hours, but was effected without discovery, and without suspicions.

2d May, Saturday.—Marched early, and in four and a quarter hours arrived at Guaxequillo; situated on the river Florada, where we were to exchange our friend Mal-

I i

gares for captain Barelo, who was a Mexican by birth, born near the capital, and entered as a cadet at Guaxequillo near twenty years past, and by his extraordinary merits (being a Creolian) had been promoted to a captain, which was even by himself considered as his ultimate promotion. He was a gentleman in his manners—generous and frank; and I believe a good soldier.

3d May, Sunday.—At Guaxequillo the captain gave up his command to Malgares. At night the officers gave a ball, at which appeared at least sixty women, ten or a dozen of whom were very handsome.

4th May, Monday.—Don Hymen Guloo arrived from Chihuahua, accompanied by a citizen and the friar, who had been arrested by order of the commandant general, and was on his way to Mexico for trial.

5th May, Tuesday.—The party marched with all the spare horses and baggage.

6th May, Wednesday.—Marched at five o'clock; ascended the river four miles, when we left it to our right and took off south 60°, east eight miles. Our friend Malgares accompanied us a few miles, to whom we bad an eternal adieu, if war does not bring us together in the field of battle opposed as the most deadly enemies, when our hearts acknowledge the greatest friendship..... Halted at ten o'clock, and marched again at four. No water on the road; detached a Spanish soldier in search of some, who did not join us until 12 o'clock at night. Encamped in the open prairie; no wood or water except what the soldier brought us in gourds. The mules came up at eleven o'clock at night. Distance 30 miles.

7th May, Thursday.—Marched very early, wind fresh from the south. The punctuality of captain Barelo as to hours was remarkable. Arrived at half past nine o'clock at a spring, the first water from Guaxequillo. The mules did not unload, but continued on 9 miles to another spring at the foot of a mountain—good pasturage round it—mountains on each side all day. Distance 28 miles.

8th, May, Friday.—Marched at five miles due west, through a gap in the mountain, then turned S. 20° E. and more south to a river about twenty feet wide—high steep banks ; now dry except in holes, but sometimes full and impassible. Halted at seven o'clock and sent on the loaded mules. Marched at five o'clock, came 10 miles and encamped without water. Distance 18 miles.

9th May, Saturday.—Marched between four and five o'clock and arrived at Pelia at eight. This is only a station for a few soldiers, but is surrounded by mines. At this place are two large warm springs, strongly impregnated with sulphur, and this is the water obliged to be used by the party who are stationed there. Here we remained all day. Captain Barelo had two beeves killed for his and my men and charged nothing to either. Here he received orders from the general to lead us through the wilderness to Montelovez, in order that we should not approximate to the frontiers of Mexico, which we should have done by the usual route of Pattos, Paras, &c.

10th May, Sunday.—Marched past one copper mine now diligently worked. At this place the proprietor had 100,000 sheep, cattle, horses, &c. Arrived at the Cadena, a house built and occupied by a priest. It is situated on a small stream at the pass of the mountains called by the Spaniards the Door of the Prison, from its being surrounded with mountains. The proprietor was at Sumbrarretto, distant six days march. This hacienda was obliged to furnish accommodations to all travellers.

Marched at five o'clock and passed the chain of mountains due east 12 miles, and encamped without water. Distance 31 miles.

11*th May*, *Monday*.—Marched and arrived at Mau-
pemie at eight o'clock, a village situated at the foot of
mountains of minerals, where they worked eight or nine
mines.   The mass of the people were naked and starved
wretches.   The proprietor of the mines gave us an elegant repast.   Here the orders of Salcedo were explained
to me by the captain.   I replied, that they excited my
laughter, as there were disaffected persons sufficient to
serve as guides should an army ever come into the
country.

Came on three miles further, where were fig-trees
and a fruit called by the French La Grain, situated on a
little stream which flowed through the gardens, and formed a terrestrial paradise.   Here we remained all day sleeping in the shade of the fig-trees, and at night continued
our residence in the garden.   We obliged the inhabitants
with a ball, who expressed great anxiety for a relief from
their present distressed state and a change of government.

12*th May*, *Tuesday*.—Was awoke in the morning by
the singing of the birds and the perfumes of the trees
around.   I attempted to send two of my soldiers to town,
when they were overtaken by a dragoon and ordered back—
they returned, when I again ordered them to go, and if a
soldier attemped to stop them to take him off his horse
and flog him.   This I did, as I conceived it was the duty
of the captain to explain his orders relative to me, which
he had not done, and I conceived that this would bring on
an explanation.   They were pursued by a dragoon
through the town, who rode after them making use of ill
language.   They attempted to catch him but could not.
As I had mentioned my intentions of sending my men to
town after some stores to captain Barelo, and he had not
made any objections, I conceived it was acting with duplicity to send men to watch the movements of my messen-

gers; I therefore determined they should punish the dragoons unless their captain had candor sufficient to explain the reasons for his not wishing the men to go to the town, in which wish I should undoubtedly have acquiesced; but as he never mentioned the circumstance, I was guardedly silent, and the affair never interrupted our harmony.

We marched at five o'clock and came on 15 miles and encamped without water. One mile on this side of the little village the road branches out into three, the right hand one by Pattos, Paras, Saltelo, &c. being the main road to Mexico and St. Antonio. The road which we took, leaves all the villages a little to the right, passing only some plantations; the left hand one goes immediately through the mountains to Montelovez, but is dangerous for small parties on account of the savages. This road is called the route by the Bolson of Maupeme, and was first travelled by Monsieur De Croix, (afterwards viceroy of Peru.) In passing from Chihuahua to Texas, by this route, you make in seven days what it takes you 15 or 20 by the ordinary one, but it is very scarce of water, and your guards must either be so strong as to defy the Appaches, or calculate to escape them by swiftness, for they fill those mountains, whence they continually carry on a predatory war against the Spanish settlements and caravans.

We this day passed on to the territories of the marquis De San Miquel, who owns from the mountains of the Rio del Norte to some distance into the kingdom of Old Mexico.

13th May, Wednesday.—Came on to the river Brasses Ranche de St. Antonio, part of the marquis' estate. My boy and self halted at the river Brasses to water our horses, having rode on ahead, and took the bridles from their mouths, in order that they might drink free, which they could not do with the Spanish bridles. The horse I rode had been accustomed to being held by his master in a peculiar manner when bridled, and would not let me put it on again for a long time, when in the mean time my boy's horse ran away, and it was out of our power to catch him again, but when we arrived at the Ranche, we soon had out a number of boys, who brought in the horse and all his different equipments which were scattered on the route. This certainly was a strong proof of their honesty, and did not go unrewarded. In the evening we gave them a ball on the green according to custom. We here learnt that one peck of corn, with three pounds of meat per week, was the allowance given a grown person.

14th May, Thursday.—Did not march until half past four o'clock, and about nine o'clock an officer arrived from St. Rosa with 24 men and two Appaches in irons. They were noble looking fellows, of large stature, and appeared by no means cast down by their misfortunes, although they knew their fate was transportation beyond the sea, never more to see their friends and relations..... Knowing as I did the intention of the Spaniards towards those people, I would have liberated them if in my power. I went near them and gave them to understand we were friends, and conveyed to them some articles which would be of service if chance offered.

This day the thermometer stood at 30° Raumauer, 99° 1-2 Farenheit and the dust and drought of the road obliged us to march in the night, when we came 15 miles and encamped without water—indeed this road which the general obliged us to take, is almost impassable at this season for want of water, whilst the other is plentifully supplied.

15th May, Friday.—Marched early and came on five miles, when we arrived at a pit dug in a hollow, which afforded a small quantity of muddy water for ourselves and beasts. Here we were obliged to remain all day in order to travel in the night, as our beasts could enjoy the benefit of water. Left this at half past five o'clock and came on 15 miles by eleven o'clock, when we encamped without water or food for our beasts. Passed a miserable burnt up soil. Distance 20 miles.

16th May, Saturday.—Marched two hours and arrived at a wretched habitation, where we drew water from a well for all the beasts. Marched in the evening and made 15 miles further. The right hand road we left on this side of Maupeme, and joined it about four miles further. Distance 15 miles.

17th May, Sunday.—Marched and about seven o'clock came in sight of *Paras*, which we left on the right and halted at the Hacienda of St. Lorenzo, a short league to the north of said village. At the Hacienda of St. Lorenzo was a young priest, who was extremely anxious for a change of government, and came to our beds and conversed for hours on the subject.

18th May, Monday.—Marched early and came through a mountainous tract of country but well watered, and houses situated here and there amongst the rocks..... Joined the main road at a Hacienda of ———— belonging to the marquis De San Miquel—good gardens and fruit—also a fine stream. The mules did not arrive until late at night, when it had commenced raining.

19th May, Tuesday.—Did not march until three o'clock, the captain not being very well. He here determined to take the main road notwithstanding the orders of general Salcedo. Came on ten miles. Met a deserter from captain Johnston's company. He returned and came to the camp, and begged of me to take him back to his company, but I would not give any encouragement to the scoundrel, only a little change, as he was without a farthing.

20th May, Wednesday.—Came to the Hacienda of Pattos by nine o'clock. This is a handsome place, where the marquis De San Miquel frequently spends his summers, the distance enabling him to come from Mexico in his coach in ten days. Here we met the Mexican post-rider going to Chewawa. Don Hymie who had left us at Paras, joined in a coach and six, in which we came out to a little settlement called the Florida, one league from Pattos, due north. Distance 18 miles.

The Hacienda of Pattos was a square enclosure of about three hundred feet, the building being one story high, but some of the apartments very elegantly furnished. In the centre of the square was a Jet d'eau, which cast forth water from eight spouts, extended from a colosean female form. From this fountain all the neighbouring inhabitants got their supply of water. The marquis had likewise a very handsome church, which, with its orna-ments cost him at least 20,000 dollars; to officiate in which, he maintained a little stiff superstitious priest. In the rear of the palace (for so it might be called) was a fish-pond, in which were immense numbers of fine fish. The population of Florida is about 2,000 souls. This was our nearest point to the city of Mexico.

21st May, Thursday.—Marched down the water course over a rough and stony road about ten miles, when we left it on the right, and came on eight miles further to a horse range of the marquis's, where he had four of his soldiers as a guarda caballo. Halted at half past nine o'clock. At this place we had a spring of bad water.

22d May, Friday.—Marched at three o'clock and came on 16 miles to a small shed, and in the afternoon to la Rancho, eight miles to the left of the main road near the foot of the mountain, where was a pond of water but no houses. Some Spanish soldiers were here. We left Pattos mountain on our left and right, but here there was a cross mountain over which we were to pass in the morning.

The marquis maintains 1500 troops to protect his vassals and property from the savages. They are all cavalry, and as well dressed and armed as the king's, but are treated by the king's troops as if vastly inferior.

23d May, Saturday.—Marched early and came to a spring in the mountain.

24th May, Sunday.—Marched at an early hour and passed through the mountain, (scarcely any road,) called the mountain of the Three Rivers. At the 13th mile joined the main road which we had left to our right on the 22d instant, and in one hour after, came to the main Mexican road from the eastern provinces; from thence north-west to the Rancho, nine miles from Montelovez, whence the captain sent in an express to give notice of our approach.

25th May, Monday.—In the afternoon lieutenant Adams, commandant of the company of Montelovez arrived in a coach and six to escort us to town, where we arrived about five o'clock, P. M. In the evening visited captain De Ferara, the commandant of the troops of Cogquilla, and inspector of the five provinces.

Lieutenant Adams who commanded this place, was the son of an Irish engineer in the service of *Spain*. He had married a rich girl of the Passo Del Norte, and they lived here in elegance and style for the country. We put up at his quarters and were very hospitably entertained.

K k

26th May, Tuesday.—Made preparations for marching the next day. I arose early before any of our people were up and walked nearly round the town ; and from the hill took a small survey, with my pencil and a pocket compass which I always carried with me—returned and found them at breakfast, they having sent three or four of my men to search for me. The Spanish troops at this place were remarkably polite, always fronting and saluting when I passed. This I attributed to their commandant, lieutenant Adams.

27th May, Wednesday.—Marched at seven o'clock, after taking an affectionate leave of Don Hymen, and at half past twelve arrived at the Haciendo of Don Melcher, situated on the same stream of Montelovez.

Don Melcher was a man of very large fortune, polite, generous and friendly. He had in his service a man who had deserted from captain Lockwood's company, first regiment of infantry, by the name of Pratt. From this man he had acquired a considerable quantity of crude indigested information relative to the United States, and when he met with us his thirst after knowledge of our laws and institutions appeared to be insatiable. He caused a fine large sheep to be killed and presented to my men.

28th May, Thursday.—Marched early and arrived at Encina Haciendo at ten o'clock. This place was owned by Don Barego.

When we arrived at the Haciendo of Encina, I found a youth of 18 sitting in the house quite genteely dressed, whom I immediately recognized from his physiognomy to be an American, and entered into conversation with him. He expressed great satisfaction at meeting a countryman, and we had a great deal of conversation. He sat at a table with us and partook of a cold collation of fruits and confectionary, but I was much surprised to learn shortly after we quit the table, that he was a deserter from our army, on which I questioned him, and he replied, that his name was Griffith, he had enlisted in Philadelphia ; arrived at New Orleans and deserted as soon as possible ; that the Spaniards had treated him much better than his own countrymen, and that he should never return. I was extremely astonished at his insolence, and mortified that I should have been betrayed into any polite conduct towards the scoundrel. I told him " that it was astonishing he " should have had the impertinence to address himself to " me, knowing that I was an American officer." He muttered something about being in a country where he was protected, &c. on which I told him, " If he again opened " his mouth to me, I would instantly chastize him, not- " withstanding his supposed protection." He was silent, and I called up one of my soldiers and told him in his hearing, that if he attempted to mix with them to turn him out of company, which they executed by leading him to the door of their room a short time after, when he entered it. When dinner was nearly ready, I sent a message to the proprietor, that " we assumed no right to say whom he " should introduce to his table, but, that we should think " it a great indignity offered to a Spanish officer to attempt " to set him down at the same board with a deserter from " their army ; and that, if the man who was at the table " in the morning, was to make his appearance again, " we should decline eating at it." He replied, " that it " was accident which produced the event of the morning ; " that he was sorry our feelings had been injured, and that " he would take care he did not appear again whilst we " were there."

Our good friend Don Melcher here overtook us, and passed the evening with us.

This day we passed the last mountains, and again entered the great Mississippi valley, it being six months and thirteen days since we first came in sight of them. Distance 20 miles.

29*th May, Friday.*—Marched at seven o'clock and came to the river Millada and Rancho.

30*th May, Saturday.*—Marched at five o'clock and arrived at the river Sabine at eight—forded it. Marched in the evening at four o'clock, at ten encamped at the Second Ridge without water. Distance 27 miles.

31*st May, Sunday.*—Marched early and at nine o'clock arrived at a Rancho, a fine running water—course east and west. Marched eight miles further to a point of woods and encamped. No water. Distance 23 miles.

1*st June, Monday.*—Arrived at the Presidio Rio Grande at eight o'clock. This place was the position to which our friend Barelo was ordered, and which had been very highly spoken of to him, but he found himself miserably mistaken, for it was with the greatest difficulty we obtained any thing to eat, which mortified him extremely. When at Chihuahua, general Salcedo had asked me if I had not lost a man by desertion, to which I replied in the negative. He then informed me that an American had arrived at the Presidio Rio Grande in the last year : that he had at first confined him, but that he was now released and practicing physic, and that he wished me to examine him on my arrival : I therefore had him sent for; the moment he entered the room I discovered he never had received a liberal education, or been accustomed to polished society. I told him the reason that I had requested to see him, and that I had it in my power to serve him if I found him a character worthy of interference.

He then related the following story ; " That his name " was Martin Henderson, that he was born in Rock Bridge

" county, state of Virginia ; that he had been brought up
" a farmer, but, that coming early to the state of Ken-
" tucky and Tennessee, he had acquired a taste for a
" frontier life, and that in the spring of 1806, himself and
" four companions, had left the Saline in the District of
" Saint Genevieve, Upper Louisiana, in order to pene-
" trate through the woods to the province of Texas ;
" that his companions had left him on the White River,
" and that he had continued on : that in swimming some
" western branch his horse sunk under him, and it was with
" difficulty he had made the shore with his gun. Here
" he waited two or three days until his horse rose, and he
" then got his saddle bags, but that all his notes on the
" country, courses, &c. were destroyed. He then pro-
" ceeded on foot for a few days, when he was met by 30
" or 40 Osage warriors, who on his telling them he was
" going to the Spaniards were about to kill him, but on
" his saying he would go to the Americans, they held a
" consultation over him, and finally seized on his clothes,
" and divided them between them ; then his pistols, com-
" pass, dirk and watch, which they took to pieces and
" hung in their noses and ears ; then stripped him
" naked, and round his body they found a belt with gold
" pieces sewed in it ; this they also took, and finally seized
" on his gun and ammunition, and were marching off to
" leave him in that situation, but he followed them, think-
" ing it better to be killed than left in that state to die by
" hunger and cold. The savages after some time halted,
" and one pulled off an old pair of leggins and gave him,
" another mockinsons, and a third a buffalo robe, and the
" one who had carried his heavy rifle had by this time be-
" came tired of his prize, (they never using rifles) and
" they counted him out 25 charges of powder and ball,
" then sent two Indians with him who put him on a war

" trace, which they said led to American establishments;
" and as soon as the Indians left him he directed his
" course as he supposed for Saint Antonio. He then killed
" deer and made himself some clothes.   He proceeded on
" and expended all his ammunition three days before he
" struck the Grand Road, nearly at the Rio Grande. He
" further added, that he had discovered two mines, one of
" silver and the other of gold, the situation of which he
" particularly described; but, that the general had taken
" the samples from him.   That he would not attempt to
" pass himself on us for a physician, and hoped as he only
" used simples and was careful to do no harm we would
" not betray him.   He further added, that since his being
" int the country, he had made (from information) maps
" of all the adjacent country, but that they had been taken
" from him."

I had early concluded that he was an agent of Burr's,
and was revolving in my mind whether I should denounce
him as such to the commandant, but felt reluctant from an
apprehension that he might be innocent, when one of my
men came in and informed me that it was Trainer, who
had killed major Bashier in the wilderness, between
Natchez and Tennessee, when he was his hireling. He
shot him (when taking a nap at noon through the head)
with his own pistols. The governor of the state and the
major's friends offered a very considerable reward for his
apprehension, which obliged him to quit the state ; and
with an Amazonian woman, who handled arms and
hunted like a savage, he retreated to the source of the
White River, but being routed from that retreat by captain
Maney, of the United States army, and a party of Cherokees, he and his female companion bore west, and she
proving to be pregnant, was left by him in the desert, and
(I was informed) arrived on the settlements of Red river,

but by what means is to me unknown.   The articles and money taken from him by the Osage's were the property of the deceased major.   I then reported the circumstance to captain Barelo, who had him immediately confined, until the will of governor Cordero was known, who informed me (when at Saint Antonio) he would have him sent to some place of perpetual confinement in the interior.   Thus vengeance has overtaken the ingrate and murderer when he least expected it.

In the evening we went to see some performers on the slack rope, who were no wise extraordinary in their performances, except in language which would almost bring a blush on the cheek of the most abandoned of the female sex in the United States.

2d June, Tuesday.—In the day time were endeavoring to regulate our watches by my compass, and in an instant that my back was turned some person stole it ; I could by no means recover it, and I had strong suspicions that the theft was approved, as the instrument had occasioned great dissatisfaction.

This day the captain went out to dine with some monks, who would have thought it profanation to have had us their guests, notwithstanding the priest of the place had escorted us round the town and to all the missions ; and we found him a very communicative, liberal and intelligent man.   We saw no resource for a dinner, but in the inventive genius of a little Frenchman who had accompanied us from Chihuahua, where he had been officiating one year as cook to the general, of whom he gave us many interesting anecdotes, and in fact he was of infinite service to us ; we supported him and he served us as cook, interpreter, &c.   It was astonishing with what zeal he strove to acquire news and information for us ; and as he had been four times through the provinces, he had acquired considerable knowledge of the country, people, &c. He went off and in a very short time returned with table-cloth, plates, and a dinner of three or four courses, a bottle of wine with a pretty girl to attend on the table. We enquired by what magic he had brought it about, and found he had been to one of the officers and notified, that it was the wish of the commandant that he should supply the two Americans with a decent dinner, (this we explained to Barelo in the evening, and he laughed heartily) which was done, but we took care to compensate them for their trouble.

We parted from the captain with regret, and assurances of remembrance. Departed at five o'clock, escorted by ensign —— and —— men, and came on to the Rio Grande, which we passed and encamped at a Rancho on the other side. Distance 7 miles.

3d June, Wednesday.—The musquetoes which had commenced the first night on this side Montelovez, now had become very troublesome. This day saw the first horse-flies—saw some wild horses—came on in the open plain, and in a dry time, where there was no water. Distance 30 miles.

4th June, Thursday.—Came 16 miles to a pond and dined—great sign of wild horses—in the afternoon to the river Noissour swiming, where we arrived, although not more than ten steps wide. Distance 36 miles.

5th June, Friday.—After loosing two horses in passing the river (the water having fallen so that we forded) crossed and continued our route. Passed two herd of wild horses, who left the road for us. Halted at a pond on the left of the road, 15 miles, where we saw the first oak since we entered New Mexico, and this was scrub oak. Passed many deer yesterday and to day. Came on to a small creek at night, where we met a party of the company of Saint Fernandez returning from the line. Distance 31 miles.

6th June, Saturday.—Marched early and met several parties of troops returning from Texas, where they had been sent to reinforce, when our troops were near the line. Immense numbers of cross roads made by the wild horses. Killed a wild hog, which on examination I found to be very different from the tame breed, smaller, brown, long hair and short legs : they are to be found in all parts between Red river and the Spanish settlements.

Passed an encampment made by the *Lee Panes*—met one of said nation with his wife. In the afternoon struck the wood land, which was the first we had been in from the time we left the Osage nation. Distance 39 miles.

7th June, Sunday.—Came on 15 miles to the river Mariano, the line between Texas and Cogquilla—a pretty little stream, Rancho. From thence in the afternoon to Saint Antonio. We halted at the mission of Saint Joseph—received in a friendly manner by the priest of the mission and others.

We were met out of Saint Antonio about three miles by governors Cordero and Herrara, in a coach. We repaired to their quarters, where we were received like their children. Cordero informed me that he had discretionary orders as to the mode of my going out of the country : that he therefore wished me to choose my time, mode, &c. and, that any sum of money I might want was at my service : that in the mean time Robinson and myself would make his quarters our home ; and that he had caused to be vacated and prepared a house immediately opposite for the reception of my men. In the evening his levee was attended by a croud of officers and priests, at which was father M'Guire and Dr. Zerbin. After supper we went to the public square, where might be seen the two governors joined in a dance with people, who in the day time would approach them with reverence and awe.

We were here introduced to the sister of lieutenant Malgares's wife, who was one of the finest women we saw —she was married to a captain Ugarte, to whom we had letters of introduction.

8th June, Monday.—Remained at Saint Antonio.

9th June, Tuesday.—A large party dined at governor Cordero's, who gave as his first toast, " The Presi-"dent of the United States."—Vive la—I returned the compliment by toasting " His Catholic Majesty." These toasts were followed by " General Wilkinson," and one of the company then gave, " Those gentleman ; their safe and " happy arrival in their own country—their honorable re-" ception, and the continuation of the good understanding " which exists between the two countries."

10th June, Wednesday.—A large party at the governor's to dinner. He gave as a toast, " His companion, " Herrara."

11th June, Thursday.—Preparing to march to-morrow. We this evening had a conversation with the two governors, wherein they exhibited an astonishing knowledge of the political character of our executive, and the local interests of the different parts of the union.

12th June, Friday.—One of the captains from the kingdom of Leon having died, we were invited to attend the burial, and accompanied the two governors in their coach, where we had an opportunity of viewing the solemnity of the interment, agreeably to the ritual of the Spanish church, attended by the military honors, which was conferred on the deceased by his late brethren in arms. Governor Cordero gave the information of my intended expedition to the commandant general as early as July. The same month I took my departure. His information was received via Natchez.

13th *June, Saturday.*—This morning there was marched 200 dragoons for the sea coast to look out for the English, and that evening colonel Cordero was to have marched to join them.

We marched at seven o'clock ; governor Cordero taking us out in his coach about two leagues, accompanied by father M'Guire, Dr. Zerbin, &c.

It may not be improper to mention here, something of father M'Guire and doctor Zerbin, who certainly treated us with all imaginable attention while at Saint Antonio. The former was an Irish priest, who formerly resided on the coast above Orleans, and was noted for his hospitable and social qualities. On the cession of Louisiana, he followed the standard of the " king, his master," who never suffers an old servant to be neglected. He received at Cuba an establishment as chaplain to the mint of Mexico, whence the instability of human affairs carried him to Saint Antonio. He was a man of chaste classical taste, observation and research.

Doctor Zerbin formerly resided at Natchez, but in consequence of pecuniary embarrassments emigrated to the Spanish territories. Being a young man of a handsome person and insinuating address, he had obtained the good will of governor Cordero, who had conferred on him an appointment in the king's hospital, and many other advantages by which he might have made a fortune ; but he had recently committed some very great indiscretions, by which he had nearly lost the favor of colonel Cordero ; but whilst we were there he was treated with attention.

We took a friendly adieu of governor Herrara and our other friends at Saint Antonio.

I will here attempt to pourtray a faint resemblance of the characters of the two governors whom we found at Saint Antonio; but whose super-excellent qualities it would require the pen of a master to do justice.

Don Antonio Cordero, is about five feet ten inches in height, fifty years of age, fair complexion, and blue eyes: he wore his hair turned back, and in every part of his deportment was legibly written "The Soldier." He yet possessed an excellent constitution, and a body which appeared to be neither impaired by the fatigues of the various campaigns he had made, nor disfigured by the numerous wounds received from the enemies of his king. He was one of the select officers who had been chosen by the court of Madrid to be sent to America about 35 years since, to discipline and organize the Spanish provincials, and had been employed in all the various kingdoms and provinces of New Spain. Through the parts which we explored, he was universally beloved and respected; and when I pronounce him by far the most *popular man* in the *internal provinces*, I risk nothing by the assertion. He spoke the Latin and French languages well—was generous, gallant, brave, and sincerely attached to his king and country. Those numerous qualifications have advanced him to the rank of colonel of cavalry, and governor of the provinces of Cogquilla and Texas. His usual residence was Montelovez, which he had embellished a great deal, but since our taking possession of Louisiana, he had removed to Saint Antonio, in order to be nearer the frontier, to be able to apply the remedy to any evil which might arise from the collision of our lines.

Don Simon de Herrara, is about five feet eleven inches high, has a sparkling black eye, dark complexion and hair. He was born in the Canary Islands, served in the infantry in France, Spain and Flanders, and speaks the

French language well, and a little of the English. He is engaging in his conversation with his equals; polite and obliging to his inferiors, and in all his actions one of the most gallant and accomplished men I ever knew.

He possesses a great knowledge of mankind from his experience in various countries and societies, and knows how to employ the genius of each of his subordinates to advantage. He had been in the United States during the presidency of general Washington, and had been introduced to that hero, of whom he spoke in terms of exalted veneration. He is now lieutenant-colonel of infantry, and governor of the kingdom of New Leon. His seat of government is Mont Elrey; and probably, if ever a chief was adored by his people it is Herrara. When his time expired last, he immediately repaired to Mexico, attended by 300 of the most respectable people of his government, who carried with them the sighs, tears and prayers of thousands that he might be continued in that government. The viceroy thought proper to accord to their wishes *pro tempore*, and the king has since confirmed his nomination.

When I saw him he had been about one year absent, during which time the citizens of Rank in Mont Elrey had not suffered a marriage or baptism to take place in any of their families, until their common father could be there, to consent and give joy to the occasion by his presence..... What greater proof could be given of their esteem and love?

In drawing a parrallel between the two friends, I should say that Cordero was the man of greatest reading, and that Herrara possessed the greatest knowledge of the world. Cordero has lived all his life a batchelor. Herrara married an English Lady in early youth, at Cadiz, who by her suavity of manners makes herself as much beloved and esteemed by the ladies as her noble husband does by the men. By her he has several children, one now an officer in the service of his royal master.

The two friends agree perfectly in one point, their hatred to tyranny of every kind; and in a secret determination never to see that flourishing part of the New World, subject to any other European lord, except *him*, whom they think their honor and loyalty bound to defend with their lives and fortunes. But should Bonaparte seize on European Spain, I risque nothing in asserting, those two gentlemen would be the first to throw off the yoke, draw their swords, and assert the independence of their country.

Before I close this subject, it may not be improper to state, that we owe to governor Herrara's prudence, that we are not now engaged in a war with Spain. This will be explained by the following anecdote which he related in the presence of his friend Cordero, and which was confirmed by him. When the difficulties commenced on the Sabine, the commandant general and the viceroy consulted each other, and they mutually determined to maintain (what they deemed) the dominions of their master, inviolate. The viceroy therefore ordered Herrara to join Cordero with 1300 men, and both the viceroy and general Salcedo, ordered Cordero to cause our troops to be attacked, should they pass the Rio Oude. Those orders were positively reiterated to Herrara, the actual commanding officer of the Spanish army on the frontiers, and gave rise to the many messages which he sent to general Wilkinson when he was advancing with our troops; but finding they were not attended to, he called a council of war on the question to attack or not; when it was given as their opinion, that they should immediately commence a predatory warfare, but avoid a general engagement; yet, notwithstanding the orders of the viceroy, the commandant general, governor Cordero's and the opinion of his officers, he had the firmness (or temerity) to enter into the agreement with general Wilkinson, which at present exists relative to our boundaries on that frontier. On his return he was received with coolness by Cordero, and they both made their communication to their superiors. Until an answer was received, said Herrara, " I " experienced the most unhappy period of my life, con- " scious I had served my country faithfully, at the same " time I had violated every principle of military duty." At length the answer arrived, and what was it, but the thanks of the viceroy and the commandant general, for having pointedly disobeyed their orders, with assurances that they would represent his services in exalted terms to the king. What could have produced this change of sentiment is to me unknown, but the letter was published to the army, and confidence again restored between the two chiefs and the troops.

Our company consisted of lieutenant Jn. Echararria, who commanded the escort. Captain Eugene Marchon, of New Orleans, and father Jose Angel Cabaso, who was bound to the camp at or near the Trinity, with a suitable proportion of soldiers. We came on 16 miles to a place called the Beson, where we halted until the mules came up. Marched again at four o'clock, and arrived at the river of Guadalupe at eight o'clock at night. Distance 30 miles.

14th June, Sunday.—When we left Saint Antonio, every thing appeared to be in a flourishing and improving state, owing to the examples and encouragement given to industry, politeness and civilization by their excellent governor Cordero and his colleague Herrara; also the large body of troops maintained at that place in consequence of the difference existing between the United States and Spain.

Came on to the Saint Mark in the morning—in the afternoon came on 15 miles further, but was late, owing to our having taken the wrong road. Distance 30 miles.

15th June, Monday.—Marched 20 miles in the morning to a small pond, which is dry in a dry season, where we halted. Here commenced the oak timber, it having been musqueet in general from Saint Antonio. Prairie like the Indiana territory. In the afternoon came on six miles further to a creek, where we encamped early. Distance 26 miles.

16th June, Tuesday.—Marched early, and at eight o'clock arrived at Red river. Here was a small Spanish station and several lodges of Tancards, tall, handsome men, but the most naked savages I ever yet saw without exception. They complained much of their situation. In the afternoon passed over hilly, stony land; occasionally saw pine timber. Encamped on a small run. Distance 26 miles. Killed one deer.

17th June, Wednesday.—Came on by nine o'clock to a large encampment of Tancards, more than 40 lodges. Their poverty was as remarkable as their independence. Immense herds of horses, &c. I gave a Camanche and Tancard, each a silk handkerchief, and a recommendation to the commandant at Natchitoches. In the afternoon came on three hours and encamped on a hill, at a creek on the right hand side of the road. Met a large herd of mules escorted by four soldiers; the lieutenant took some money from them which they had in charge. Distance 30 miles.

18th June, Thursday.—Rode on until half past ten o'clock, when we arrived at the river Brassos. Here is a stockade guard of one corporal, six men, and a ferry boat. Swam our horses over—one was drowned and several others near it, owing to their striking each other with their feet.   We then came on about two miles on this side of a bayou called the Little Brassos, which is only a branch of the other, and which makes an impassable swamp at certain seasons between them.   Distance 31 miles.

19*th June, Friday.*—Came on through prairies and woods alternately 20 miles to a small creek, *Corpus Christi* well wooded rich land.   In the afternoon came on ten miles, and passed a creek which in high water is nearly impassable four miles.   Overflows swamps, ponds, &c. Encamped about one mile on this side on high land to the right of the road.   Met the mail, Indians and others.   Distance 30 miles.

20*th June, Saturday.*—Came on 16 miles in the morning—passed several herds of mustangs or wild horses, good land, ponds and small dry creeks, prairie and woods alternately.   It rained considerably.   We halted to dry our baggage long before night.   Distance 20 miles.

21*st June, Sunday.*—Came on to the river Trinity by eight o'clock.   Here was stationed two captains, two lieutenants and three ensigns, with nearly 100 men, all sick, one scarcely able to assist the other.   Met a number of runaway negroes, some French and Irishmen.   Received information of lieutenant Wilkinson's safe arrival.   Crossed with all our horses and baggage with much difficulty. Distance 20 miles.

22*d June, Monday.*—Marched the mules and horses in the forenoon, but did not depart ourselves until three o'clock, P. M.   Father Jose Angel Cabaso, separated from us at this place for the post of ——— where he was destined.   Passed thick woods and a few small prairies with high rich grass.   Sent a dispatch to Nacogdoches. Distance 22 miles.

23*d June, Tuesday.*—Came on 20 miles in the forenoon to a small creek of standing water ; good land and well timbered. Met a sergeant from Nacogdoches. In the afternoon made 20 miles and crossed the river Natchez, running N. W. & S. E. 20 yards wide; belly deep to horses at that time, but sometimes impassable. Two miles on this side encamped on a hill in a little prairie—mules and loads arrived at twelve o'clock. The sandy soil and pine timber began again this afternoon, but good land near the river. Distance 40 miles.

24*th June, Wednesday.*—The horses came up this morning; lost six over night. We marched early and in 15 miles came to the river Angeline, about the width of the Natchez, running N. & S. Good land on its borders —two miles further was a settlement of Barr and Davenport's, where were three of our lost horses—one mile further found two more of our horses where we halted for dinner. Marched at four o'clock, and at half past eight arrived at Nacogdoches—were politely received by the adjutant and inspector, and captain Herrara, Davenport, &c. This part of the country is well watered, but sandy; hilly soil—pine, scrub oak, &c. Distance 37 miles.

25*th June, Thursday.*—Spent in reading a gazette from the United States, &c. A large party at the adjutant and inspector's to dinner. 1st toast, " The President of the United States." 2nd. " The King of Spain." 3d. " Governors Herrara and Cordero."

26*th June, Friday.*—Made preparations to march the next day. Saw an old acquaintance, also Lorrimier's son-in-law from the district of cape Jerardeau. Dined with the commandant, and spent the evening at Davenport's.

27*th June, Saturday.*—Marched after dinner and came only 12 miles. Was escorted by lieutenant Guodiana and a military party. Mr. Davenport's brother-in-law who was taking in some money also accompanied us.

Don Francis Viana, adjutant and inspector of the Internal provinces, who commanded at Nacogdoches, is an old and veteran officer, and was one of those who came to America at the same time with colonel Cordero ; but possessing a mind of frankness, he unfortunately spoke his opinions too freely in some instances, which finding their way to court, prevented his promotion. But he is highly respected by his superiors, and looked up to as a model of military conduct by his inferiors. He unfortunately does not possess flexibility sufficient to be useful in the present state of the Spanish kingdoms. He is the officer who caused major Sparks and Mr. Freeman to return from their expedition on the Red river.

28th June, Sunday. Marched early and at nine o'clock crossed the little river called ———, from whence we pushed on in order to arrive at the house of ———, a Frenchman, —— miles distant from the Sabine. We stopped at a house on the road, where the lieutenant informed me an American by the name of Johnson lived, but was surprized to find he had crossed the line with his family, and a French family in his place. When we began conversing with them they were much alarmed thinking we had come to examine them, and expressed great attachment to the Spanish government, but was somewhat astonished to find I was an American officer, and on my companions stepping out, expressed themselves in strong terms of hatred to the Spanish nation. I excused them for their weakness, and gave them a caution. Fine land, well watered and timbered, hickory, oak, sugar-tree, &c. Distance 40 miles.

29th June, Monday.—Our baggage and horses came up about ten o'clock, when we dispatched them on.... Marched ourselves at two o'clock, and arrived at the river Sabine by five. Here we saw the cantonment of the Spanish troops, when commanded by colonel Herrara, on the late affair between the two governments. Crossed the Sabine river and came about one league on this side to a little prairie, where we encamped. Parted with lieutenant Guodiana and our Spanish escort. And here I think proper to bear testimony to the politeness, civility and attention of all the officers, who at different periods and in different provinces commaded my escort, (but in a particular manner, to Malgares and Barelo, who appeared studious to please and accommodate, all that lay in their power) also the obliging, mild dispositions evinced in all instances by their rank and file. On this side of the Sabine I went up to a house where I found 10 or 15 Americans hovering near the line, in order to embrace an opportunity of carrying on some illicet commerce with the Spaniards, who on their side were equally eager. Here we found Tharp and Sea, who had been old sergeants in general Wayne's army. Distance 15 miles.

30th June, Tuesday.—Marched early and came on to a house at a small creek 15 miles, where lived a Dutch family named Faulk, where we left a small roan horse which had given out. Marched twelve miles further to a large bayou, where had been an encampment of our troops, which I recognized by its form, and took pleasure in imagining the position of the general's marquee and the tents of my different friends and acquaintances. Distance 28 miles.

1st July, Wednesday.—Finding that a horse of doctor Robinson's, which had come all the way from Chihuahua, could not proceed, was obliged to leave him here. Yesterday and to day passed many Choctaws, whose clothing, furniture,&c. evidently marked the superiority of situation of those who bordered on our frontiers, to those of the naked, half starved wretches whom we found hanging round the Spanish settlements. Came on and passed a string of huts, supposed to be built by our troops, and at a small run a fortified camp but a half mile from the hill, where anciently stood the village Adyes.

We proceeded on to a spring where we halted for our loads, and finding the horses much fatigued, and not able to proceed, left them and baggage and proceeded on, when we arrived at Natchitoches about four o'clock, P. M.

Language cannot express the gaiety of my heart, when I once more beheld the standard of my country waved aloft!—" All hail cried I, the ever sacred name of " country, in which is embraced that of kindred, friends, " and every other tie which is dear to the soul of man!!" Was affectionately received by colonel Freeman, captains Strong and Woolstoncraft, lieutenant Smith, and all the officers of the post.

Z. M. PIKE.

Meteorological observations made by captain Pike during a tour he made through the Internal Provinces of New Spain, in the year 1807.

days.	months.	sun-rise.	3 P. M.	sun-set.	Sky.	Course.	Force.
3		4	-	-	cloudy & snow	W	fresh
4		1	-	2	snow	E	do.
5		4	-	-	clear	N W	gentle
6		-	-	2	cloudy & snow	N	do.
7		1	-	-	hail	N	-
8		-	-	3	cloudy	W	-
9		3	-	4	clear	W	-
10		0	-	6	hail and snow	S W	-
11		1	-	6	-	W	fresh
12		3	-	3	-	W	gentle
13		1	-	-	-	N	fresh
14		3	-	6	cloudy	S W	-
15	MARCH.	0	-	6	-	W	-
16		7	-	2	clear	S W	gentle
17		4 1-2	-	7	-	E	-
18		6	-	6	-	E	fresh
19		2	-	7	-	-	-
20		-	-	-	-	E	-
21		9	-	-	clear & cold	-	-
22		-	-	-	snow and hail	S E	-
23		-	-	-	-	-	-
24		2	-	6	clear	E	gentle
25		-	-	-	do.	-	-
26		1	-	6	do.	E	gentle
27		1	-	-	do.	S	fresh
28		2	-	8	do.	S	gentle
29		2	-	9	-	N	fresh
30		1	14	4	-	N	-
31		5	-	11	-	W	gentle
4		13	16	15	-	-	-
5		14	17	15	-	9	-
6		15	16	14	-	-	-
7		13	15	16	cloudy	-	-
8		14	16	17	-	-	-
9		13	17	15	-	-	-
10		14	16	14	-	-	-
11		15	18	15	-	-	-
12		13	19	17	-	-	-
13		14	17	18	light snow	-	-
14	APRIL.	15	19	15	-	-	-
15		14	20	18	-	-	-
16		13	18	16	-	-	-
17		16	20	15	-	-	-
18		17	19	16	-	-	-
19		18	18	15	-	-	-
20		15	18	16	-	-	-
21		14	13	15	-	-	-
22		16	18	16	-	-	-
23		15	19	17	-	-	-
24		13	19	16	-	-	-

Meteorological observations made by captain Pike, during a tour he made through the Internal Provinces of New Spain, in the year 1807.

Time of observation.		Thermometer.			Sky.	Wind.	
days.	months.	sun-rise.	3 P. M.	sun-set.		Course.	Force.
25	APRIL.	15	19	16	clear	-	-
26		14	18	17	-	-	-
27		15	19	17	-	-	-
28		14	17	16	-	-	-
29		15	24	20	-	-	-
30		15	-	20	-	-	-
							-
1	MAY.	11	-	-	-	-	-
2		12	24	17	-	-	-
3		15	23	16	some rain	-	-
4		14	24	17	clear	-	-
5		17	23	16	-	W	-
6		17	28 1-2	16	-	S	-
7		14	29	15	-	S W	-
8		12	27	15	-	W	-
9		9	26	20	-	-	-
10		11	24	17	-	W	-
11		-	25	-	-	-	-
12		15	27	-	-	-	-
13		27	20	-	-	E	-
14		10	30	20	-	S W	-
15		11	32 1-2	-	clear	S E	-
16		-	25	-	cloudy	S	-
17		-	23	20	some rain	-	-
18		29	24	21 1-2	rain	-	-
19		20 1-2	-	15	cloudy	E	gentle
20		13	24	-	some rain	-	-
21		-	22	19	cloudy	-	-
22		-	24	-	rainy morning	-	-
23		15	23	15	clear	W	-
24		14	22	21	-	-	-
25		16	24	23	-	-	-
26		15	23	22	cloudy and rain	W	-
27		14	21	18	rain	-	-
28		15	23	15	cloudy	S	-
29		19	-	-	do.	-	-
30		-	30	20	do.	-	-
31		22	27	25	do.	S	-
1	JUNE.	17	2	-	-	-	-
2		-	25	-	cloudy	S E	-
3		-	26	-	-	-	-
4		-	30	-	-	-	-

N. B. The foregoing are from Reaumer's Thermometer.

PIKE.

APPENDIX TO PART I.

_____

[No. 1.]

Head of the rapids de Moyen, Aug. 20, 1805.

DEAR GENERAL,

I arrived here this day, after what I have considered as rather an unfortunate voyage, having had a series of rainy weather for the first six days, by which means all our biscuit was more or less damaged, they being in very bad and open barrels, and having got twice so fast on forked sawyers or old trees, as to oblige me partly to unload, and staving in a plank in another, which nearly sunk our boat before we got on shore, and detained us one whole day. These all occasioned unavoidable detentions of two days, and the innumerable islands and sand bars (which, without exaggeration, exceeds the river below the Ohio) has been the cause of much unexpected delay : but I calculate on getting to Prairie de Chien in at least the same time I was coming here. We were met yesterday on the Rapids by a Mr. William Ewing, who is sent here by the government of the United States to teach the savages agriculture ; and I perceive in governor Harrison's instructions is termed an agent of the United States, under the instructions of P. Choteau (and, he says, with a salary of 500 dollars per annum. I conceived you did not know of this functionary, or that you would have mentioned him to me. He was accompanied by a Monsieur Louis Tisson Houire, who informed me he had calculated on going with me as my interpreter, and that you had spoken to him on the occasion,

1

and appeared much disappointed when I told him I had no instructions to that effect; he said he had promised to discover mines, &c. which no person knew but himself, but, as I conceive him much of a hypocrite, and possessing great gasconism, I am happy he was not chosen for my voyage. They brought with them three perogues of Indians, who lightened my barge and assisted me up the Rapids. They expressed great regret at the news of two men having been killed on the river below (which I believe to be a fact, as I have it from various channels), and was very apprehensive they would be censured by our government as the author, which from every enquiry, they conceive not to be the case, and seem to ascribe the murder to the Kickapoos, and strongly requested I would hear what they had to say on the subject: this, with an idea that this place would be a central position for a trading establishment, for the Sacs, Reynards, Iowas of the de Moyen, the Sioux from the head of said river and Paunte of the riviere de Roche, has induced me to halt part of the day to-morrow. I should say more relative to Messrs. Ewings and Houire, only that they propose visiting you with the Indians who descend (as I understand by your request) in about 30 days, when your penetration will give you *le tout ensemble* of their characters. I have taken the liberty of inclosing a letter to Mrs. Pike to your care.

My compliments to lieutenant Wilkinson, and the tender of my highest respects for your lady, with the best wishes for your health and prosperity,

I am, general,

Your obedient servant,

(Signed)   Z. M. PIKE.

General Wilkinson.

[No. 2.]

Prairie de Chien, Sept. 5, 1805.

DEAR GENERAL,

I arrived here the day before yesterday, and found my interpreter gone in the employ of Mr. Dickson. I then endeavored to gain information relative to crossing the falls; and amidst the igno-

rance of the Canadians, and all the contradiction in the world, I have
learned it is impossible to carry my large barge round the shoot, I
have therefore hired two Schenectady barges, in which I shall embark
the day after to-morrow, with some expectation and hope of seeing
the head of the Mississippi and the town of Saint Louis yet this
winter.

I have chosen three places for military establishments; the
first on a hill about 40 miles above the river de Moyen rapids, on
the W. side of the river, in about 41° 2ʹ N. latitude. The channel
of the river runs on that shore; the hill in front is about 60 feet
perpendicular, nearly level on the top.   400 yards in the rear is a
small prairie fit for gardening, and over on the E. side of the river
you have an elegant view on an immense prairie, as far as the eye
can extend, now and then interrupted by clumps of trees, and to
crown all, immediately under the hill is a limestone spring, sufficient for the consumption of a regiment.   The landing is good and
bold, and at the point of the hill a road could be made for a waggon
in half a day.   This place I conceive to be the best to answer the
general's instructions relative to the intermediate post between
Prairie de Chien and St. Louis; but if its being on the W. bank is
a material objection, about 30 miles above the second Sac village at
the third yellow bank on the E. side, is a commanding place, on a
prairie, and most elegantly situated, but is scarce of timber, and no
water but that of the Mississippi. When thinking on the post to be
established at the Ouiscousing, I did not look at the general's instructions. I therefore piched on a spot on the top of the hill on
the W. side of the Mississippi, which is   feet high, level on the
top, and completely commands both rivers, the Mississippi being
only one half mile wide and the Ouiscousing about 900 yards when
full. There is plenty of timber in the rear, and a spring at no great
distance on the hill. If this position is to have in view the annoyance of any European power who might be induced to attack it with
cannon, it has infinitely the preference to a position called the *Petit
Gris* on the Ouiscousing, which I visited and marked the next day.
This latter position is three miles up the Ouiscousing on a prairie
hill, on the W. side, where we should be obliged to get our timber
from the other side of the river, and our water out of it; there is
likewise a small channel which runs on the opposite side, navigable
in high water, which could not be commanded by the guns of the
fort, and a hill about three quarters of a mile, in the rear from
which it could be cannonaded.   These two positions I have marked
by blazing trees, &c.   A Mr. Fisher of this place, will direct any

officer who may be sent to occupy them. I found the confluence of the Ouiscousing and Mississippi be in lat. N. 43º 28' 8''.

The day of my arrival at the lead mines, I was taken with a fever, which, with Monsieur Dubuque having no horses about his house, obliged me to content myself with proposing to him the inclosed queries; the answers seem to carry with them the semblance of equivocation.

Messrs. Dubuque and Dickson were about sending a number of chiefs to St. Louis, but the former confessing he was not authoized, I have stopped them without in the least dissatisfying the Indians.

Dickson is at Michilimackinac. I cannot say I have experienced much spirit of accommodation from his clerks, when in their power to oblige me; but I beg leave to recommend to your attention a Mr. James Aird, who is now in your country, as a gentleman to whose humanity and politeness I am much indebted; also a Mr. Fisher of this place, the captain of militia and justice of the peace. A band of Sioux between here and the Missouri have applied for two medals, in order that they may have their chiefs distinguished as friends of the Americans: if the general thinks proper to send them here to the care of Mr. Fisher, with any other commands, they may possibly meet me here, or at the falls of St. Anthony on my return.

* * * * * * * * *

* * * * * * * *

The above suggestion would only be acceptable under the idea of our differences with Spain being compromised; as should there be war, the field of action is the sphere for young men, where they hope, and at least aspire, to gather laurels or renown, to smooth the decline of age; or a glorious death. You see, my dear general, I write to you like a person addressing a father: at the same time I hope you will consider me not only in a professional, but a personal view, one who holds you in the highest respect and esteem: My compliments to lieutenant Wilkinson, and my highest respects to your lady.

I am, general,
Your obedient servant,
(Signed)   Z. M. PIKE, Lt.

General Wilkinson.

QUERIES

Proposed to Mr. Dubuque—with his answers.

1. What is the date of your grant of the mines from the savages?

Answer. The copy of the grant is in Mr. Soulard's office at St. Louis.

2. What is the date of the confirmation by the Spaniards?

Ans. The same as to query first.

3. What is the extent of your grant?

Ans. The same as above.

4. What is the extent of the mines?

Ans. Twenty-eight or twenty-seven leagues long, and from one to three broad.

5. Lead made per annum?

Ans. From 20 to 40,000 pounds.

6. Quantity of lead per cwt. of mineral?

Ans. Seventy-five per cent.

7. Quantity of lead in pigs?

Ans. All he makes, as he neither manufactures bar, sheet-lead, nor shot.

8. If mixed with any other mineral?

Ans. We have seen some copper, but having no person sufficiently acquainted with chymistry to make the experiment properly, I cannot say as to the proportion it bears to the lead.

Dubuque.

(Signed)   Z. M. PIKE.

Lead mines, Sept. 1, 1805.

[No. 3.]

CONFERENCES

HELD WITH DIFFERENT BANDS OF INDIANS, ON A VOYAGE UP THE
MISSISSIPPI, IN THE YEARS 1805 AND 1806.

---

*Speech delivered to the Sioux, at the entrance of the river St. Peter's,
23d September,* 1805.

BROTHERS—I am happy to meet you here at this council fire, which your father has sent me to kindle, and to take you by the hands as our children. We having but lately acquired from the Spanish the extensive territory of Louisiana.—Our general has thought proper to send out a number of his young warriors to visit all his red children—to tell them his will, and to hear what request they may have to make of their father. I am happy the choice has fell on me to come this road; as I find my brother's, the Sioux, ready to listen to my words.

BROTHERS—It is the wish of our government to establish military post's on the Upper Mississippi, at such places as might be thought expedient—I have, therefore, examined the country, and have pitched on the mouth of the river St. Croix. This place and the falls of St. Anthony—I therefore, wish you to grant to the United States, nine miles square, at St Croix, and at this place, from a league below the confluence of the St. Peter's and Mississippi, to a league above St. Anthony, extending three leagues on each side of the river; and as we are a people who are accustomed to have all our acts wrote down, in order to have them handed to our children—I have drawn up a form of an agreement, which we will both sign in the presence of the traders now present. After we know the terms we will fill it up, and have it read and interpreted to you.

BROTHERS—Those posts are intended as a benefit to you. The old chiefs now present must see, that their situation improves by a communication with the whites. It is the intention of the United Statesto establish at those posts, factories, in which the Indians may procure all their things at a cheaper and better rate than they do now; or, than your traders can afford to sell them to you, as they are single men who come far in small boats. But your fathers are many and strong, and will come with a strong arm, in large boats. There will also be chiefs here, who can attend to the wants of their brothers, without their sending or going all the way to St. Louis, and will see the traders that go up your rivers, and know that they are good men.

BROTHERS—Another object your father has at heart, is to endeavour to make peace between you and the Chipeway's. You have now been a long time at war, and when will you stop ? If neither side will lay down the hatchet, your paths will always be red with blood ; but if you will consent to make peace, and suffer your father to bury the hatchet between you, I will endeavour to bring down some of the Chipeway chiefs with me to St. Louis, where the good work can be completed, under the auspices of your mutual father. I am much pleased to see that the young warriors have halted here to hear my words this day ; and as I know it is hard for a warrior to be struck and not strike again, I will send (by the first Chipeway I meet) word to their chiefs :—That, if they have not yet felt your tomahawk, it is not because you have no legs or the hearts of men, but because you have listened to the voice of your father.

BROTHERS—If the chiefs do not listen to the voice of their father, and continue to commit murders on you and our traders, they will call down the vengeance of the Americans ; for they are not like a blind man walking into the fire. They were once at war with us, and joined to all the northern Indians, were defeated at Roche De Bœuf, and were obliged to sue for peace—that peace we granted them. They know we are not children, but, like all wise people, are slow to shed blood.

BROTHERS.—Your old men probably know, that about 30 years ago, we were subject to, and governed by the king of the English ; but he not treating us like children, we would no longer acknowledge him as father—and after ten years war, in which he lost 100,000 men, he acknowledged us a free and independent nation. They know that not many years since, we received Detroit, Michilimackinac, and all the posts on the lakes from the English, and now but the other day, Louisiana from the Spanish ; so that we put one foot on the sea at the east, and the other on the sea at the west ; and if once children, are now men ; yet, I think, the traders who come from Canada are bad birds amongst the Chipeways, and instigate them to make war on their red brothers the Sioux, in order to prevent our traders from going high up the Mississippi. This I shall enquire into, and if so, warn those persons of their ill conduct.

BROTHERS—Mr. Choteau was sent by your father to the Osage nation, with one of his young chiefs. He sailed some days before me, and had not time to procure the medals which I am *told* he promised to send up, but they will be procured.

BROTHERS—I wish you to have some of your head chiefs to be ready to go down with me in the spring. From the head of the St. Pierre also, such other chiefs as you may think proper, to the number of four or five. When I pass here on my way I will send you word at what time you will meet me at the Prairie des Chiens.

BROTHERS—I expect that you will give orders to all your young warriors to respect my *flag* and *protection* which I may extend to the Chipeway chiefs who may come down with me in the spring : for was a dog to run to my lodge for safety, his enemy must walk over me to hurt him.

BROTHERS—Here is a flag, which I wish to send to Gens de Feuilles, to shew them they are not forgot by their father. I wish the comrade of their chief to take it on himself to deliver it with my words.

BROTHERS—I am told that hitherto the traders have made a practice of selling rum to you. All of you in your right senses must know that it is injurious ; and occasions quarrels, murders, &c. amongst yourselves. For this reason your father has thought proper to prohibit the traders from selling you any rum. Therefore, I hope, my *brothers* the *chiefs*, when they know of a trader to sell an Indian rum, will prevent that Indian from paying his credit. This will break up the pernicious practice and oblige your father. But I hope you will not encourage your young men to treat our traders ill from this circumstance, or from a hope of the indulgence formerly experienced ; but make your complaints to persons in this country, who will be authorised to do you justice.

BROTHERS—I now present you with some of your father's tobacco, and some other trifling things, as a memorandum of my good will, and before my departure I will give you some liquor to clear your throats.

WHEREAS, at a conference held between the United States of America and the Sioux nation of Indians : lieutenant Z. M. Pike, of the army of the United States, and the chiefs and the warriors of said tribe, have agreed to the following articles, which, when ratified and approved of by the proper authority, shall be binding on both parties.

Art. 1. That the Sioux nation grant unto the United States, for the purpose of establishment of military posts, nine miles square at the mouth of the St. Croix,* also from below the confluence of the Mississippi and St. Peters up the Mississippi to include the falls of St. Anthony, extending nine miles on each side of the river, that the Sioux nation grants to the United States the full sovereignty and power over said district for ever.

Art 2. That, in consideration of the above grants, the United States shall pay (filled up by the senate with 2000 dollars.)

Art.3. The United States promise, on their part, to permit the Sioux to pass and repass, hunt, or make other use of the said districts as they have formerly done without any other exception than those specified in article first.

In testimony whereof we, the undersigned, have hereunto set our hands and seals, at the mouth of the river St. Peters, on the 23d day of September, 1805.

Z. M. PIKE, 1st lieut.   (L. S.)
          and agent at the above conference.

                                        his
LE PETIT CORBEAU,   ✗   (L. S.)
                                        mark

                                        his
WAY AGO ENAGEE,   ✗   (L. S.)
                                        mark

[No. 4.]

St. Peters, 23d Sept. 1805 ; 9 *miles below the falls of St. Anthony.*
DEAR GENERAL,

          I ARRIVED here two days since, but shall not be able to depart before the day after tomorrow ; three of my men have been up to view the falls, but their reports are so contradictory, that no opinion can be formed from them. All the young warriors (of the two villages of Sioux near this place) and many chiefs had marched against the Chipeways, to revenge a stroke made on their people, the very day after their return from their visit to the Illinois (when

* My demand was one league below : their reply was " from below."—I imagine (without iniquity) they may be made to agree.

2

ten persons were killed on this ground. I yesterday saw the mausoleum in which all their bodies are deposited, and which is yet daily marked with the blood of those who swear to revenge them) but a runner headed them, and yesterday they all arrived—about 250 persons ; in company with those who were in the ponds gathering rice. Amidst the yelling of the mourners and the salutes of the warriors, there was a scene worthy the pen of a Robertson.

To-day I held a council on the beech, and made them a speech, in which I touched on a variety of subjects, but the principal points were the obtaining the lands as specified in the within articles,* making peace with the Chipeways, and granting such chiefs as might accompany me down (to visit you) a safe conduct through their country. These ends were accomplished. You will perceive that we have obtained about 100,000 acres for a song. You will please to observe, general, that the 2d article relative to consideration is blank. The reasons for it were as follow—that I had to fee privately two of the chiefs, and besides that, to make them presents at the council, of articles which would in this country be valued at 200 dollars, and the others about 50 dollars—part of these things were private property, purchased here ; such as a few scarlet shrouds, &c. These I was not furnished by the United States ; and although the chiefs in the council presented me with the land, yet, it is possible your excellency may think proper to insert the amount of those articles as the considerations to be specified in article 2d. They have bound me up to many assurances that the posts shall be established ; also, that if the Chipeways are obstinate, and continue to kill the Indians who bear our flags (the Chipeways on the upper Mississippi bearing the English flag) and our traders, we would take them in hand, and teach them to lay down the hatchet, as we had once already done. This I was the rather induced to say, as there were some persons present, who, although trading under your licences, I know to be British subjects. A chief by the name of the Elan Levie, then told me to look round on those young warriors on the beach ; that not *only them*, but those of six villages more were at our command. If possible, I will endeavor to note down their several speeches, and shew them you on my return. I have not a doubt of making Lake Sable in pretty good season ; but they inform me the source of the river is in Lake La Sang Sue, about 60 leagues further—this I must also see, and hope the general approves of my determination. At those two lakes, there are establishments of the N. W.

* See preceding convention signed on the 23d September.

company. These are both in our country, and time and circumstances only can determine in what manner I shall conduct myself toward them. *A Mr. M'Gillis, (whose father was a refugee, and had his estate confiscated by the Americans,) has charge of those factories. He, they say, is a sworn enemy of the United States—this was told me by a man, who I expect was a friend of the N. W. company ; but had quite a contrary effect than what he intended it to have : as I am determined, should he attempt any thing malicious towards me, (open force he dare not) to spare no pains to punish him. In fact. the dignity and honor of our government requires, that they should be taught to gather their skins in quiet, and even then not in a clandestine manner—added to which, they are the very instigators of the war between the Chipeways and Sioux, in order that they may monopolize the trade of the Upper Mississippi.

The chiefs who were at Saint Louis this spring, gave up their English medals to Mr. Chouteau. He promised them to obtain American medals in return, and send them up by some officer. They applied to me for them, and said they were their commissions ; their only distinguishing mark from the other warriors. I promised to write you on the occasion, and that you would remedy the evil. The chiefs were very loth to sign the articles relative to the land, asserting that their word of honor for the gift was sufficient, and that it was an impeachment of their probity, to require them to bind themselves further, &c. &c. This is a small sample of their way of thinking. I must mention something to your excellency relative to the man recommended to me by Mr. Chouteau as interpreter ; at the time he solicited the employ, he was engaged to Mr. Dickson, and on my arrival at the Prairie was gone up the St. Peters. I understand he is to be recommended for the appointment of the interpreter to the United States in this quarter : ou the contrary, I beg leave to recommend for that appointment, a Mr. Joseph Reinville, who has served as interpreter for the Sioux last spring at the Illinois, and who has gratuitously and willingly, (by the permission of Mr. Frazer, to whom he is engaged,) served as my interpreter in all my conferences with the Sioux. He is a man respected by the Indians, and I believe an honest one. I likewise beg leave to recommend to your attention Mr. Frazer, one of the two gentlemen who dined with you, and was destined for the Upper Mississippi. He waited eight or ten days at the Prairie for me, detained his inter-

* Incorrect—he being a Scotchman, a gentlemen, and a man of honor ; but this was the information I received at the St. Peters.

preter, and from thence forward has continued to evince a zeal to promote the success of my expedition, by every means in his power. He is a Vermonter born, and although not possessing the advantages of a polished education, inherits that, without which, an education serves but to add to the frivolity of the character, candor, bravery, and that amor patria, which distinguishes the good of every nation, from Nova Zembla to the line. Finding that the traders were playing the devil with their rum ; I yesterday in council informed the Indians, that their father had prohibited the selling of liquor to them, and that they would oblige him and serve themselves, if they would prevent their young men from paying the credits of any traders who sold rum to them, at the same time charging the chiefs to treat them well ; as their father although good, would not again forgive them, but punish with severity any injuries committed on their traders. This I presume, general, is agreeable to the spirit of the laws. Mr. Frazer immediately set the example, by separating his spirits from the merchandize in his boats, and returning it to the Prairie—although it would materially injure him if the other traders retained theirs and sold.

In fact, unless there are some persons at our posts here, (when established) who have authority effectually to stop the evil by confiscating the liquors, &c. it will still be continued by the weak and malevolent.

I shall forbear giving you a description of this place until my return, except only to observe, that the position for the post, is in the point between the two rivers, which equally commands both ; and at St. Croix on the hill on the lower side of the entrance on the E. bank of the Mississippi ; owing to cloudy weather, &c. I have taken no observation here ; but the head of Lake Pepin is in 44° 58′ 8″ N. and we have made very little northing since. The Mississippi is 130 yards wide, and the St. Peters 80 yards at their confluence.

24th Sept.—This morning the Little Corbeau came to see me from the village, (he having recovered an article, which I suspected to be taken by the Indians) he told me many things which the ceremony of the council would not permit his delivering there ; and added, he must tell me, that Mr. Roche, who went up the river St. Peters, had in his presence gave two kegs of rum to the Indians ; he (the chief) asked him " why he did so, as he knew it was con-" rary to the orders of his father ; that Messrs. Mareir and Tremer " had left their rum behind them, but that he alone had rum contrary " to the orders." He then gave the chief 15 bottles of rum, as I suppose to bribe him to silence. I presume he should be taught the impropriety of his conduct, when he applies for his licence the next year.

26th Sept. above the falls of St. Anthony.

The cloudy weather still continues, and I have not been able to to take the latitude. Mr. Frazer has been kind enough to send two of his people across from the Sioux town,~on the St. Peters, for my dispatches, and the place being dangerous for them, I must haste to dispatch them ; of course, general, the following short sketch of the falls, will merely be from *le coup d'œil.* The place where the river falls, over the rocks, appears to be about 15 feet perpendicular, the sheet being broken by one large island on the E. and a small one on the W. the former commencing below the shoot, and extending 500 yards above ; the river then falls through a continued bed of rocks, with a descent of at least 50 feet perpendicular in the course of half a mile—from thence to the St. Peters, a distance of eleven miles by water, there is almost one continued rapid, aggravated by the interruption of 12 small islands. The carrying place has two hills, one of 25 feet, the other 12, with an elevation of 45°, and is about three fourths of a mile in length. Above the shoot, the river is of a considerable width, but below, (at this time) I can easily cast a stone over it. The rapids or suck, continues about half a mile above the shoot, when the water becomes calm and deep. My barges are not yet over, but my trucks are preparing, and I have not the least doubt of succeeding.

The general, I hope, will pardon the tautologies and egotisms of my communications, as he well knows Indian affairs are productive of such errors, and that in a wilderness, detached from the civilized world every thing, even if of little import, becomes magnified in the eyes of the beholder, and when I add, my hands are blistered in working over the rapids, I presume it will apologise for the manner and style of my communications.

I am, general,

Your obedient servant,

(Signed)   Z. M. PIKE, Lt.

General Wilkinson.

N. B. I flatter myself with hearing from you at the Prairie, on my way down.

[No. 5.]

N. W. establishment, on Lake Leech, Feb. 1806.

SIR,

AS a proprietor of the N. W. company, and director of the Zond du Lac department, I conceive it my duty as an officer of the United States, (in whose territory you are) to address you solely on the subject of the many houses under your instructions. As a member of the greatest commercial nation in the world, and a company long renowned for their extent of connections and greatness of views, you cannot be ignorant of the rigor of the laws of the duties of imports of a foreign power.

Mr. Jay's treaty, it is true, gave the right of trade with the savages to British subjects in the United States territories, but by no means exempted them from paying the duties, obtaining licences, and subscribing unto all the rules and restrictions of our laws. I find your establishments at every suitable place along the whole extent of the south side of Lake Superior to its head, from thence to the source of the Mississippi, and down Red River, and even extending to the centre of our newly acquired territory of Louisiana, in which it will probably yet become a question between the two governments, if our treaties will authorise the British subjects to enter into the Indian trade on the same footing, as in the other parts of our frontiers; this not having been an integral part of the United States, at the time of said treaty. Our traders to the south, on the Lower Mississippi, complain to our government, with justice, that the members of the N. W. company, encircle them on the frontiers of our N. W. territory, and trade with the savages upon superior terms, to what they can afford, who pay the duties of their goods imported from Europe, and subscribe to the regulations prescribed by law.

These representations have at length attracted the attention of our government to the object in question, and with an intention to do themselves as well as citizens justice, they the last year took some steps to ascertain the facts, and make provision against the growing evil. With this, some geographical, and also local objects in view was I dispatched with discretionary orders, with a party of troops to the source of the Mississippi. I have found, sir, your commerce and establishments, extending beyond our most exaggerated ideas, and in addition to the injury done our revenue, by the evasion of the duties, other acts which are more particularly injurious to the *honor* and *dignity* of our government. The transactions alluded to, are the presenting *medals* of his Britannic majesty, and *flags* of the said government, to the chiefs and warriors resident in the territory of the United States. If political subjects are strictly prohibited to our traders, what would be the ideas of the executive to see foreigners making chiefs, and distributing flags, the standard of an European power. The savages being accustomed to look on that standard, which had been the only prevailing one for years, as that which alone has authority in the country, it would not be in the least astonishing to see them revolt from the United States, limited subjection which is claimed over them by the American government, and thereby be the cause of their receiving a chastisement : although necessary, yet unfortunate as they have been led astray by the policy of the traders of your country.

I must likewise observe, sir, that your establishments, if properly known, would be looked on with an eye of dissatisfaction by our government, for another reason, viz. there being so many furnished posts in case of a rupture between the two powers, the English government would not fail to make use of those as places of deposit of arms, ammunition, &c. to be distributed to the savages who joined their arms ; to the great annoyance of our territory, and the loss of the lives of many of our citizens. Your flags, sir, when hoisted in inclosed works, are in direct contradiction of the laws of nations, and their practice in like cases, which only admits of foreign flags being expanded on board of vessels, and at the residence of Ambassadors, or consuls. I am not ignorant of the necessity of your being in such a position as to protect you from the sallies of the drunken savages, or the more deliberate plans of the intended plunderer ; and under those considerations, have I considered your stockades.

You, and the company of which you are a member, must be conscious from the foregoing statement that strict justice would demand, and I assure you that the law directs, under similar circumstances, a total confiscation of your property, personal imprisonment and fines. But having discretionary instructions and no reason to think the above conduct was dictated through ill will or disrespect to our government, and conceiving it in some degree departing from the character of an officer, to embrace the first opportunity of executing those laws, I am willing to sacrifice my prospect of private advantage, conscious that the government look not to interest, but its *dignity* in the transaction, I have therefore to request of you, assurances on the following heads, which setting aside the chicanery of law, as a gentleman, you will strictly adhere to: viz.—

That you will make representations to your agents, at your head quarters, on Lake Superior, of the quantity of goods wanted the ensuing spring, for your establishments in the territory of the United States, in time sufficient, or as early as possible, for them to enter them at the C. H. of Michilimackinac, and obtain a clearance and licence to trade in due form.

2d. That you will give immediate instruction to all your posts in said territory, under your direction, at no time and on no pretence whatever to hoist, or suffer to be hoisted, the English flag. If you conceive a flag necessary, you may make use of that of the United States, which is the only one which can be admitted.

3d. That you will on no further occasion, present a flag or medal to an Indian: hold councils with them on political subjects, or others foreign from that of trade: but on being applied to on those heads, refer them to the American agents, informing them that they are the only persons authorised to hold councils of a political nature with them.

There are many other subjects, such as the distribution of liquor, &c. which would be too lengthy to be treated of in detail. But the company will do well to furnish themselves with our laws, regulating the commerce with the savages, and regulate themselves in our territories accordingly. I embrace this opportunity, to acknowledge myself and command under singular obligations to yourselves and agents, for the assistance which you have rendered us, and the polite treatment with which I have been honored. With sentiments of high respect, for the establishment and yourself.

I am, sir,

Your obedient servant,

Z. M. PIKE.

Hugh M'Gillis, Esq.
Proprietor and agent of the N. W. company,
established at Zond Du Lac.

[No. 6.]

Leech Lake, 15th February, 1806.

Sir,

YOUR address presented on the 6th inst. has attracted my most serious consideration to the several objects of duties on importations, of presents made to, and our consultations with Indians ; of enclosing our stores and dwelling houses, and finally, of the custom obtaining to hoist the British flag on the territory belonging to the United States of America.   I shall at as early a period as possible present the agents of the N. W. Company with your representations regarding the paying duties on the importation of goods to be sent to our establishments within the bounds of the territory of the United States, as also their being entered at the custom house of Michilimackinac, but I beg to be allowed to present for consideration, that the major part of the goods necessary to be sent to the said establishments for the trade of the ensuing winter, are now actually in our stores at Kamanitiguia, our head quarters on Lake Superior, and that it would cause us vast expense and trouble to be obliged to convey those goods back to Michilimackinac to be entered at the custom house office ; we therefore pray that the word of gentlemen with regard to the quantity and quality of the said goods to be sent to said establishment, may be considered as equivalent to the certainty of a custom house register.   Our intention has never been to injure your traders, paying the duties established by law.   We hope those representations to your government respecting our concerns with the Indians, may have been dictated with truth, and not exaggerated by envy to prejudice our interests, and to throw a stain on our character, which may require time to efface from the minds of a people, to whom we must ever consider ourselves indebted for the lenity of procedure, of which the present is so notable a testimony.   The enclosures to protect our stores and dwelling houses from the insults and barbarity of savage rudeness, have been erected for the security of my property and person in a country, till now, exposed to the wild will of the frantic Indians : we never formed the smallest idea that the said enclosures might ever be useful in the juncture of a rupture between the two powers, nor do we now conceive that such poor shifts will ever be employed by the British government, in a country overshadowed with wood, so adequate to every purpose.   Forts might in a short period of time be built far superior to any stockades we may have occasion to erect.

3

We were not conscious, sir, of the error I acknowledge we have been guilty to commit, by exhibiting to view on your territory any standard of Great Britain. I will pledge myself to your government, that I will use my utmost endeavors, as soon as possible, to prevent the future display of the British flag, or the presenting of medals, or the exhibiting to public view, any other mark of European power, throughout the extent of territory known to belong to the dominion of the United States. The custom has long been established and we innocently and inoffensively, as we imagined, have conformed to it till the present day.

Be persuaded that on no consideration, shall any Indian be entertained on political subjects, or on any affairs foreign to our trade ; and reference shall be made to the American agents, should any application be made worthy such reference ; and be assured that we as a commercial company must find it ever our interests to interfere as little as possible with affairs of government in the course of trade ; ignorant as we are in this rude and distant country of the political views of nations.

We are convinced that the inestimable advantages arising from the endeavors of your government, to establish a more peaceful course of trade in this part of the territory belonging to the United States, are not acquired through the mere liberality of a nation, and are ready to contribute to the expense necessarily attending them. We are not averse to pay the common duties established by law, and will ever be ready to conform ourselves to all rules and regulations of trade that may be established according to common justice.

I beg to be allowed to say, that we have reason to hope, that every measure will be adopted to secure and facilitate the trade with the Indians ; and these hopes seem to be confirmed beyond the smallest idea of doubt, when we see a man sent among us, who instead of private considerations to pecuniary views, prefers the honor, dignity and lenity of his government, and whose transactions are in every respect so conformable to equity. When we behold an armed force ready to protect or chastise as necessity or policy may direct, we know not how to express our gratitude to that people whose only view seems to be to promote the happiness of all, the savages that rove over the wild confines of their domain not excepted.

It is to you, sir, we feel ourselves most greatly indebted, whose claim to honor, esteem and respect, will ever be held in high estimation by myself and associates. The danger and hardships by your fortitude vanquished, and by your perseverance overcome, are signal, and will ever be preserved in the annals of the N. W. Company. Were it solely from the considerations of those who have exposed their lives in a long and perilous march through a country, where they had every distress to suffer, and many dangers to expect (and this with a view to establish peace in a savage country,) we should think ourselves under the most strict obligation to assist them ; but we know we are in a country where hospitality and gratitude are to be considered above every other virtue, and therefore have offered for their relief what our poor means can allow : and, sir, permit me to embrace the opportunity, to testify that I feel myself highly honored by your acceptance of such accommodations as my humble roof could afford.

With great consideration and high respect for the government of the United States, allow me to express my esteem and regard for you.

I am, sir,
Your obedient humble servant,

(Signed)   H. M'GILLIS,
                                                        Of N. W. Company.

Lieut Pike,
1st. Regt. United States infantry.

[No. 7.]

A SPEECH

DELIVERED TO THE SAUTEAUX IN A COUNCIL, AT LEECH LAKE, 16TH FEBRUARY, 1806.

BROTHERS—A few months since the Spaniards shut up the mouth of the Mississippi, and prevented the Americans from floating down it to the sea. This your father, the president of the United States would not admit of. He, therefore, took such measures as to open the river, and remove the Spaniards from both sides of the Mississippi to a great distance on the other side of the Missouri, and to open the road from the ocean of the east to that of the west. The Americans being then at peace with all the world, your great father, the president of the United States, began to look round on his red children, in order to see what he could do to render them happy and sensible of his protection. For that purpose he sent two of his captains, Lewis and Clark up the Missouri, to pass on to the west sea, in order to see all his new children, to go round the world that way and return by water. They stayed the first winter at the Mandane's village, where you might have heard of them. This year your great father directed his great war chief (general Wilkinson) at St. Louis, to send out a number of his young warriors up the Missouri, Illinois, Osage river, and other courses, to learn the situation of his red children, to encourage the good, punish the bad, and make peace between them all, by persuading them to lay by the hatchet, and follow them to St. Louis, where the great war chief will open their ears, that they may hear the truth, and their eyes, to see what is right.

Brothers—I was chosen to ascend the Mississippi, to bear to his red children the words of their father ; and the *Great Spirit* has opened the eyes and ears of all the nations that I have passed, to listen to my words. The Sauks and Reynards are planting corn and raising cattle. The Winebagos continue peaceable, as usual, and even the Sioux have laid by the hatchet at my request. Yes, my brothers, the *Sioux*, who have so long and so obstinately waged war against the Chipeways, have agreed to lay by the hatchet, smoke the calumet, and become again your brothers, as they were wont to be.

Brothers—You behold the pipe of Wabasha, as a proof of what I say. The Little Corbeau, Tills De Pinchow, and the L'Aile Rouge had marched 250 warriors to revenge the blood of their women and children, slain last year at the St. Peters. I sent a runner after them, stopped their march, and met them in council at the mouth of St. Peters, where they promised to remain peaceable until my return ; and if the Ouchipawah chiefs accompanied me to receive them as brothers, and to accompany us to St. Louis, there to bury the hatchet and smoke the pipe in the presence of our great war chief ; and to request him to punish those who first broke the peace.

Brothers—I sent flags and a message up the St. Peters to the bands of Sioux on that river, requesting them to remain quiet, and not to go to war. The people of the Leaves received my message, and sent me word that they would obey ; but the Yanctongs and Sussitongs had left the St. Peters previous to my message arriving, and did not receive it. But when I left my fort they had appointed a day for 50 of their chiefs and warriors to come and see me, but I could not wait for them ; so that, as to their dispositions for peace or war, I cannot answer positively.

BROTHERS—I have, therefore, come to fetch some of your approved chiefs with me to St. Louis.

BROTHERS—In speaking to you I speak to brave warriors. It is, therefore, not my intention to deceive you :—possibly we might meet with some bad people who may wish to do us ill ; but, if so, we will die together, certain that our fathers, the Americans, will settle with them for our blood.

BROTHERS—I find you have received from your traders English medals and flags. These you must deliver up, and your chiefs who go with me shall receive others from the American government, in their room.

BROTHERS—Traders have no authority to make chiefs ; and in doing this they have done what is not right. It is only great chiefs, appointed by your fathers, who have that authority. But at the same time you are under considerable obligations to your traders, who come over large waters, high mountains, and up swift falls, to supply you with clothing for your women and children, and ammunition for your hunters, to feed you, and keep you from perishing with cold.

BROTHERS—Your chiefs should see your traders done justice, oblige your young men to pay their credits, and protect them from insults ; and your traders, on their part, must not cheat the Indians, but give them the value of their skins.

BROTHERS—Your father is going to appoint chiefs of his own to reside amongst you, to see justice done to his white and red children, who will punish those who deserve punishment, without reference to the color of their skin.

BROTHERS—I understand that one of your young men killed an American at Red Lake last year, but that the murderer is far off: let him keep so—send him where we never may hear of him more ; for was he here I would be obliged to demand him of you, and make my young men shoot him. My hands on this journey are yet clear of blood ; may the Great Spirit keep them so !

BROTHERS—We expect, in the summer, soldiers to come to the St. Peters : your chiefs who go with me, may either come up with them, or some traders who return sooner. They may make their selection.

BROTHERS—Your father, finding that the rum with which you are supplied by the traders, is the occasion of quarrels, murders, and bloodshed ; and that, instead of buying clothing for your women and children, you spend your skins in liquor, &c. has determined to direct his young warriors and chiefs to prohibit it, and keep it

from amongst you.   But I have found the traders here with a great
deal of rum on hand; I have, therefore, given them permission to
sell what they have, that you may forget it by degrees, against next
year, when none will be suffered to come in the country.

———

[No. 8.]

ANSWERS

OF SEVERAL INDIAN CHIEFS MADE TO AN ADDRESS FROM LIEUTE-
NANT PIKE, AT LEECH LAKE, 16th FEBRUARY, 1806.

1st. Sucre of Red Lake (Wiscoup).

MY FATHER—I have heard and understood the words of our
great father.   It overjoys me to see you make peace among us.   I
should have accompanied you had my family been present, and
would have gone to see my father, the great war chief.

This medal I hold in my hand I received from the English
chiefs.   I willingly deliver it up to you.   Wabasha's calumet,
with which I am presented, I receive with all my heart.   Be assured
that I will use my best endeavors to keep my young men quiet.
There is my calumet, I send it to my father the great war chief.
What does it signify that I should go to see him.   Will not my
pipe answer the same purpose?

MY FATHER—You will meet with the Sioux on your return.
You may make them smoke in my pipe, and tell them that I have
let fall my hatchet.

MY FATHER—Tell the Sioux on the upper part of the river
St. Peters that they mark trees with the figure of a calumet; that
we of Red lake who may go that way, should we see them, that we
may make peace with them, being assured of their pacific disposition when we shall see the calumet marked on the trees.

2d. The chief de la Terre of Leech lake (Obigouitte).

MY FATHER—I am glad to hear that we and the Sioux are
now brothers, peace being made between us.   If I have received a
medal from the English traders, it was not as a mark of rank or
distinction, *as I considered it*, but merely because I made good
hunts and payed my debts.   Had the Sucre been able to go and see
our father, the great war chief I should have accompanied him; but

I am determined to go to Michilimackinac the next spring to see my brothers the Americans.

3d. *The Gcuelle Platte of Leech lake (Eskibugeckoge.)*

MY FATHER—My heart beat high with joy, when I heard that you had arrived, and that all the nations through which you passed had received and made peace among them.

You ask me to accompany you to meet our father, the great war chief: this I would willingly do, but certain considerations prevent me. I have sent my calumet to all the Sauteaux who hunt round about, to assemble to form a war party : should I be absent, they, when assembled, may strike those with whom we have made peace, and may kill our brothers. I must, therefore, remain here, to prevent them from assembling, as I fear that there are many who have begun already to prepare to meet me. I present you with the medal of my uncle here present. He has received it from the English chiefs as a recompense for his good hunts. As for me, I have no medal here ; it is at my tent, and I will cheerfully deliver it up. That medal was given me by the English traders, from a consideration of something that I had done ; and I can say that the three-fourths of those here present belong to me.

MY FATHER—I promise you, and you may confide in my word, that I will preserve peace, that I bury my hatchet ; and, that even should the Sioux come and strike me, for the first time I would not take up my hatchet ; but should they come and strike me a second time, I will dig up my hatchet and revenge myself.

[No. 9.]

Extract of a letter from LIEUT. PIKE, *to Mr. Dickson, dated Lower Red Cedar Lake,* 26th Feb. 1806.

" Mr. Grant was prepared to go on a trading voyage, amongst the Fols Avoins ; but it was what I could not by any means admit of, and I hope on a moment's reflection, you will admit the justice of my refusal ; for what could be a greater piece of injustice, than for me to admit you to send goods, *illegally* brought into the country, down into the same quarter, to trade for the credits of men who have paid their duties, regularly taken out licenses, and in other respects acted conformably to law. They might exclaim with justice—What ! Lt. Pike not content with suffering the laws to slumber, when it was his duty to have executed them—has now suffered the N. W. company's agents to come even here to violate them, and injure the citizens of the United States ; certainly he must be corrupted to admit this.

" This, sir, would be the natural conclusion of all persons."

[No. 10.]

Copy of a letter to a trader, on the subject of selling spirituous liquors to Indians.

Grand Isle, Upper Mississippi, 9th April, 1806.

MR. LA JENNESSE,

SIR,

BEING informed that you have arrived here with an intention of selling spirituous liquors to the savages of this quarter, together with other merchandize under your charge. I beg leave to inform you, that, the making sale of spirituous liquors on the Indian territories to any savages whatsoever, is contrary to a law of the United States for regulating the trade with the savages ; and preserving peace on the frontiers. And that, notwithstanding the custom has hitherto obtained on the Upper Mississippi, no person whatsoever has authority therefor ; and as the practice may have a tendency to occasion broils and dissentions amongst the savages, and thereby occasion bloodshed, and an infraction of the good understanding which now (through my endeavors) so happily exists. I have (at your particular request) addressed you this note in writing, informing you that in case of an *infraction*, I shall conceive it my duty, as an officer of the United States, to prosecute according to the *pains* and *penalties* of the law.

I am, sir,

With all due consideration,

Your obedient servant,

(Signed)   Z. M. PIKE, Lt.

[No. 11.]

Prairie De Chien, 18*th April,* 1806.

DEAR GENERAL,

I ARRIVED here within the hour, and as Mr. Jearreau of Cahokia, embarks for St. Louis early to-morrow morning, I embrace this opportunity, to give a slight sketch of the events of my expedition; and being obliged to steal the hours from my repose, I hope the general will pardon the conciseness of my epistle.

I pushed forward last October, with all eagerness, in hopes to make Lake De Sable, and return to St. Louis in the autumn; the weather was mild and promising, until the middle of the month, when a sudden change took place, and the ice immediately commenced running. I was then conscious of my inability to return, as the falls and other obstacles would retain me until the river would close. I then conceived it best to station part of my men, and push my discovery with the remainder on foot. I marched with eleven soldiers and my interpreter, seven hundred miles to the source of the Mississippi, through (I may without vanity say) as many hardships as almost any party of Americans ever experienced, by cold and hunger. I was on the communication of *Red* river and the Mississippi, the former being a water of Hudson's bay. The British flag, (which was expanded on some very respectable positions) has given place to that of the United States wherever we passed: likewise, we have the faith and honor of the N. W. company, for about $13,000 duties this year; and by the voyage, peace is established between the Sioux and Sauteurs. These objects I have been happy enough to accomplish without the loss of one man, although once fired on. I expect hourly the Sussitongs, Yanctongs, Wachpecoutes, and three other bands of Sioux ; they are some from the head of the St. Peters, and some from the plains west of that river. From here I bring with me a few of the principal men only, (agreeably to your orders) also some chiefs of the Fols Avoins (or Menomenes) and Winebagos, the latter of whom have murdered three men since my passing here last autumn : the murderers I shall demand, and am in expectation of obtaining two, (for whom I now have irons making) and expect to have them with me on my arrival. Indeed, sir, the insolence of the savages in this quarter is unbounded, and unless an immediate example is made, we shall certainly be obliged to enter into a general war with them.

My party has been some small check to them this winter, as I was determined to preserve the dignity of our flag, or die in the attempt.

I presume, general, that my voyage will be productive of much new matter, useful and interesting information to our government, although detailed in the unpolished diction of a soldier of fortune.

The river broke up at my Stockade, (600 miles above here on the 7th instant, and Lake Pepin was passable for boats *only*, on the 14th. Thus you may perceive, sir, I have not been slow in my descent, leaving all the traders behind me. From the time it will take to make my arrangements, and the state of the water, I calculate on arriving at the cantonment on the 4th of May ; and hope my general will be assured, that nothing but the most insurmountable obstacles shall detain me one moment.

> I am, dear sir,
>> With great consideration,
>>> Your obedient servant,
> (Signed)   Z. M. PIKE, Lt.

N. B. I beg leave to caution the general against attending to the reports of any individuals, as it relates to this country, as the most unbounded prejudices and party rancour pervade almost generally.

> (Signed)   P.

[No. 12.]

A SPEECH

DELIVERED TO THE PUANTS, AT THE PRAIRIE DES CHEINS, THE
20TH DAY OF APRIL, 1806.

BROTHERS—When I passed here last autumn, I requested to see you on my return. I am pleased to see you have listened to my words. It has pleased the great spirit to open the ears of all the nations through which I passed, to hear and attend to the words of their father. Peace has been established between two of the most powerful nations in this quarter.

Notwithstanding all this, some of your nation have been bold enough to kill some of the white people. Not content with firing on the canoes, in descending the Ouiscousing last autumn, they have killed a man on Rock river, when sitting peaceably in his tent.

Also—they have more recently murdered a young man near this place, without any provocation whatever. As an officer of the United States, it is my duty to demand the murderers ; and *I do now demand them.*

BROTHERS—In this action I am not influenced or urged by any individual of this place, or the people generally : no more than, as it is my duty to give all our citizens all the protection in my power. I will not deceive you. If the prisoners are delivered to me, I sha'l put them in *irons*, under my *guards ;* and in all instances treat them as men guilty of a capital crime ; and on their arrival below, they will be tried for their lives, and if it be proved they have killed the people without provocation, in all probability they will be put to *death.* If on the contrary, it is proved that the whites were the aggressors, and it was only self defence, it will be deemed justifiable, and they will be sent back to their nation.

It becomes you to consider well, if in case of a refusal, you are sufficiently powerful to protect those men against the power of the United States—who has always since the treaty of 1795, treated all the savages as their children ; but if obliged to march troops to punish the many murders committed on their citizens ; then the innocent will suffer with the guilty.

My demand will be reported in candor and truth below—when the general will take such steps as he may deem proper. But I hope for the sake of your innocent women and children, you will do us and yourselves justice. I was directed to invite a few chiefs down with me to St. Louis. Many of different bands are about to descend with me. I now give an invitation to two or three of your principal men, to descend with me. Whatever are your determinations, I pledge the faith of a *soldier*, for a safe conduct back to your nation. At present, I am not instructed to act by force, to procure those men—therefore, you will consider yourselves as acting without restraint, and under free deliberations.

They replied—" That they thanked me for the generous and " candid manner in which I had explained myself, and that they " would give me an answer to-morrow."

21*st April.*—The Puants met me in council, agreeably to promise, and Karamone, their chief, addressed me and said—" They " had come to reply to my demand of yesterday. He requested that " I, with the traders would listen." A soldier, then called the *Little Thunder*, arose and said—" The chiefs were for giving up the " murderer present ; but, that it was the opinion of the soldiers, that " they should themselves take him with the others to their father

" But, that if I prefered their taking one down now, they would
" do it ; but, if on the contrary, I expected all three, they would
" immediately depart in pursuit of the others, and bring them alto-
" gether to their father.   That if he did not bring them, he would
" deliver himself up to the Americans."   I replied—" He must not
" attempt to deceive, that I had before told him that I was not au-
" thorised to seize their men by force of arms ; but, that I wished
" to know explicitly, the time when we might expect them at St.
" Louis, in order that our general should know what steps to take
" in case they did not arrive.   That the consequence of a non-com-
" pliance would be serious to themselves and their children.   Also,
" that they had recently hoisted a British flag near this place, which,
" had I have been here, I should have prevented.   I advised them
" to bring their British flags and medals down to St. Louis, to de-
" liver them up, and receive others in exchange."   Their reply was,
" in ten days to the Prairie, and from thence to St. Louis, in ten
" days more."

Held a council with the Sioux, in which the chiefs of the Yanctongs, Sussitongs, Sioux, of the head of the De Moyen, and part of the
Gens Du Lac was present. Wabasha first spoke, in answer to my
speech, wherein I recapitulated the conduct of the Sauteurs—their
desire and willingness for peace—their arrangements for next summer—the pipes they had sent, &c.   Also, the wish of the general
for some of the chiefs to descend below.   Recommended the situation and good intentions of the young chiefs at the mouth of the St.
Peters, to the others ; and that they should give them assistance to
keep the bad men in awe.

They all acquiesced in the peace with the Sauteurs, but said
generally, that they doubted their bad faith ; as they had experienced
it many a time.   The Nez Corbeau said he had been accused of
being hired to kill Mr. Dixon, which he here solemnly denied ever
having been instigated to any such action.

The *Tonnere Rouge*, then arose and said—*Jealousy* was in a great
measure, the principal cause of his descending. That if ever any trader had any cause to complain of him, that, now let him do it publicly.
That last year an officer went up the Missouri—gave flags and medals
—made chiefs, and played the devil and all. That this year the liquor
was restricted to the Indians on the Louisiana side, and permitted
on this.   He wished to know the reason of those arrangements.

I replied, that the officer who ascended the Missouri, was
authorised by their father ; and that to make chiefs of them, &c.

was what I now invited them down. But that for the liquor, it was too long an explanation to give them here; but that it would be explained to them below—and that in a very short time the liquor would be restricted on both sides of the river.

The Puants in the evening, came to the house, and Macraragah, alias the Merchant, spoke—That last spring he had embarked to go down to St. Louis; but, that at De Buques, the Reynards gave back. That when he saw me last autumn, he gave me his hand without shame; but, that since it had pleased the father of life to cover them with shame—that now they felt themselves miserable. But implored me to present their *flags* and *medals* to the general, as a proof of their good intentions; and that when I arrived at St. Louis, to assure the general they were not far behind. (The chiefs and the soldiers would follow with the murderers; but begged I would make their road clear, &c. &c.) Delivered his pipe and flag.

Karamone then spoke (with apparent difficulty), assured of the shame, disgrace and distress of their nation, that he would fulfil what the others had said; and that he sent by me the medal of his father, which he considered himself as no longer worthy to wear (putting it round my neck trembling), and begged me to intercede with the general in their favor, &c. &c.

I assured him that the American nation was a generous nation, not confounding the innocent with the guilty; that when they had delivered up the *three* or *four* dogs who had covered them with blood, we would again look on them as our children; to take courage, that, if they did well they should be treated well; that I would tell the general every thing relative to the affair; also, their repentance, and determination to deliver themselves and the murderers, and explain about their flags and medals.

[No. 13.]

Notice to Messrs. Campbell and Fisher, for taking depositions against the murderers of the Puant nation.

Prairie des Chiens, 20th April, 1806.

GENTLEMEN,

Having demanded of the Puants the authors of the late atrocious murders; and understanding that it is their intentions to deli-

ver them to me, I have to request of you, as magistrates of this
territory, that you will now have all the depositions of those facts
taken, which it is in your power to procure ; and, if, at any future
period previous to the final decisions of their fate, further proofs can
be obtained, that you will have them properly authenticated and forwarded to his excellency general Wilkinson.

I am, gentlemen,

With respect,

Your obedient servant,

(Signed)   Z. M. PIKE, Lt.

————◆————

[No. 14.]

Fort St. Louis, 26*th May*, 1806.

DEAR SIR,

I had hitherto detained the medals and flags, intending to have
presented them to you at the final conclusion of my vouchers, on
the subject of my correspondence with the savages. But in order
that the general might know of whom I had obtained medals and
flags, I gave him a memorandum when I handed in my vouchers on
the subject of the N. W. company.

But I have thought proper to send them by the bearer, marked
with the names of the chiefs from whom I detained them.

I also send you a pipe and beaver robe of the Tonnere Rouge,
as they are the handsomest of any which I received on the whole
route. I have several other pipes, two sacks, and one robe ; but as
they bore no particular message, I conceived the general would look
on it as a matter of no consequence ; and indeed, none except the
Sauteurs were accompanied by a talk, but just served as the em-
blem of the good will of the moment. I likewise send the skins
of the Lynx and Brelaw, as the general may have an opportunity to
forward them.

Some gentlemen have promised me a mate for my dog : if I
obtain him, the pair, or the single one with the sleigh, is at the general's service to be transmitted to the states as we had determined
on. I mentioned in my memorandums the engagements I was
under relative to the flags or medals, and should any early communications be made with that country, I hope the subject may not be
forgotten. I have labelled each article, with the name of those

from whom I obtained them—also, the names of the different animals.

I am, sir,

With esteem and high consideration,

Your obedient servant,

(Signed)   Z. M. PIKE, Lt.

General James Wilkinson.

[My faith was pledged to the savage chiefs for the replacing of the medals and flags of the British government, which they surrendered me, by others of the same magnitude of the United States; but owing to the change of agents, and a variety of circumstances, it was never fulfilled. This has left a number of the Sioux and Sauteur chiefs without their distinguishing marks of dignity, and has induced them to look on my conduct toward them as a premeditated fraud, and would render my life in danger, should I ever return amongst them, and the situation of any other officer who should presume to make a similar demand extremely delicate; besides it has compromitted the *faith* of our government with those savage warriors, which, to enable any government ever to do good, should be held inviolate.]

[No. 15.]

Bellefontaine, 2d *July*, 1806.

DEAR SIR,

I have at length finished all my reports, observations, and journals, which arose from my late voyage to the source of the Mississippi, and hope they may prove interesting, from the information, on different subjects, which they contain.

I perceive that I differ materially from capt. Lewis, in my account of the numbers, manners, and morals of the Sioux. But our reception by that nation (at the first interview) being so different, it no doubt left an impression on our minds, which may have (unknown to ourselves) given a cast to our observations; but I will not only vouch for the authenticity of my account as to numbers, arms, &c. from my own notes, but from having had them revised and corrected by a gentleman of liberal education, who has resided eighteen years in that nation, speaks their language, and for some years past has been collecting materials for their natural and philosophical history.

I have not attempted to give an account of nations of Indians whom I did not visit except the *Assinniboins*, who, from their intimate connection with the Sioux (in a lineal point of view) it would have been improper to have left out of the catalogue.

The correctness of the geographical parts of the voyage I will vouch for, as I spared neither time, fatigue, nor danger, to see myself every part connected with my immediate route.

The general already knows, at the time I left St. Louis, there were no instruments proper for celestial observations (excepting those which he furnished me, which were inadequate to taking the longitude); neither had I the proper tables nor authors to accomplish that object, but it can no doubt be ascertained, by various charts, at different points of my route; neither had I proper time-pieces nor instruments for meteorological observations. Those made were from an imperfect instrument I purchased in the town of St. Louis.

I do not possess the qualifications of the naturalist, and even had they been mine, it would have been impossible to have gratified them to any great extent, as we passed with rapidity over the country we surveyed, which was covered with snow six months out of the nine I was absent. And indeed, my thoughts were too much engrossed in making provisions for the exigencies of the morrow, to attempt a science which requires time and a placidity of mind which seldom fell to my lot.

The journal in itself will have little to strike the imagination, but a dull detail of our daily march, and containing many notes which should have come into the geographical part; others, of observations on the savage character, and many that were never intended to have been included in my official report.

The daily occurrences were written at night, frequently by fire-light, when extremely fatigued, and the cold so severe as to freeze the ink in my pen, of course have little claim to elegance of expression or style; but they have truth to recommend them, which, i· always attended to, would strip the pages of many of our journalists, of their most interesting occurrences. The general will please to recollect also, that I had scarcely returned to St. Louis, before the voyage now in contemplation was proposed to me, and after some consideration, my duty (and inclination in some respects) induced me to undertake it.

The preparations for my new voyage prevented the possibili of my paying that attention to the correction of my errors, that should otherwise have done. This, with the foregoing reasons, will, I hope, be deemed a sufficient apology for the numerous errors, tautologies and egotisms which will appear.

I am, dear general,
With great respect,
Your obedient servant,
(Signed)   Z. M. PIKE, Lt. 1st. Regt. Infty.
General James Wilkinson.

———

[No. 16.]

Instructions delivered to sergeant Henry Kennerman, at
Pine creek rapids, Oct. 1, 1805.

YOU are to remain here with the party under your command, subject to the following instructions : viz.—Your guards to consist of one non-commissioned officer and three privates, yourself mounting in regular rotation, making one centinel by day and by night ; and, until your position is inclosed by pickets, every man is to be employed on that object ; after which Sparks is to be employed in hunting : but this will by no means excuse him from his tour of guard at night when in the stockade ; but he must be relieved during the day by another man.

Should any Indians visit you previous to having your works complete, divide your men between the two block houses, and on no conditions suffer a savage to enter into the one where the stores are, and not more than one or two into the other : but should you be so fortunate as not to be discovered until your works are completed, you may admit three, without arms, and no more, to enter at once— at the same time always treating them with as much friendship as is consistent with your own safety.

You are furnished with some tobacco to present them with ; but on no condition do you ever give them one drop of liquor, informing them I have taken it all with me. From the arrangements I have made with the Sioux it is presumable they will treat you with friendship ; but the Chipeways may be disposed to hostilities, and, should you ever be attacked, calculate on surrendering with your life. Instruct your men not to fire at random, nor ever, unless the enemy is near enough to make him a *point blank* shot. This you must particularly attend to, and punish the first man found acting in contradiction thereto. The greatest economy must be used with

5

the ammunition and provisions : of the latter I shall furnish Sparks his proportion ; and at any time should a man accompany him for a day's hunt, furnish him with four or five balls and extra powder, and on his return, take what is left away from him.   The provisions must be issued agreeably to the following proportion.   For four days N. 80 lbs. of fresh venison, elk, or buffaloe, or 60 lbs. fresh bear meat, with one quart of salt for that period.   The remainder of what is killed keep in the open air and frozen, if so, as long as possible, or salt and smoke it, so as to lay up meat for my party, and us all, to descend the river with.   If you are obliged, through the failure of your hunter, to issue out of our reserved provisions, you will deliver, for four days, 18 lbs of pork or bacon, and 18 lbs. of flour only.   This will be sufficient, and must, in no instance, be exceeded.

No whiskey will be issued after the present barrel is exhausted, at half a gill per man per day.   Our boats are turned up near your gate : you will make a barrel of pitch, and give them a complete repairing ready for us to descend in.

I have delivered to you my journals and observations to this place, with a letter accompanying them to his excellency general James Wilkinson, which, should I not return by the time hereafter specified, you will convey to him and deliver personally, requesting his permission to deliver the others committed to your charge.

You will observe the strictest discipline and justice in your command.   I expect the men will conduct themselves in such a manner that there will be no complaints to be made on my return, and that they will be ready to account to a higher tribunal.   The date of my return is uncertain ; but let no information or reports, except from under my own hand, induce you to quit this place until one month after the ice has broke up at the head of the river, when, if I am not arrived, it is reasonable to suppose that some disastrous events detain us, and you may repair to St. Louis.   You are taught to discriminate between my baggage and the United States' property.   The latter deliver to the assistant military agent at St. Louis, taking his receipts for the same—the former, if in your power, to Mrs. Pike.

Your party is regularly supplied with provisions, to include the 8th December, 1805, only, from which time you are entitled to draw of the United States.

(Signed)   Z. M. PIKE, Lt.

[No. 17.]

OBSERVATIONS

ON THE TRADE, VIEWS, AND POLICY OF THE NORTH WEST COM-
PANY, AND THE NATIONAL OBJECTS CONNECTED WITH THEIR
COMMERCE, AS IT INTERESTS THE GOVERNMENT OF THE UNI-
TED STATES.

THE fur trade in Canada, has always been considered as an
object of the first importance to that colony ; and has been cherish-
ed by the respective governors of that province, by every regulation
in their power, under both the French and English administrations.
The great and almost unlimited influence the traders of that country had acquired over the savages, was severely felt, and will long
be remembered by the citizens on our frontiers.   Every attention
was paid by the cabinet of St James, in our treaty with Great Britain, to secure to their subjects, (the Canadians) the privilege
of the Indian trade within our territories, and with what judgment
they have improved the advantages obtained, by the mother country, time will soon unfold.

In the year 1766, the trade was first extended from Michilimackinac, to the north west, by a few desperate adventurers, whose
mode of life on the voyage, and short residence in civilized society, obtained for them, the appellation of " Coureurs des Bois."
From those trifling beginings, arose the present north west company,
who notwithstanding the repeated attacks made on their trade, have
withstood every shock, and are now, by the coalition of the late X.
Y. company, established on so firm a basis, as to bid defiance to
every opposition, which can be made by private individuals.

They, by a late purchase of the king's posts in Canada, extend
their line of trade from Hudson's Bay, to the St. Lawrence, up that
river on both sides, to the Lakes—from thence to the head of Lake
Superior, at which place the north west company have their head
quarters ; from thence to the source of Red river, and on all its
tributary streams, through the country to the Missouri—through
the waters of Lake Winipie, to the Saskashawin, on that river to
its source—up Elk river to the lake of the Hills—up Peace river to
the Rocky mountains—from the lake of the Hills, up Slave river to
Slave Lake, and this year have dispatched a Mr. Mackenzie on a
voyage of trade and discovery down Mackenzie's river, to the north
sea ; and also a Mr. M'Coy, to cross the Rocky mountains, and proceed to the western ocean with the same objects in view.   They
have had a gentleman by the name of Thompson, making a geographical survey of the north west part of the continent—who, for

three years, with an astonishing spirit of enterprise and perseverance, passed over all that extensive and unknown country. His establishment, although not splendid, (the mode of travelling not admitting it) was such, as to admit of the most unlimited expences in every thing necessary to facilitate his enquiries; and he is now engaged in digesting the important results of his enterprise. I find from the observations and suggestions of Mr. Thompson, that when at the source of the Mississippi, it was his opinion the line of limits between the United States and Great Britain, must run such a course, from the head of the lake of the Woods, as to touch the source of the Mississippi; and this I discovered to be the opinion of the north west company, whom, we may suppose, or reasonably conclude, speak the language held forth by their government. The admission of this pretension, will throw out of our territory all the upper part of Red river, and nearly two fifths of the territory of Louisiana. Whereas, if the line be run due west from the head of the lake of the Woods, it will cross Red river nearly at the entrance of Reed river, and it is conjectured strike the western ocean at Birch Bay, in Queen Charlotte Sound. Those differences of opinion, it is presumed, might be easily adjusted between the two governments, at the present day, but it is believed that delays by unfolding the true value of the country, may produce difficulties, which do not at present exist. The north west company, have made establishments at several places on the south side of Lake Superior, and on the head waters of the rivers Sauteaux and St. Croix, which discharge themselves into the Mississippi. The first I met with on the voyage up, was at Lower Red Cedar Lake, about one hundred and fifty miles, above the Isle de Corfeau, being on the east side of the river, and distant therefrom six miles. It is situated on the north point of the lake, and consists of log buildings, flanked by picketed bastions on two of its angles. The next establishment I met with, was situated on Sandy Lake; for a description of which, see document marked A*. Midway between Sandy Lake and Leech Lake, is a small house not worthy of notice. On the south west side of the latter lake, from the outlet of the Mississippi, stand the head quarters of the Fond du Lac department; for information relative to which, have reference to document marked B.† Here resides the director of this department. In document C.‡ is a recapitulation of the specific articles of 115 packs of peltry, which will give an idea of the whole, amounting per said voucher to 233 packs per annum in the Fond du

* See A. Appendix part I. page 38.   † ib. B. p. 38.   ‡ Ib. table C. facing page 40.

Lac department.   Document D.* will explain the relative price of goods in that district, but the trading prices are various, according to situations and circumstances.   Voucher E.† shews the number of men, women, and children in the service of the north west company, in the district aforesaid, with their pay per annum, &c. &c. This department brings in annually forty canoes, which by a calculation made by a gentleman of veracity and information, who has been eighteen years in the Indian trade, and in the habit of importing goods by Michilimackinac, it appears that the annual amount of duties would be about thirteen thousand dollars.   The Lower Red River (which I conceive to be within our territory) would yield about half that sum, viz. 6,500, and the Hudson's bay company's servants, who import, by the way of Lake Winipie, six thousand five hundred dollars more.

Thus is the United States defrauded annually, of about twenty six thousand dollars.   From my observations, and information, I think it will be an easy matter to prevent the smuggling of the Fond du Lac department.   By establishing a post with a garrison of one hundred men, and an office of the customs, near the mouth of the river St. Louis, where all goods for the Fond du Lac department must enter ; this is at present the distributing point, where the company have an establishment, and the goods on being received from Kamanitiquia, are embarked for their different destinations. That Point also commands the communication with Lake de Sable, Leech Lake, Red Lake, &c. &c. &c.   I am also of opinion, the goods for Red River (if it is within our boundary) would enter here, in preference to being exposed to seizure.   It is worthy of remark, that the charter of the Hudson's Bay company extends to all its waters, and if the British government conceived they had authority to make such a grant, they certainly would claim the country therein specified, which would extend far south of the west line, from the head of the lake of the Woods.

The north west company, were about to push their trade down the Mississippi, until they would have met the traders of Michilimackinac ; but I gave them to understand, that it could not be admitted ; as appears per letter to Mr. Dickson.‡

Z. M. PIKE, 1st Lt. 1st U. S. Regt. Infty.

* See D, appendix part I, page 39.   † See E. appendix part I. page 40. ‡ See appendix part I, page 23.

N. W.

Recapitulation of Furs and Peltries, Fond du Lac department, Mark[...]

Marks	Numbers	Weight of Packs	Bears	Do. Cubs	Beaver Mixed	Do. Large	Do. Small	Do. Wt. in Pounds	Badgers	Carcajoux	Deer	Foxes	Fishers	Lynxes	Martens	Minks	Orig. Skin dressed	Do. Parchment	Do. Green	Otters	Racoons
N.W. L.L.	1	92	.	.	.		.		.	.	45										
	2	92	.	.	.		.		.	.	47										
	3	93	.	.	.		.		.	.	47										
	4	91	.	.	.		.		.	.	45										
	5	90	.	.	.		.		.	.	47										
	6	91	.	.	.		.		.	.	37										
	7	92	.	.	.		.		.	.	39										
	8	87	.	.	.		.		.	.	40										
	9	92	.	.	.		.		.	.	38										
	10	91	.	.	.		.		.	.	38										
	11	92	.	.	.		.		.	.	38										
	12	87	.	.	.		.		.	.	38										
	13	90	.	.	.		.		.	.	44										
	14	92	.	.	.		.		.	.	39										
	15	93	.	.	.		.		.	.	35										
	16	93	.	.	.		.		.	.	40										
	17	99	.	.	.		.		.	.	40										
	18	88	.	.	.		.		.	.	35										
	19	96	.	.	.		.		.	.	2	.	.	.	.	.	.	.	.	.	.	.
	20	95	.	.	.		.		.	.	2	.	.	.	.	.	.	.	.	.	.	.
	21	90	.	.	68		.	90													
	22	89	.	.	66		.	89													
	23	92	.	.	64		.	92													
	24	92	.	.	71		.	92													
	25	92	.	.	68		.	92													
	26	92	.	.	65		.	92													
	27	91	.	.	73		.	91													
	28	89	.	.	75		.	89													
	29	90	.	.	75		.	90													
	30	90	.	.	85		.	90													
	31	91	.	.	61	.	.	91													
	32	92	.	.	60		.	92													
	33	91	.	.	67		.	91													
	34	91	.	.	74		.	91													
	35	91	5	.	.		.		.	.	.	.	.	.	.	.	.	.	.	.	60	.
	36	99	4	.	.		.		.	.	1	.	.	.	.	.	.	.	.	.	60	.
	37	92	18	.	.		.		.	.	.	.	.	.	.	.	.	.	.	.	.	.
	38	93	4	.	.		.		.	.	3	.	11	25	.	.	.	.	.	.	22	.
	39	92	6	.	.		.		.	.	.	.	11	4	.	2	.	.	.	.	16	.
	40	87	6	.	.		.		.	1	2	1	11	.	5	11	.	.	.	.	27
	41	92	6	.	29		.	10		.	7	.	1	1	.	5	.	.	.	16	10
	42	93	.	.	66		.	93													
	43	93	.	.	79		.	93													
	44	90	.	.	70		.	93													
	45	93	2	.	.		.		1	.	11	.	3	.	14	2	13	.	.	7½	2
	46	91	.	.	79		.	91													
	47	90	.	.	89		.	90													
	48	91	.	.	69		.	91													
	49	91	.	.	73		.	91													
	50	87	2	.	.		.		1	2	.	11	1	3	15	4	.	.	45	
	51	104	2	.	36		.		.	1	.	2	2	.	2	2	.	.	10	1
	52	117	1	.	46		.		.	.	.	4	.	4	3	2	.	.	11	2
N.W. R.	1	94	.	.	.	57	9	94													
	2	91	.	.	.	51	14	91													
	3	91	.	.	.	50	11	91													
	4	92	.	.	.	49	19	92													
	5	92	.	.	.	54	31	92													
	6	92	.	.	.	59	6	92													
	7	95	7	1	.	2								3		.	11			.	.	3
	8	91	.	.	.	2															

and Numbers as per margin. North West Company, 1804-5.

(Table C. to face p. 42, Appendix, Part I.)

Marks	Numbers	Weight of Packs	Bears	Do. Cubs	Beaver Large	Do. Small	Do. Wt. in Pounds	Carcajous	Deer	Foxes	Fishers	Lynxs	Martens	Minks	Orig. Skins dressed	Do. Parchment	Do. Green	Otters	Racoons	Musk Rats	Wolves
N.W.R.	9	92	.	.	.	.	.	1	1	.	15	.	.	.	.	.	1	67	.	.	1
	10	90	.	.	1	.	.	.	1	.	3	.	.	.	11	.	.	.	.	.	.
	11	90	8	2	2	.	.	.	.	1	3	7	37	24	5	.	.	.	.	3	
Red Lake	12	95	.	.	45	8	.	.	.	.	2	.	.	.	.	.	.	11	13	.	
	13	93	4	4	.	.	.	.	.	11	.	7	19	9	1	.	1	3	58		
	14	93	2	2	13	9	.	.	.	7	.	1	1	11	.	.	6	4	6		
	15	92	.	.	3	6	14	.	.	.	.	2	1	.	2	1	1	.	1		
N.W.S.	1	86	.	.	.	.	.	.	14	1	18	.	3	7	.	.	.	25	7		
	2	91	.	.	.	.	.	.	6	.	.	.	.	.	.	.	.	.	.	500	
	3	88	.	.	40	29	88														
	4	91	.	.	37	32	91														
	5	91	.	.	37	30	91														
	6	90	.	.	31	37	90														
	7	89	.	.	38	26	89														
	8	92	.	.	42	33	92														
	9	86	.	.	43	17	86														
	10	87	.	.	32	40	87														
	11	88	.	.	42	28	88														
	12	90	.	.	44	22	90														
	13	87	.	.	35	38	87														
	14	92	.	.	43	23	92														
	15	95	.	.	.	.	.	.	5	.	22	.	.	.	.	.	.	63			
	16	92	.	.	.	.	.	.	25	.	6	3	15	14	.	.	.	.	.	26	
	17	86	.	.	.	.	.	.	32												
	18	90	.	.	.	.	.	.	31												
	19	91	.	.	.	.	.	.	59												
	20	95	.	.	.	.	.	.	33												
	21	87	7	1	30	.	43	.	6												
	22	83	.	.	38	33	83														
	23	93	.	.	34	42	93														
	24	87	.	.	34	43	87														
	25	89	.	.	36	37	89														
	26	92	.	.	57	14	92														
	27	94	16	1	.	.	.														
	28	94	4	.	.	.	.	.	2	.	11	.	.	.	.	.	.	58			
	29	90	.	.	.	.	.	.	2	.	.	.	.	.	.	.	.	.	.	400	
	30	91	.	.	.	.	.	.	.	.	5	1	43	22	1	11	.	.	.	20	
	31	93	.	.	.	.	.	.	39												
	32	93	.	.	.	.	.	.	43												
	33	90	.	.	.	.	.	.	43												
	34	91	.	.	.	.	.	.	35												
	35	99	.	.	.	.	.	.	41												
	36	86	.	.	.	.	.	.	44												
	37	72	.	.	.	.	.	.	7	.	.	.	.	2	13	1	.	1	.	55	
	38	92	1	.	35	33	.	.	5	.	.	.	.	.	1	.	.	5			
F.L.	Summr. Nos.	.	1	.	7	.	12	.	.	.	1	.	.	3	.	1	.	4	.	166	
	1	91	.	.	2	.	4	.	.	.	.	.	.	.	.	.	.	.	.	625	
	2	93	.	.	51	14	93														
	3	92	.	.	45	24	92														
	4	93	.	.	44	25	93														
	5	88	.	.	41	34	88														
	6	95	5	.	.	.	.	.	.	.	.	.	199	40	8						
	7	95	5	.	.	.	.	.	.	.	16	.	.	.	6	.	.	35			
	8	95	4	.	.	.	.	.	.	.	.	.	.	.	1	.	.	.	.	473	
	9	93	9	4	.	.	.	.	2	1	.	3	.	.	6	.	.	6	6	49	
	10	98	.	1	30	19	.	.	1	.	.	.	.	.	2	.	2	.			
A. Pacton.		.	.	11	.	15	.	.	.	.	.	.	2	.	2	.	3				

Amount of the above return, ... 115 Packs.
Different establishments not included, . . 54
Amount of the E. of the X. Y. company, . . 84

TOTAL AMOUNT.   ...

NOTES

TO THE PRECEDING " OBSERVATIONS," &c.

A.

Description of the N. W. company's fort at Sandy lake.

The fort at Sandy lake is situated on the south side of the lake, near the E end, and is a stockade of 100 feet square, with Bastions at the S. E. and N. W. angles, pierced for small arms.

The pickets are squared on the outside, round within of about one foot diameter, and are 13 feet above ground.

There are three gates: the principal one fronts the lake on the N. and is 10 feet by 9, the one on the W. 6 feet by 4, the one on the E. 6 feet by 5. As you enter by the main gate you have on the left a building of one story 20 feet square, the residence of the superintendant. Opposite to this house, on the left of the E. gate is a house 25 feet by 15, the quarters of the men. On entering the W. gate you find the store house on the right, 30 feet by 20, and, on your left, a building 40 feet by 20 which contains rooms for clerks, a work-shop, and provision-store.

On the W. and N. W. is an enclosure of about 4 acres picketed in; in which last year they raised 400 bushels of Irish potatoes, cultivating no other vegetable. In this enclosure is a very *ingeniously* constructed vault to contain the potatoes, but which likewise has *secret* apartments, to conceal liquors, dry goods, &c.

B.

Description of the N. W. company's fort at Leech lake, in February, 1806.

The fort is situated on the W. side of the lake, in 47° 16' 13" N. lat. It is built near the shore, on the declivity of a rising ground, having an enclosed garden of about 5 acres on the N. W. It is a square stockade of 150 feet, the pickets being 16 feet in length, 3 feet under, and 13 above the ground, and are bound together by horizontal bars, each 10 feet long. Pickets of 10 feet are likewise drove into the ground, on the inside of the work, opposite the apertures between the large pickets. At the W. and E angles are square bastions pierced for fire arms.

The main building in the rear, fronting the lake, is 60 feet by 25, 1 1-2 story high; the W. end of which is occupied by the director of the Fond du Lac department. He has a hall 18 feet square, bed-room and kitchen, with an office. The centre is a trading shop of 12 1-2 feet square, with a bed-room in the rear of the same dimensions. The E. end is a large store 25 feet by 20, under which there is an ice-house well filled. The loft extends over the whole building, and contains bales of goods, packs of peltries; also chests with 500 bushels of wild rice. Besides the ice-house there are cellars under all the other parts of the building. The doors and window-shutters are musket-proof.

On the W. side is a range of buildings 54 by 18 feet, fronting the parade, the N. end of which is a cooper's shop 18 by 14, with a cellar; joining to which is a room called the Indian hall (expressly for the reception of Indians, and in which the chiefs who met me in council were entertained). In this hall are two closed bunks for interpreters: its dimensions are 22 feet by 18. Adjoining to this is a room 18 feet square, for the clerks (in which my small party were quartered). Under both of the latter rooms are cellars.

On the E. side is a range of buildings 50 feet by 18, which has one room 20 feet and one of 15 feet, for quarters for the men; also a blacksmith-shop of 15 feet, which is occupied by an excellent workman. On the left of the main gate, fronting the river, is the flag-staff 50 feet in height.

They intended building a small block house over the main gate, fronting the lake, to place a small piece of artillery in. There are, likewise, gates on the N. and E. flanks of about 10 feet by 8.

D.

The price of goods in exchange with the Indians of this quarter, viz.

		Dollars.
Blankets, 3 and 2 1-2 point each	plus 4	8
Ditto 2 ditto,	2	4
Ditto 1 1-2 ditto,	1	2
Blue strouds, per fathom,	4	8
Scarlet cloth, 8-6	6	12
Worsted binding, per piece,	4	8
Vermillion, per pound,	4	8
Molten, blue and white, per fathom,	2	4
Gunpowder, per half pint,	1	2
Balls, 30 per	1	2
Shot of all sorts, per handful,	1	2
Tobacco, per carrot,	4	8
Twist tobacco, per fathom,	1	2
Beaver traps, each,	4	8
Half axes,	2	4
Castites,	1	2
N. W. Guns, each,	10	20
Knives,	1	2

Wampum and silver works, there is no regulation, as well as Rum; but the real price of goods here in exchange for Peltry, is about two hundred and fifty per cent on the prime cost.

GEO. ANDERSON.

E.

Return of men employed in the N. W. company's department of Fond du Lac, with the amount of their wages per annum, &c.

Accountants.	Clerks and men receiving interpreter's wages.	Interpreters.	Canoe men.	Total.	Women and children belonging to the establishment.		
					Women.	Children.	Total.
3	19	2	85	109	29	50	79

Sum of the wages per annum of the above 109 men, .	63,913	livres.
Average wages of each man, ...	586	7
Due by the N. W. company, ...	38,566	8
Due to ditto, ...	24,326	16

FOR 1805.

N. B. The above women are all Indians, there not being a single white woman N. W. of Lake Superior.

[No. 18.]

OBSERVATIONS

ON THE SOIL, SHORES, QUARRIES, TIMBER, ISLANDS, RAPIDS, CON-
FLUENT STREAMS, HIGHLANDS, PRAIRIES ; THE SAVAGES AND
SETTLEMENTS WHICH I MET WITH ON MY VOYAGE UP THE MIS-
SISSIPPI, FROM ST. LOUIS TO ITS SOURCE.

From St. Louis to the mouth of the Missouri on the east, is
a rich sandy soil, timbered with buttonwood, ash, cottonwood, hackberry, &c. The west side is highlands for a small distance above
the town ; then it is bordered by a small prairie, after which is
bottom land with the same timber as on the east. The current is
rapid, and the navigation, in low water, obstructed by sand bars.

Immediately on the peninsula formed by the confluence of the
rivers Mississippi and Missouri is a small Kickapoo settlement, occupied in summer only. On the west shore a rich prairie, with
small skirts of woods ; and on the east shore is generally high hills,
from eighty to one hundred feet, extending to the mouth of the Illinois. The current of the Mississippi, above the entrance of the
Missouri is quite mild, until you arrive at the mouth of the Illinois ;
where, owing to the large sand-bars and many islands, it is rendered
extremely rapid. The Illinois river is about four hundred and fifty
yards wide at its mouth, and bears from the Mississippi N. 75° W.
The current appears not to exceed two and a half miles per hour.
The navigation and connecting streams of this river are too well
known to require a description at the present day. From the Illinois
to the Buffalo river the E. shore is hills, but of easy ascent. On
the W. is continued the prairie, but not always bordering on the
river. Timber, on both sides, generally hackberry, cottonwood, and
ash. The Buffalo river comes in on the W. shore, and appears to
be about 100 yards wide at its mouth. It bears from the Mississippi
S. 30° W. From the Illinois to this river the navigation is by no
means difficult, and the current mild.

From thence to Salt river (or Oahahah) the east shore is either
immediately bounded by beautiful cedar cliffs, or the ridges may be
seen at a distance. On the W. shore there is a rich low soil, and
two small rivers which increase the waters of the Mississippi. The
first I called Bar river, about twenty yards in width. The second is
about fifteen yards. Salt river bears from the Mississippi N. 75°

6

W. and is about 100 or 120 yards wide at its entrance, and, when I passed, appeared to be perfectly mild, with scarcely any current. About one day's sail up the river there are salt springs, which have been worked for four years; but I am not informed as to their qualities or productions. In this distance the navigation of the Mississippi is very much obstructed by bars and islands; indeed, to such a degree as to render it difficult to find (in many places) the proper channel. The shores are generally a sandy soil, timbered with sugar maple, ash, pecan, locust, and black walnut. The E. side has generally the preference as to situations for building. From this to the river Jaustioni (which is our boundary between the Sac nation and the United States, on the west side of the Mississippi) we have the hills on the W. shore, and low lands on the E. the latter of which is timbered with hickory, oak, ash, maple, pecan, &c. The former the same, with an increase of oak. The E. is a rich sandy soil, and has many very eligible situations for cultivation. About seven miles below the Jaustioni a Frenchman is settled on the W. shore. He is married to a woman of the Sac nation, and lives by a little cultivation and the Indian trade. The river before mentioned is about 30 yards wide at its mouth, and bears from the Mississippi about S. W. In this part of the river the navigation is good.

From this to the Wyaconda river the navigation is easy, with very few impediments; and the soil on both sides pretty good. This river pays its tribute to the Mississippi by a mouth 100 yards wide, and bears from the latter nearly due W. Just below its entrance is a small stream 15 yards wide, which discharges itself into the Mississippi. Between this river and the river de Moyen, there is one small river emptying itself into the Mississippi, on the W. of about 55 yards in width, and bears S. by W. The first part of the distance is obstructed by islands, and the river expands itself to a great width, so as to render the navigation extremely difficult; but the latter part affords more water, and is less difficult. The timber is principally oak and pecan. The soil as the river below; for a description of de Moyen see the chart herewith, and for that of the rapids my diary of the 20th of August.

Above the rapid de Moyen, on the W. bank of the Mississippi, is situated the first Sac village, consisting of 13 lodges; and immediately opposite is the establishment of Mr. Ewing, the American agent at that place. From whence to a large prairie on the E. side, on which is situated the second Sac village, the E. side of the river is beautiful land, but principally prairie. The W. is in some part high land, both sides timbered with oak, ash, &c. The naviga-

tion is by no means difficult. From thence to the Iowa river the navigation is much obstructed with islands. * The Iowa river bears
from the Mississippi S. W. and is 150 yards wide at its mouth. The
E. shore of the Mississippi is high prairie, with yellow clay banks,
and in some places red sand. On the W. shore is prairie, also, but
bounded on the shore by skirts of woods. About 10 miles up the
Iowa river, on its right bank, is a village of the Iowas.

From this place to Rock river,† we generally had beautiful
prairies on the W. but in some places very rich land, with black
walnut and hickory timber. Stony river is a large river which empties into the Mississippi on the E. shore, and is about 300 yards
wide at its mouth. It bears from the Mississippi almost due E.
About three miles up this river, on the S. bank, is situated the third
town of the Sac nation, which (I was informed by a Mr. James
Aird) was burnt in the year 1781 or 2, by about 300 Americans,
although the Indians had assembled 700 warriors to give them battle. For a description of the rapids of Stony river, see my diary of
the 28th August.‡

A little above the rapids of Rock river, on the W. side of the
Mississippi, is situated the first Reynard village : it consists of about
18 lodges. From this place to the lead mines the Mississippi evidently becomes narrower; but the navigation is thereby rendered
much less difficult. The shores are generally prairie, which, if not
immediately bordering on the river, can be seen through the skirts
of forests which border the river. The timber is generally maple,
birch and oak, and the soil very excellent. To this place we had
seen only a few turkies and deer, the latter of which are pretty numerous from the river de Moyen up. For a description of the lead
mines, see my report from the prairie des Chiens, of the 5th Sept.‖
From the lead mines unto Turkey river, the Mississippi conti-

* In ascending Iowa river 36 miles you come to a fork, the right branch of
which is called Red Cedar river (from the quantity of that wood on its banks),
which is navigable for batteaux near 300 miles, where it branches out into three
forks, called the Turkey's foot. Those forks shortly after lose themselves in Rice
lakes.

† Rock river takes its source near Green bay of Lake Michigan more than
450 miles from its mouth, and is navigable upwards of 300 miles.

‡ Between the Iowa river and Turkey river, on the W. you find the Wabisi-
pinekan river. It coasts along the Red Cedar river in a parallel direction, and
scarcely any wood on its banks. The next water met with was the Great Maco-
keth, and 20 leagues higher is the little river of the same name. These two rivers
appear to approach each other, and have nothing remarkable excepting lead mines,
which are *said* to be in their banks.

‖ See Appendix to part I. [No. 2.] page 2.

nues about the same width; and the banks, soil and productions are entirely similar. The Turkey river empties in on the W. bears from the Mississippi about S. W. and is about 100 yards wide at its mouth. Half a league up this river, on the right bank, is the third village of the Reynards, at which place they raise sufficient corn to supply all the permanent and transient inhabitants of the Prairie des Chiens. From thence to the Ouiscousing, the high hills are perceptible on both sides, but on the W. almost border the river the whole distance. The Ouiscousing at the entrance is nearly half a mile wide, and bears from the Mississippi nearly N. E. * This

* The voyage from Michilimackinac to the Prairie des Chiens, by the Ouiscousing and Fox rivers is as follows :—viz.

The distance between Michilimackinac and the settlement at the bottom of Green bay is calculated to be 80 leagues. On leaving Michilimackinac there is a traverse of five miles to point St. Ignace, which is the entrance into Lake Michigan. Four leagues from Michilimackinac is an island of considerable extent, named St. Helens, and may be seen from that place in a clear day. The shore from Michilimackinac to the Point du Chene, which is a league distant from the island, is rocky; and from this to the island of Epouvette, which is a very small one, and stands near the banks of the lake, is high and covered with pine—the soil very barren. From this island to the river Mino Cockien is five leagues. Two small islands on the way, and a river where boats and canoes may take shelter from a storm. The river Mino Cockien is large and deep, and takes its rise near Lake Superior. From this to Shouchoir is ten leagues. The shore is dangerous, from the number of shoals that extend a great way into the lake. This rock, called Shouchoir, is an excellent harbor for canoes, but its entrance, when the wind blows from the lake, is difficult; but when once in, canoes and boats may lay during any storms without unlading. A custom prevails here among the voyagers for every one to have his name carved on the rocks the first time he passes, and pay something to the canoe-men. From this to the river Manistique is five leagues: it is a large river. The entrance is difficult, from a sand-bank at its mouth, and the waves are very high when the wind blows from the lake. At certain seasons is found here sturgeon in great numbers. The banks of this river are high and sandy, covered with pine. It takes its rise from a large lake, and nearly communicates with Lake Superior. From this to the Detour is ten leagues. The shore is rocky, flat, and dangerous. Here begins the Traverse at the mouth of Green bay. The first island is distant from the main land about a league, and is called the Isle au Detour, and is at least three leagues in circumference. There are generally a few Sauteaux lodges of Indians on this island during the summer months. From this to Isle Brule is three leagues. There are two small islands from these to Isle Verte, and two leagues to Isle de Pou, called so from the Poutowatomies having once a village here, but now abandoned. In the months of May and June there is a fishery of trout, and they are taken in great quantities by trolling. And there are also white fish in vast numbers. The ship *channel* is between this island and Isle Verte. From thence to Petit D'Etroit to the main land is three leagues, where some lodges of Ottowas and Sauteaux raise small quantities of corn; but their subsistence, during the summer river is the grand source of communication between the lakes and the Mississippi, and the route by which all the traders of Michilimackinac convey their goods, for the trade of the Mississippi, from St. Louis to the river de Corbeau, and the confluent streams which

months, chiefly depends upon the quantities of sturgeon and other fish, with which the lake here abounds. From Petit D'Etroit to the main land is three leagues, and is called the Port de Mort, from a number of Reynard canoes having been wrecked at this place, where every one perished. The shore is bold and rocky. From this is four leagues to the *Isle Racro*, which is a safe harbor, inaccessible to all winds. From this to Sturgeon bay is eight leagues. The shore is bold and rocky, and several large islands lie a few miles distant. A few Sauteaux families raise corn here and reside during the summer season. Trout and sturgeon are here in great numbers. Sturgeon's bay is two miles across and about four leagues in length, and communicates by a portage with Lake Michigan, near Michilimackinac. Distant from the lake about two leagues is the Isle Vermillion. Here were, a few years ago, a number of Fols Avoin inhabitants, who were accustomed to raise corn; but from what reasons they have left this place I cannot learn. From this is thirteen leagues to the entrance of the Fox river. On leaving Isle Vermillion, the woods and general appearance of the country begins to change, and has a very different aspect from the more northern parts of this lake. A small river called Riviere Rouge falls into the lake, about half way between Isle Vermillion and La Baye. On approaching La Baye, the water of the latter assumes a whiter appearance, and becomes less deep. A channel which winds a good deal may be found for vessels of 50 and 60 tons burden; and loaded vessels of these dimensions have gone up the Fox river to the French settlement, opposite to which is the Fols Avoin village, which consists of ten or twelve bark lodges. A great number of Sauteaux, and some Ottowas, come here in the spring and fall. Three leagues from La Baye is a small village of the same nation, and another three leagues higher, at the portage of Kakalin. This portage is a mile long : the ground even and rocky. There is a fall of about ten feet, which obstructs the navigation for three leagues higher, and almost continual rapids until the fall of Grand Konimee. About five feet high, above this, the river opens into a small lake, at the end of which is a strong rapid, called Puant's rapid, which issues from a lake of that name. This lake is ten leagues long, and from two to three wide. At its entrance is the first Puant village, of ten or twelve lodges. At the upper end of the lake is another Puant village, of about the same number of lodges, and at this end is a small river, which, with the interval of a few portages communicates with rock river. About midway between the two Puant villages is a Fols Avoin village, on the south side of the lake, of 50 or 60 men. Five leagues from the entrance of the lake, on the north side, the Fox river falls in, and is about 200 yards wide. Ascending two leagues higher, is a small Fols Avoin village, where is a lake of more than two leagues long; and about a league above this lake the river de Loup joins the Fox river, near a hill called the But de Mort, where the Fox nation were nearly extirminated by the French and confederate Indians. The rivers and lakes are, at certain seasons, full of wild rice. The country on the borders of this river is finely diversified with woods and prairies. Any quantity of hay may be made, and is as fine a country for raising stock as any in the same latitude through all America.

are in those boundaries. * The village of the Prairie des Chiens is situated about one league above the mouth of the Ouiscousing river. On the E. bank of the river there is a small pond or marsh which runs parallel to the river in the rear of the town, which, in front of the marsh, consists of 18 dwelling-houses, in two streets; 16 in Front-street, and 2 in First-street. In the rear of the pond are 8 dwelling-houses: part of the houses are framed, and in place of weatherboarding, there are small logs let into mortises made in the uprights, joined close, daubed on the outside with clay, and handsomely white-washed within. The inside furniture of their houses

From the But de Mort to the Lac a Puckway is twenty-eight leagues. Here is another Puant village of seven or eight large lodges. This lake is three leagues long: four leagues above it Lac du Bœuf begins, which is also four leagues long, and is full of wild rice, and a great many fowls in their season. From Lac du Bœuf to the forks, which is five leagues from the portage of the Ouiscousing, and ten leagues above the forks is a very small lake, called Lac *Vaseux*, and is so choaked with wild rice as to render it almost impassable. The river, although very winding, becomes here more and more serpentine on approaching the portage, and the river narrows so much as almost to prevent the use of oars. The length of the portage to the Ouiscousing is two miles, and when the waters are high, canoes and boats loaded pass over. Here the waters at that time separate, the one part going to the gulph of Mexico, and the other to that of St. Lawrence. In wet seasons the portage road is very bad, the soil being of a swampy nature. There is for nearly half way a kind of natural canal, which is sometimes used, and I think a canal between the two rivers might be easily cut. The expense at present attending the transport is one third of a dollar per hundred weight; for a canoe five dollars, and a boat eight dollars but this is not cash, but in goods, at the rate of 200 per cent on the sterling. There are at present two white men, who have establishments there; but they are much incommoded by the Puants of the Rock river, who are troublesome visitors. The Ouiscousing is a large river, its bottom sandy, full of islands and sand-bars during the summer season. The navigation is difficult even for canoes, owing to the lowness of the water. From the portage to its confluence with the Mississippi is 60 leagues. The Saques and Reynards formerly lived on its banks, but were drove off by the Sauteaux. They were accustomed to raise a great deal of corn and beans, the soil being excellent. Opposite to the Detour de Pin, half way from the Portage, on the south side, are lead mines, said to be the best in any part of the country, and may be wrought with great ease. Boats of more than four tons are improper for the communication between the Mississippi and Michilimackinac. [*Dickson.*]

* The present village of the Prairie des Chiens, was first settled in the year 1783, and the first settlers were Mr. Giard, Mr. Antaya, and Mr. Dubuque. The old village is about a mile below the present one, and had existed during the time the French were possessed of the country. It derives its name from a family of Reynards who formerly lived there, distinguished by the appellation of Dogs. The present village was settled under the English government, and the ground was purchased from the Reynard Indians.

is decent, and indeed, in those of the most wealthy displays a degree of elegance and taste.

There are eight houses scattered round the country, at the distance of one, two, three and five miles : also, on the W. side of the Mississippi, three houses, situated on a small stream called the Giards river, making, in the village and vicinity, 37 houses, which it will not be too much to calculate at 10 persons each, the population would be 370 souls ; but this calculation will not answer for the spring or autumn, as there are then, at least 5 or 600 white persons. This is owing to the concourse of traders and their engagees from Michilimackinac and other parts, who make this their last stage, previous to their launching into the savage wilderness. They again meet here in the spring, on their return from their wintering grounds, accompanied by 3 or 400 Indians, when they hold a *fair ;* the one disposes of remnants of goods, and the others reserved peltries. It is astonishing there are not more murders and affrays at this place, as there meets such an heterogeneous mass to trade ; the use of spirituous liquors being in no manner restricted ; but since the American government has become known, such accidents are much less frequent than formerly. The prairie on which the village is situated is bounded in the rear by high bald hills. It is from one mile to three quarters of a mile from the river, and extends about eight miles from the Mississippi, to where it strikes the Ouiscousing at the *Petit Grey,* which bears from the village S. E. by E.

If the marsh before spoken of was drained (which might be easily done), I am of the opinion it would render the situation of the prairie healthy, which now subjects its inhabitants to intermitting fevers in the spring and autumn.

There are a few gentlemen residing at the Prairie des Chiens, and many others claiming that appellation ; but the rivalship of the Indian trade, occasions them to be guilty of acts at their wintering grounds, which they would blush to be thought guilty of in the civilized world. They possess the spirit of generosity and hospitality in an eminent degree ; but this is the leading feature in the character of frontier inhabitants. Their mode of living had obliged them to have transient connexion with the Indian women ; and what was at first *policy* is now so confirmed by habit and inclination, that it is become (with a few exceptions) the ruling practice of all the traders ; and, in fact, almost one half of the inhabitants under 20 years have the blood of the aborigines in their veins. From the village to Lake Pepin we have, on the W. shore, first Yellow river:

of about 20 yards wide, bearing from the Mississippi nearly due W
second, the Iowa river, about 100 yards wide, bearing from the Mississippi about N. W. third, the Racine river, about 20 yards wide,
bearing from the Mississippi nearly W. and navigable for canoes 60
miles ; fourth, the rivers Embarra and Lean Claire, which join
their waters just as they form a confluence with the Mississippi, and
are about 60 yards wide, and bear nearly S. W.

On the E. shore, in the same distance, is the river de la Prairie
la Cross, which empties into the Mississippi, at the head of the
prairie of that name. It is about 20 yards wide, and bears N. N. W.

We then meet with the Black river, a very considerable stream
about 200 yards wide at its mouth, on which the traders frequently
winter with the *Puants* and *Fols Avoins*. Next pass the river of the
Montaigne qui Trompes dans l'Eau, a small stream in the rear of the
hill of that name ; and then we find the Riviere au Bœuf, of about 30
yards wide, bearing N. by W. and, at the entrance of Lake Pepin,
on the E. shore joins the Sauteaux river, which is at least half a
mile wide, and appears to be a deep and majestic stream. It bears
from the Mississippi nearly due N. This river is in size and
course (some distance up) scarcely to be distinguished from the
Ouiscousing, and has a communication with the Montreal river by a
short portage, and by this river with Lake Superior. The agents of
the N. W. company supply the Fols Avoin Sauteaux, who reside
at the head of this river, and those of Michilimackinac, the Sioux
who hunt on its lower waters.

In this division of the Mississippi the shores are more than
three-fourths prairie on both sides, or, more properly speaking, bald
hills, which, instead of running parallel with the river, form a continual succession of high perpendicular cliffs and low vallies : they
appear to head on the river, and to traverse the country in an angular
direction. Those hills and vallies give rise to some of the most
sublime and romantic views I ever saw. But this irregular scenery is sometimes interrupted by a wide extended plain, which
brings to mind the verdant lawn of civilized life, and would almost
induce the traveller to imagine himself in the centre of a highly
cultivated plantation. The timber of this division is generally birch,
elm and cottonwood, all the cliffs being bordered by cedar.

The navigation unto the Iowa river is good ; but from thence
to the Sauteaux river is very much obstructed by islands; and in
some places the Mississippi is uncommonly wide, and divided into
many small channels, which from the cliffs appear like so many distinct rivers, winding in a parallel course through the same im-

mense valley. But there are few sand-bars in those narrow channels : the soil being rich, the water cuts through it with facility.

La Montaigne qui Trompe dans l'Eau stands in the Mississippi
near the E. shore. about 50 miles below the Sauteaux river, and is
about two miles in circumference, with an elevation of two hundred
feet, covered with timber. There is a small river which empties
into the Mississippi, in the rear of the mountain, which, I conceive,
once bounded the mountain on the lower side, and the Mississippi
on the upper, when the mountain was joined to the main by a neck
of prairie low ground, which in time was worn away by the spring
freshes of the Mississippi ; and thus formed an island of this celebrated mountain. Lake Pepin (so called by the French,) appears
to be only an expansion of the Mississippi. It commences at the
entrance of the Sauteaux river, and bears N. 55 W. to Point de
Sable 12 miles, which is a neck of land making out about one mile
into the lake from the W. shore, and is the narrowest part of the
lake. From here to the upper end the course is nearly due W.
about 10 miles, making its whole length 22 miles, and from four to
one and a half miles in width, the broadest part being in the bay
below Point de Sable. This is a beautiful place ; the contrast of
the Mississippi full of islands, and the lake with not one in its whole
extent, gives more force to the grandeur of the scene. The French,
under the government of M. Frontenac, drove the Reynards (or
Ottaquamies) from the Ouiscousing, and pursued them up the Mississippi, and, as a barrier, built a stockade on Lake Pepin, on the
W. shore, just below Point de Sable ; and, as was generally the case
with that nation, blended the military and mercantile professions, by
making their fort a factory for the Sioux. The lake, at the upper
end, is three fathoms deep ; but this, I am informed, is its shoalest
part. From the Iowa river to the head of Lake Pepin, the elk are
the prevailing species of wild game, with some deer, and a few bear.

From the head of Lake Pepin about 12 miles to the Cannon
river, the Mississippi is branched out into many channels, and its
bosom covered with numerous islands. There is a hill on the W.
shore, about six miles above the lake called the Grange, from the
summit of which you have one of the most delightful prospects in
nature. When turning your face to the E. you have the river winding in three channels at your feet; on your right the extensive
bosom of the lake, bounded by its chain of hills, in front over the
Mississippi, a wide extended prairie ; on the left the valley of the
Mississippi, open to view quite to the St. Croix, and partly in your
rear, the valley through which passes the Riviere *au Canon ;* and

when I viewed it, on one of the islands below, appeared the spotted lodges of the Red Wing's band of Sioux.   The white tents of the traders and my soldiers, and three flags of the United States waving on the water, which gave a contrast to the still and lifeless wilderness around, and increased the pleasure of the prospect.

From the Cannon river to the St. Croix, the Mississippi evidently becomes narrower, and the navigation less obstructed by islands. The St. Croix river joins the Mississippi on the E. and bears from the latter almost due N.   It is only 80 yards wide at its mouth, and 500 yards up commences Lake St. Croix, which is from one and a half to three miles wide, and 36 long.   This river communicates with Lake Superior by the Burnt river, by a portage of half a mile only, and in its whole extent has not *one fall or rapid* worthy of notice.   This, with the mildness of its current, and its other advantages, render it by far the most preferable communication which can be had with the N. W. from this part of our territories.   Its upper waters are inhabited by the Fols Avoins and Sauteaux, who are supplied by the agents of the north west company ; and its lower division by the Sioux and their traders.

The Mississippi from the Cannon river is bounded on the E. by high ridges, but the left is low ground.   The timber is generally ash and maple, except the cedar of the cliffs.   From the St. Croix to the river St. Peters the Mississippi is collected into a narrow compass (I crossed it at one place with forty strokes of my oars) and the navigation very good.   The E. bank generally bounded by the river ridges, but the W. sometimes timbered bottom or prairie.   The timber is generally maple, sugar-tree, and ash.   About twenty miles below the entrance of the river St. Peters, on the E. shore, at a place called the Grand Morais, is situated the Petit Corbeau's village of eleven log houses.   For a description of the river St. Peters, see the chart herewith.   From the river St. Peters to the falls of St. Anthony, the river is contracted between high hills, and is one continual rapid or fall, the bottom being covered with rocks which (in low water) are some feet above the surface, leaving narrow channels between them.   The rapidity of the current is likewise much augmented by the numerous small rocky islands, which obstruct the navigation.   The shores have many large and beautiful springs issuing forth, which form small cascades as they tumble over the cliffs into the Mississippi.   The timber is generally maple.   This place we noted for the great quantity of wild fowl.   As I ascended the Mississippi, the falls of St. Anthony did not strike me with that majestic appearance which I had been taught to expect from the description of former travellers. On an actual survey, I find the portage to be 260 poles; but when the river is not very low, boats ascending may be put in 31 pole below, at a large cedar tree, which would reduce it to 229 poles. The hill over which the portage is made, is 69 feet ascent, with an elevation at the point of debarkation of 45°. The fall of the water between the place of debarkation and re-loading is 58 feet; the perpendicular fall of the shoot 16 1-2 feet. The width of the river above the shoot 627 yards; below 209. For the form of the shoot, see a rough draught herewith. In high water, the appearance is much more sublime, as the great quantity of water *then* forms a spray, which in clear weather reflects from some positions the colors of the rainbow, and when the sky is o'ercast, cover the falls in gloom and chaotic majesty. From the Falls of St. Anthony to Rum river, the Mississippi is almost one continual chain of rapids, with the eddies formed by winding channels. Both sides are prairie, and scarcely any timber but small groves of scrub oak. Rum river is about 50 yards wide at its mouth, and takes its source in Le Mille Lac, which is but 35 miles S. of Lower Red Cedar Lake. The small Indian canoes ascend this river quite to the lake, which is considered as one of the best fur hunting grounds for some hundreds of miles; and has been long a scene of rencounters between the hunting parties of the Sioux and Sauteaux. The last winter a number of the Fols Avoins and Sioux, and some Sauteaux, wintered in that quarter. From Rum river to Leaf river, (called by father Hennipin and Carver, the river St. Francis, and was the extent of their travels) the prairies continue with a few interruptions. The timber scrub oak, with now and then a lonely pine. Previous to your arrival at Leaf river, you pass Crow river on the W. about 30 yards wide, which bears from the Mississippi S. W. Leaf river is only a small stream of not more than 15 yards over, and bears N. by W.

The elk begin to be very plenty; some buffalo, quantities of deer, racoons, and on the prairie a few of the animals called by the French brelaws.

From thence to Sac river, a little above the Grand Rapids, both sides of the river are generally prairie, with skirts of scrub oak. The navigation still obstructed with ripples, but with some intermissions of a few miles.

At the Grand Rapids the river expands itself to about 3-4 of a mile in width, (its general width not being more than 3-5 of a mile) and tumbles over an unequal bed of rocks for about two miles, through which there cannot be said to be any channel: for notwith.-

standing the rapidity of the current, one of my invalids, who was on the   . shore waded to the E. (where we were encamped.) The E. bank at the Rapids is a very high prairie; the W. scrubby wood land. The Sac river is a considerable stream, which comes in on the W. and bears about S. W. and is 200 yards wide at its mouth.

The quantity of game still increasing from the Sac river to Pine creek, the place where I built my stockade, and left part of my party the borders are prairie, with groves of pine on the edge of the bank; but there are some exceptions where you meet with small bottoms of oak, ash, maple, and lynn. In this distance there is an intermission of rapids for about 40 miles, when they commence again, and are full as difficult as ever. There are three small creeks emptying in on the W. scarcely worthy of notice, and on the E. are two small rivers called Lake and Clear Rivers; the former quite a small one, bears N. W. and is about 15 yards wide at its mouth; about 3 miles from its entrance, is a beautiful small lake, around which, resort immense herds of elk and buffalo. Clear river is a beautiful little stream, of about 80 yards in width, and heads in some swamps and small lakes on which the Sauteaux of Lower Red Cedar Lake, and Sandy Lake frequently come to hunt. The soil of the prairies from above the falls is sandy, but would raise small grain in abundance; the bottoms rich, and fit for corn or hemp. Pine creek is a small stream which comes in on the W. shore, and bears nearly W. It is bordered by large groves of *white* and *red* pine. From Pine creek to the Isle De Corbeau, (or river of that name) two small rivers come in on the W. shore. The first is of little consequence; but the second called Elk river, is entitled to more consideration, from its communication with the river St. Peters. They first ascend it to a small lake, cross it, then ascend a small stream to a large lake; from which they make a portage of four miles W. and fall into the Sauteaux river, which they descend into the river St. Peters. On the E. side is one small stream which heads towards Lower Red Cedar Lake, and is bounded by hills. The whole of this distance is remarkably difficult to navigate, being one continued succession of rapid shoals and falls; but there is *one* deserves to be more particularly noticed, viz: The place called by the French Le Shute de la Roche Peinture, which is certainly the 3d obstacle in point of navigation, which I met with in my whole route. The shore where there is not prairie, is a continued succession of pine ridges. The entrance of the river De Corbeau, is partly hid by the island of that name, and discharges its waters into the Mississippi above and below it: the lowest channel bearing from the Mississippi

N. 65°, W. the upper due W. This (in my opinion) should be termed the Forks of the Mississippi, it being nearly of equal magnitude, and heading not far from the same source ; although taking a much more direct course to their junction.   It may be observed on the chart, that, from St. Louis to this place, the course of the river had generally been N. to the W. and, that from here it bore N. E. This river affords the best and most approved communication with the Red river ; and the navigation is as follows :   You ascend the river De Corbeau 180 miles, to the entrance of the river Des Feuilles, which comes from the N. W.   This you ascend 180 miles also ; then make a portage of half a mile into the Otter Tail Lake, which is a principal source of Red river.   The other branch of the river De Corbeau bears S. W. and approximates with the St. Peters.   The whole of this river is rapid, and by no means affording so much water as the Mississippi.   Their confluence is in latitude 45° 49′ 50″ N. In this division the elk, deer, and buffalo, were probably in greater quantities than in any other part of my whole voyage.   From thence to Pine river the Mississippi continues to become narrower, and has but few islands.   In this distance I discovered but one rapid, which the force of the frost had not entirely covered with ice.   The shores in general presented a dreary prospect of high barren nobs, covered with dead and fallen pine timber.   To this there were some exceptions of ridges of yellow and pitch pine ; also some small bottoms of lynn, elm, oak, and ash.   The adjacent country is (at least two thirds) covered with small lakes, some of which are 5 miles in circumference.   This renders the communication impassible in summer, except with small bark canoes.   In this distance we first met with a species of pine called the sap pine.   It was equally unknown to myself and all my party.   It scarcely ever exceeds the height of 35 feet, and is very full of projecting branches.   The leaves are similar to other pines ; but project out from the branches on each side, in a direct line, thereby rendering the branch flat ; and this formation occasions the natives and voyagers to give it the preference on all occasions to the branches of all other trees for their beds, and to cover their temporary camps ; but its greatest virtue arises from its medicinal qualities.   The rind is smooth, with the exception of little protuberances of about the size of a hazel nut ; the top of which being cut, you squeeze out a glutinous substance of the consistence of honey.   This gum or sap gives name to the tree, and is used by the natives and traders of that country as a balsam for all wounds made by sharp instruments, or on parts frozen, and almost all other external injuries which they receive.   My poor fellows experienced its beneficial qualities by the application made of it to their frozen extremities in various instances. The *Pine river* bears from the Mississippi N. 30° E. although it empties in on that which has been hitherto termed the W. shore. It is 80 yards wide at its mouth, and has an island immediately at the entrance. It communicates with Lake Le Sang Sue, by the following course of navigation : In one day's sail from the confluence, you arrive at the first part of White Fish Lake, which is about 6 miles long and two wide. From thence you pursue the river about two miles, and come to the 2d White Fish Lake, which is about 3 miles long and 1 wide ; then you have the river three miles to the 3d lake, which is 7 miles long and two in width. (which I crossed on my return from the head of the Mississippi, on the   of February; and is in 46° 32′ 32″ N. latitude) From thence you follow the river a quarter of a mile to the 4th lake, which is a circular one of about 5 miles in circumference. From thence you pursue the river one day's sail to a small lake ; from thence two day's sail to a portage, which conveys you to another lake, from whence by small portages from lake to lake, you make the voyage to Leech Lake. The whole of this course lays through ridges of pines or swamps of pinenet, sap pine, hemlock, &c. &c. From the river De Corbeau to this place, the deer are very plenty, but we found no more buffalo or elk. From this spot to Red Cedar Lake, the pine ridges are interrupted by large bottoms of elm, ash, oak, and maple ; the soil of which would be very proper for cultivation. From the appearance of the ice, (which was firm and equal) I conceive there can be but one ripple in this distance. Red Cedar lake lays on the E. side of the Mississippi, at the distance of 6 miles from it, and is near equally distant from the river De Corbeau and Lake De Sable. Its form is an oblong square, and may be 10 miles in circumference. From this to Lake De Sable on the E. shore, you meet with Muddy River, which discharges itself into the Mississippi by a mouth 20 yards wide, and bears nearly N. E. We then meet with Pike river on the W. about 77 miles below Sandy lake, and bears nearly due N : up which, you ascend with canoes 4 day's sail, and arrive at a wild Rice lake, which you pass through and enter a small stream, and ascend it two leagues ; then cross a portage of two acres into a lake 7 leagues in circumference ; then two leagues of a river into another small lake. From thence you descend the current N. E. into Leech lake. The banks of the Mississippi are still bordered by the pines of the different species, except a few small bottoms of elm, lynn and maple. The game scarce, and the Aborigines, subsist almost entirely on the beaver, with a few moose, and the wild rice or oats.

Sandy Lake river (or the discharge of said lake) is large, but is only six miles in length from the lake to its confluence with the Mississippi. Lake De Sable is about 25 miles in circumference, and has a number of small rivers running into it: one of those is entitled to particular attention, viz: the river Savanna, which by a portage of three miles and three quarters communicates with the river St. Louis, which empties into Lake Superior at the Fond Du Lac; and is the channel by which the N. W. company bring all their goods for the trade of the Upper Mississippi. Game is very scarce in this country. In ascending the Mississippi from Sandy lake, you first meet with Swan river on the east, which bears nearly due E. and is navigable for bark canoes, 90 miles to Swan lake. You then meet with the Meadow river, which falls in on the E. and bears nearly E. by N. and is navigable for Indian canoes 100 miles. You then in ascending meet with a very strong ripple, and an expansion of the river where it forms a small lake. This is three miles below the falls of Packegamau, and from which the noise of the shoot might be heard. The course of the river at the falls, was N. 70° W. and just below, the river is a quarter of a mile in width, but above the shoot not more than 20 yards. The water thus collected, runs down a flat rock, which has an elevation of about 30 degrees. Immediately above the fall is a small island of about 50 yards in circumference, covered with sap pine. The portage which is on the E. (or N.) side, is no more than 200 yards; and by no means difficult. Those falls, in point of consideration, as an impediment to the navigation, stand next to the falls of St. Anthony, from the source of the river to the Gulf of Mexico. The banks of the river to the Meadow river; have generally either been timbered by the pine, pinenett, hemlock, sap pine, or the aspen tree. From thence it winds through high grass meadows, (or savannas) with the pine swamps, at a distance appearing to cast a deeper gloom on the borders. From the falls in ascending, you pass the lake Packegamau on the W. celebrated for its great productions of wild rice; and next meet with the Deer river on the E. the extent of its navigation unknown. You next meet with the Riviere Le Cross, on the E. side, which bears nearly N. and has only a portage of one mile to pass from it into the Lake Winipeque Branch of the Mississippi. We next come to what the people of that quarter call the forks of the Mississippi. The right fork of which bears N. W. and runs eight leagues to Lake Winipeque, which is of an oval form of about 36 miles in circumference. From Lake Winipeque the river continues 5 leagues to Upper Red Cedar Lake, which may be termed the Upper Source of Mississippi. The Leech Lake Branch bears (from the forks) S. W. and runs through a chain of meadows. You pass Muddy lake, which is scarcely any thing more than an extensive marsh of 15 miles in circumference; the river bears through it nearly N. after which it again turns W. In many places this branch is not more than ten or fifteen yards in width, although 15 or 20 feet deep. From this to Leech Lake, the communication is direct, and without any impediment. This is rather considered as the main source, although the Winipeque Branch is navigable the greatest distance. To this place the whole face of the country has an appearance of an impenetrable morass, or boundles savanna. But on the borders of the lake is some oak and large groves of sugar maple, from which the traders make sufficient sugar for their consumption the whole year. Leech Lake communicates with the river De Corbeau by seven portages, and the river Des Feuilles also, with the Red river, by the Otter Tail Lake on the one side, and by Red Cedar Lake and other small lakes to Red Lake on the other. Out of these small lakes and ridges, rises the upper waters of the St. Lawrence, Mississippi, and Red river,* the latter of which discharges itself into the ocean by Lake Winipie and Hudson's Bay. All those waters have their upper sources within 100 miles of each other, which I think plainly proves this to be the most elevated part of the N. E. continent of America. But we must cross (what is commonly termed) the Rocky Mountains, or a Spur of the Cordeliers, previous to our finding the waters, whose currents run westward, and pay tribute to the western ocean

In this quarter we find moose, a very few deer and bear, but a vast variety of fur animals of all descriptions.

The first nation of Indians whom we met with in ascending the Mississippi from St. Louis, were the Sauks, who principally reside in four villages. The 1st at the head of the rapids De Moyen on the W. shore, consisting of 13 log lodges. The 2d on a prairie on the E. shore, about 60 miles above. The 3d on the Riviere De Roche, about three miles from the entrance, and the last on the river Iowa.

They hunt on the Mississippi and its confluent streams, from the Illinois to the river Des Iowa; and on the plains west of them, which border the Missouri. They are so perfectly consolidated with

* Red river discharges itself into Hudson's Bay, by Lake Winipie and Nelson's river.

the Reynards, that they scarcely can be termed a distinct nation ; but recently there appears to be a schism between the two nations : the latter not approving of the *insolence* and *ill will*, which has *marked* the conduct of the former towards the United States, on many late occurrences. They have for many years past made war (under the auspices of the Sioux) on the Sauteaux, Osages, and Missouries ; but as recently a peace has been (through the influence of the United States) made between them and the nations of the Missouri, and by the same means between the Sioux and Sauteaux, (their principal allies) it appears that it would by no means be a difficult matter to induce them to make a general peace, and pay still greater attention to the cultivation of the earth : as they now raise a considerable quantity of corn, beans, and melons. The character that they bear with their savage brethren, is, that they are much more to be dreaded for their deceit and inclination for stratagem, than for open courage.

The Reynards reside in three villages. The 1st. on the W. side of the Mississippi, six miles above the rapids of the river De Roche. The 2d. about 12 miles in the rear of the lead mines, and the 3d. on Turkey river, half a league from its entrance. They are engaged in the same wars, and have the same alliances as the Sauks, with whom they must be considered as indissoluble in war or peace. They hunt on both sides of the Mississippi from the river Iowa, (below the Prairie Des Chiens) to a river of that name above said village. They raise a great quantity of corn, beans, and melons ; the former of those articles in such quantities, as to sell many hundred bushels per annum.

The Iowas reside on the rivers De Moyen and Iowa in two villages. They hunt on the west side of the Mississippi, the river De Moyen, and westward to the Missouri ; their wars and alliances are the same as the Sauks and Reynards ; under whose special protection they conceive themselves to be. They cultivate some corn ; but not so much in proportion as the Sauks and Reynards. Their residence being on the small streams in the rear of the Mississippi, out of the high road of commerce, renders them less civilized than those nations.

The Sauks, Reynards, and Iowas, (since the treaty of the two former with the United States) claim the land from the entrance of the Jauflioni on the W. side of the Mississippi, up the latter river to the Des Iowa, above the Prairie Des Chiens and westward to the Missouri ; but the limits between themselves are undefined. All the land formerly claimed by those nations E. of the Mississippi, is

8

now ceded to the United States; but they reserved to themselves the privilege of hunting and residing on it as usual.

By killing the celebrated Sauk chief Pontiac, the Illinois, Cahokias, Kaskaskias and Piorias, kindled a war with the allied nations of Sauks and Reynards, which has been the cause of the almost entire destruction of the former nations.

The Winebagos, or Puants, are a nation who reside on the rivers Ouiscousing, De Roche, Fox and Green Bay, in seven villages, which are situated as follows viz:

1st. At the entrance of Green Bay.
2d. End of do.
3d. Wuckan, on the Fox river.
4th. At Lake Puckway.
5th. Portage of the Ouiscousing.
6th and 7th. Both on Roche river.

Those villages are so situated, that the Winebagos can embody the whole force of their nation, at any one point of their territory in four days. They hunt on the Ouiscousing, Rock river, and E. side of the Mississippi; from the Rock river to the Prairie Des Chiens; on Lake Michigan, Black river, and the country between Lakes Michigan, Huron, and Superior. From the tradition amongst them, and their speaking the same language of the Otos, of the Riviere Platte, I am confident in asserting that they are a nation who have emigrated from Mexico, to avoid the oppression of the Spaniards; and the time may be fixed at about one and a half centuries past, when they were taken under the protection of the Sioux, to whom they still profess to owe faith, and *at least brotherly* attention. They have formerly been at war with the nations west of the Mississippi, but appear recently to have laid down the hatchet. They are reputed brave, but from every circumstance their neighbors distinguish their bravery as the ferocity of a tiger, rather than the deliberate resolution of a man. And recently, their conduct has been such as to authorise the remark made by a chief of a neighboring nation, " That a white man never should lay down to sleep, without precaution in their villages."

The Menomene or Fols Avoins (as termed by the French) nation, reside in seven villages, situated as follows, viz. 1st. At the river Menomene, 15 leagues from Green Bay, north side of the lake. 2d. At Green Bay. 3d. At Little Kakalin. 4th. Portage of Kakalin. 5th. Stinking Lake. 6th. Entrance of a small lake on Fox river; and 7th. Behind the Bank of the Dead. Their hunting grounds are similar to the Winebagos ; only, that owing to the very high estimation in which they are held, both by Sioux and Chipeways, they are frequently permitted to hunt near the Raven river on the Mississippi ; which may be termed the battle ground between those two great nations. The language which they speak is singular ; for no white man has ever yet been known to acquire it, but this may probably be attributed to their all understanding the Algonquin, in which they and the Winebagos transact all conferences with the whites or other nations ; and the facility with which that language is acquired, is a further reason for its prevalence.

The Fols Avoins although a small nation, are respected by all their neighbors for their bravery, and independent spirit, and esteemed by the whites as their friends and protectors. When in the country, I have heard their *chief* assert in council with the Sioux and Chipeways, " That although they were reduced to few in num- " ber, yet they could say, we never were slaves." As they had always preferred, " that their women and children should die by their " own hands, to their being led into slavery by their enemies." The boundary of their territory is uncertain. The Sauks, Reynards, Puants, and Menomenes, all reside (when not at their villages) in lodges in the form of an ellipsis, and some are from 30 to 40 feet in length, by 14 or 15 wide, which are sufficiently large to shelter 60 people from the storm, or for 20 to reside in. Their covering are rushes plaited into mats, and carefully tied to the poles. In the centre are the fires, immediately over which is a small vacancy in the lodge, which, in fair weather, is sufficient to give vent to the smoke ; but in bad weather you must lay down on the ground to prevent being considerably incommoded by it.

We next come to that powerful nation the Sioux, the dread of whom is extended over all the savage nations, from the confluence of the Mississippi and Missouri, to the Raven river on the former, and to the Snake Indians on the latter ; but in those limits are many nations whom they consider as allies ; on similar footing with the allies of ancient Rome, i. e. humble dependants. But the Chipeway nation is an exception who have maintained a long contest with them, owing to their country being intersected by numerous small lakes, water courses, impenetrable morasses, and swamps ; and have hitherto bid defiance to all the attacks of their neighbors. It is necessary to divide the Sioux nation into the different bands, as distinguished amongst themselves, in order to have a correct idea of them. Agreeably to this plan, I shall begin with the *Minowa Kantong*, (or Gens De Lac) who extend from the Prairie Des Chiens, to La

Prairie du Francois, 35 miles up the St. Peters. This band is again sub-divided into four divisions, under different chiefs. The first of which most generally reside at their village on the Upper Iowa river, above the Prairie Des Chiens, and are commanded by Wabasha, a chief, whose father was considered as the first chief of all the Sioux nation. This sub-division hunts on both sides of the Mississippi, and its confluent streams from the Prairie Des Chiens to the riviere du Bœuf. The second sub-division resides near the head of Lake Pepin, and hunt from the riviere du Bœuf near to the river St. Croix. Their chief's name is Tantangamani, a very celebrated war chief. The third sub-division resides between the riviere au Canon and the entrance of the St. Peters, are headed by Chatewaconamani. Their principal hunting ground is on the St. Croix. They have a village at a place called the Grand Marais, 15 miles below the entrance of the St. Peters. It is situated on the east bank of the Mississippi, and consists of eleven log huts. The fourth sub-division is situated from the entrance of the St. Peters, to the Prairie Des Francois; they are headed by a chief called Chatamutah, but a young man, Wyaganage, has recently taken the lead in all the councils and affairs of state of this sub-band. They have one village nine miles up the St. Peters, on the N. side. This band (Minowa Kantong) are reputed the bravest of all the Sioux; and have for years been opposed to the Fols Avoin Sauteurs, who are reputed the bravest of all the numerous bands of Chipeways.

The 2d. band of Sioux, are the Washpetong (or Gens Des Fieulles) who inhabit the country from the Prairie De Francois, near to Roche Blanche, on the St. Peters. Their first chief is Wasonquianni. They hunt on the St. Peters; also on the Mississippi, up Rum river, and sometimes follow the buffalo, on the plains. Their sub-divisions I am unacquainted with.

The 3d. band are the Sussitongs; they extend from the Roche Blanche, to Lac de Gross Roche, on the river St. Peters; they are divided into two sub-divisions. The 1st. band called the Cawrees, are headed by the chief called Wuckiew Nutch, (or the Tonnere Rouge.) The 2d. called the *Sussitongs proper*, and headed by Wacantoe, (or Esprit Blue.) Those two sub-bands hunt eastward to the Mississippi, and up that river as far as the Riviere De Corbeau.

The 4th. great band are the Yanctongs, who are dispersed from the Montaignes De la Prairie, (which extends from St. Peters to the Missouri) to the river De Moyen. They are divided into two grand divisions, generally termed the Yanctongs of the north, and the Yanctongs of the south. The former are headed by a chief called Muckpeanutah ; (or Nuage Rouge) and those of the Prairie by Petessung. This band are never stationary, but with the Titongs are the most erratic bands of all the Sioux, sometimes to be found on the borders of the Lower Red River, sometimes on the Missouri, and on those immense plains which are between the two rivers.

The 5th. great band are the Titongs, who are dispersed on both sides of the Missouri. On the north principally from the river Chienne up ; and on the south, from the Mahas to the Minetares, (or Gross Ventres.) They may be divided into the Titongs of the north and south ; but the immense plains over which they rove with the Yanctongs, renders it impossible to point out their place of habitation.

The 6th. last and smallest band of the Sioux, are the *Washpecoute*, who reside generally on the lands west of the Mississippi, between that river and the Missouri. They hunt most generally on the head of the river De Moyen. They appeared to me to be the most stupid and inactive of all the Sioux.

GENERAL OBSERVATIONS.

The Minowa Kantongs are the only band of Sioux who use canoes, and by far the most civilized, they being the only ones who have ever built log huts, or cultivated any species of vegetables ; and those only a very small quantity of corn and beans ; for although I was with them in September or October, I never saw one kettle of either, always using the wild oats for bread. This production nature has furnished to all the most uncultivated nations of the N. W. continent, who may gather a sufficiency in autumn, which, when added to the productions of the chase and the net, ensures them a subsistence through all the seasons of the year. This band is entirely armed with fire arms, but is not considered by the other bands as any thing superior on that account, especially on the plains.

The Washpetong are a roving band ; they leave the river St. Peters in the month of April, and do not return from the plains, until the middle of August. Sussitongs of Roche Blanche, have the character of being the most evil disposed Indians, on the river St. Peters. They likewise follow the buffalo in the spring and summer months. Sussitongs of the Lac de Gross Roche (under the Tonnere Rouge) have the character of good hunters and brave warriors, which may principally be attributed to their chief the *Tonnere Rouge*, who, at the present day is allowed by both white people and the savages of the different bands, to be (after their own chiefs) the first man in the Sioux nation. The Yanctongs and Titongs are the most independent Indians in the world; they follow the buffalo as chance directs; clothing themselves with the skin, and making their lodges, bridles, and saddles of the same materials, the flesh of the animal furnishing their food. Possessing innumerable herds of horses, they are here this day, 500 miles off ten days hence, and find themselves equally at home in either place, moving with a rapidity scarcely to be imagined by the inhabitants of the civilized world.

The trade of the Minowa Kantong, Washpetong, Sussitongs, and part of the Yanctongs, is all derived from the traders of Michilimackinac; and the latter of those two bands supply the Yanctongs of the north, and Titongs, with the small quantities of iron works which they require. Fire arms are not in much estimation with them. The Washpecoute trade principally with the people of Prairie Des Chiens; but for a more particular explanation of this subject, please to refer to the table.*

The claims of limits of the Sioux nation, are allowed by all their neighbors, to commence at the Prairie Des Chiens, and ascends the Mississippi on both sides, to the Riviere De Corbeau, up that river to its source; from thence to the source of the St. Peters; from thence to the Montaigne De La Prairie; from thence to the Missouri down that river to the Mahas, bearing thence N. E. to the source of the river De Moyen; and from thence to the place of begining. They also claim a large territory south of the Missouri, but how far it extends is uncertain. The country E. of the Mississippi, from Rum river to the Riviere De Corbeau is likewise in dispute between them and the Chipeways; and has been the scene of many a sharp encounter for near one hundred and fifty years past.

From my knowlege of the Sioux nation, I do not hesitate to pronounce them the most warlike and independent nation of Indians within the boundaries of the United States, their every passion being subservient to that of war; but at the same time, their traders feel themselves perfectly secure of any combination being made against them, but it is extremely necessary to be careful not to injure the honor or feelings of an individual, which is certainly the principal cause of the many broils which occur between them. But

* See table F. appendix to part I, facing page 66.

never was a trader known to suffer in the estimation of the nation by rese ting any indignity offered him ; even if it went to taking the life of the offender. Their guttural pronunciation ; high cheek bones; their visages, and distinct manners, together with their own traditions, supported by the testimony of neighboring nations, puts it in my mind, beyond the shadow of a doubt that they have emigrated from the N. W. point of America, to which they had come across the narrow streights, which in that quarter divides the two continents ; and are absolutely descendants of a Tartarean tribe.

The only personal knowledge which I have of the Chipeway nation, is restricted to the tribes on the south side of Lake Superior, head waters of the Chipeway river, and the St. Croix ; and those who reside at Sandy Lake, Leech Lake, Rainy Lake, Red Lake, and the head of the rivers Rouge, Mississippi, and De Corbeau. They are divided into many bands (like the Sioux) the names of seven of which I am only acquainted with. I shall begin with those who reside on the south side of Lake Superior, and on Lakes De Sable and Sang Sue, with the adjacent country. They are generally denominated by the traders, by the name of Sauteux; but those of the head waters of the Chipeways and St. Croix river, are called Fols Avoin Sauteurs. I am unacquainted with the names of their chiefs. Those of Sandy Lake are headed by a chief called Catawabata, (or De Breche.) They hunt on the Mille Lacs, Red Lake, and the east bank of the Mississippi, from Rum river up to the river Des Corbeau, and from thence on both sides of the Mississippi to Pine river; on that river also, up the Mississippi to Lake De Sable, and about 100 miles above that lake. Those of Leech Lake hunt on its streams, Lake Winipie, Upper Red Cedar Lake, the Otter Tail Lake, head of the river De Corbeau, and the upper part of Lower Red river. Their chief is Le Gieulle Platte, (or Eskibugeckoge.)

2d. The Crees reside on Red lake, and hunt in its vicinity, and on Red river. Their first chief's name is Wiscoup, (or Le Sucre.)

3d. The Nepesangs reside on Lake Nippising, and on Lake St. Joseph.

4th. The Algonquins reside on the lake of the two Mountains, and are dispersed along the north side of Lakes Ontario and Erie. From this tribe the language of the Chipeways derives its name, and the whole nation is frequently designated by that appellation.

5th. The Otoways reside on the N. W. side of Lake Michigan, and Lake Huron ; and hunt between those lakes and Lake Superior.

6th. The Iroquois Chipeways, are dispersed along the banks of all the Great Lakes, from Ontario to the Lake of the Woods.

7th. The Muscononges reside on the waters of Lower Red river, near to Lake Winipie, and are the farthest band of Chipeways. The Chipeways were the *great* and almost natural enemies of the Sioux, with whom they had been waging a war of extermination for near two centuries. On my arrival among them, I succeeded in inducing both sides to agree to a peace, and no blood was shed from Sept. 1805, to April 1806, when I left the country. This object had frequently been (in vain) attempted by the British government, who often brought the chiefs of the two nations together, at Michilimackinac ; made them presents, &c. but the Sioux, still haughty and overbearing, spurned the proferred *calumet ;* and returned to renew the scenes of slaughter and barbarity. It may then be demanded, how could a subaltern with 20 men, and no presents worthy of notice, effect that, which the governors of Canada, with all the immense finances of the Indian department had attempted in vain ; although they frequently and urgently recommended it ? I reply, that, the British government, it is true, requested, recommended, and made presents ; but all this at a distance ; and when the chiefs returned to their bands, their thirst of blood soon obliterated from their recollection the lectures of humanity, which they had heard in the councils of Michilimackinac. But, when I appeared amongst them, the United States had lately acquired the jurisdiction over them, and the names of the Americans (as warriors) had frequently been sounded in their ears ; and when I spoke to them on the subject, I *commanded* them, in the name of their great father, to make peace ; and offered them the benefit of the mediation and guarantee of the United States : and spoke of the peace, not as a benefit to us, but a step taken to make themselves and children happy. This language held up to both nations, with the assistance of the traders ; a happy coincidence of circumstances ; and (may I not add ?) the assistance of the almighty, affected that which had long been attempted in vain. But I am perfectly convinced, that, unless troops are sent up between those two nations, with an agent, whose business it would be to watch the rising discontents ; and check the brooding spirit of revenge : that the weapons of death will again be raised, and the echoes of savage barbarity will resound through the wilderness.

The Chipeways are uncommonly attached to spirituous liquors ; but may not this be owing to their traders, who find it much to their interest to encourage their thirst after an article, which enables them to obtain their peltries at so low a rate, as scarcely to be denominated a consideration, and have reduced the people near the establishments, to a degree of degradation unparalleled? The Algonquin language is one of the most copious and sonorous languages of all the savage dialects in North America; and is spoken and understood by the various nations (except the Sioux) from the Gulf of St. Lawrence to Lake Winipie.

This nation is much more mild and docile than the Sioux; and (if we may judge from unprejudiced observers) more cool and deliberate in action; but the latter possess a much higher sense of the *honor* of *their nation:* the others *plan for self-preservation.* The Sioux attack with impetuosity, the other defends with every necessary precaution. But the superior number of the Sioux, would have enabled them to have annihilated the Chipeways long since, had it not been for the nature of their country, which entirely precludes the possibility of an attack on horseback. Also, gives them a decided advantage over an enemy, who, being half armed with arrows, the least twig of a bush would turn the shaft of death out of its direction. Whereas, the whizzing bullet holds its course, nor spends its force short of the destined victim. Thus, we generally have found, that, when engaged in a Prairie the Sioux came off victorious; but if in the woods, even, if not obliged to retreat, the carcases of their slaughtered brethren shew how dearly they purchase the victory.

The Sioux are bounded on the N. E. and N. by these two powerful nations, the Chipeways and Knisteneaux, whose manners, strength, and boundaries, are ably described by sir Alexander Mackenzie. The Assinniboins (or Stone Sioux) who border the Chipeways on the N W. and W. are a revolted band of the Sioux, and have maintained a war with the parent nation for about a century; and have now rendered themselves their most violent enemies. They extend from the Red river west, nearly to the Rocky Mountains, and are computed at 1500 warriors. They reside on the plains, and follow the buffalo, consequently they have very little occasion for traders or European productions.

Z. M. PIKE,
1st, Lieut. 1st United States Regt. Infty.

Abstract of the number, &c. of the Nations of Indians residing on the Mississippi and its confluent

Names of the different nations, as pronounced in the English language.	Primitive names, as given by the savages themselves.	Names given them by the French.	No. of Warriors.	No. of Women.	No. of Children.	No. of Villages.	Probable No. of Souls.	No. of Lodges of the Roving Bands.	No. of Fire Arms.	Primitive Language.	Traders or Bands with whom they trade.	Amount of merchandise necessary for their annual consumption.	Annual return of Peltry in packs.	Species of Peltry
Sauke	Sawkee	Saque	700	750	1400	3	2850		700	Sauk	Of Michilimackinac, St. Louis, with the people of the Prairie des Chiens	15000	600	Principally Deer-skins, Bear, and a few Otter and Racoon
Foxes	Ottagamie	Reynards	400	500	850	3	1750		400	Sauk, with a small difference in the idiom.	Ditto	2500	400	Principally Deer, and with a small proportion of furs.
Iowas	Aiouais	Ne Perce	300	400	700	2	1400		250	Missouries	Of Michilimackinac	10000	300	Deer-skins, Black Bear, Beaver, Mink, Racoon, Fox, and Musk-rat.
Winebagos	Ochangras	Puants	450	500	1000	7	1950		450	Missouries, or Zoto	Of Ditto	9000	200	The same as the Foxes.
Menomenes	Monomene	Fols Avoin	300	350	700	7	1350		300	Menomene	Of Michilimackinac	9000	250	Beaver, Marten, Mink, Muskrat, Otter-skins, Elk-skins, &c.
Sioux	Narcotah	Sioux												
1st Band: People of the Lakes	Minowa Kantong	Gens du Lac	305	600	1200	3	2105	125	305	Narcotah	Of Michilimackinac	13500	230	Deer-skins, a few Beaver, Racoon, &c.
2d Band: People of the Leaves	Washpetong	Gens des Feuilles	180	350	530		1060	70	160	Ditto	Of Ditto	6000	115	Deer-skins, a few Buffalo, some Beaver, Otter, &c.
3d Band: Sisitons	Sisitong	Sisitong	360	700	1100		2160	155	260	Ditto	Of Ditto	12500	160	Deer-skins and a large proportion of robes, with Fox... ed from the Raven...
4th Band: Yanktons	Yanctong	Yanctong	900	1600	2700		4380	270	550	Ditto	Of Ditto	8000	130	Principally Buffalo...
5th Band: Tetons	Titong	Titong	2000	3600	6000		11600	600	100	Ditto	With Yanktongs and part of the Sisitong			Buffalo robes.
6th Band: People of the Leaves detached	Washpecoute	Gens des Feuilles tirees	90	180	170		450	50	90	Ditto	People of the Prairie des Chiens and on the head of de Moyen	2000	50	Deer-skins, Beaver, &c.
			3835	6433	11800	3	21675	1270	1370					
	This is merely a band of vagabonds, who are formed by refugees from all the other bands, which they have left for some bad deed.													
Chipeways	Ouchipawah	Sauteurs												
Leapers		Sauteurs proper												
Of Sandy Lake			45	79	224		345	24		Algonquin	N. W. company			Beaver, Muskrat, Otter, Black and Silver...
Of Leech Lake			150	280	690		1120	65		Ditto	Ditto			Ditto.
Of Red Lake			150	260	610		1020	64		Ditto	Ditto			Ditto.
Of St. Croix and the Chipeway river			104	165	420		689	50		Ditto	Ditto			Ditto.
Of the other bands generally			1600	1400	4000		8000	400		Ditto	Ditto and others	Uncertain.		Unknown.
		Total,	2049	3184	5944		11177	630	2049					

(Chipeway bands: "From actual estimate." Merchandise column: "See my reports on the trade of the N. W. Company.")

...s most proper for establishments.	Nations with whom at war.	Nations with whom at peace, or in alliance.	Names of the Chiefs or Principal Men.			Remarks.
			Indian.	French.	English.	
of the rapid de	Chipeways.	Reynards, Puants, Sioux, Osage, Potowatomies, Fols Avoins, Ioways, and all the nations of the Missouri.	Washione			
			Pochquinike	Bras Casse	Broken Arm	
stream called Gi-	Chipeways.	Ditto.	Olopiar			First Fox Chief.
early opposite the			Pecit	Le Petit Corbeau	Little Raven	
Chiens, or at the			Akaque	La Peau Blanche	White Skin	The man who killed the Osage when on their way to St. Louis, and who is now raising a war party to make a marche on the Santeaux.
of the Mississippi crossing.						
de Moyen and	Chipeways.	Ditto.				
Cockalin, on Fox	Since the peace was made be-	In alliance with the Sauks,	New Okat	—	—'	First chief of the nation—received a commission as first chief.
se Grand Calumet.	tween the Osages, Sauks, and	Reynards, Sioux, Fols Avoins,	Sanamani Chenoway's Son	—	—	Commissioned.
	Reynards, the Puants have ta-	&c. and at peace with all other	Karwnene	—	—·	Ditto.
	citly ceased to make war on	nations.	Du Quarre	—	—	Ditto.
	the former.		Macraragah	—	—	Ditto.
Perre, on the Fox	None.	Ottoway, Chipeway, and O-	Tonaw	Thomas Carron	Thomas Carron	First chief of the nation—received a commission as first chief and a flag.
		changras; and at peace with	Shawnoe			
		all nations.	Neckech			
			Wabasha	La Feuille	The Leaf	First chief of the nation. Literally translated—received a commission and flag.
st Croix.	Recently with the Chipeways,	With the Sauks, Reynards,	Talangamane	L'Aile Rouge	The Red Wing	Ditto ditto.
	but now at peace with the As-	Ioways, and Fols Avoins.	Chatewacoonamani	Petit Corbeau	Little Raven	Received a commission and flag.
	siniboins and some nations on		Tahamie	L'Orignal Leve	Rising Moose	Literally translated.
	the Missouri.		Tatamane	Bras Corbeau	Raven Moon	Literally the Wind that walks—commissioned.
			Wassaquinani	L'Arrignes Jaune	Yellow Spider	First chief of the nation.
le	Ditto.	Ditto.	Wakunena	Tonnerre qui Sonne	The Rolling Thunder	Literally translated.
ere.			Heoho Otah	Le Noyeau	The Stone of Fruit	Received a commission and flag.
Roche,	Ditto.	Ditto.	Wacante	Esprit Bleu	Blue Spirit	First chief of his band.
ers.			Wamimishah	Killieu Noir	Black Eagle	Literally translated.
			Itoya	Gross Calumet	Big Pipe	
			Wuchiew Nutch	Tonnerre Rouge	Red Thunder	A literal translation—first chief of all the Sioux.
			Petesung	La Vache Blanche	White Buffalo	Literally translated.
			Muckpemutah	Nuage Rouge	Red Cloud	Ditto. First chief of the nation.
			Champanage			
	Various nations of the Mis-	Ditto.	Chantaouteka	Le Coeur Mauvais	The Bad Heart	Of Bois Brulé.
	souri.		Shenoukar	La Couverte Blanche	White Blanket	Ohandandas.
			Wamancopenutah	Le Coeur du Killeur Rouge	The Heart of the Red Eagle	
			Tantangrahatah	Le Boeuf que Joue	The Playing Buffalo	Liberal translation.
Chiens.	Ditto.	Ditto.	Kachiwasigon	Le Corbeau Francois	The French Raven	Ditto.
	Recently the Sioux; but now	With the Fols Avoins and all	Catawbaxta	De Bruche	Broken Tooth	First chief of his band.
	at peace. At war with the	the nations of Canada.				
	Sauks, Foxes, and Ioways.					
	Ditto.	Ditto.	Eshibugetchaye	Genelle Platte	Flat Mouth	First chief of his band.
			Obigouixte	Chef de la Terre	Chief of the Land	
			Oole	La Brule	The Burnt	
	Ditto.	Ditto.	Wiscoup	Le Sucre	The Sweet	First chief of his band.
f Lake Superior.	Ditto.	Ditto.				
			Neckzame	Premier	Head Chief.	Resides on Lac La Plair river.

N. B. Wynganage, or the Fils de Pinchow, a chief of the Gens du Lac, and head of the village at the entrance of the St. Peters, omitted. He has received a flag and commission.

RECAPITULATION.

NAMES OF THE NATIONS.	No. of Warriors.	No. of Women.	No. of Children.	No. of Villages.	Probable number of Souls.	No. of Lodges of the Roving Bands.	No. of Fire Arms.
SAUKS,	700	750	1400	3	2850		700
FOXES,	400	500	850	3	1750		400
IOWAS,	300	400	700	2	1400		250
WINEBAGOS,	450	500	1000	7	1950		450
MENOMENES,	300	350	700	7	1350		300
SUES,	3835	6430	11800	3	21675	1270	1265
CHIPEWAYS,	2049	3185	5944		11177	603	2049
Total	8034	12114	22394	25	45152	1873	5414

APPENDIX TO PART II.

A DISSERTATION

ON THE SOIL, RIVERS, PRODUCTIONS, ANIMAL AND VEGETABLE, WITH GENERAL NOTES ON THE INTERNAL PARTS OF LOUISIANA, COMPILED FR OMOBSERVATIONS MADE BY CAPT. Z. M. PIKE, IN A LATE TOUR FROM THE MOUTH OF THE MISSOURI, TO THE HEAD WATERS OF THE ARKANSAW AND RIO DEL NORTE, IN THE YEARS 1806 AND 1807 ; INCLUDING OBSERVATIONS ON THE ABORIGINES OF THE COUNTRY.

FROM the entrance of the Missouri, on the south bank, the land is low, until you arrive at Belle Fontaine, four miles from its entrance. In this distance are several strata of soil, one rising above the other. As the river is cutting off the north point, and making land on the south, this is well timbered with oak, walnut, ash, &c. &c.

From Belle Fontaine to St. Charles, the north side of the Missouri is low, bounded on its banks by timbered land, extending from half a mile to one mile from the river. On the south side the bottoms are narrow, the hills frequently coming in on the river. Six miles below St. Charles, on the south side, in front of a village called Florissant, is a coal hill, or as it is termed by the French, La Charbonniere. This is one solid stone hill, which probably affords sufficient fuel for all the population of Louisiana. St. Charles is situated on the west side of the Missouri, where the hill first joins the river, and is laid out parallel to the stream.

The main street on the first bank, the 2nd. on the top of the hill. On this street is situated a round wooden tower, formerly occupied by the Spaniards as a fort or guard house, now converted into a prison. From this tower you have an extensive view of the river below. St. Charles consists of about 80 houses, principally occupied by Indian traders or their engagees. It is the seat of justice for the district of St. Charles.

From St. Charles to the village of La Charrette, the west side is generally low, but hills running parallel at a great distance back from the river: on the south side, more hilly with springs. Scattering settlements on both sides.

La Charrette, is the last settlement we saw on the Missouri, although there is one above, at a saline on the west side. From La Charrette to the Gasconade river, you find on the north, low land heavily timbered. On the south, hills, rivulets and a small number of small creeks; very high cane. The Gasconade is 200 yards wide at its entrance; is navigable at certain seasons 100 miles. At the time we were at it, it was backed by the Mississippi, but was clear and transparent, above their confluence. On the opposite side to their confluence, commences the line between the Sac Indians and the United States.

From the Gasconade to the entrance of the Osage river, the south side of the river is hilly, but well timbered. On the north are low bottoms and heavy timber; In this space of the Missouri, from its entrance to the Osage river, we find it well timbered, rich soil, and very proper for the cultivation of all the productions of our middle and western states. It is timbered generally with cotton wood, ash, oak, pecan, hickory and with some elm ; but the cotton wood predominates on all the made bottoms. From the entrance of the Osage river, to the Gravel river, a distance of 118 miles, the banks of the Osage are covered with timber, and possess a very rich soil. Small hills, with rocks, alternately border the eastern and western shores ; the bottoms being very excellent soil, and the country abounding in game. From thence to the Yungar, the river continues the same appearance ; the shoals and islands being designated on the chart. The Yungar (or Ne-hem-gar) as termed by the Indians, derives its name from the vast number of springs at its source ; it is supposed to be nearly as extensive as the Osage river, navigable for canoes 100 miles, and is celebrated for the abundance of bear, which are found on its branches. On it hunt the Chasseurs du Bois of Louisiana, Osage, and Creeks (or Muskogees) a wandering party of which have established themselves in

Louisiana; and between whom and the French hunters, frequent skirmishes have passed on the head of the Yungar.

A few miles above this river, the Osage river becomes narrower, and evidently shews the loss experienced by the deficiency of the waters of the Yungar. On the E. shore is a pond of water, about 20 paces from the bank of the river, and half a mile in circumference; it was elevated at least 20 feet above the surface of the river. This appeared the more singular, as the soil appeared to be sandy, from whence it would be concluded, that the waters of the pond would speedily discharge itself through the soil into the river; but there appeared to be no reason for any such deduction.

From thence to a few miles below the Park, (see chart) the banks of the river continue as usual. We now, for the first time, were entertained with the sight of prairie land, but it still was interspersed with clumps of woodland, which diversified the prospect.

In this district the cliffs which generally bordered one of the sides of the river, were covered with the largest and most beautiful cedars I ever saw. From thence to the Grand Forks, the banks of the river continue the same, but from hence up to the Osage town, there is a larger proportion of prairie. At the place where Mr. Chouteau formerly had his trading establishment, the east bank of the river is an entire bed of stone coal; from whence by land to the villages, is but 9 miles, but by water at least 50. The country round the Osage villages, is one of the most beautiful the eye ever beheld. The three branches of the river, viz: the large east fork, the middle one (up which we ascended,) and the northern one, all winding round and past the villages, giving the advantages of wood and water—and at the same time, the extensive prairies crowned with rich and luxuriant grass and flowers—gently diversified by the rising swells, and sloping lawns—presenting to the warm imagination the future seats of husbandry, the numerous herds of domestic animals, which are no doubt destined to crown with joy those happy plains. The best comment I can make on the navigation of the Osage river, is a reference to my chart and journal on that subject. From the last village on the Missouri to the prairies on the Osage river, we found plenty of deer, bear, and some turkies. From thence to the towns, there are some elk and deer, but near the villages they become scarce.

From the Osage towns to the source of the Osage river, there is no difference in the appearance of the country, except that on the south and east, the view on the prairies becomes unbounded, and is only limited by the imbecility of our sight.   The waters of the White river and the Osage, are divided merely by a small ridge in the prairie, and the dry branches appear to interlock at their head. From thence to the main branch of said river, the country appeared high and gravelly ridges of prairie land.   On the main White river is large timber and fine ground for cultivation.   Hence a doubt arises as to the disemboguing of this stream.   Lt. Wilkinson from some authority, has drawn the conclusion, that it discharges itself into the Arkansaw, a short distance below the Vermillion river— but from the voyages of capt. Maney, on the *White* river, the information of hunters, Indians, &c. I am rather induced to believe it to be the White river of the Mississippi—as at their mouths there is not so great a difference between their magnitude ; and all persons agree in ascertaining that the White river heads between the Osage river, Arkansaw and Kanses rivers, which would still leave the Arkansaw near 800 miles more lengthy than the White river. From these proofs, I am pretty confident in asserting, that this was the White river of the Mississippi which we crossed.   At the place where we traversed it, the stream was amply navigable for canoes, even at this dry season (August) of the year.

Up this river to the dividing ridges, between it and the Verdigrise river, the bottom is of some magnitude and importance, but the latter river is bounded here in a narrow bed of prairie hills, affording not more than sufficient timber for fire wood for a limited number of inhabitants for a few years.   From the Verdigrise, our course again lay over gravelly hills and a prairie country, but well watered by the branches of the Verdigrise and White rivers (alias Grand river.) From this point to the source of White river, there is very little timber, the grass short, prairies high and dry.   From the head of White river over the dividing ridge between that and the Eastern branch of the Kans river, the ridge is high, dry, and has many appearances of iron ore, and on the West side some spaw springs—Here the country is very deficient of water, from the East Branch of the Kans river (by our route) to the Pawnee republic on the republican fork, (see chart) the prairies are low, high grass, and the country abounds with salines, and the earth appears to be impregnated with nitrous and common salts.   The immediate border of the republican fork near the village is high ridges, but this is an exception to the general face of the country.   All the country, between the forks of the Kans river, a distance of 160 miles, may be called prairie, notwithstanding the borders of wood land which ornament the banks of those streams, but are no more than a line traced on a sheet of paper, when compared to the immense tract of meadow country.

For some distance from the Osage villages, you only find deer, then elk, then cabrie and finally buffalo. But it is worthy of remark, that although the male buffalo were in great abundance, yet in all our route from the Osage to the Pawnees we never saw one female. I acknowledge myself at a loss to determine, whether this is to be attributed to the decided preference the savages give to the meat of the female ; and that consequently they are almost exterminated in the hunting grounds of the nations—or to some physical causes, for I afterwards discovered the females with young in such immense herds, as gave me no reason to believe, they yielded to the males in numbers. From the Pawnee town on the Kanses river, to the Arkansaw, the country may almost be termed mountainous, but want of timber gives the hills less claim to the appellation of mountains. They are watered and created as it were by the various branches of the Kans river. One of those branches, a stream of considerable magnitude (say 20 yards) which I have designated on the chart by the name of the Saline—was so salt at where we crossed it, on our route to the Arkansaw, that it salted sufficiently, the soup of the meat which my men boiled in it. We were here, very eligibly situated, had a fresh spring, issuing from a bank near us ; plenty of the necessaries of life all around, viz : buffalo ; a beautiful little sugar loaf hill, for a look out post ; fine grass for our horses ; and a saline in front of us. As you approach the Arkansaw (on this route) within 15 or 20 miles the country appears to be low and swampy ; or the land is covered with ponds extending out from the river some distance. The river at the place where I struck it, is nearly 500 yards wide, from bank to bank. Those banks not more than four feet high, thinly covered with cotton wood. The north side a swampy low prairie, and the south a sandy sterile desert. From thence, about half way to the mountains, the country continued the low prairie hills, with scarcely any streams putting into the river ; and on the bottom many bare spots, on which when the sun is in the meridian, is congealed a species of salt, sufficiently thick to be accumulated, but it is so strongly impregnated with nitric qualities, as to render it unfit for use until purified. The grass in this district on the river bottoms, has a great appearance of the grass on our salt marshes. From the first south fork (see chart) the borders of the river have more wood, and the hills are higher, until you arrive at its entrance, into the mountains. The whole of the timber is cotton wood, from the entrance of the Arkansaw, in the mountains, to its source, a distance of about 170 miles ; (by the meanders) it is alternately bounded by perpendicular precipices in small narrow prairies, on which the buffalo and elk have found the means to arrive, and are almost secure from danger, from their destroyer—Man.

In many places the river precipitates itself over rocks, so as at one moment to be visible only in the foaming and boiling of its waters ; at the next moment it disappears in the charms of the o'er hanging precipices.

The Arkansaw river, taking its meanders agreeably to Lt. Wilkinson's survey of the lower part, is 1981 miles from its entrance into the Mississippi to the mountains, and from thence to its source 192 miles, making its total length 2,173 miles, all of which may be navigated with proper boats, constructed for the purpose ; except the 192 miles in the mountains. It has emptying into it, several small rivers navigable for 100 miles and upwards.* Boats bound up the whole length of the navigation, should embark at its entrance, on the 1st of February ; when they would have the fresh quite to the mountains, and meet with no detention. But if they should start later, they would find the river 1500 miles up nearly dry. It has one singularity, which struck me very forcibly at first view, but on reflection, I am induced to believe it is the same case with all the rivers which run through a low, dry, and sandy soil in warm climates. This I observed to be the case with the Rio del Norte, viz : for the extent of 4 or 500 miles before you arrive near the mountains, the bed of the river is extensive, and a perfect sand bar, which at certain seasons is dry ; at least the water is standing in ponds, not affording sufficient to procure a running course. When you come nearer the mountains, you find the river contracted, a gravelly bottom, and a deep navigable stream. From these circumstances it is evident, that the sandy soil imbibes all the waters which the sources project from the mountains, and renders the river (in dry seasons) less navigable *five hundred miles ;* than 200 miles from its source. The borders of the Arkansaw river may be termed the paradise (terrestrial) of our territories, for the *wandering savages.* Of all countries ever visited by the footsteps of civilized man, there never was one probably that produced game in greater abundance, and we know that the manners and morals of the erratic nations, are such (the reasons I leave to be given by the ontologists) as never to give them a numerous

* See Lt. Wilkinson's report of the lower Arkansaw.

population ; and I believe that there are buffalo, elk, and deer sufficient on the banks of the Arkansaw alone, if used without waste, to feed all the savages in the United States territory one century. By the route of the Arkansaw and the Rio Colorado of California, I am confident in asserting (if my information from Spanish gentlemen of information is correct) there can be established the best communication on this side the Isthmus of Darien between the Atlantic and Pacific oceans, as, admitting the utmost, the land carriage would not be more than 200 miles, and the route may be made quite as eligible as our public high ways over the Alleghany mountains. The Rio Colorado is to the great Gulph of California, what the Mississippi is to the Gulph of Mexico, and is navigable for ships of considerable burden, opposite to the upper part of the province of Senora.

From the Arkansaw to the Rio del Norte (the route I passed) the country was covered with mountains of small prairies, (as per chart) but the game became much more scarce owing to the vicinity of the Spanish Indians and the Spaniards themselves.

In this western *traverse* of Louisiana, the following general observations may be made, viz : that from the Missouri to the head of the Osage river, a distance in a straight line of probably 300 miles, the country will admit of a numerous, extensive and compact population ; from thence on the rivers Kanses, La Platte, Arkansaw, and their various branches. It appears to me to be only *possible*, to introduce a limited population on their banks. The inhabitants would find it most to their advantage, to pay attention to the multiplication of cattle, horses, sheep, and goats ; all of which they can raise in abundance, the earth producing spontaneously sufficient for their support, both winter and summer, by which means their herds might become immensely numerous ; but the wood now in the country, would not be sufficient for a moderate share of population, more than 15 years, and then it would be out of the question to think of using any of it in manufactories, consequently their houses would be built entirely of mud-brick (like those in New Spain) or of the brick manufactured with fire. But possibly time may make the discovery of coal mines, which would render the country habitable.

The source of the La Platte, is situated in the same chain of mountains with the Arkansaw, (see chart) and comes from that grand reservoir of snows and fountains which gives birth on its north eastern side to the Red river ;* of the Missouri, (its great south wes-

---

* The yellow stone river of Lewis.

tern branch) and the La Platte ; on its south western side, it produces the Rio Colorado of California ; on its east the Arkansaw, and on its south the Rio del Norte of North Mexico. I have no hesitation in asserting, that I can take a position in the mountains from whence I can visit the source of any of those rivers in one day.

Numerous have been the hypothesis formed by various naturalists, to account for the vast tract of untimbered country which lies between the waters of the Missouri, Mississippi, and the western Ocean, from the mouth of the latter river to the 48° north latitude. Although not flattering myself to be able to elucidate *that*, which numbers of highly scientific characters, have acknowleged to be beyond their depth of research ; still, I would not think I had done my country justice, did I not give birth to what few lights my examination of those internal deserts has enabled me to acquire. In that vast country of which we speak, we find the soil generally dry and sandy, with gravel, and discover that the moment we approach a stream, the land becomes more humid with small timber ; I therefore conclude, that this country never was timbered, as from the earliest age, the aridity of the soil having so few water courses running through it, and they being principally dry in summer, has never afforded moisture sufficient to support the growth of timber. In all timbered land, the annual discharge of the leaves, with the continual decay of old trees and branches, creates a manure and moisture, which is preserved from the heat of the sun not being permitted to direct his rays perpendicularly, but only to shed them obliquely through the foliage. But here a barren soil, parched and dried up for eight months in the year, presents neither moisture nor nutrition sufficient, to nourish the timber. These vast plains of the western hemisphere, may become in time equally celebrated as the sandy desarts of Africa ; for I saw in my route, in various places, tracts of many leagues, where the wind had thrown up the sand, in all the fanciful forms of the ocean's rolling wave, and on which not a speck of vegetable matter existed.

But from these immense prairies may arise one great advantage to the United States, viz : The restriction of our population to some certain limits, and thereby a continuation of the union. Our citizens being so prone to rambling and extending themselves, on the frontiers, will, through necessity, be constrained to limit their extent on the west, to the borders of the Missouri and Mississippi, while they leave the prairies incapable of cultivation to the wandering and uncivilized aborigines of the country. The Osage Indians appear to have emigrated from the north and west, and from their speaking the same language with the Kans, Otos, Missouries, and Mahaws ; together with the great similarity of manners, morals, and customs, there is left no room to doubt, but that they were originally the same nation ; but seperated by that great law of nature, self-preservation, the love of freedom, and the ambition of various characters, so inherent in the breast of man.   As nations purely erratic must depend solely on the chase for subsistence, (unless pastoral, which is not the case with our savages) it requires large tracts of country, to afford subsistence for a very limited number of souls ; consequently, self-preservation obliges them to expand themselves over a large and extensive district.   The power of certain chiefs becoming unlimited, and their rule severe, added to the passionate love of liberty, and the ambition of other young, bold, and daring characters, who step forward to head the malcontents, and like the tribes of Israel, to lead them through the wilderness to a new land ; the land of promise, which flowed with milk and honey. (alias abounded with deer and buffalo)   These characters soon succeed in leading forth a new colony, and in process of time establishing a new nation.   The Mahaws, Missouries, and Otos, remained on the banks of the Missouri river, such a distance up, as to be in the reach of that powerful enemy, the Sioux, who with the aid of the small pox, which the former nations unfortunately contracted by their connection with the whites, have reduced the Mahaws (formerly a brave and powerful nation) to a mere cypher, and obliged the Otos and Missouries to join their forces, who now form but one nation.   The Kanses and Osage, came farther to the east, and thereby avoided the Sioux, but fell into the hands of the Iowas, Sacs, Kickapous, Potowatomies, Delawares, Shawanese, Cherokees, Chickasaws, Chactaws, Arkansaws, Caddoes, and Tetaus ; and what astonished me extremely, is that they have not been entirely destroyed by those nations.   But it must only be attributed to their ignorance of the enemies' force, their want of concert, wars between themselves, and the great renown the invaders always acquire by the boldness of the enterprise, on the minds of the invaded.

Their government is oligarchical, but still partakes of the nature of a republic, for although the power nominally is vested in a small number of chiefs, yet they never undertake any matter of importance, without first assembling the warriors, and proposing the subject in council, there to be discussed and decided on by a majority.

Their chiefs are hereditary, in most instances, but yet there are many men who have risen to more influence than those of illustrious ancestry, by their activity and boldness in war.

Although there is no regular code of laws, yet there is a tacit acknowledgment of the right, which some have to command on certain occasions ; whilst others are bound to obey, and even to submit to corporeal punishment ; as is instanced in the affair related in my diary of the 29th July ; when Has-ha-ke-da-tungar (or the Big Soldier) whom I had made a partisan to regulate the movements of the Indians, flogged a young Indian with arms in his hands.

On the whole, their government may be termed an oligarchical republic, where the chiefs propose, and the people decide on all public acts.

The manners of the Osage are different from those of any nation I ever saw (except those before mentioned of the same origin) having their people divided into classes. All the bulk of the nation being warriors and hunters (with them, the terms being almost synonimous) the remainder is divided into two classes, cooks and doctors, the latter of whom likewise exercise the functions of priests or magicians, and have great influence on the councils of the nation by their pretended divinations, interpretations of dreams, and their magical performances ; an illustration of which will be better given by the following anecdote, which took place during my stay at the nation, in August 1806, viz : Having had all the doctors or magicians assembled in the lodge of Ca-ha-ga-tonga, (alias Cheveux Blancs) and about 500 spectators. They had two rows of fires prepared, around which the sacred band was stationed. They commenced the tragic-comedy, by putting a large butcher knife down their throats ; the blood appearing to run during the operation very naturally ; the scene was continued, by putting sticks through the nose, swallowing bones and taking them out of the nostrils, &c. At length one fellow demanded of me what I would give if he would run a stick through his tongue, and let another person cut off the piece. I replied, " a shirt." He then apparently performed his promise, with great pain, forcing a stick through his tongue, and then giving a knife to a bye-stander, who appeared to cut off the piece, which he held to the light, for the satisfaction of the audience : and then joined it to his tongue ; and by a magical charm healed the wound immediately. On demanding of me what I thought of the performance : I replied I would give him 20 shirts,

if he would let me cut off the piece from his tongue ; this disconcerted him a great deal, and I was sorry I made the observation.

The cooks are either for the general use, or attached particularly to the family of some great man, and what is the more singular, that frequently men who have been great warriors, and brave
men having lost all their families by disease, in the war, and themselves becoming old and infirm, they frequently take up the profession of cook, in which they do not carry arms, and are supported by
the public, or their particular patron.

They likewise exercise the functions of town criers, calling
the chiefs to council and to feasts ; or if any particular person is
wanted, you employ a crier, who goes through the village crying
his name, and informing him he is wanted at such a lodge. When
received into the Osage village, you immediately present yourself
at the lodge of the chief, who receives you as his guest, where you
generally eat first after the old patriarchal style. You are then invited to a feast by all the great men of the village ; and it would be
a great insult if you did not comply, at least, as far as to taste of
their victuals. In one instance, I was obliged to taste of fifteen different entertainments, the same afternoon. When you will hear
the cooks crying, " come and eat," such an one gives a feast, " come
and eat of his bounty." Their dishes were generally boiled sweet
corn in buffalo grease ; or boiled meat and pumpkins ; but San
Oriel (alias Tetobasi) treated me with a dish of tea in a wooden
dish, new horn spoons, boiled meat and crullers : he had been in
the United States. Their towns hold more people in the same
space of ground, than any places I ever saw. Their lodges being
posted with scarcely any regularity ; each one building in the manner, directions, and dimensions which suits him best, by which
means they frequently leave only room for a single man to squeeze
between them ; added to this, they have pens for their horses, all
within the village, into which they always drive them at night, in
case, they think, there is any reason to believe there is an enemy
lurking in the vicinity.

The Osage lodges are generally constructed with upright posts,
put firmly in the ground, of about 20 feet in height, with a crotch at
the top ; they are generally about 12 feet distant from each other ; in
the crotch of those posts, are put the ridge poles, over which are bent
small poles, the end of which are brought down and fastened to a
row of stakes of about 5 feet in height ; these stakes are fastened
together with three horizontal bars, and from the flank walls of the
lodge. The gable ends are generally broad slabs and rounded off

to the ridge pole. The whole of the building and sides are covered with matting made of rushes, of two or three feet in length, and four feet in width, which are joined together, and entirely exclude the rain. The doors are in the side of the building, and generally are one on each side. The fires are made in holes in the centre of the lodge ; the smoke ascending through apertures left in the roof for the purpose; at one end of the dwelling is a raised platform, about three feet from the ground, which is covered with bear skins, and generally holds all the little choice furniture of the master, and on which repose his honorable guests.

In fact with neatness and a pleasing companion, they would compose a very comfortable and pleasant summer habitation, but are left in the winter for the woods ; they vary in length from 36 to 100 feet.

The Osage nation is divided into three villages, and in a few years you may say nations, viz ; the Grand Osage, the Little Osage, and those of the Arkansaw.

The Little Osage separated from the Big Osage, about 100 years since ; and their chiefs on obtaining permission to lead forth a colony from the great council of the nation, moved on to the Missouri, but after some years finding themselves too hard pressed by their enemies, they again obtained permission to return, and put themselves under the protection of the grand village, and settled down about 6 miles off. (See chart.)

The Arkansaw schism was effected by Mr. Pierre Choteau, 10 or 12 years ago, as a revenge on Mr. Manuel De Sezei, who had obtained from the Spanish government the exclusive trade of the Osage nation, by the way of the Osage river, after its having been in the hands of Mr. Choteau for nearly 20 years. The latter having the trade of the Arkansaw, thereby nearly rendered abortive the exclusive privilege of his rival. He has been vainly promising to the government, that he would bring them back to join the grand village. But his reception at the Arkansaw village, in the autumn of 1806, must have nearly cured him of that idea. And in fact, every reason induces a belief, that the other villages are much more likely to join the Arkansaw, (which is daily becoming more powerful) than the latter to return to its ancient residence. For the Grand and Little Osage are both obliged to proceed to the Arkansaw every winter, to kill the summer's provision ; also all the nations with whom they are now at war, are situated to the westward of that river, and from whence they get all their horses. Those inducements are such, that the young, the bold, and the enterprising are daily emigrating from the Osage village, to the Arkansaw village. In fact, it would become the interest of our government to encourage that emigration ; *if they intend to encourage the extension of the settlement of Upper Louisiana ; but if on the contrary (their true policy) every method should be taken to prevent their elongation from the Missouri.*

They are considered by the nations to the south and west of them, as a brave and warlike nation ; but are by no means a match for the northern nations, who make use of the rifle, who can combat them two for one, whilst they again may fight those armed with bows, arrows, and lances at the same disproportion.

The humane policy which the United States have held forth to the Indian nations, of accommodating their differences, and acting as mediators between them, has succeeded to a miracle with the Osage of the Grand village, and the Little Osage. In short, they have become a nation of Quakers, as it respects the nations to the north and east of them ; at the same time that they continue to make war on the naked and defenceless savages of the west. An instance of their forbearance was exhibited by an attack made on a hunting party of the Little Osage, in the autumn of 1808, on the grand river of the Osage, by a party of Potowatomies, who crossed the river Missouri by the Saline, and found the women and children alone and defenceless. The men, 50 or 60, having found plenty of deer the day before, had encamped out all night. The enemy struck the camp about 10 o'clock in the morning, killed all the women and boys who made resistance, also some infants ; the whole number amounting to 34, and led into captivity near sixty, forty-six of whom were afterwards recovered by the United States, and sent under my protection to the village. When the men returned to the camp, they found their families all destroyed, or taken prisoners. My narrator had his wife and four children killed on the spot ! ! and yet in obedience to the injunctions of their great father, they forebore to revenge the blow ! !

As an instance of the great influence the French formerly had over this nation ; the following anecdote may be interesting : Chtoka (alias Wet Stone) aL ittle Osage, " said he was at Braddock's de- " feat, with all the warriors who could be spared from both villages : " that they were engaged by Mr. M'Cartie, who commanded at fort " Chartres, and who supplied them with powder and ball ; that the " general place of rendezvous was near a lake and large fall (sup- " pose Niagara) the Kans did not arrive until after the battle ; but " that the Otos were present. They were absent from their villages

" seven months ; and were obliged to eat their horses on their re-
" turn."

AGRICULTURE—The Osage raise large quantities of corn,
beans and pumpkins, which they manage with the greatest economy, in order to make it last from year to year. All the Agricultural labor is done by women.

FACTORIES—If the government think it expedient to establish
factories for the grand and little villages, equi-distant from both,
which would answer for the grand and little villages. The other
establishment should be on the Arkansaw, near the entrance of the
Verdigrise river, (as stated by Lt. Wilkinson) for the Arkansaw
Osage.

The Pawnees are a numerous nation of Indians, who reside on
the rivers Platte and Kans ; they are divided into three distinct nations, two of them being now at war ; but their manners, language,
customs, and improvements, are in the same degree of advance-
ment.

On the La Platte, reside the grand Pawnee village, and the Pawnee loups on one of its branches, with whom the Pawnee Republi-
cans are at war.

Their language is guttural, and approaches nearer to the language of the Sioux, than the Osage, and their figure tall, slim,
and high cheek bones, clearly indicate their Asiatic origin ; but
their emigration south, and the ease with which they live on the
buffalo plains, have probably been the cause of a degeneracy of
manners, for they are neither so brave nor honest, as their more
northern neighbors. Their government is the same as the Osage,
an hereditary aristocracy ; the father handing his dignity of chieftain down to his son ; but their power is extremely limited, notwithstanding the long life they have to establish their authority and influence. They merely recommend, and give counsel in the great
assemblage of the nation.

They are not so cleanly, neither do they carry their internal policy so far as the Osage ; but out of the bounds of the village, it
appeared to me, that they exceeded them ; as I have frequently seen
two young soldiers come out to my camp, and instantly disperse a
hundred persons, (by the strokes of long whips) who were assembled there to trade with my men.

In point of cultivation, they are about equal to the Osage, raising a sufficiency of corn and pumpkins, to afford a little thickening
to their soup during the year.

Their pumpkin they cut into thin slices, and dry it in the sun, which reduces it to a small size, and not more than a tenth of its original weight.

With respect to raising horses, the Pawnees are far superior to the Osage, having vast quantities of excellent horses which they are daily increasing, by their attention to their breeding mares, which they never make use of; and in addition, frequently purchase from the Spaniards.

Their houses are a perfect circle, (except where the door enters) from whence there is a projection of about 15 feet; the whole being constructed after the following manner, viz: 1st. there is an excavation of a circular form, made in the ground, of about 4 feet deep and 60 diameter, where there is a row of posts about 5 feet high, with crotches at the top, set firmly in all round, and horizontal poles from one to the other. There is then a row of posts, forming a circle of about 10 feet width in the diameter of the others, and 10 feet in height; the crotches of those are so directed, that horizontal poles are also laid from one to the other; long poles are then laid slanting, perpendicularly from the lower poles over the upper, and meeting nearly at the top, leaving only a small aperture for the smoke of the fire to pass out, which is made on the ground in the middle of the lodge. There is then a number of small poles put up round the circle, so as to form the wall, and wicker work ran through the whole. The roof is then thatched with grass, and earth thrown up against the wall until a bank is made to the eves of the thatch; and that is also covered with earth one or two feet thick, and rendered so tight, as entirely to exclude any storm whatsoever, and make them extremely warm. The entrance is about 6 feet wide, with walls on each side, and roofed like our houses in shape, but of the same materials as the main building. Inside there are numerous little apartments constructed of wicker work against the wall with small doors; they have a great appearance of neatness and in them the members of the family sleep and have their little deposits. Their towns are by no means so much crowded as the Osage, giving much more space, but they have the same mode of introducing all their horses into the village at night, which makes it extremely crowded. They keep guards with the horses during the day. They are extremely addicted to gaming, and have for that purpose a smooth piece of ground cleared out on each side of the village for about 150 yards in length, at which they play the following games, viz: one is played by two players at a time, and in the following manner: They have a large hoop of about four feet diameter, in the centre of which is a small leather ring attached to leather thongs, which is extended to the hoop, and by that means keeps it in its central position ; they also have a pole of about 6 feet in length, which the player holds in one hand, and then rolls the hoop from him, and immediately slides the pole after it, and the nearer the head of the pole lies to the small ring within the hoop, (when they both fall) the greater is the cast. But I could not ascertain their mode of counting, sufficiently to decide when the game was won.

Another game is played with a small stick, with several hooks, and a hoop about four inches diameter, which is rolled along the ground, and the forked stick darted after it, when the value of the cast is estimated by the hook on which the ring is caught. This game is gained at 100. The third game alluded to, is that of La Platte, described by various travellers, and is played at by the women, children, and old men, who like grasshoppers, crawl out to the circus to bask in the sun, probably covered only with an old buffalo robe.

The Pawnees, like the Osage, quit their villages in the winter, making concealments under ground of their corn, in which it keeps perfectly sound until spring. The only nations with whom the Pawnees are now at war, are the Tetaus, Utahs, and Kyaways. The two latter of whom reside in the mountains of North Mexico, and shall be treated of, when I speak of the Spanish Indians. The former generally inhabit the borders of the Upper Red river, Arkansaw, and Rio del Norte.

The war has been carried on by those nations for years, without any decisive action being fought, although they frequently march with 2 or 300 men.

The Pawnees have much the advantage of their enemies in point of arms, having at least one half fire arms, whilst their opponents have only bows, arrows, lances, shields and slings.

The Pawnees always march to war on foot, their enemies are all cavalry. This nation may be considered as the one equi-distant between the Spanish population, and that of our settlements of Louisiana, but are at present decidedly under Spanish influence, and should a war commence to-morrow, would all be in their interest. This circumstance does not arise from their local situation, because they are all situated on navigable waters of the Missouri ; nor from their interest, because from the Spaniards they obtain nothing except horses and a few coarse blankets of W. Mexico ; whilst from us they receive all their supplies of arms, ammunition, and clothing, but all those articles in very small quantities, not more than half having a blanket, and many without breech cloths to cover their nakedness.

But the grand principle by which the Spaniards keep them in their influence, is fear; frequently chastising their small parties on their frontiers. Their sending out the detachment of 600 horsemen in 1806, has made such an impression, that they may safely calculate on them in case of war.

This detachment took with them some of the Pawnees to Chihuahua, at the same time I entered the Spanish provinces.

But, by withholding their supplies of arms, ammunition, and clothing one or two years, bringing on their backs the Osage and Kans, they would be in great distress, and feel the necessity of a good understanding with the United States.

If there should ever be factories established for their accomodation, they should be at the entrance of the La Platte and Kans rivers, as those waters are of so uncertain navigation, (only in freshes) that it would be folly to attempt any permanent establishments high up them; and to make those establishments useful to the Pawnees, we must presuppose our influence sufficient to guarantee to them peace and a safe passage through the nations of the Kans, Otos, and Missouries; the former on the Kans river; the two latter on the river Platte. My journey will give various other striking traits of the national character of the Pawnees, and my dissertation on the subject of the Spanish claims, will further elucidate the political and relative situation of that nation.

The Kans are a small nation, situated on the river of that name (see the chart) and are in language, manners, customs, and agricultural pursuits, precisely similar to the Osage : with whom I believe them, as before observed, to have had one common origin.

It may be said, however, that their language differs in some degree, but not more than the dialect of our eastern states, differs from that of the southern.

But in war, they are yet more brave than their Osage brethren, being (although not more than one third their number) their most dreaded enemies, and frequently making the Pawnees tremble.

The Tetaus or Camanche, as the Spaniards term them, Padoucas by the Pawnees, are a powerful nation, which are entirely erratic, without the least species of cultivation, and subsisting solely by the chase. But their wanderings are confined to the frontiers of New Mexico on the west; the nations on the Lower Red river on the S. the Pawnees and Osage on the E. and the Utahs, Kyaways, and various unknown nations on the N. This nation although entirely in our territories, is claimed exclusively by the Spaniards, and may be said to be decidedly in their interest, notwithstanding the few who lately paid a visit to Natchitoches.

They are the only nation who border on the Spanish settlements, which that nation treat as an independent people. They are by the Spaniards reputed brave, indeed they have given them some very strong evidences of it; for when I first entered the province of New Mexico, I was shewn various deserted villages and towers beat down, which had been destroyed by the Tetaus in an invasion of that province, when they were at war with the Spaniards about ten years since.

From the village Agua Caliente, (see chart) they carried off at one time 2,000 head of horses, but they now have an excellent understanding with the Spaniards, which Don Facundo Malagare's late expedition has served very much to increase. He personally related his rencounter with the Tetaus in the following manner: " Having been personally apprised of each other's approximation, " and appointed a time for the Indians to receive him on an exten- " sive prairie, he sallied forth from his camp with 500 men, all on " white horses, excepting himself and his two principal officers, " who rode jet black ones, and was received on the plain by 1500 of " those savages, dressed in their gay robes, and displaying their va- " rious feats of chivalry." I leave this subject to the judicious, whether the circumstance would not be handed down to the latest posterity, as an instance of the good will and respect which the Spaniards paid their nation; as no doubt Malgare had policy sufficient to induce them to believe that the expedition principally was fitted out with a view to pay them a visit.

As I was not in their country, and did not meet with any of the wandering parties, I shall not attempt to describe their manners, customs, &c. but in my statistical tables, I shall include them agreeably to the best information obtained of their nation.

I shall here conclude my account of the nations with which I became acquainted in our boundaries; as I conceive the Spanish Indians require a different discussion and attention in a different point of view, as their missionaries have succeeded with their nations beyond what we can form an idea of.

My diary will present numerous additional circumstances, to form an idea of those savages, their manners, customs, principles, and biases, political and local.

Z. M. Pike, Capt. 1st U. S. Regt. Infty.
Washington City, January 1808.

THE following *Report* was written by lieutenant Wilkinson, at a time when it was expected I had been cut off by the savages; it consequently alluded to transactions relative to the expedition *previous* to our separation, which I have since corrected: but the adventures of his party, *after* our separation, are given in his own words.

Z. M. PIKE.

LIEUTENANT WILKINSON'S REPORT

OF HIS

PASSAGE DOWN THE ARKANSAW, &c.

—————————————

New-Orleans, April 6, 1807.

Sir,

AGREEABLY to your order dated in June, 1806, I took my departure from Belle Fontaine, under the command of lieutenant Pike, early in July. The Missouri being well up, we found the navigation as favorable as could have been expected. On the 28th of the same month, we reached the mouth of the Osage river, which we found a pellucid, tranquil stream, with the exception of a few trifling ripples, and a fall of about six feet in two-thirds of a mile, called the Old Man's Rapid. The river abounds with various kinds of good fish, especially the soft-shelled turtle, which we took in great numbers. The banks of the river are generally formed by craggy cliffs, and not unfrequently you perceive stupendous rocks projecting over the water, out of which issue excellent springs. The most remarkable natural curiosity which I observed is a pond of water, about three hundred toises in circumference, six miles above the Yanga, on a rising piece of ground, considerably above the level of the river, which keeps one continued height, is perfectly pure and transparent, and has no outlet by which to discharge itself.

On the 12th of August the Osages appeared dissatisfied with the tedious movement of our barges, and expressed a wish to cross the prairie to their villages, in case an escort was allowed them. I immediately volunteered my services, and we parted with the boats at the mouth of Grand river, the spot where our ransomed prisoners were taken the preceding winter by the Potowatomies.

We reached the village of the little Osages, after a fatiguing and laborious march of six days, across an arid prairie.

When within a mile of the town, the chief *Tuttasuggy* or the *Wind*, desired a regular procession might be observed and accordingly he placed me between himself and his first warrior, and the ransomed captives followed by files. Half a mile from the village we were met by one hundred and eighty horsemen, painted and decorated in a very fanciful manner : those were considered as a guard of honor, and on our approach, opened to the right and left, leaving a sufficient space for us to pass through. A few yards in advance on the right I perceived sixty or more horsemen painted with a blue chalk, which, when the chief observed, he commanded a halt, and sent forward his younger brother *Nezuma* or the *Rain that Walks*, with a flag and silk handkerchief as a prize for the swiftest horseman. At a given signal they started off at full speed. The two foremost taking the flag and handkerchief, and the rest contenting themselves with having shewn their agility and skill.

As I entered the village, I was saluted by a discharge from four swivels (which the Indians had taken from an old fort erected by the Spaniards on the river) and passed through a crowd of nearly a thousand persons, part of whom I learnt were of the grand village. I was immediately, but with ceremony, ushered into the lodge of the *Soldier of the Oak*, who, after having paid me some very handsome compliments, courteously invited me to eat of green corn, buffalo meat and water-melons about the size of a twenty-four-pound shot, which, though small, were highly flavored.

After lieutenant Pike's arrival with the boats, we formed our camp on the bank of the river, equi-distant from the villages of the Grand and Little Osages, and he selected a situation for making his observations, which he did not complete until the 28th of the month. The 29th and 30th were devoted to packing as conveniently and carefully as possible the mathematical instruments and a small quantity of provisions, and on the 1st of September we commenced our march for the Pawnee republic, and entered on that vast and extensive prairie, which lies between the Missouri and the Rio del Norte.

We coursed the Osage river to its source, and almost immediately after crossed some of the small branches of Grand river which enters the Arkansaw about seven hundred miles from the Mississippi. After passing Grand river, which we found to be sixty or eighty yards wide, we marched a whole day before we reached the waters of the Kanses, and were agreeably surprised to find ourselves on the bank of a bold running stream. Between this and the village of the Pawnees, we crossed two strongly impregnated salines, which passed over a sandy country, almost destitute of herbage, and after a painful march, under an oppressive sun, over an irregular and broken surface we arrived at the town of the Republican Pawnees on the 25th of September. We (the day before) were met by a number of warriors, whom curiosity had led thus far to see us, among whom was the third consequential character of the republican party; for you must know that the village is composed of the followers of a dissatisfied warrior, who first made this establishment, and the adherents of a regular chief of the *Grand* Pawnees, who migrated thither some few years since with his family, and usurped the power of the republican warrior To such a pitch does this party spirit prevail that you easily perceive the hostility which exists between the adherents of the two chiefs. Early on the morning of the 25th we were joined by a few more savages of distinction, headed by the brother of *Characterish*, or the *White Wolf*, chief of the nation, who was to act as master of the ceremonies to our formal entry. Preparatory to our march, we had our men equipped as neatly as circumstances would admit. About mid-day we reached the summit of a lofty chain of ridges, where we were requested to halt and wait the arrival of the chief, who was half a mile from us, with three hundred horsemen, who were generally naked (except buffalo robes and breech cloths) and painted with white, yellow, blue, and black clay. At the word of the chief the warriors divided, and pushing on at full speed, flanked us on the right and left, yelling in a most diabolical manner. The chief advanced in front, accompanied by *Iskatappe*, or the *Rich Man*, the second great personage of the village, and his two sons, who were clothed in scarlet cloth. They approached slowly, and when within a hundred yards, the three latter halted, and Characterish advanced in great state, and when within a few paces of us, stretched out his hand and cried " *Bon jour.*" Thus ended the first ceremony. We moved on about a mile farther, and having gained the summit of a considerable hill, we discovered the village directly at its base. We here were again halted, and the few Osages who accompanied us were ordered in front and seated in rank entire. The chief squatted on his hams in front of them and filled a calumet, which several different Indians took from him, and handed the Osages to smoke. This was called the *horse-smoke*, as each person who took the pipe from the chief intended presenting the Osages a horse. Mr. Pike and Dr. Robinson afterwards accompanied the chief to his lodge, and I moved on with the detachment and formed our camp on the opposite bank of the republican fork of the Kanses river, on a commanding hill, which had been selected as the most favorable situation for making observations, though very inconvenient on account of wood and water, which we had to transport nearly a quarter of a mile.

At a council held some few days after our arrival, lieutenant Pike explained to them the difference of their present situation, and that of a few years past; that now they must look up to the president of the United States as their great father, and that he had been sent by him to asure them of his good wishes, &c. &c.; that he perceived a Spanish flag flying at the council lodge door, and was anxious to exchange one of their great father's for it, and that it was our intention to proceed on further to the westward, to examine this our newly acquired country. To this a singular and extraordinary response was given—in fact, an objection, started in direct opposition to our proceeding further to the west; however they gave up the Spanish flag, and we had the pleasure to see the American standard hoisted in its stead.

At the same council Characterish observed that a large body of Spaniards had lately been at his village, and that they promised to return and build a town adjoining his. The Spanish chief, he said, mentioned that he was not empowered to council with him; that he came merely to break the road for his master, who would visit him in the spring with a large army, and that he further told him the Americans were a little people, but were enterprising, and one of those days would stretch themselves even to his town, and that they took the lands of Indians and would drive off their game; and how very true, says Characterish, has the Spanish chieftain spoken! We demanded to purchase a few horses, which was prohibited us, and the friendly communication which had existed between the town and our camp was stopped. The conduct of our neighbours assumed a mysterious change; our guards were several times alarmed, and finally appearances became so menacing as to make it necessary for us to be on our guard day and night.

It was obvious that the body of Spaniards who preceded us but a few weeks in their mission to this village, were the regular cavalry and infantry of the province of Santa Fee, as they had formed their camps in regular order, and we were informed they kept regular guards, and that the beats of their drum were uniform morning and evening. The Spanish leader, further, delivered to Character-ish a grand medal, two mules, and a commission bearing the signature of the governor, civil and military, of Santa Fee. He also had similar marks of distinction for the Grand Pawnees, the Pawnee Mahaws, Mahaws Proper, Otos and Kanses.

On the 6th of October we made some few purchases of miserable horses at the most exorbitant prices, and on the 7th, unmoved by the threats of the chief relative to our proceeding farther to the west, we marched in a close and compact body until we passed their village, and took the large Spanish beaten trace for the Arkansaw river. We passed the following day, an encampment of the Spaniards, where we counted sixty-nine fires. On the 9th, as usual, made an easy march, and about noon, when we halted to refresh ourselves, were overtaken by three hundred Pawnees, on their way to the salines of the Kanses to hunt buffalo. Their every act shewed a strong disposition to quarrel, and in fact they seemed to court hostility; but, finding us without fear and prepared, to a man, they offered no outrage, and having grazed our horses an hour, we parted from this turbulent band, slung our packs and proceeded on to Solomon's Fork of the Kanses, and pitched our tents on an old encampment of the Spaniards, whose trace we were following, as we found the next morning many tent-pins made of wood, different from any in that country. At mid-day lieutenant Pike, Dr. Robinson, and the interpreter Baroney, pushed on to search for water, and I remained with the troops. I pushed on as briskly as our poor half-famished horses would permit, and at night fall could discover nothing of Mr. Pike, and had not a tree in view. This induced me to quicken my pace, and, as darkness had rendered my compass useless, I coursed by the polar star; but the horizon becoming overcast, I halted on a naked stony prairie, without water or grass for our horses. On the following morning I directed my course more to the southward, and about ten o'clock came to the creek and encampment of lieutenant Pike. Late in the evening of the same day, after passing over a mountainous tract of country, we reached the Grand Saline, which we found so strongly impregnated, as to render unpalatable corn, when boiled in it. On the 12th after a distressing day's march, we reached the Second, or Small Saline, and on the following day encamped on the most western branch of the Kanses river.

We were detained, on the morning of the 13th, by a small rain, but as time was pressing, we marched about noon, crossed the dividing ridge of the Kanses and Arkansaw rivers, and halted on a small branch of the latter. For several days past we had been so bewildered by buffalo paths, that we lost the Spanish trace, and this being an object of moment, we resolved to make search for it. Accordingly, on the following day at noon, Mr. Pike and Dr. Robinson struck off from the party a due west course, and I marched the detachment for a copse of wood, which we could barely discern in the south-west, and reached it about midnight. At day-break I was awoke by my old and faithful Osage, who informed me that we were on the banks of the Arkansaw river. I immediatly arose, and discovered my tent to have been pitched on the margin of a water-course, nearly four hundred yards wide, with banks not three feet high, and a stream of water running through it about twenty feet in width, and not more than six or eight inches deep.

I remained here four days in great anxiety and suspence, as neither Mr. Pike nor Dr. Robinson made their appearance, nor could be found, although I had all my hunters out in search of them. But I was agreeably surprised on the fifth day, early in the morning, by their arrival. It appeared our apprehensions were mutual, as they expected I had been cut off, and I believed they had been murdered.

On the 17th it commenced raining and continued for several days, during which time the river rose so much as to fill its bed, from bank to bank; and lieutenant Pike having determined that I should descend the Arkansaw, we cut down a small green cottonwood, and with much labor split out a canoe, which being insufficient, we formed a second of buffalo and elk skins.

After the rain had ceased the weather became extremely cold, and on the 27th, in the evening, a severe snow-storm commenced, and continued nearly all night. In the morning the river was almost choaked with drifting ice; but the sun bursting out at noon, the ice disappeared, and I took leave of Mr. Pike, who marched up the river at the moment I embarked on board my newly constructed canoe; but, unfortunately, we had not proceeded more than one hundred yards when my boats grounded, and the men were obliged to drag them through sand and ice five miles, to a copse of woods on the south-western bank. I here hauled up my canoe, formed a kind of a cabin of it, and wrapped myself up in my buffalo robe, disheartened and dissatisfied with the commencement of my voyage. The night was severely cold, and in the morning the river was so full of ice as to prevent all possibility of proceeding. The day continued stormy, with snow from the north-west.

On the 30th the river was frozen up, and towards evening the water had ran off, and left the bed of the river covered with ice. This circumstance determined me to leave my canoes and course the river by land. Accordingly, on the 31st of October, after having thrown away all my clothing and provision, except half a dozen tin cups of hard corn for each man, I slung my rifle on my shoulder, and with my buffalo robe at my back and circumferentor in my hand, I recommenced my march with a light and cheerful heart. My only apprehension was the meeting with detached bands of the Pawnees, who, I am confident, would have brought me and my five men to action, and the consequence was very obvious.

On the 1st, 2d, and 3d of November I marched over high and barren hills of sand, and at the close of each day, passed strongly impregnated salines, and perceived the shores of the river to be completely frosted with nitre. The face of the country, as I descended, looked more desolate than above, the eye being scarcely able to discern a tree; and if one was discovered, it proved to be a solitary cotton-wood, stinted in growth by the sterility of the soil. The evening of the 3d instant I encamped on the bank of the river, without a tree or even a shrub in view. On the 4th we experienced a heavy rain; but hunger and cold pressed me forward. After marching ten miles I reached a small tree, where I remained in a continued rain for two days, at the expiration of which time having exhausted my fuel, I had again to push off in a severe storm, and formed my camp at the mouth of a bold running stream, whose northern bank was skirted by a chain of lofty ridges.

On the 8th, in the morning, it having cleared up, I began my march early, and it appeared as if we had just gotten into the region of game, for the herds of buffalo, elk, goat, and deer surpassed credibility. I do solemnly assert, that, if I saw one, I saw more than nine thousand buffalos during the day's march.

On the 10th, in the evening, after a severe day's march, I encamped on the bank of a large creek, and discovered, for the first time, on the river, a species of wood differing from the cotton tree. I assure you the sight was more agreeable than a person would imagine: it was like *meeting* with an old *acquaintance*, from whom you had been separated a length of time; I even began to think myself approximating civilized settlements, although I was just entering on the hunting ground of the Osages.

The buffalo and goats disappeared on the 12th, or rather we had passed their range and entered that of the deer only. Our marches now lay through rich narrow bottoms, from one hundred and fifty, to two hundred yards wide.

On the 15th discovering timber sufficiently large to form canoes, I felled a couple of trees, and commenced *splitting out*. I would have proceeded further by land, but as my men were almost worn out with fatigue, and as the game grew scarce, I conceived it most adviseable to rest for a short time, and kill my winter's store of meat. This I effected by the 24th, and on the same day completed the canoes. On the 25th I again attempted the navigation of the river, but was as unfortunate as at first, for my boat grounded, after floating a few hundred yards, and the men were consequently compelled to ply with their shoulders instead of their paddles.

The following day I passed the Negracka, at whose mouth commence the craggy cliffs, which line a great part of the shores of the Arkansaw.

On the 28th the provision canoe oversat, and I lost nearly all my stock of meat; this accident was rendered the more distressing by an almost total loss of my ammunition, which unfortunately was in the same canoe.

On the 30th, I fell in with a band of Grand Osages, who were in pursuit of buffalo cows; the chief of the party insisted on my remaining with him a day, and sent out his young men to hunt for me. In the afternoon two Indians of the Little Osage nation joined us, with a horse and mule, and brought me a message from Tuttasuggy, or the *Wind*, who it appeared was lying very ill, about twenty miles across the prairie, and wished to see me. As he was a particular favorite of mine, I left my canoes in charge of the men, and passed with a guide to the chief's temporary village. I found him extremely unwell, with what I conceived to be a dropsy, for his abdomen was very much swollen. He seemed gratified at the sight of me, and observed, " That he was poor and pitiful, for the reason that he was a friend to the Americans. He said that Chouteau after he had arrived at their villages last fall, had treated him like a child, and had taken on to Washington his younger brother *Nezuma*, or *the rain that walks*, and intended making him chief of the nation; that Chouteau told him he was a *bad man*, was an American, but that the Spaniards were going to war with America, and that in a short time they would claim all this country again." That he prevented the traders allowing a credit, whereby his family were much distressed, as I clearly perceived, for they were even destitute of a whole blanket.

This *Nezuma*, whom Chouteau took on to Washington last fall with his wife, I am better acquainted with, than perhaps Mr. Chouteau himself. In the first place, I marched with him from St. Louis to his town, and he started with us to visit the Pawnees, but the mean and pitiful wretch, got alarmed and sneaked off without even advising us of his departure. He has no more command in the village than a child, is no warrior, and has not even the power to controul the will of a single man of his nation. Whether this youth is entitled to a grand medal, you may judge from the foregoing statement. Indeed, sir, our grand medals have become so common, that they do not carry with them the respect which they should. I recollect one of the deputation who was at the seat of government, the year before the last, came out with a large medal, and an intermediate sized one. On our arrival at the villages, I calculated on his acting a conspicuous part, but to my utter astonishment, he was not permitted to sit among the chiefs, or even the warriors at the council.

You well know, sir, how particular the Spaniards, and the British especially, have been in their distribution of medals, and if I mistake not, an Iowa chief, who had been to the seat of government, and there received a small medal, returned it in preference to giving up a large British medal, as he valued it more because it was a *certain* distinguishing mark of a chief.

You gave to Mr. Pike an intermediate sized medal, for one of the Pawnee chiefs, which he presented Iskatappe, who having, remarked the medals pendant from the necks of the *two Pawnee young men*, who were on at Washington, demanded of what *utility it would be to him*. The only Spanish medals in the Pawnee nation, are those worn by Characterish, or the *White Wolf* and his son.

The following sarcastic remark was made by the son of the " Bel Oiseau," a chief of the first standing among the Grand Osages whilst living, and who unfortunately was killed by the Sacs on his way to Washington with the first deputation.

The son of White Hairs, with " Shenga Wassa," or *Beautiful Bird*, was to accompany us to the Pawnee village ; but the former proved recreant, and at the crossing of Grand River, said he would return home. " Shame on you," says the latter, " what a pity it is " so great and honorable a medal, should be disgraced by so mean a " heart."

You will pardon this digression, but I would wish to convince you, from what I have seen of Indians, how very requisite it is to use the utmost caution in the distribution of our presents and marks of distinction.

Before I set out to visit Tuttasuggy, the ice had commenced drifting in large sheets, and on my return, I found it running from shore to shore, I however pushed off and drifted with it.

The night of the 2d of December was intensely cold, but hunger obliged me to proceed, and we fortunately reached the mouth of the Neskalonska, river, without accident or injury, excepting that one of my men got frosted. This day we passed two salines which enter on the south western side.

The severity of the weather increased, and the river froze over on the morning of the 3d. This circumstance placed me in a situation truly distressing, as my men were almost naked ; the tatters which covered them were comfortless, and my ammunition was nearly exhausted.

The men solicited me to hut, but I was resolved by perseverance and exertion, to overcome, if in my power, the obstacles opposed to my progress.

The Neskalonska, is about 120 yards wide, shoal and narrow at its mouth, but deepens and spreads after you turn the first point. On this stream, the Grand and Little Osages form their temporary fall hunting camps, and take their peltries. When the severity of winter sets in, the Grand Osages retire to " *Grosse Isle*," on the Verdigrise, or Wasetihoge ; and the Little Osages to one of its small branches called Possitonga, where they remain during the hard weather, and from thence return to their towns on the Neska, or *Osage* river.

On the 6th the ice began to drift, and immediately pushed off with it ; but as my evil stars would have it, my boats again grounded, and being in the middle of the river, my only alternative was to get out and drag them along for several miles, when we halted to warm our benumbed feet and hands. The next day several large cakes of ice had blocked up the river, and we had to cut our way through them with axes ; the boats as usual grounded, and the men bare legged and bare footed, were obliged to leap into the water. This happened so frequently, that two more of my men got badly frosted.

On the 8th one of my canoes was driven on a bank of ice, during a snow storm, and did not overtake me until the evening of the 9th, and in so shattered a condition, that she could hardly be kept above water, and the poor fellows who were in her, were almost frozen.

On the 10th, about noon, I passed the Grand Saline, or the *Newsewketonga*, which is a reddish color, though its water is very clear. About two days march up this river, you find the prairie grass on the S. W. side incrusted with salt, and on the N. E. bank, fresh water springs, and lakes abounding with fish. This salt the Arkansaw Osages, obtain by scraping it off of the prairie with a turkey's wing into a wooden trencher. The river does not derive its name from its saline properties, but the quantities that may always be found on its banks, and is at all seasons of the year potable.

On the 20th in the afternoon, we passed another saline with water equally as red as the *Newsewketonga*, and more strongly impregnated with salt.

After encountering every hardship, to which a voyage is subject in small canoes, at so inclement a season of the year, I arrived on the 23d inst. in a storm of hail and snow, at the wintering camp of Cashesegra, or " *Big Track*," chief of the Osages, who reside on Verdigrise rivers. On the following day I gave him your talk, and received his reply, which it is unnecessary to recount fully, as it was merely a description of his poverty and miserable situation. He however said, that he had been informed, the United States intended erecting factories, on the Osage river, and that he was anxious to have one near to his own village, and for the purpose, he was willing to give the United States the tract of country lying between the Verdigrise and Grand rivers. A factory with a garrison of troops stationed there, would answer the double purpose of keeping in order those Indians, who are the most desperate and profligate part of the whole nation, and more fully impressing them with an idea of our consequence, and gaining more firmly their friendship. It also would tend to preserve harmony among the Chactaws, Creeks, Cherokees, and Osages of the three different villages, who are in a constant state of warfare, and further it would prevent the Osages making excursions into the country of the poor and peaceably disposed Caddoes, and might have some effect in confining the Spaniards to their own territorial limits.

On the 27th I passed the mouths of the Verdigrise and Grand rivers, the former being about a hundred, and the latter one hundred and thirty yards wide ; those streams enter within a quarter of a mile of each other. Below the mouth of Grand river, commence the rapids, which continue for several hundred miles down the Arkansaw.

About 58 or 60 miles up the Verdigrise, is situate the Osage village. This band some four or five years since, were led by the chief Cashesegra, to the waters of the Arkansaw, at the request of Pierre Chouteau, for the purpose of securing their trade. The *exclusive trade* of the *Osage river*, having at that time been purchased from the Spanish governor, by Manuel Lisa, of St. Louis, but though Cashesegra be the nominal leader; Clermont, or the *Builder of Towns*, is the greatest warrior, and most influential man, and is now more firmly attached to the interests of the Americans, than any other chief of the nation. He is the lawful sovereign of the Grand Osages, but his hereditary right was usurped by Pahuska, or *White Hair*, whilst Clermont was yet an infant. White Hair, in fact, is a chief of Chouteau's creating, as well as Cashesegra, and neither have the power, or disposition to restrain their young men from the perpetration of an improper act, fearing least they should render themselves unpopular.

On the 29th I passsed a fall of near seven feet perpendicular, and at evening was visited by a scout from an Osage war party, and received from them a man by the name of M'Farlane, who had been trapping up the Pottoe. We passed about noon this day, the mouths of the river des Illinois, which enters on the N. E. side, and the Canadian river, which puts in from the S. W. The latter river is the main branch of the Arkansaw, and is equally as large.

On the 31st I passed the mouth of Pottoe, a deep, though narrow stream, which puts in on the S. W. and also the river au " Millieu" that enters from the N. E.

On the evening of the 6th January I reached the plantation of a Mr. Labomme, and was more inhospitably treated than by the savages themselves.

On the 8th passed the two upper Arkansaw or Quapaw villages, and on the 9th, after passing the lower Quapaw town, and a settlement of Chactaws, arrived at the post of Arkansaw.

The surface of the country between the Osage towns and the Pawnee village is generally broken and naked; the soil sterile, and abounding with flint and lime stones. As you approach the waters of the Kanses, it becomes hilly and sandy; the same may be said of the country between the Pawnee village and the Arkansaw, but after passing the ridge which separates the waters of the Kanses and Arkansaw, the surface becomes more regular and less stoney.

Below the Verdigrise, the shores of the Arkansaw are generally lined with cane, and consequently rich bottoms. I was informed by the Indians that the country to the north west of the Osage village, abounds with valuable lead mines, but I could make no discovery of any body of mineral.

The survey from the Arkansaw post to the Mississippi, I fear is not correct, as I was so ill when I descended that part of the river, as to be confined to my blanket.

The chart which accompanies this report, of the course of the Arkansaw, I hope will prove satisfactory, not only to yourself, but the president.

   I have the honor to subscribe myself,
     Your faithful and obliged
      Humble and obedient servant,
    (Signed)   JAMES B. WILKINSON,
       1st Lieut. 2d U. S. Regt. of Infantry.

His excellency
General James Wilkinson,
  Commander in chief of the U. S. army.

[No. 3.]

St. Charles, 17th July, 1806.

DEAR SIR,

  WE arrived here last evening all well, except some of the soldiers from fatigue, as in the present state of the water we are obliged to row altogether.

  We were disappointed in obtaining any information from St. Louis, or baggage for our Panis. I do not know how it will be digested by them.

* * * * * * * * * * *

  We likewise were disappointed in receiving a line from you, as we had here expected, and in the hopes of which I shall yet detain until 12 o'clock, and then take my departure. Our Osage conduct themselves pretty well, and are very obedient to orders; at first they had an idea a little too free relative to other people's property, but at present stand corrected.

  I understood from you that they were equipped by Mr. Tillier, with every thing necessary for their voyage to their towns, consequently, although they have been applying to me for a variety of articles, none of which have they been gratified with, but powder and ball, which is necessary for their own defence.

The general will pardon this scrawl, and should he send an express after us, please to let Mrs. Pike know of the opportunity.

> I am, dear sir,
>> With high respect,
>>> Your obedient servant,
>>>> (Signed)   Z. M. PIKE, Lt.

General Wilkinson.

[No. 4.]

St. Charles, 19th July, 1806.—In the morning.

DEAR GENERAL,

ENCLOSED you have one of the articles, subscribed by Mr. Henry, mentioned in my note of yesterday. I hope the general may approve of the contents.

Lieut. Wilkinson and Dr. Robinson marched (with one soldier) this morning, and the boats have proceeded under the conduct of Ballenger; I shall overtake them in an hour or two.

Numerous reports have been made to the Indians, calculated to impress them with an idea that there is a small army of their enemies waiting to receive us at the entrance of the Grand Osage. But I have partly succeeded in scouting the idea from their minds.

No news of Chouteau nor Panis' Trunks.

> I am, dear general,
>> Your obedient servant,
>>> (Signed)   Z. M. PIKE, Lt.

General Wilkinson.

[No. 5.]

Village De Charette, 22d July, 1806.

DEAR GENERAL,

I HAVE the honor to acknowledge the receipt of your two obliging favors of the 18th and 19th inst. the particular contents of each, shall be punctually attended to.

I assure you sir, that I am extremely pleased with the idea, that Messrs. ——— and ———, will meet with their merited reward, and I on my part, am determined to shew them, that it is not their sinister movements that can derange the objects of our voyage; the greatest embarrassment they have yet occasioned me, has been by the detention of the Panis's baggage, who have been much mortified on the occasion. But I question much if under similar impressions and circumstances, many white men would have borne their loss with more philosophy, than our young savages.

I conceive that I cannot dispose of one of my guns better, than to give it to *Frank*, whose *fusee* was left at Chouteau's; also, each of them a soldier's coat; this is all the remuneration I will pretend to make them, and I hope may bring them to a good humor.

You will probably be surprised at the slow progress we have made, but, are already informed of the cause of our detention at St. Charles; and since have been detained two days, on account of the rain; and although we were able to prevent the water from entering immediately on the top of the boat where covered, yet the quantity which she made at both ends, occasioned so much dampness under the loading, as to injure both my own corn, and that of the Indians, with other small articles, which they had at various times taken from under the loading, and not returned to their proper places; but they appear satisfied, that we have paid all possible attention to prevent injury, as much, and indeed more, to their baggage than our own.

In consequence of the above, (and with a design to write you) I halted here to day, which I hope we shall usefully employ in drying our baggage, cleaning our arms, and putting ourselves in a posture of defence. Lieut. Wilkinson has experienced no inconvenience from his march by land with the Indians; and the event has proved the necessity of some officer accompanying them, as he informs me, he found it necessary to purchase some beeves for their consumption on the route, for which he drew on the superintendant of Indian affairs, and will write to you more particularly on the subject. They were absent from the boat four days, and had he not been with them, they would have supplied themselves by marauding, to the great offence of our *good* citizens.

I am informed, that a party of 40 Sacs were at Boon's Lick, above the Osage river, a few days since; but, I by no means conceive on the route to intercept us, as the people pretend at this place.

Three days since, one of my men complained of indisposition, and went on shore to march; he has never joined the party, and from various reasons, I conceive has deserted. I have therefore enclosed an advertisement, which if the general will please to cause to be posted at St. Louis, Kaskaskias, and Lusk's Ferry on the Ohio, I conceive he will be caught.

I have written to capt. Danl. Bissell on the occasion ; but hope the general will enforce my request to that gentleman, as to his being brought to trial. I was much mortified at the event, not only on account of the loss of the man, but that my peculiar situation prevented me from pursuing him, and making him an example.

With respect to the Tetaus, the general may rest assured, I shall use every precaution previous to trusting them ; but as to the mode of conduct to be pursued towards the Spaniards, I feel more at a loss, as my instructions lead me into the country of the Tetaus, part of which is no doubt claimed by Spain, although the boundaries between Louisiana and New Mexico, have never yet been defined, in consequence of which, should I encounter a party from the villages near Santa Fe, I have thought it would be good policy to give them to understand, that we were about to join our troops near Natchitoches, but had been uncertain about the head waters of the rivers over which we passed ; but, that *now*, if the commandant approved of it, we would pay him a visit of politeness, either by deputation, or the whole party, but if he refused, signify our intention of pursuing our direct route to the post below ; but if not I flatter myself secure us an unmolested retreat to Natchitoches. But if the Spanish jealousy, and the instigation of domestic traitors should induce them to make us prisoners of war, (in time of peace) I trust to the magnanimity of our country for our liberation, and a due reward to their opposers, for the insult and indignity offered their national honor. However, unless they give us ample assurances of just and honorable treatment, according to the custom of nations in like cases, I would resist, *even* if the inequality was as great as at the affair of Bender, or the streights of Thermopylæ.

Will you pardon the foregoing as the enthusiasm of a youthful mind, yet, not altogether unimpressed by the dictates of prudence.

I hope the general will be persuaded, that with his son, I shall act as I would to a brother, endeavoring in all cases to promote his honor and prosperity.

> I am, dear general,
>> Your sincere friend,
>>> And obedient humble servant,
>> (Signed)   Z. M. PIKE.

General J. Wilkinson.

N. B. In consequence of indisposition, &c. lieut. Wilkinson will stear one boat and I the other.

[No. 6.]

Village de Charette, evening of the 22d *July*, 1806.

DEAR SIR,

FINDING no prospect of meeting with a private conveyance of our letters, in time sufficient to find you previous to your setting sail, which would be entirely too late to secure my deserter, and give you the other information they contain, I have hired the bearer to ride express to Belle Fontaine, for which I have promised him eight dollars; which taking into view, his ferriages, &c. it cannot be deemed high, and I hope the general will please to order the military agent to discharge the same.

The weather hath at length became settled, and we set sail to-morrow with our boats newly, and much better, arranged.

I am, general, with sincere esteem,

And high respect,

Your obedient servant,

(Signed)   Z. M. PIKE.

General Wilkinson.

[No. 7.]

Five leagues below the river Osage, 26th *July*, 1806.

DEAR GENERAL,

I HALT a moment, in order to say we have arrived thus far all safe, although our savages complain much of fatigue, &c.

The bearer had been sent by Mr. Sangonet to examine the Osage river, and reports that they could not get their canoes up the river more than 60 miles: if so, we have a bad prospect before us; but go we will, if God permits.

I am, dear general,

Your obedient servant,

(Signed)   Z. M. PIKE.

Gen. James Wilkinson.

We have been detained several days by the Indians.

[No. 8.]

Park on the Osage river, 14*th Aug.* 1806.

DEAR SIR,

BY Baptiste la Tulip I send this letter, who informs me he bears letters to Chouteau, informing him that a party of the *Little Osages* have marched to war against the Kanses ; and a party of the *Grand Osages* left the village expressly to make war on the white people on the Arkansaw. This latter step the White Hair did every thing in his power to prevent, but could not. If true, what are we to think of our *bons amis* the Osage ?

But to ———— must we ascribe the stroke against the *Kanses*, who I am informed sent a message to the Osage nation to *raze* the Kanses village entirely. On this subject I intended to have been more particular, and substantiate it by proofs ; but present circumstances seem to give credit to it. On my arrival at the village, more particular enquiry shall be made on the subject.

Yesterday morning lieutenant Wilkinson, the doctor, interpreter, and one soldier, marched with the Indians, as they were very apprehensive of an attack. The people in the canoe heard them crying and saw them on their march.

Nothing extraordinary has yet taken place on our route, except our being favored with a vast quantity of rain, which I hope will enable us to ascend to the village.

What face will the Indians receive us with ? and to whom are we to ascribe their hostile disposition, unless the traitors of St Louis ?

Lieutenant Wilkinson is in very good health, and will lament his having missed this opportunity of assuring his parents of his love and affection.

I am, dear general,

Your obedient servant,

(Signed)   Z. M. PIKE

Gen. James Wilkinson.

[No. 9.]

Cantonment, Missouri, August 6, 1806.

SIR,

IN consequence of the receipt of the enclosed letters, I have thought proper to send you an express, to enable you to announce to the Osage the designs of their enemies, that they may take seasonable measures to circumvent them.   You will not fail, in addition to the within talk, to enhance our paternal regard for this nation, by every proper expression; but are to keep clear of any conflict in which they may be involved, though you are to avoid the appearance of abandoning them.   If it should be the Potowatomies' intention to carry their threat into execution.   It is probable they will not attempt to make the blow before the falling of the leaves, and in the mean time the Osages should establish a chain of light scouts, along the coast of the Missouri, to ascertain with certainty the approach of their enemy.

It is reduced to a certainty that ———— and a society of which he is the ostensible leader, have determined on a project to open some commercial intercourse with Santa Fe, and as this may lead to a connection injurious to the United States, and will, I understand, be attempted without the sanction of law or the permission of the executive : you must do what, consistently, you can to defeat the plan. No good can be derived to the United States from such a project, because the prosecution of it will depend entirely on the Spaniards, and they will not permit it, unless to serve their political, as well as their personal interests.   I am informed that the ensuing autumn and winter will be employed in reconnoitring and opening a connection with the Tetaus, Panis, &c. that this fall, or the next winter, a grand magazine is to be established at the Osage towns, where these operations will commence ; that ———— is to be the active agent, having formed a connection with the Tetaus.   This will carry forward their merchandise within three or four days travel of the Spanish settlements, where they will deposit it, under a guard of 300 Tetaus.   ———— will then go forward with four or five attendants, taking with him some jewelry and fine goods.   With those he will visit the governor, to whom he will make presents, and implore his pity by a fine tale of sufferings which have been endured by the change of government : that they are left here, with goods to be sure, but not a dollar's worth of bullion, and therefore they have adventured to see him, for the purpose of praying his leave for the in-

troduction of their property into the province. If he assents, then
the whole of the goods will be carried forward ; if he refuses, then
———— will invite some of his countrymen to accompany him to his
deposit, and having there exposed to them his merchandise, he will
endeavor to open a forced or clandestine trade ; for he observes, the
Spaniards will not dare to attack his camp. Here you have the plan,
and you must take all prudent and lawful means to blow it up.

In regard to your approximation to the Spanish settlements,
should your route lead you near them, or should you fall in with any
of their parties, your conduct must be marked by such circumspection and discretion, as may prevent alarm or conflict, as you will be
held responsible for consequences. On this subject I refer you to
my orders. We have nothing new respecting the pending negotiations in Europe ; but from colonel Cushing I understand the Spaniards below are behaving now with great courtesy.

By the return of the bearer you may open your correspondence
with the secretary of war; but I would caution you against anticipating a step before you, for fear of deception and disappointment.
To me you may, and must, write fully and freely, not only giving a
minute detail of every thing past worthy of note, but also of your
prospects and the conduct of the Indians. If you discover that any
tricks have been played from St. Louis, you will give them to me
with names, and must not fail to give particulars to the secretary of
war, with names, to warn him against improper confidence and deception. Enclose your dispatch for me to colonel Hunt, and it will
follow me by a party which I leave for the purpose. It is interesting to you to reach Nachitoches in season to be at the seat of government pending the session of congress ; yet you must not sacrifice any essential object to this point. Should fortune favor you on
your present excursion, your importance to our country will, I think,
make your future life comfortable.

To shew you how to correct your watch by the quadrant, after
it has been carefully adjusted, preparatory to your observing on the
eclipses of the satellites of Jupiter, I send you a very simple plan,
which you will readily understand : a bason of water, in some place
protected from the motion of the air, will give you a fairer artificial
horizon than Mercury. I think a tent, with a suitable aperture in the
side of it would do very well. I have generally unroofed a cabin.
Miranda has botched his business. He has lost his two schooners
captured, and himself in the Leander returned to Jamaica. The
French have a squadron of four frigates at Porto Rico, and of five

sail of the line with Jerome Bonaparte at Martinique. I consider them lost.

Your children have been indisposed; but Mrs. Pike writes you. She appears well. My regards to your associates, and may God protect you.

(Signed)   J. WILKINSON.

Lieutenant Pike.

[No. 10.]

Camp Independence, near the Osage Towns, August 28, 1806.

DEAR GENERAL,

You will no doubt be much surprised to perceive by the date of this letter, that we are still here; but we have been unavoidably detained by a variety of circumstances.

I had the happiness to receive your express the day of my arrival, the bearer having arrived the night before, and have attended particularly to its contents.

On the 19th inst. I delivered your *parole* to the Cheveux Blanche, and on the 21st held a grand council of both towns, and made the necessary communications and demands for horses, on the subject of making peace with the Kans, accompanying me to the Panis, down the Arkansaw, and if there was any *brave* enough to accompany me the whole voyage.

They requested one day to hold council in the villages previous to giving an answer. It was three before I received any; their determination was as follows:—From the *Grand Osage* village, or the Cheveux Blanche we are accompanied by his son, and *Jean La Fon*, the second chief of the village, with some young men not known, and he furnishes us four horses.

The *Little Osage* sends the brother of the chief (whom I really find to be the third chief of the village) and some young men unknown, and furnishes *six* horses!! This is their present promise, but four of the ten are yet deficient. With these I am merely capable of transporting our merchandise and ammunition. I shall purchase two more, for which I find we shall be obliged to pay extravagant prices.

I sincerely believe that the two chiefs, *White Hair* and *The Wind*, have exerted all their influence; but it must be but *little* when they could only procure *ten* horses out of seven or eight hundred.

I have taken an exact survey of the river to this place, noting particular streams, &c. a protracted copy of which lieutenant Wilkinson forwards by this opportunity. Since our arrival here I have ascertained the variation of the compass to be 6° 30′ E. the latitude, by means of several observations, 37° 26′ 17″ N. and by an observation of three different nights, obtained two immersions of Jupiter's satellites, which will enable us to ascertain every geographical object in view.

On the same night I arrived near the village, there was a Mr. Baptist Duchouquette, alias Larme, with two men, in a small canoe arrived and went immediately to the lodge of the White Hair, whose conduct, with that of our resident interpreter, appears (in my estimation) to have changed since I sent lieutenant Wilkinson to demand to see Baptist's passport, if he had one : if not, to bring him to camp—which was done. I detained him two days, until I had made an enquiry of White Hair, who said he had merely mentioned him that *Labardie* was coming with a quantity of goods. Finding I could substantiate nothing more criminal against him than his having entered the Indian boundaries without a passport, and not being able to send him back a prisoner, detained him sufficient time to alarm him, and then took his deposition (a copy of which is inclosed to the attorney-general), and wrote Dr. Brown on the occasion, and requested him to enter a prosecution against these men.

Barroney informs me that he has not the least doubt but ———— was at the bottom of this embassy, although in the name of ————, as after the arrival of Baptist, the Indians frequently spoke of ———— and declared, if he had come he could have obtained horses plenty.

Our interpreter, also (Maugraine), I do believe to be a perfect creature of ————: he has almost positively refused to accompany me (although I read your order on the subject), alledging he was only engaged to interpret at this place, notwithstanding he went last year to the Arkansaw for Mr. Chouteau without difficulty. I have not yet determined on the line of conduct to be pursued with him, but believe, on his giving a positive refusal, I shall use military law. What the result will be is uncertain; but to be thus braved by a scoundrel, will be lessening the dignity of our government. He is married into a powerful family, and appears, next to the White Hair, to have the most influence in the Grand village. The general will please to observe that much of the foregoing rests on conjecture, and therefore will give it its due weight. But to him I not only write as my general, but as a paternal friend, who would not make use of my open communications, when not capable of being substantiated by proofs.

We have heard nothing of the Potowatomies; but should they come in a few days, they will meet with a warm reception, as all are ready to receive them.

Since my arrival here many Spanish medals have been shown me, and some commissions. All I have done on the subject is merely to advise their delivery below, when they would be acknowledged by our government. Many have applied for permission to go to Saint Louis; none of which I have granted, except to the son of Sans Orielle, who goes down to make enquiry for his sister.

I have advanced our express some things on account, and forward his receipts; also, some trifles to Barroney, who I have found to be one of the finest young men I ever knew in his situation, and appears to have entirely renounced all his Saint Louis connections, and is as firm an American as if born one: he of course is entirely discarded by the people of Saint Louis; but I hope he will not suffer for his fidelity.

On the chart forwarded by lieutenant Wilkinson is noted the census which I caused to be taken of the village of the *Little Osage*; that of the big one I shall likewise obtain—which are from actual enumeration. Lieutenant Wilkinson will (if nothing extraordinary prevents) descend the Arkansaw, accompanied by Ballenger and two men, as the former is now perfectly acquainted with the mode of taking courses and protracting his route, and the latter appears as if he had not the proper capacity for it, although a good dispositioned and brave man.

I am, dear sir,

Your obedient servant,

(Signed)   Z. M. PIKE, Lt.

Gen. Wilkinson.

[No. 11.]

29th August, 1806.

DEAR SIR,

I WILL continue my communications, by relating that the *Wind* has come in and informed me that the other two horses which he promised have been withdrawn by their owners. He appeared really distressed, and I conceive I do him justice in believing that he is extremely mortified at the deceptions which have been passed on him.

It is with extreme pain I keep myself *cool* amongst the difficulties which those people appear to have a disposition to throw in my way ; but I have declared to them that I should go on, even if I collected our tents and other baggage (which we will be obliged to leave together) and burn them on the spot.

I have sold the batteaux which I brought up (and which was extremely rotten) for 100 dollars, in merchandize, the price of this place, which I conceive was preferable to leaving her to destruction, as I am afraid I do the barge (for which I demanded 150 dollars), although I leave her under charge of the *Wind* and shall report her to colonel Hunt.

I shall dispatch the express to-morrow, as he complains much of the detention, &c. and as I hope nothing worthy of note will occur at this place previous to our departure. I hope the general will believe me to be, and should this be my last report, to have been, his sincerely attached friend and

obedient servant,

(Signed)   Z. M. PIKE, Lt.

Gen. Wilkinson.

[No. 12.]

30th August, Osage Towns, 1806.

DEAR SIR,

I HAVE brought Mr. Noal, alias Maugraine, to reason, and he either goes himself or hires, at his expence, a young man who is here who speaks the Panis language, and in many other respects is preferable to himself; but he will be the bearer of the express to Saint Louis.

The Cheveux Blanche requested me to inform you that there is a murderer (an Osage) in his village, who killed a Frenchman on the Arkansaw; but owing to the great dissentions and schism of the Arkansaw faction, he is fearful to deliver him up, without some of his friends having agreed to it, and his authority being strengthened by a *formal* demand from you, when he assures me he shall be brought down a prisoner. Indeed the Cheveux Blanche appears to be very delicately situated, as the village on the Arkansaw serves as a place of refuge for all the young, daring, and discontented; and added to which, they are much more regularly supplied with ammunition, and, should not our government take some steps to prevent it, they will ruin the Grand village, as they are at liberty to make war without restraint, especially on the nations who are to the west, and have plenty of horses. The chief says he was promised, at Washington, that these people should be brought back to join him ; but, on the contrary, many of his village are emigrating there.

Owing to the difficulty of obtaining horses, Mr. Henry returns from this place. In descending the Mississippi I will request him to pay his respects to you.

I last evening took the census of the Grand village, and found it to be—

Men	.	.	.	502
Boys	.	.	.	341
Women and Girls				852
			Total	1695
		Lodges	. . .	214

The express waits, which I hope the general will accept as an excuse for this scrawl, having written him fully on the 28th and 29th inst.

I am, dear general,
Your ever sincere friend
and obedient servant,
(Signed)   Z. M. PIKE, Lt.

Gen. J. Wilkinson.

[No. 13.]

Pawnee Republic, 1*st Oct.* 1806.

SIR,

WE arrived here on the 25th ult. after a tedious march of 375 miles, the distance (as I conceive) being very much augmented by the Osages, who accompanied us, leading us too far to the south, owing to their great fear of the Kans. We suffered considerably with thirst, but our guns furnished us amply with buffalo meat.

We delivered in safety to the chief the two young Pawnees who had lately visited Washington, and caused to be explained to the nation, the parole which they bore from the president of the United States.

On our arrival, we found the Spanish and American flags both expanded in the village, and were much surprised to learn, that it was not more than three or four weeks, since a party of Spanish troops (whose number were estimated by the Indians of this town, at 300) had returned to Santa Fe ; and further learnt that a large body of troops had left N. Mexico, and on their march had met with the villagers of the Pawnee Mahaws, who were on one of their semi-annual excursions ; that they encamped together, and entered into a treaty, but after this the Pawnees raised their camp in the night, and stole a large portion of the Spaniards' horses. This circumstance induced them to halt on the Arkansaw with the main body of the troops, and to send forward the party who appeared at this village ; who proposed to this chief to join a party of his warriors to their troops, march to and entirely destroy the village of the Pawnee Mahaws ; this proposition he had prudence enough to reject, although at war with that nation. The Spanish officer informed him that his superior, who remained at the Arkansaw, had marched from Santa Fe, with an intention of entering into a treaty with the following nations of Indians, viz : The Kanses, the Pawnee Republic, the Grand Pawnees, Pawnee Loups, Otos, and Mahaws ; and had with him a grand medal, commissions, and four mules for each ; but by the stroke of the Pawnee Mahaws, the plan was disconcerted, except only as to this nation. The commissions are dated Santa Fe, 15th June 1806, and signed governor general, &c. &c. of New Mexico, and run in the usual style of Spanish commissions to savages, as far as I was capable of judging of their contents.

The chief further informed me, that the officer who commanded said party, was too young to hold councils, &c. that he had *only* come to open the road, but that in the spring his superior would be here, and teach the Indians what was good for them ; and that they would build a town near them. In short, it appears to me to have been an expedition expressly for the purpose of striking a dread into those different nations of the Spanish power, and to bring about a general combination in their favor. Under these impressions, I have taken the earliest opportunity of reporting the infringement of our territory, in order that our government may not remain in the dark, as to the views of her neighbor. I effected a meeting at this place, between a few Kans and Osages, who smoked the pipe of peace and buried the hatchet, agreeably to the wishes of their great father ; in consequence of which a Kans has marched for the Osage nation, and some of the latter propose to accompany the former to their village ; whether this good understanding will be permanent, I will not take on me to determine ; but at least, a temporary good effect has succeeded. From the Osage towns, I have taken the courses and distances, by the route we came, marking each river or rivulet we crossed, pointing out the dividing ridges, &c. The waters which we crossed, were the head of the Osage, White, and Verdigrise rivers, (branches of the Arkansaw) and the waters of the Kans river. The latitude of this place, I presume, will be in about 39° 30′ N. and I hope to obtain every other astronomical observation, which will be requisite to fix its geographical situation beyond dispute. I expect to march from here in a few days, but the future prospects of the voyage are entirely uncertain, as the savages strive to throw every impediment in our way, agreeably to the orders received from the Spaniards. Being seated on the ground, and writing on the back of a book, I hope will plead my excuse for this scrawl.

I am, sir,

With high respect,

Your obedient servant,

(Signed)   Z. M. PIKE, Lt.

The hon. Henry Dearborn,

    Secretary war department.

[No. 14.]

Pawnee Republic, 2d *Oct*. 1806.

DEAR GENERAL,

INCLOSED you have a copy of my letter from this place, to the secretary of war, in order, that should you think any communication on the contents necessary, you may have a perfect command of the information given the war department, and will be the more capable of illustrating the subject.

You will perceive by said communication, that we were led considerably out of our course by our guides, and in my opinion not less than 100 miles ; this was entirely owing to the pusillanimity of the Osage, who were more afraid of the Kans, than I could possibly have imagined.

You will likewise perceive the council which took place between those nations (under our auspices) and its effects, but which I candidly confess, I have very little hopes will be productive of a permanent peace, as none of the principal men of either nation were present ; but as both are anxious for a cessation of hostilities perhaps it may have the desired effect.

Two of the Kans chiefs have said they will pursue the voyage with me agreeably to my orders ; I do not yet know whether they will descend the Arkansaw with lieut. Wilkinson, or continue on to Red river with me, but they have their own selection.

The general will no doubt be struck with some surprize, to perceive that so large a party of Spanish troops have been so lately in our territory ; no doubt at first you would conclude that it must have been militia ; but when informed that their infantry was armed with muskets and bayonets, and had drums ; that the men wore long mustaches and whiskers, which almost covered the whole of their faces ; their cavalry armed with swords and pistols, and that regular guards and patroles were kept by horse and foot, you may probably change your opinion.

The route by which they came, and returned, was by no means the direct one from Santa Fe, and why they should have struck so low down as the Grand Saline, unless they had an idea of striking at the village of the *Grand Pest :* or conceived the Saline in their territory, I cannot imagine.

On our arrival here, we were received with great pomp and ceremony, by about 300 men on horseback, and with great apparent friendship by the chief. The Osage (one chief and four warriors,

were presented with eight horses, the Kans who arrived two days
after, were also presented with horses. The day after, we assembled
the four principal chiefs to dine, after which I presented the principal, with a doubled barrel'd gun, gorget, and other articles, (this
man wore the grand Spanish medal) and to the second the small
medal you furnished me, with other articles; and to each of the
others a gorget in their turn. Those presents I conceived would
have a good effect, both as to attaching them to our government,
and in our immediate intercourse.

At the council which was held a day or two afterwards, I presented them with merchandize (which at this place should be valued
at $250) and after explaining their relative situation as to the Span-
ish and American governments, I asked on my part, *if they would
assist us with a few horses*, a Tetau prisoner *who spoke Pawnee, to
serve as an interpreter, an exchange of colors ; and finally, for some
of their chiefs to accompany us, to be sent to Washington.* The exchange of the colors was the only request granted at the time ; and
for particular reasons (which lieut. Wilkinson related) I thought
proper to return them to the chief; and after spending two or three
anxious days, we were given to understand, that our requests could not
be complied with in the other points, and were again strongly urged
by the head chief, to return the way we came, and not prosecute
our voyage any further ; this brought on an explanation as to our
views towards the Spanish government ; in which the chief declared, that it was the intention of the Spanish troops to have proceeded
further towards the Mississippi, but, that he objected to it, and they
listened to him and returned ; he therefore hoped we would be
equally reasonable ; but finding I still determined on proceeding, he
told me in plain terms (if the interpreter erred not) that it was the
will of the Spaniards we should not proceed ; which not *answering*,
he painted innumerable difficulties which he said lay in the way ;
but finding all his arguments had *no effect*, he said, " It was a pity,"
and was silent.

This day I sent out several of my party to purchase horses, but
know not yet how we shall succeed, as the Kans have intimated an
idea, that the chief will prohibit his people from trading with us.

The Pawnees and the Tetaus are at war ; the latter killed six of
the former in August last, consequently the effecting any communication with the Tetaus by means of this nation is impossible.

If God permits, we shall march from here in a few days, and
at the Arkansaw I shall remain, until I build two small canoes for

lieut. W. (whose party will consist of Ballenger and two or three men, with three Osage.) Those canoes will be easily managed, and in case of accident to one, the other will still be sufficient to transport their baggage.

I am informed, that in a few days he will meet French hunters, and probably arrive at the village of the *Grand Pest* in a fortnight; and as all the Osage nation are apprized of his descent, I conceive he will meet with no insurmountable difficulties.* The Tetaus are at open war with the Spaniards, so that could we once obtain an introduction, I conceive we should meet with a favorable reception. Yet how it is to be brought about, I am much at a loss to determine, but knowing that, at this *crisis* of *affairs*, an intimate connection with that nation, might be extremely serviceable to my *country*, I shall proceed to *find* them; in hopes to find some means through the French, Osage, and Pawnee languages, of making ourselves understood.

Any number of men (who may reasonably be calculated on) would find no difficulty in marching the route we came with baggage waggons, field artillery, and all the usual appendages of a small army; and if all the route to Santa Fe should be of the same description in case of war, I would pledge my life (and what is infinitely dearer, my honor) for the successful march of a reasonable body of troops, into the province of New Mexico.

I find the savages of this country less brave; but possessing much more duplicity, and by far a greater propensity to lying and stealing, than those I had to pass through in my last voyage.

I am extremely doubtful if any chief of those nations, can be induced to prosecute the voyage with us, as their dread of the Tetaus, and the objections of the Pawnees, seems to outweigh every argument, and inducement to the contrary.

3d *October*—The Pawnee chief has induced the Kans to return to their villages, by giving them a gun and promising horses, with many frightful pictures drawn if they proceeded.

The Osages lent me five horses, which their people who accompanied us were to have led back, but receiving fresh ones from the Pawnees, they would not be troubled with them. In fact, it was a fortunate circumstance, as four of the horses I obtained of the Osage, have such bad backs, they cannot proceed, and we will be obliged to leave them; and not purchasing here with facility, I

---

* This was erroneous, but it was my impression at the time.

would have been obliged to have sacrificed some of our baggage. I therefore sent them a certificate for each horse, on the Indian agent below, which I hope the general will order him to discharge·

I know the general's goodness will excuse this scrawl, as he is well acquainted with the situation it must be written in, and at the same time, believe me to be his sincere friend and

> Most obedient
> Humble servant,
> (Signed)   **Z. M. Pike**, Lt.

General J. Wilkinson.

[No. 15.]

Arkansaw, 24*th Oct.* 1806.   *Latitude* 37° 44′ 9″ *N.*
Dear General,

OUR party arrived here on the 15th inst. myself and Doctor Robinson on the 19th, we having been out to seek the trace of the Spanish troops missed the party, and were not able to join them until the 4th day.

The river being very regular, lieut. Wilkinson had calculated to proceed on the day following, on the most direct route for the Red river, but shortly after my joining, a considerable rain fell and raised the river, and we have been ever since preparing wooden and skin canoes, for that gentleman and party to descend in.

The river is between three and four hundred yards in width; generally flat low banks, not more than two or three feet high, and the bed a sand bank from one side to the other.

The want of water will present the greatest obstacle to the progress of the party who descend the Arkansaw, as they have no cause to fear a scarcity of provision, having some bushels of corn on hand, and at their option to take as much dried meat as they think proper, hundreds of pounds of which are lying on scaffolds at our camp; and they are likewise accompanied by the choice of our hunters.

Under those circumstances, and those stated in my letter from the Pawnees, I can assert with confidence, there are no obstacles I should hesitate to encounter, although those inseparable from a voyage of several hundred leagues through a wilderness inhabited only by savages, may appear of the greatest magnitude to minds unaccustomed to such enterprizes.

Lieut. Wilkinson and party appear in good spirits, and shew a disposition which must vanquish every difficulty.

We were eight days travelling from the Pawnee village to the Arkansaw, (our general course S. 10° W.) several of which we lay by nearly half, owing to various circumstances; my course made it 150 miles, but could now march it in 120. Lieut. Wilkinson has copied and carries with him a very elegant protracted sketch of the route, noting the streams, hills, &c. that we crossed; their courses, bearings, &c. and should I live to arrive, I will pledge myself to shew their connexions, and general direction with considerable accuracy, as I have myself spared no pains in reconnoitring or obtaining information from the savages in our route.

From this point, we shall ascend the river until we strike the mountains, or find the Tetaus; and from thence bear more to the S. until we find the head of the *Red river*, where we shall be detained some time, after which nothing shall cause a halt until my arrival at Natchitoches.

I speak in all those cases in the positive mood, as, so far as lies in the compass of human exertions, we command the power; but I pretend not to surmount impossibilities, and I well know the general would pardon my anticipating a little to him.

The general will probably be surprized to find that the expences of the expedition will more than double the contemplated sum of our first calculations; but I conceived, the Spaniards were making such great exertions to debauch the minds of our savages, economy might be very improperly applied. And I likewise have found the purchase of horses to be attended with much greater expence than was expected at St. Louis. Those reasons, and when I advert to the expences of my two voyages, (which I humbly conceive might be compared with the *one* performed by captains Lewis and Clark) and the appropriations made for *theirs*, I feel a consciousness, that it is impossible for the most rigid to censure my accounts.

I cannot yet say if I shall sacrifice my horses at Red river, but every exertion shall be made to save them for the public; some if in good condition would be fine ones, and average between fifty and sixty dollars. Should the fortune of war at length have honored me with a company, I hope the general will recollect his promise to me, and have my command attached to it; and on my arrival I shall take the liberty of soliciting his influence, that they may obtain the same, or similar rewards, to those who accompanied capt. Lewis, as I will make bold to say, that they have in the two voyages, incurred as great dangers, and went through as many hardships.

I am, dear general,

Your ever attached friend,

And obedient servant,

(Signed)   Z. M. PIKE.

General J. Wilkinson.

N. B. Doctor Robinson presents his respectful compliments, and is sanguine in the success of our expedition.

RECAPITULATION.

NAMES OF THE NATIONS.	No. of Warriors.	No. of Women.	No. of Children.	No. of Villages.	Probable No. of Souls.	No. of Lodges of the Roving Bands.	No. of Fire Arms.
OSAGE, - - - - - - - - -	1,252	1,793	974	3	4,019	516	1,200
KANS, - - - - - - - -	465	500	600	1	1,565	204	450
PAWNEES, - - - - - - -	1,993	2,170	2,060		6,223	174	700
TETAUS, - - - - - - - -	2,700	3,000	2,500	3	8,200	1,020	270
TOTAL, - - - - - - -	6,410	7,463	6,134	7	20,007	1,914	2,620

A Statistical Abstract of the nations of Indians who inhabit that part of Louisiana visi

Names of the different nations of Indians, as pronounced in the English language.	Primitive names, as given by the Savages themselves.	Names given them by the French or Spaniards.	No. of Warriors.	No. of Women.	No. of Children.	No. of Villages.	Probable No. of Souls.	No. of Lodges of the Roving Bands.	No. of Fire Arms.	Primitive Language.	Traders or Bands with whom they traffic.	Amount of merchandise necessary for their annual consumption.	Annual return of Peltry in packs.	Species of Peltry.
Osage Grand Village	Wasbasha	Grand Osage	502	852	341 Male	1	1695	214	500	Osage	Of St. Louis	*Dollars.* 10000	1000	Deer-skins, black Bear skins, Otter, Beaver, and some few Buffalo robes.
Ditto	Ditto	Petit Osage	250	241	{ 174 G. 159 B. — 333 T. }	1	824	102	250	Ditto	Ditto	8000	300	Ditto.
Ditto	Ditto		500	700	300 B.	1	1500	200	450	Ditto	Of Arkansaw			
		Total..Osage	1252	1793	974	3	4019	516	1200					
Kans	Kansa	Kan	465	500	600	1	1565	204	450	Ditto	St. Louis	8000	{ 250 deer, 15 beaver, 100 otter. — 365 total. }	Deer, Beaver Otter, Bear and Buffalo skins.
Pawnee Village of the Republic.	Pawnane	Panis	508	550	560	1	1618	30 & this nation in this village.	200	Pawnee	St. Louis and Kans	8000		Deer, Buffalo, and a few Beaver and Otter.
Pawnee Grand Village	Ditto	Ditto	1000	1120	1000	1	3120	90	300	Ditto	St. Louis, and possibly once in three years a few Spaniards	15000		Deer, Buffalo, and a few Beaver and Otter.
Pawnee Village of Pawnee Loups	Ditto	Ditto	485	500	500	1	1485	40	200	Ditto	Ditto.	8000		Ditto.
		Total..Pawnees	1993	2170	2060	3	6223	174	700					
Tetau	Camanches		2700	3000	2500		8200	1020	270	Camanche	Spaniards of North Mexico.	30000		Buffalo robes and Horses

by captain Z. M. Pike, in his tour of discovery in that country, in the years 1806 and 1807.

The positions most proper for trading establishments.	Nations with whom at war.	Nations with whom at peace or in alliance.	Names of the Chiefs or Principal Men.			Remarks.
			Indian.	French.	English.	
…the middle branch of …Osage river, between …Grand and Little vil-…ge.	Tetaus.	Little Osage.	Cahagatonga.	Cheveux Blanche.	White Hair.	Grand and little medal, colors, &c. 1st …
	Potowatomics.	All the Pawnees.	Watchawaha.	Jean La Fon.		Second chief, son-in law to White Hai…
	Arkansaws.	Sacs.	Tawangaha.	Fils de Canard.	He who drives villages.	Literally from the Indian.
	Cherokees.	Reynards.	Ichesohungar.		Wise Family.	Son Cheveux Blanche.
	Chickasaws.	Delawares.	Hapause.		Pointed Horn.	First Soldier.
	Chactaws.	Shawanese.	Chaporanga.	Bonnet du Bœuf.		
	Creeks.	Kickapous.	Gihagatche.		The Chief himself.	
	Padoucas.	Otos.	Shenga Wassa	Belle Oiseau.	Beautiful Bird.	Accompanied me to the Pawnees.
	Caddoes.	Missouries.	Wasaba Tunga.	Sans Nerve.	Without Nerve.	
		Mahaws, &c.	Ogahawasa.		The Son-in-Law.	
		Kans uncertain.	Tourmansara.		Heart of the Town.	
…tto and above the Gr. …age, on the Arkansaw …d on the side of the …issouri.	Ditto.	Ditto.	Tuttasuggy	Le Vent.	The Wind.	First chief Little Osage.
			Watchkesingar.	Soldat de Chien.	Soldier's Dog.	Second do.
			Nezuma		The Rain which Walks.	Brother first chief.
			Tetobasi.	Sans Oreille.	Without Ears.	First Soldier.
			Tarchem.		The Yellow Skin Deer.	N. B. 49 of the Little Osage have be… killed since under our government.
			Maugraine.		The Big Rogue.	
	Ditto.	Ditto.				The enumeration of the Grand and Lit… Osage village was taken by myself. Th… calculation of the Arkansaw village is b… the estimates of the chiefs of the Gra… Osage. For further explanation relati… to that village, see lieutenant Wilkinso… report, Appendix, Part II. [No. 2.] p. 2
…he entrance of the Kans …ver, or at the village.	None, if at peace with the Osage.	With all their neighbors.				The men are from actual enumeratio… the women and children by estimation.
…itto.	Tetaus and the Indians of Kans, Osages, and all the New Mexico, also Panis Loups.	Indians of the east.	Characterish.	Loup Blanche.	The White Wolf.	
			Iskatappe.	l.'Homme Riche.	The Rich Man.	
			———	———	Republican Chief.	N. B. The population of the Pawnee …public is from actual enumeration; … the others from information.
					Two sons of Charac-terish.	
…ntrance of the La Platte	Ditto, except the Panis Loups.	Ditto.				
…itto.	Ditto, and Pawnee repub-lic.	Ditto.				
…igh up the Red river …d near the mountains …a the Arkansaw.	Pawnees and Utahs, Osage and Kans.	With all the Spanish In-dians.				

APPENDIX TO PART III.

―――――――

THE kingdom of New Spain, lies between the 16° and 44° N. lat. and 96° and 118° W. long. is divided into two separate and independent governments, and these again into various sub-divisions.

The vice royalty includes the administrations of Guadalaxara, which lies between 18° 30,′ and 24° 30′ N. latitude, and 104° and 109° W. longitude, and is bounded south and west, by the South Sea, north by the province of Biscay and Sinaloa ; N. E. by the administration of Zacatecas ; E. by the administration of Guanaxuato and S· E. by that of Valladolid, and is 350 miles in length from north west to south east, and 250 in width, east and west. Its population may be estimated at 100,000. It is one of the most luxuriant and rich administrations in the vice royalty ; and is watered from east to west by the great river de Santego, which receives most of its waters from Lac de Chapala. Guadalaxara the capital, was built by one of the Gusman family in 1551, and in 1570, the bishopric was removed from Compostela to that place. It is the seat of the audience of Guadalaxara, which includes Guadalaxara and the administration of Zacatecas. The population of this city may be estimated at 75,000, and stands in N. latitude 20° 50′, W. longitude 105°.

The administration of Valladolid lies between 22° 10′, and 18° 12′ N. longitude, and 102° and 105° W. longitude, and is bounded south by the South sea, and part of Mexico, east and north east by the latter, and north by that of Guanaxuato. Its greatest length from north east to south west is 230 miles, and its greatest width east and west 190 miles. Its population may be estimated at 360,000. Its capital of the same name, is situated in about the 20° N. latitude, 103° 25″ W. longitude. Population unknown.

The administration of Mexico lies between 21° 30′, and 16° 30′ N. latitude, 99° and 105° W. longitude, and is bounded south by the South Sea ; east by the governments of La Puebla and La Vera Cruz ; north by that of St. Louis, and west by Valladolid and Guanaxuato. Its greatest length north and south, may be 360 miles. and its greatest width, which is on the Western Ocean, is 200 miles, Its population may be estimated at 1,500,000 souls. The capital of this administration and of the whole kingdom, is Mexico ; a particular description of which is deemed unnecessary. From every information I could obtain from persons who had resided in it for years, it does not contain more than 200,000 inhabitants. Its being the residence of the vice roy, whose court is more splendid than that of Madrid ; its central position as to the ports of Acapulco and Vera Cruz, together with the rich and luxuriant vale which surrounds it, will whenever the Spanish Americans burst the present bonds of slavery in which they are bound, give to Mexico all those advantages which great wealth, a large population, and a commanding situation concentrate and assuredly make it one of the greatest cities in the world. In point of population, it is now in the second rank, and in beauty, riches, magnificence, and splendor in the first.

The administration of Oxaca lies between 18° and 16° N. latitude, 98° and 112° W. longitude, and is bounded south by the South Sea, west by the government of La Puebla, north by Mexico and La Vera Cruz, and east by the province of Gualamalia. Its greatest length east and west 230 miles, and its width north and south 175 miles. Its population may be estimated at 520,000 souls. Its capital is Oxaca in 17° 30′ N. latitude, 99° 25′ W. longitude.

The administration of Vera Cruz lies between 17° and 22° N. latitude and 98° and 101° W. longitude, and is bounded north and east by the gulf of Mexico, south by Oxaca, west by Puebla and Mexico. Its greatest length N. W. and S. E. is 430 miles, and its width E. and W. not more than 60 miles. Its population may be estimated at 220,000. Its capital is Vera Cruz, which is the sole port of entry for all the kingdom on the Atlantic ocean, as that of Acapulco is on the Western. Its population may be estimated at 30,000 souls, and is in 19° 10′ N. latitude and 98° 30′ W. longitude. This city was taken and sacked by the English on the 17th May, 1683, since which the works for its defence have been made so very strong, as almost to bid defiance to an attack from the sea.

The administration de la Puebla lies between 20° and 16° N. latitude and 100° and 102° W. longitude, and is bounded south by the South sea, east by Oxaca and Vera Cruz, north and west by Mexico, and is near 300 miles in its greatest length from north to south, and 120 in its greatest width from east to west. Its population may be estimated at 800,000 souls. Its capital is the city of La Puebla, estimated at 80,000 souls, which is in 19° 12′ N. latitude, 100° 50′ W. longitude.

The administration of Guanaxuato lies between 21° 30′ and 22° 30′ N. latitude and 103° and 105° W. longitude, and is bounded south by Valladolid, east by Mexico, north by St. Louis Zacataca, and west by Guadalaxara. Its greatest extent, from north to south, is 75 miles, and from east to west 85. Its population may be estimated at 500,000 souls. Its capital city is Guanaxuato, in latitude 21° N. longitude 103° W.

The administration of Zacataca lies between 21° 20′ and 24° 52′ N. latitude and 103° and 105° 30′ W. longitude, and is bounded north by the internal province of Biscay, east by St. Louis, west by Guadalaxara and south by Guanaxuato. Its greatest length is 210 miles, north and south, and its greatest width is 145 miles, from east to west. Its population may be estimated at 250,250 souls. The capital, Zacataca, stands in 23° N. latitude and 104° W. longitude.

The administration of St. Louis lies between 21° 20′ and 28° 50′ N. latitude and 99° and 102° W. longitude, and includes Texas and St. Ander in this dimension, and is bounded north by New Leon, east by the province of St. Ander, south by Guanaxuato and Mexico, and west by Zacataca. Its greatest length from north to south is 200, and its width from east to west is 170 miles. Its population may be estimated at 311,500 souls. Its capital, St. Louis de Potosi the population of which is 60,000: it stands in 22° N. latitude, 103° W. longitude, and was founded in 1568.

The province of Nuevo San Ander is bounded north by the province of Texas, west by Nuevo Leon and Cogquillo, south by St. Louis, and east by the Atlantic ocean, and from north to south is about 500 miles in length, but from east to west not more than 150. Its population may be estimated at 38,000 souls. The capital, New

San Ander, is on the river of that name, about 40 miles from the sea, in 23° 45′ N. latitude and 101° W. longitude.

The kingdom of New Leon is bounded east by New San Ander, north by Cogquilla, west by Biscay, and south by St. Louis and Zacataca; its greatest length north and south is 250 miles, width east and west 100 miles. Its population may be estimated at 30,000 souls. Its capital, Mont El Rey, is situated on the head waters of Tiger river, which discharges itself into the gulf of Mexico. The city of Mont El Rey contains about 11,000 souls, and is the seat of the bishop, Don Dio Premiro, who visited the port of Nachitoches when commanded by captain Turner, of the 2d United States regiment of infantry. His episcopal jurisdiction extends over Nuevo San Ander, New Leon, Cogquilla and Texas, and his salary is equal to $100,000 per annum. Mont El Rey is situated in 26° N. latitude and 102° W. longitude. There are many and rich mines near the city of Mont El Rey, from whence, I am informed, there are taken, to be coined, 100 mule-loads of bullion in silver and gold monthly, which may be presumed to be not more than the three-fifths of what is taken from the mines, as there are many persons who prefer never getting their metal coined, as then it is not so easily ascertained what they are worth, which is an all-important secret in a despotic government.

The foregoing nine administrations or intendencias, the kingdom of Leon, and the province of Nuevo San Ander are included in the two audiences of Guadalaxara and Mexico, and form, as I believe, the whole political government of the vice-roy of Mexico ; but I am not positive whether his jurisdiction does not include the audience of Guatimalia, which lies to the south, and includes the province of that name, that of Chiapa, Yucatan, Veraqua, Costa Rica and Honduras. An audience is the high court of appeals in which the vice-roy presides and has two votes : it is intended as a check on his power and authority.

The administrations are governed by intendants, who are officers of high rank, and always Europeans. The longitude given is from the meridian of Paris.

In the general view of New Spain, I shall take some notice of the manners, customs, political force, &c. of the vice-royalty ; but, as I do not pretend to be correctly informed as to that quarter of the kingdom, and there have been so many persons who have given statements on those heads, I shall confine my observations principally to the internal provinces through which I passed, and on which I made my observations.

INTERNAL PROVINCES.

New Mexico lies between 30° 30′ and 44° N. latitude and 104 and 108° W. longitude, and is the most northern province of the kingdom of New Spain ; it extends north-west into an undefined boundary, is bounded north and east by Louisiana, south by Biscay and Cogquilla, and west by Senora and California. Its length is unknown, its breadth may be 600 miles, but the inhabited part is not more than 400 miles in length and 50 in breadth, lying along the river del Norte, from the 37° to the 31° 30′ N. latitude ; but in this space there is a desert of more than 250 miles.

Air and Climate.—No persons accustomed to reside in the temperate climate of 36 and 37 degrees of north latitude in the United States can form any idea of the piercing cold which you experience in that parallel in New Mexico ; but the air is serene and unaccompanied by damps or fogs, as it rains but once a year, and some years not at all. It is a mountainous country. The grand dividing ridges which separate the waters of the rio del Norte from those of California border it on the line of its western limits, and are covered, in some places, with eternal snows, which give a keenness to the air that could not be calculated upon nor expected in a temperate zone.

Timber and Plains.—The cotton tree is the only tree of this province, except some scrubby pines and cedars at the foot of the mountains. The former borders the banks of the rio del Norte and its tributary streams. All the rest of the country presents to the eye a barren wild of poor land, scarcely to be improved by culture, and appears to be only capable of producing sufficient subsistence for those animals which live on succulent plants and herbage.

Mines, Minerals, and Fossils —There are no mines known in the province, except one of copper situated in a mountain on the west side of the rio del Norte, in latitude 34° N. It is worked and produces 20,000 mule-loads of copper annually. It also furnishes that article for the manufactories of nearly all the internal provinces. It contains gold ; but not quite sufficient to pay for its extraction ; consequently it has not been pursued.

There is, near Santa Fe, in some of the mountains, a stratum of talc, which is so large and flexible as to render it capable of being subdivided into thin flakes, of which the greater proportion of the houses in Santa Fe, and all the villages to the north, have their window-lights made.

Rivers.—The river del Norte takes its source in the mountains (which give birth to the head-waters of California, the Plata, Pierre Jaune of the Missouri and Arkansaw of the Mississippi) in 40° N. latitude and 110° W. longitude. Its distance from its source to the gulf of Mexico may be, by its meanders, estimated at 2000 miles, passing through the provinces of New Mexico, part of Biscay, Cogquilla, and New San Ander, where it falls into the gulf in 26° N. latitude. It cannot, in any part of its course, be termed a navigable stream, owing to the sand-bars. In the flat country and mountains in the upper part, with which its course is interrupted, small boats might ascend as high as the Presidio de rio Grande in Cogquilla, and it might be navigable for canoes in various parts of its course. In the mountains above Santa Fe it afforded amply sufficient water for canoe navigation, and even more than appeared to be flowing in its bed in the plains. This must be attributed to numerous canals and the dry sandy soil through which the river courses and where much of the water which flowed from the mountains must be absorbed and lost. In the province of New Mexico it is called the Rio del Norte ; below it is termed the Rio Grande ; but in no instance did I hear it called the Rio Bravo, as many of our ancient maps designate it.

There are also, in the limits of this province, to the west, the rivers San Rafael, San Xavier, river de los Dolores, also de los Anamas or Nabajoa, all of which join and form the Great Rio Colorado of California. The two first take their sources in the same mountains as the Rio del Norte, but on the west side.

The river Colorado, by its meanders, may be about 1000 miles in length, from its sources to its discharge into the head of the gulf of California, in the 33d degree of N. latitude. It has been represented to me, by men of information and research, to be navigable for square rigged vessels at least 300 miles from the gulf. By this river and the Arkansaw there could be the best communication established between the Pacific and the Atlantic oceans. There are represented to be various, numerous and warlike nations of Indians on its banks. Through the whole of its course its banks are entirely destitute of Timber, and indeed I was informed that for 300 miles there was not a tree ten inches in diameter.

The river S. Buenaventura empties into the Pacific ocean to the north of California in 39° 30′ N. latitude, and takes its source in the Sierra Madre to the north of the Colorado and del Norte.

The Rio Gila heads opposite to the copper-mines, and discharges itself into the gulf of California, just below the Colorado, in the 33d degree of N. latitude.

The Rio Puerto is a branch of the Rio del Norte, and comes from the north and joins that river about 100 miles below the Presidio del Norte.

None of the foregoing streams present any evidences of civilization on their shores but the Rio del Norte.

Lakes.—I heard of no lakes in the province, except that of Tampanagos, the existence of which I consider very doubtful. It is said to commence (according to Father Escalante) in the 40th deg. N. latitude, and to have been explored to the 42d deg. in a N. W. direction, where it enlarged its dimension, and the discoverer thought proper to return.

Animals.—North Mexico produces deer, elk, buffalo, cabrie, the gresley, black bear, and wild horses.

Population.—Its population is not far short of 30,000 souls, one-twentieth of which may be Spaniards from Europe (or Chapetones), four-twentieths Creoles, five-twentieths Metifs, and the other half civilized Indians.

The capital is Santa Fe, situated on a small stream which empties into the east side of the Rio del Norte, at the foot of the mountains which divide the waters of that river from the Arkansaw and Red river of the Mississippi, in 36° N. latitude and 109° W. longitude. It is an oblong square, extending about one mile from east to west on the banks of the creek. In the centre is the public square, one side of which forms the flank of the soldiers' square, which is closed and in some degree defended by round towers in the angles which flank the four curtains : another side of the square is formed by the palace of the governor, his guard-houses, &c. The third side is occupied by the priests and their suit, and the fourth by the Chapetones who reside in the city. The houses are generally only one story high, flat roofs, and have a very mean appearance on the out-side, but some of them are richly furnished, especially with plate.

The second cities in the province are Albuquerque and Passo del Norte. The latter is the most southern city of the province, as Tons is the most northern. Between the village of Sibilleta and the Passo there is a wilderness of near 200 miles.

Trade and Commerce.—New Mexico carries on a trade direct with Mexico through Biscay, also with Senora and Sinaloa : it sends out about 30,000 sheep annually, tobacco, dressed deer and cabrie skins, some fur, buffalo robes, salt, and wrought copper vessels of a superior quality. It receives in return, from Biscay and Mexico, dry goods, confectionary, arms, iron, steel, ammunition, and some choice European wines and liquors, and from Senora and Sinaloa, gold, silver, and cheese. The following articles sell as stated (in this province), which will shew the cheapness of provisions and the extreme dearness of imported goods :

Flour sells, per hundred at	2 dollars
Salt, per mule-load,	5
Sheep, each,	1
Beeves, each,	5
Wine del Passo, per barrel,	15
Horses, each,	11
Mules, each,	30
Superfine cloths, per yard,	25
Fine do. do.	20
Linen, per yard,	4

and all other dry goods in proportion.

The journey with loaded mules from Santa Fe to Mexico, and returning to Santa Fe, takes five months. They manufacture rough leather, segars, a vast variety and quantity of potters' ware, cotton, some coarse woolen cloths, and blankets of a superior quality. All those manufactures are carried on by the civilized Indians, as the Spaniards think it more honorable to be agriculturalists than mechanics. The Indians likewise far exceed their conquerors in their genius for, and execution of, all mechanical operations.

New Mexico has the exclusive right of cultivating tobacco.

About two miles above the town of the Passo del Norte is a bridge over the river, where the road passes to the west side, at which place is a large canal, which takes out an ample supply of water for the purpose of cultivation, which is here carried on in as great perfection as at any place that I visited in the provinces. There is a wall bordering the canal the whole way on both sides, to protect it from the animals ; and when it arrives at the village, it is distributed in such a manner that each person has his fields watered in rotation. At this place were as finely cultivated fields of wheat and other small grain as I ever saw. Numerous vineyards, from which were produced the finest wine ever drank in the country, which was celebrated through all the provinces, and was the only wine used on the table of the commanding general.

Agriculture.—They cultivate corn, wheat, rye, barley, rice, tobacco, vines, and all the common culinary plants cultivated in the same latitude in the United States. They are, however, a century

behind us in the art of cultivation; for, notwithstanding their numerous herds of cattle and horses, I have seen them frequently breaking up whole fields with the hoe. Their oxen draw by the horns,
after the French mode. Their carts are extremely awkward and
clumsily made. During the whole of the time we were in New
Spain I never saw a horse in a vehicle of any description, mules
being made use of in carriages as well as for the purposes of labour.

Antiquities.—On the river St. Francis, a large branch of the
river Gila, which heads near the copper mines in New Mexico and
discharges itself into the Red river of California, are the remains of
old walls and houses which are ascertained to have been the work of
the Mexicans on their route emigrating from the north-west to the
plains of Mexico, where they finally established themselves. Those
walls are of a black cement, the durability of which increases with
its age, so that it has hitherto bid defiance to the war of time. Its
composition is now entirely lost. There is also found at this place
many broken pieces of earthen ware, which still possess the glazing
as perfect as when first put on.

Aborigines.—The Kyaways wander on the sources of the La
Platte and are supposed to be 1000 men strong. They possess immense herds of horses and are at war with both Pawnees and Tetaus,
as well as Sioux. They are armed with bows, arrows and lances,
and hunt the buffalo. This nation with the Tetaus and Utahs all
speak the same language. The Utahs wander at the sources of the
Rio del Norte, are supposed to be 2000 warriors strong, are armed
in the same manner, and pursue the same game as the Kyaways.
They are, however, a little more civilized, from having more connection with the Spaniards, with whom they are frequently at war,
but were then at peace, and waging war with the Tetaus.

A battle was fought between them and the Tetaus in September
1806, near the village of Tons: there were about 400 combatants
on each side, but they were separated by a Spanish alcade riding out
to the field of battle. There were eight or ten killed on each side.
The Utahs gave all the horses taken to the Spaniards. This shews
in a strong degree, the influence the Spaniards have over those Indians. The Nanahaws are situated to the north-west of Santa Fe,
are frequently at war with the Spaniards, and are supposed to be
2000 warriors strong. They are armed in the same manner as the
two preceding nations. This nation, as well as all others to the west
of them bordering on California, speak the language of the Appaches and Le Panis, who are in a line with them to the Atlantic.

17

The Appaches are a nation of Indians who extend from the black mountains in New Mexico to the frontiers of Cogquilla, keeping the frontiers of three provinces in a continual state of alarm, and making it necessary to employ nearly two thousand dragoons to escort the caravans, protect the villages, and revenge the various attacks they are continually making on the subjects of his Catholic majesty. This nation formerly extended from the entrance of the Rio Grande to the gulf of California, and have waged a continual warfare, except short truces, with the Spaniards, from the time they pushed their enterprises back from Mexico into the internal provinces. It is extremely difficult to say what are their numbers at the present day, but they must be very much reduced, from their long and constant warfare, the wandering and savage life they lead in the mountains, which is so injurious to an increase of population, and in which they are frequently extremely pinched by famine.

At the commencement of their warfare the Spaniards used to take their prisoners and make slaves of them ; but finding that their unconquerable attachment to liberty made them surmount every difficulty and danger in returning to their mountains, they adopted the mode of sending them to Cuba, which the Appaches no sooner learned than they refused to give or receive quarters, and in no instance have there been any taken since that period, except surprised when asleep or knocked down and overpowered.

Their arms are the bow and arrow and the lance. Their bow forms two demi-circles, with a shoulder in the middle : the back of it is entirely covered with sinews, which are laid on in so nice a manner, by the use of some glutinous substance, as to be almost imperceptible ; this gives great elasticity to the weapon. Their arrow is more than the " cloth yard" of the English, being three feet and a half long, the upper part consisting of some light rush or cane, into which is inserted a shaft of about one foot, made of some hard, seasoned light wood ; the point is of iron, bone, or stone, and, when the arrow enters the body, in attempting to extract it, the shaft comes out of its socket and the point remains in the wound. With this weapon they shoot with such force as to go through the body of a man at the distance of 100 yards, and an officer told me that, in an engagement with them, one of their arrows struck his shield and dismounted him in an instant. Their other weapon of offence is a lance of 15 feet in length, with which they charge with both hands over their heads, managing their horses principally with their knees. With this weapon they are considered an overmatch for the Spanish dragoons single handed, but, for want of a knowledge of tactics, they can never stand the charge of a body which acts in concert. They all carry a shield. Some few are armed with guns and ammunition taken from the Spaniards. Those, as well as the archers, generally march to war on foot; but the lancemen are always mounted. Numerous are the anecdotes I have heard related of their personal bravery and the spirit of their partisan corps. Not long before I went into that country a cornet, with 63 dragoons, between New Mexico and Biscay, was surrounded by about 200 Appaches infantry, and instead of charging through them, as it was on the plain, he ordered his dragoons to dismount and fight with their carabines, in consequence of which he and his whole party fell a sacrifice.

Malgares related an instance when he was marching with 140 men and they were attacked by a party of Appaches, both horse and foot, who continued the fight for four hours. Whenever the Spanish dragoons would make a general charge, the Appaches' cavalry would retreat behind their infantry, who met the Spaniards with a shower of arrows, who immediately retreated, and even the gallant Malgares spoke of the Spanish cavalry's breaking the Appaches' infantry as a thing not to be thought of.

Malgares assured me that, if the Appaches had seconded the efforts and bravery of their chieftain, the Spaniards must have been defeated and cut to pieces; that in various instances he rallied his men and brought them up to the charge, and that when they flew, he retired indignantly to the rear. Seeing Malgares very actively engaged in forming and bringing up the Spaniards, the Appache chieftain rode out a-head of his party and challenged him to single combat with his lance. This my friend refused, as he said that the chief was one of the stoutest men he knew, carried a remarkably heavy lance, and rode a very fine charger; but one of his corporals, enraged to see the Spaniards thus braved by this savage, begged permission to meet the "infidel." His officer refused his request and ordered him to keep his ranks; but he reiterating the request, his superior in a passion told him to go. The Indian chief had turned his horse to join his party, but seeing an enemy advancing, he turned, gave a shout, and met him at full speed. The dragoon thought to parry the lance of his antagonist, which he in part effected, but not throwing it quite high enough, it entered his neck before and came out at the nape, when he fell dead to the ground, and his victorious enemy gave a shout of victory, in which he was joined by all his followers: this enraged the Spaniards to such a degree that they made a general charge, in which the Indian cavalry again retreated notwithstanding the entreaties of their gallant leader.

In another instance a small smoke was discovered on the prairie; three poor savages were surrounded by 100 dragoons and ordered to lay down their arms: they smiled at the officer's demand and asked him if he could suppose that men who had arms in their hands would ever consent to become slaves. The officer, being loath to kill them, held a conference for an hour, when finding that his threats had as little effect as his entreaties, he ordered his men to attack them at a distance, keeping out of the reach of their arrows, and firing at them with their carabines, which they did, the Indians never ceasing to resist as long as life remained.

In a truce which was held a Spanish captain was ordered to treat with some of the bands. He received their deputies with hauteur, and they could not come upon terms. The truce was broken and the Indians retreated to their fastnesses in the mountains. In a day or two this same officer pursued them: they were in a place called the door in the mountain, where but two or three dragoons could enter at a time, and there were rocks and caves on the flanks behind which the Indians secreted themselves until a number of the Spaniards had come in, when the Indians sounded a trumpet and the attack began and continued on the side of the Appaches until the Spanish captain fell, when the Indian chief caused the firing to cease, saying that "the man who had so haughtily spurned the proffered peace was now dead." On this occasion they deviated from their accustomed rule of warfare and made prisoner of a young officer, who, during the truce, had treated them with great kindness, and sent him home safe and unhurt. Some of the bands have made temporary truces with the Spaniards and received from them 25 cents per diem each. Those people hang round the fortifications of the country, drink, shoot, and dissipate their time; they are haughty and independent. Great jealousy exists between them and the Spaniards. An officer was under trial, when I was in the country, for anticipating an attack on his fortress by attacking the chiefs of the supposed conspiracy, and putting them to death before they had time to mature and carry their plan into execution. The decision of his case I never learnt; but those savages who have been for some time about the forts and villages, become by far the most dangerous enemies the Spaniards have, when hostile, as they acquire the Spanish language, manners, and habits, and passing through the populated parts under the disguise of the civilized and friendly Indians, commit murders and robberies and are not suspected. There is in the province of Cogquilla a partisan by the name of Ralph, who, they calculate, has killed more than 300 persons. He comes into the towns under the disguise of a peasant, buys provisions, goes to the gambling tables and to mass, and before he leaves the village, is sure to kill some person or carry off a woman, which he has frequently done. Sometimes he joins people travelling on the road, insinuates himself into their confidence, and takes his opportunity to assassinate them. He has only six followers, and from their knowledge of the country, activity, and cunning, he keeps about 300 Spanish dragoons continually employed. The government have offered 1000 dollars for his head.

The civilized Indians of the province of New Mexico are of what was formerly twenty-four different bands, the different names of which I did not become acquainted with, but the Keres were one of the most powerful; they form at present the population of St. Domingo, St. Philips, and Deis, and one or two other towns. They are men of large stature, round full visage, fine teeth, appear to be of a gentle, tractable disposition, and resemble the Osage more than any nation of whom I possess any knowledge. They are not the vassals of Individuals, yet may properly be termed the slaves of the state, for they are compelled to do military duty, drive mules, carry loads, or in fact perform any other act of duty or bondage that the will of the commandant of the district, or any passing military tyrant chooses to ordain. I was myself eye-witness of a scene which made my heart bleed for those poor wretches, at the same time that it excited my indignation and contempt, that they would suffer themselves, with arms in their hands, to be beat and knocked about by beings no ways their superiors, unless a small tint of complexion could be supposed to give that superiority. Before we arrived at Santa Fe, one night, we were near one of the villages where resided the families of two of our Indian horsemen. They took the liberty to pay them a visit in the night. Next morning the whole of the Indian horsemen were called up, and because they refused to testify against their imprudent companions, several were knocked down from their horses by the Spanish dragoons with the butt of their lances; yet, with the blood streaming down their visages, and arms in their hands, they stood cool and tranquil : not a frown, not a word of discontent or palliation escaped their lips. Yet what must have been the boiling indignation of their souls at the indignities offered by the wretch clothed with a little brief authority; but the day of retribution will come in thunder and in vengeance.

Those savages are armed with bow and arrows and with lances, or escopates.

Although they are said to be converted to Christianity, they still retain many of their ancient rituals, feasts, and ceremonies, one of which is so remarkable it must not be passed unnoticed. Once a year there is a great feast prepared for three successive days, which they spend in eating, drinking, and dancing. Near to this scene of amusement is a dark cave, into which not a glimpse of light can penetrate and in which is prepared places to repose on. To this place persons of all descriptions, of both sexes and of all ages, after puberty, and repair in the night, where there is an indiscriminate commerce of the votaries, as chance, fortune, and events direct. Those revels certainly have great affinity to some of the ancient mystic rights of Greece and Rome.

Government and Laws.—The government of New Mexico may be termed military, in the pure sense of the word ; for although they have their alcades or inferior officers, their judgments are subject to a reversion by the military commandants of districts. The whole male population are subject to military duty, without pay or emolument, and are obliged to find their own horses, arms and provision. The only thing furnished by the government is ammunition, and it is extraordinary with what subordination they act when they are turned out to do military duty, a strong proof of which was exhibited in the expedition of Malgares to the Pawnees. His command consisted of 100 dragoons of the regular service and 500 drafts from the province. He had continued down the Red river until their provision began to be short : they then demanded of the lieutenant where he was bound and the intention of the expedition ? To this he haughtily replied, " wherever his horse led him." A few mornings after he was presented with a petition, signed by 200 of the militia, to return home. He halted immediately, and caused his dragoons to erect a gallows ; then beat to arms. The troops fell in : he separated the *petitioners* from the others, then took the man who had presented the petition, tied him up, and gave him 50 lashes, and threatened to put to death, on the gallows erected, any man who should dare to grumble. This effectually silenced them, and quelled the rising spirit of sedition ; but it was remarked that it was the first instance of a Spaniard receiving corporal punishment ever known in the province.

Morals, Manners, &c.—There is nothing peculiarly characteristic in this province that will not be embraced in my general observations on New Spain, except that being frontier, and cut off, as it were, from the more inhabited parts of the kingdom, together with their continual wars with some of the savage nations who surround them, render them the bravest and most hardy subjects in New Spain; being generally armed, they know the use of them. Their want of gold and silver renders them laborious, in order that the productions of their labor may be the means of establishing the equilibrium between them and the other provinces where those metals abound. Their insolated and remote situation also causes them to exhibit, in a superior degree, the heaven-like qualities of hospitality and kindness, in which they appear to endeavor to fulfil the injunction of the scripture, which enjoins us to feed the hungry, clothe the naked, and give comfort to the oppressed in spirit, and I shall always take pleasure in expressing my gratitude for their noble reception of myself and the men under my command.

Military Force.—There is but one troop of dragoons in all New Mexico of the regular force, which is stationed at Santa Fe, and is 100 strong. Of this troop the governor is always the captain, entitling himself captain of the royal troop of Santa Fe dragoons; but they are commanded by a first lieutenant, who is captain by brevet.

The men capable of bearing arms in this province may be estimated at 5000 : of those probably 1000 are completely armed, 1000 badly, and the rest not at all.

Religion.—The catholic religion is practised in this province after the same manner as in the other provinces, and will hereafter be taken notice of generally.

History.—In the year 1594 two friars came out from Old Mexico to New Mexico, and were well received by the savages. They returned, and the ensuing year Juan de Ouate, a monk, went out, explored the country, and returned. After this 100 troops and 500 men, women, and children came out and settled on the Rio del Norte, some, no very great, distance from where Santa Fe now stands. They entered into an arrangement with the Indians on the subject of their establishment ; but a few years after the Indians rose *en masse*, fell on the Spaniards by surprise, killed most of the soldiers, and obliged them to retreat to the Passo del Norte (from whence it acquired its name). Here they waited a reinforcement from Biscay, which they received, of 70 men and two field-pieces, with which they recommenced their march and finally arrived at Santa Fe, then the capital Indian village, to which they immediately laid siege. The Indians maintained themselves twenty-two days, when they surrendered and entered into a second negotiation, since which time the Spaniards have been engaged in continual warfare with the various savage tribes which surround them on all sides, and who have been near ruining themselves several times, and obliged them to apply for reinforcements from Biscay and Senora. A few years since the Tetaus carried on a warm and vigorous war against them, but are now at peace and considered as their firmest allies.

In the history of New Mexico it may not be improper to record the name of James Pursley, the first American who ever penetrated the immense wilds of Louisiana, and shewed the Spaniards of New Mexico that neither the savages who surround the deserts which divide them from the habitable world, nor the jealous tyranny of their rulers, was sufficient to prevent the enterprising spirit of the Americans penetrating the arcanum of their rich establishment of the new world. Pursley was from near Baird's town, Kentucky, which he left in 1799. In 1802, with two companions, he left St. Louis and travelled west, on the head of the Osage river, where they made a hunt: from thence they struck for the White river of the Arkansaw, and intended to descend it to Orleans ; but, while making preparations, the Kans stole their horses. They secured their peltries and pursued them into the village. The horses were there, but the Indians refused to give them up. Pursley saw his horse, with an Indian on him, going to the water at the edge of the town, pursued him, and with his knife ripped open the horse's bowels. The Indian returned to the village, got his gun, and came and snapped it at Pursley, who pursued him into the village with his knife. The Indian took refuge in a lodge surrounded by women and children. This struck the chiefs with astonishment and admiration of the " mad Americans," as they termed them, and they returned the other horses to the hunters. This anecdote was related by traders who were in the village at the time. Pursley and his companions then returned to where they had buried their peltry, and determined to pursue the route by land to St. Louis : but some persons stole their horses a second time, when they were at no great distance from the Osage river, on which they formed a rough canoe and descended that stream. Near the entrance of the Missouri they overset their canoe and lost their whole year's hunt, but saved their arms and ammunition, which is always the primary object in a desert. In the Missouri they met Monsieur ———— in his barge, bound to the Mandanes. Pursley embarked with him for the voyage : his two companions prefered returning to their homes. On their arrival at the point of destination, his employer dispatched Pursley on a hunting and trading tour, with some bands of the Padducas and Kyaways, with a small quantity of merchandise. In the ensuing spring they were driven from the plains by the Sioux into the mountains which give birth to the La Platte, Arkansaw, &c. &c. and it was their sign which we saw in such amazing abundance on the head waters of La Platte. Their party consisted of near 2,000 souls, with 10,000 beasts. The Indians, knowing they were approximating to New Mexico, determined to send Pursley, with his companions and two of their body, into Santa Fe, to know of the Spaniards if they would receive them friendly and enter into a trade with them. This being acceded to by the governor (Allencaster) the Indian deputies returned for their bands; but *Pursley* thought proper to remain with a civilized people, which a fortuitous event had thrown him among, a circumstance which, he assured me, he had at one time entirely despaired of. He arrived at Santa Fe in June 1805, and had been following his trade, a carpenter, ever since, at which he made a great deal of money, except when working for the officers, who paid him little or nothing. He was a man of strong natural sense and dauntless intrepidity. He entertained me with numerous interesting anecdotes of his adventures with the Indians, and of the jealousy of the Spanish government. He was once near being hanged for making a few pounds of gun-powder, which he innocently did, as he had been accustomed to do in Kentucky, but which is a capital crime in these provinces. He still retained the gun which he had with him his whole tour, and spoke confidently that if he had two hours start not all the province could take him. He was forbidden to write, but was assured he should have a passport whenever he demanded it, but was obliged to give security that he would not leave the country without permission of the government. He assured me that he had found gold on the head of La Platte, and had carried some of the virgin mineral in his shot-pouch for months ; but that being in doubt whether he should ever again behold the civilized world, and losing in his mind all the *ideal value* which mankind have stamped on that metal, he threw the sample away : that he had imprudently mentioned it to the Spaniards, who had frequently solicited him to go and shew a detachment of cavalry the place, but that conceiving it in our territory he had refused, and was fearful that the circumstance might create a great obstacle to his leaving the country.

Geography.—BISCAY lies between 33° and 24° N. latitude and 105° and 111° W. longitude, is bounded on the north by New Mexico, on the west by Senora and Sinaloa, and on the east by New Leon and Cogquilla. It is 600 miles in length from north-west to south-

east, and 400 miles in width from east to west, taking it at its greatest extent.

Air and Climate.— The air is dry and the heat very great at
that season of the year, which precedes the rainy season, which
commences in June and continues until September by light show-
ers. During the other part of the year there is not the least rain
or snow to moisten the earth. The atmosphere had therefore become so electrified, that when we halted at night, in taking off our
blankets the electric fluid would almost cover them with sparks, and
in Chihuahua we prepared a bottle with gold-leaf, as a receiver, and
collected sufficient of the electric fluid from a bear-skin to give a
considerable shock to a number of persons. This phenomenon
was more conspicuous in the vicinity of Chihuahua than in any
other part that we passed over.

Mines and Minerals.— This province abounds in silver and gold
mines, which yield an immense quantity of those metals, but not
so great a revenue to the king as those which are nearer the mint,
and consequently present a greater facility to coinage. I am not
acquainted with the proportion of the metals which the mineral
yields in any instance, except in one of the silver mines at Chihuahua, which belonged to a friend of mine, who informed me that his
mine yielded him 13 1-2 dollars per cwt. I one day, with Robinson,
went through many of these furnaces and noticed the manner
which they pursued in analysing the mineral and extracting the
metals, but, as I had previously asked several Spanish officers to accompany me, who had always declined or defered it to a future period, I conceived it probable it was too delicate a subject to make a
minute inquiry into. I, however, so far observed the process as to
learn that the mineral was brought from the mines in bags, on
mules, to the furnace : it was then ground or pounded into small
lumps, not more than the size of a nut, and precipitated into water,
in a sieve which permitted the smaller particles to escape into a tub,
through several progressive operations. From the small particles
which remained at the bottom of the tubs, after it had been purified
of the earthy qualities, there was a proportion of metal extracted
by a nicer process ; but the larger parts were put into a furnace similar to our iron furnaces, and when it was in a state of fusion, it was
let out into a bed of sand prepared for it which formed it into
bars about the size of our common pig iron, averaged in value at
about 2,500 dollars. The gold was cast into a mould similar to a
bowl and stamped, as was each bar of silver, by the king's essayer
of metals, with its value. They were worth from 8 to 10,000 dol-

iars. These masses of silver and gold are then received into the king's treasury in payment, and in fact have a currency through the kingdom ; but there are vast speculations made on the coinage, as people who have not large capitals prefer selling their bullion, in the internal provinces, at a considerable discount, to being obliged to transport it to Mexico, in order to have it converted into specie. The present C————, I was informed, was engaged in this traffic, on which, from the province of Senora, he sometimes made 25 per cent. Numbers of the proprietors who have no immediate use for their bullion put it into their cellars, where it remains piled up for their posterity, of no service to themselves or the community. There are at Chihuahua and its vicinity fifteen mines, thirteen silver, one gold, and one copper, the furnaces of all of which are situated round the town and suburbs, and present, except on Sundays, volumes of smoke arising to the eye in every direction, which can be seen from a distance long before the spires of the city strike the view. It is incredible the quantity of cinders which surround the city in piles ten or fifteen feet high : next the creek they have formed a bank of it to check the encroachments of the stream, and it presents an effectual barrier.

I am told that an European employed some hands and wrought at the cinders and that it yielded one dollar and twenty-five cents for each per day; but that this not answering his expectations, he ceased his proceedings. At Mausseme there is one gold and seven silver mines.

At Durango there are many and rich mines, but the number to me is unknown.

There are also gold mines in the Sierra Madre, near Alomas, and many others of which I have no knowledge. There is in the province, about one hundred miles south of Chihuahua, a mountain or hill of loadstone. Walker, who had been on the ground and surveyed it, informed me it appeared to be solid strata, as regular as that of limestone, or any other of the species. He had brought home a square piece of near a foot and a half, was preparing some to be sent to Spain, and likewise forming magnets to accompany it, in order that their comparative strength might be ascertained with magnets formed in Europe.

Rivers.—Rio Conchos is the largest in the province. It takes its source in the Sierra Madre, near Batopilis in 28° N. latitude, and discharges itself into the Rio del Norte in the 31°, after a course of about 300 miles. It is the largest western branch of the Rio del Norte, and receives in its course the Rio Florido from the east and San Paubla from the west, where we struck the Conchos. It appeared to be nearly as large as the Rio del Norte at the Passo.

The Rio San Paubla is the largest western branch of the Conchos, and heads in 28° 50′ N. latitude, and empties into the latter at Bakinoa. Its whole course is about 150 miles : in summer it is nearly dry, and in the rainy seasons impassable.

The Rio Florido takes its rise in latitude 26 1-2 N. and after a course of about 150 miles, discharges itself into the Conchos. Guaxequillo is situated on its east bank about its centre.

The Rio Nassas is in part the line between Biscay and Cogquilla : it runs north and sinks in the lake du Cayman ; it is nearly dry in the dry seasons, but at *some* seasons it is impassable.

Lakes.—Lac du Cayman and lac du Parras are two small lakes, situated at the foot of the mountains and are full of fish.

Animals, insects, &c.—There are some few bears, deer, and wild horses, but they are not in abundance. The scorpions of Durango are one of the most remarkable instances of the physical effects of climate or air that I ever saw recorded. They come out of the walls and crevices in May, and continue about a fortnight in such numbers that the inhabitants never walk in their houses after dark without a light, and always shift or examine the bed-clothes and beat the curtains previous to going to bed, after which the curtains are secured under the bed, similar to the precautions we take with our musquito curtains. The bite of those scorpions has been known to prove mortal in two hours. The most extraordinary circumstance is that by taking them ten leagues from Durango, they become perfectly harmless and lose all their venemous qualities. Query, Does it arise from a change of air, sustenance, or what other cause ?

Population and Chief Towns.—The population of Biscay may be estimated at 200,000 : of these three-twentieths may be Spaniards from Europe, five-twentieths Creoles, five-twentieths Metifs and Quatroons, and seven-twentieths Indians. Durango was founded in 1550. It is the principal city, the seat of government for the province of Biscay and of the bishoprick of Durango. Its population may be estimated at 40,000 souls. It is situated in 25° N. latitude and 107° W. longitude.

Pallalein, situated somewhere at the foot of the Sierra Madria, is supposed to contain 25,000 souls.

Chihuahua, the place of residence of the commandant general of the internal provinces, was founded in 1691, is situated in 29° N. latitude, 107° 30′ W. longitude. Its population may be estimated at 7,000. It is an oblong square, on the east side of a small stream which discharges itself into the river Conchos. On its south extremity is a small but elegant church. In the public square stands the principal church, royal treasury, town-house, and the richest shops. At the western extremity is another church for the military, a superb hospital, belonging formerly to the Jesuits' possessions, the church of the monks of St. Francis, St. Domingo, the military academy, and quartel del tropa. On the north-west were two or three missions very handsomely situated on a small stream which comes in from the west. About one mile to the south of the town is a large aqueduct which conveys the water round it, to the east, into the main stream below the town, in the centre of which is raised a reservoir for the water, from whence it is to be conducted by pipes to the different parts of the city, and in the public square is to be a fountain and *jet d'eau*, which will be both ornamental and useful. The principal church at Chihuahua was the most superb building we saw in New Spain. Its whole front was covered with statues of the apostles and the different saints, set in niches of the wall, and the windows, doors, &c. ornamented with sculpture. I never was within the doors, but was informed by Robinson that the decorations were immensely rich. Some men, whom we supposed entitled to credit, informed us that the church was built by a tax of 12 1-2 cents laid on each ingot of gold or silver taken out of the mines in the vicinity in ―― years. Its cost, with decorations, was 1,500,000 dollars, and when it was finished there remained 300,000 dollars of the fund unappropriated. At the south side of Chihuahua is the public walk, formed by three rows of trees whose branches nearly entwined over the heads of the passengers below. At different distances there are seats for persons to repose themselves on. At each end of the walks there were circular seats, on which, in the evening, the company collected and amused themselves with the guitar, songs in Spanish, Italian, and French, adapted to the voluptuous manners of the country. In this city, as well as all others of any consideration, there are patroles of soldiers during the night, who stop every person at 9 o'clock and examine them. My countersign was " Americans."

Trade, Commerce, and Manufactures.—Biscay trades with North Mexico, Senora, and the vice-royalty, from the latter of which they bring on mules all their dry goods, European furniture, books, ammunition, &c. They furnish a great quantity of horses, mules, sheep, beeves, goats, &c. to the parts of the kingdom which are more populous and have less spare ground for pasturage, &c. Some persons make large fortunes by being the carriers from Mexico to

Chihuahua, the freight being eight dollars per cwt. and they generally put 300 pounds on each mule. The merchants make their remittances twice a year in bullion. Goods sell at Chihuahua about 200 per cent on the prices of our Atlantic sea port towns. Their horses average at six dollars, but some have sold as high as 100 : their trained mules at 20 dollars ; but extraordinary matches for carriages have sold at 400 dollars per pair. Rice sells at four dollars per cwt.

They manufacture some few arms, blankets, stamped leather, embroidery, coarse cotton and woollen cloths, and a species of rough carpeting. Their blankets average two dollars, but some sell as high as 25 dollars.

Agriculture.—They cultivate wheat, corn, rice, oats, cotton, flax, indigo, and vines. What I have said relative to the cultivation of those articles in New Mexico will equally apply to this province, but it may be proper to observe here that one of Nolan's men constructed the first cotton gin they ever had in the province, and that Walker had caused a few churns to be made for some private families, and taught them the use of them.

Timber, Plains and Soil.—To the north of Chihuahua, about 30 miles to the right of the main road, there is some pine timber, and at a spring on this side of Carracal we saw one walnut-tree, and on all the small streams there are shrubby cotton-trees. With these few exceptions the whole province is a naked, barren plain, which presents to the eye an arid, unproductive soil, and more especially in the neighborhood of mines ; even the herbage appears to be poisoned by the mineral qualities of the soil.

Antiquities.—There are none in the province which came within my notice but the Jesuits' college and church at Chihuahua, which were about a century old, and are used as hospitals. In these there was nothing peculiar, except a certain solidity and strength, which appeared to surpass the other public buildings of the city.

Aborigines.—There are no uncivilized savages in this province except the Appaches, of whom I have spoken largely. (Vide Ap. to Part III. p. 10.) The Christian Indians are so incorporated amongst the lower grades of metifs that it is scarcely possible to draw the line of distinction, except at the ranelios of some nobleman or large landholder, where they are in a state of vassalage. This class of people laid a conspiracy, which was so well concerted as to baffle the inquiries of the Spaniards for a length of time, and to occasion them the loss of several hundred of the inhabitants. · The Indians used to go out from their villages in small parties : in a short time a part would return with the report that they had been attacked by the Indians ; the Spaniards would immediately send out a detachment in pursuit, when they were led into an ambuscade and every soul cut off. They pursued this course so long that the whole province became alarmed at the rapid manner in which their enemies multiplied ; but some circumstances leading to a suspicion, they made use of the superstition of those people for their ruin. Some officers disguised themselves like friars and went round amongst the Indians, pretending to be possessed of the spirit of prophecy. They preached up to the Indians that the day was approaching when a general deliverance from the Spanish tyranny was about to take place, and invited the Indians to join in concerting with them the work of God. The poor creatures came forward, and in their confessions stated the great hand that had already been put to the work. After these pretended friars had ascertained the nature and extent of the conspiracy, and had a body of troops prepared, they commenced the execution and put to death about 400 of the unsuspecting Indians. This struck terror and dismay through the Indian villages, and they dared not rise and declare their freedom and independence.

Government and Laws.—In this province there is some shadow of civil law ; but it is *merely a shadow,* as the following anecdote may illustrate. An officer, on arriving at a village, demanded quarters for himself and troops. The supreme civil officer of the place sent him word that he must show his passport. The military officer immediately sent a file of men, who brought the judge a prisoner before him, when he severely reprimanded the judge for his insolence and obliged him to obey his orders instantly. This has been done by a subaltern, in a city of 20,000 inhabitants. The only laws which can be said to be in force are the military and ecclesiastic, between which there is a perfect understanding.

The governor is a brigadier-general, resides at Durango, and receives 5000 dollars, in addition to his pay in the line. It is proper to observe that there are ordinances to bear on each subject of civil discussion, but the administration of them is so corrupt, that the influence of family and fortune generally procure the determination that they have *right* on their side.

In each town is a public magazine for provisions, where every farmer brings whatever grain and produce he may have for sale, where he is sure to meet with a market ; and should there be a scarcity the ensuing year, it is retailed out to the inhabitants at a reasonable rate. To this place all the citizens of the town repair to purchase.

Morals, Manners, &c.—There is nothing peculiar in the manners or morals of the people of this province, but a much greater degree of luxury among the rich, misery among the poor, and a corruption of morals more general than in New Mexico. As to military spirit they have none. At a muster of a regiment of militia at Chihuahua one of my men attended, and informed me that there were about 25 who had fire-arms and lances, 50 with bows and arrows and lances, and the balance with lances or bows and arrows only.

Military Force.—The regular military force of Biscay consists of 1100 dragoons, distributed as follows: On the frontiers of the deserts of New Mexico and Senora, at the forts of Elisiaira, Carracal, and San Buenaventura, Presidio del Norte, Janos, Tulenos, and San Juan Baptist. Farther south are Chihuahua, Jeronime, Cayone, San Paubla, Guaxequillo, and Conchos, with several other places which are appendages of those positions. The complement of each of those posts is 150 men, but may be averaged at 1100 in all, say 100 at each post. The militia are not worthy of particular notice.

Regilion.—Biscay is in the diocese of Durango, the bishop's salary being estimated at 100,000 dollars per annum. The catholic religion is here in its full force, but the inferior clergy are very much dissatisfied. The people's superstition is so great that they are running after the holy father in the streets, and endeavoring to kiss the hem of his garment, and should the bishop be passing the street, the rich and poor all kneel.

History.—I shall not presume to say any thing on this subject except that I believe this province has been populated about 270 years.

Geography.—Senora lies between the 33° and 27° N. latitude and 110° and 117° W. longitude. Its greatest length from north to south is about 420 miles, and its width from east to west 380 miles. It is bounded north by New Mexico, west by California, south by Sinaloa and the gulf, east by Biscay and New Mexico.

Air and Climate.—Dry, pure, and healthy generally, but near the gulf the ground is marshy, and it is, in some of the districts, unhealthy.

Mines, Minerals, and Fossils.—On this subject I can only speak in general. Senora abounds in rich gold and silver mines, but more especially the former, inasmuch as the gold does not preserve its usual exchange with silver in this province. General Salcedo told me that in this province the largest piece of pure gold had been found ever yet discovered in New Spain, and that it had been sent to the king to be put in his cabinet of curiosities, &c.

Rivers.—Rio de l'Ascencion is a short river which enters the gulf of California about the 31° N. latitude.

Rio Yaqui heads on the borders of Biscay and Senora and discharges itself into the gulf of California at Guyamas at the 28° N. latitude.

Timber, Plains, and Soil.—This province is, like Biscay, destitute of timber, but has some rich soil near the gulf.

Animals.—There are deer, cabrie, and bear; there are also remarkably large lizards, which are said to weigh ten pounds, and are perfectly harmless, tamed by the inhabitants and trained to catch mice.

Population and Chief Towns.—The population of Senora may be estimated at 200,000 souls, of which three-twentieths probably are Spaniards, four-twentieths Creoles, six-twentieths Metifs, and seven-twentieths Indians.

Arispea, the capital of Senora, and until 20 years past the seat of government of the internal provinces, is situated in 31° N. latitude and 111° W. longitude, near the head of the river Yaqui. It is celebrated throughout the kingdom for the urbanity and hospitality of its inhabitants and the vast quantity of gold table utensils made use of in their houses. Its population is 3,400 souls.

Sonora and Terenate are the next cities in magnitude in the province, the latter to the north and the former to the south of the capital.

Trade and Commerce.—Senora trades with New Mexico and Biscay for the productions of those different provinces, and with Old Mexico both by land and sea, through the gulf of California. It is celebrated for its cheese, horses, and sheep.

Agriculture.—They cultivate the same as in Biscay.

Aborigines.—There are a number of savage nations bordering on Senora, which oblige the king to keep up a number of military posts on the north and western frontiers; but the names of the tribes, or any of their distinguished characters, I am unacquainted with; however, it may not be improper to observe that they are armed with bows, arrows, shield and lance, like their savage neighbors. The civilized Indians are in the same situations as in the other provinces.

Government and Laws.—Similar to Biscay, the governor being a brigadier-general and receives 7000 dollars, in addition to his pay in the line.

Morals and Manners.—In every respect similar to Biscay, except that they are more celebrated for hospitality.

Military Force.—The regular military force of this province is 900 dragoons and 200 infantry, stationed as follows: Tubson, San Cruz, Tubac, and Altac on the north, with 100 dragoons each for a garrison; Fiuntenas, Bacuachi, Bavista, and Horcasites in the centre, with 300 dragoons and 200 infantry; Buenavista on the south, with 100 dragoons as a garrison. The infantry mentioned above are of a nation of Indians called the Opejas, and are said to be the best soldiers in New Spain. I saw a detachment of them at Chihuahua who appeared to be fine, stout, athletic men, and were the most subordinate and faithful troops I ever knew, acting like a band of brothers and having the greatest attachment for their officers.

Religion.—Catholic in the diocese of the bishop of Durango.

History—I am unacquainted with, except that the seat of government of the internal provinces was formerly at Arispea, at which time the government of California was also under the commandant-generalcy of the internal provinces; but the removal of the seat of government to Chihuahua and the disjunct situation of California induced his majesty to annex it to the government of the vice-royalty. The increasing magnitude of the relations of New Spain with the United States also gave an importance to the eastern interests which induced the continuance of the seat of government at Chihuahua.

Geography.—SINALOA lies between the 23° and 28° N. latitude and 108° and 111° W. longitude and is bounded north by Senora and Biscay, east by the latter, south by the administration of Guadalaxara, and west by the gulf of California, and in its greatest length is 300 miles, north and south, and in width from east to west 150 miles.

Air and Climate.—On the sea coast humid, but back dry and pure.

Mines, Minerals, and Fossils.—There are both gold and silver mines; but as to their relative value or productions, I am unacquainted.

Rivers.—Rio Fuerte takes its source in 27° N. latitude and 110° W. longitude and disembogues itself into the gulf of California. It crosses the whole province and is nearly 150 miles long.

Rio Culican is not more than 50 miles in length and enters the gulf of California in 25° N. latitude.

Timber, Plains, and Soil.—No timber; soil similar to Senora.

Animal·.—Domestic only.

Population and Chief Towns.—Its population may be estimated at 60,000, not more than three-twentieths of whom are Spaniards; the remainder Creoles, Metifs, and Indians.

Sinaloa is the capital, but its population, extent, &c. to me is unknown.

Trade and Commerce—Unacquainted with.

Agriculture.—The same as Senora.

Aborigines.—None who are not civilized.

Government and Laws—Unacquainted with.

Military Force.—One hundred dragoons for expresses and a guard for the governor.

Religion.—Catholic in the diocese of the bishop of Durango.

History.—To me unknown.

Geography.—The province of COGQUILLA lies between the 31° and 33° 30′ N. latitude and 101° and 105° W. longitude, and its greatest length north and south may be 500 miles, and in its greatest width east and west 200 miles. It is bounded north by New Mexico and Texas, east by the latter, San Ander, and New Leon, south by the administration of Zacataca, and west by Biscay.

Air and Climate.—Pure and healthy, except about the middle of May, when the heat is intense, and sometimes a scorching wind is felt, like the flame issuing from an oven or furnace, which frequently skins the face and affects the eyes. This phenomenon is felt more sensibly about the setting of the sun than at any other period of the twenty-four hours.

Mines, Minerals, and Fossils.—I know of no mines in this province, except at Montelovez and San Rosa, with the value of which I am unacquainted; but those of San Rosa are reputed to be as rich as any silver mines in the kingdom. Montelovez has none very considerable.

Rivers.—This province has no river of magnitude or consequence but the Rio Grande, which crosses its northern part in a south-east direction.

Lakes.—There is a small lake, called the Aqua Verde, situated on its western extremities, which gives rise to a small stream that discharges itself into the Rio del Norte.

Timber, Plains, and Soil.—From the river Nassus to the east there is the palmetto, which grows to the height of 20 and 25 feet, with a trunk of two feet diameter. Its leaves are in the shape of a spear, and cover all the trunk when young, but fall off as the tree grows old. Its wood is of a spongy nature, and from every information I could procure, is of the same species as that of the same name in the southern states. One hundred miles to the east of the Rio Grande, oak timber commenced, being the first we had seen in the provinces; but it was very small and scrubby, and presented, from this to the line of Texas (the river Mariana), a very perceptible gradation of the increase of timber, both in quantity, luxuriance, and variety. The country now became very similar to the Indiana territory.

Animals.—Deer, wild horses, a few buffalo and wild hogs.

Population and Chief Towns.—Montelovez is the capital of Cogquilla. It is situated on a small stream of water in 26° 30' N. latitude and 103° 30' W. longitude. It is about one mile in length, on a course N. 70° E. by the main street. It has two public squares, seven churches, a powder magazine, mills, king's hospital, and quartel del tropa. This is the principal military depot for the provinces of Cogquilla and Texas. Its population may be estimated at 3,500 souls. This city being the stated residence of his excellency governor Cordero, he has ornamented it with public walks, columns, and fountains, and made it one of the handsomest cities in the internal provinces.

Santa Rosa is about 38 miles to the north-west of Montelovez, is represented to be the most healthy situation in the province, and to have the best water and fruit. It is on the head waters of the river Millada. Its population is represented at 4,000 souls. Paras is situated on a small stream; with its suburbs it is supposed to contain 7000 souls, and San Lorenzo, three miles to the north, five hundred souls. This place may be termed the vineyard of Cogquilla, the whole population pursuing no other occupation than the cultivation of the grape. Its name denotes the *Branches of the Vine*. At the Hacienda of San Lorenzo, where we halted, there were fifteen larger stills, large cellars, and a greater number of casks than I ever saw in any brewery of the United States. Its gardens were delightfully interspersed with figs, vines, apricots, and a variety of fruits which are produced in the torrid zone; fine summer-houses, where were wine, refreshments, and couches to repose on and where the singing of the birds was delightful.

There were, likewise, mills and a fine water-fall. The presidio of Rio Grande is situated on that river, and is remarkable for nothing but three or four handsome missions with which it is surrounded, a powder magazine, quarters for the troops, and a few iron field-pieces on miserable truck carriages. Population 2,500 souls.

The population of this province may be estimated at 70,000 souls, not more than 10,000 of whom are Spaniards.

Trade, Commerce, and Manufactures.—This province receives all its merchandise from Mexico by land, and in return gives horses, mules, vines, gold, and silver. There is an annual fair held at Saltelo, in New Leon, where there is an immense quantity of merchandise disposed of, and where merchants of very large capitals reside.

Agriculture.—They cultivate the vine principally with grain and corn sufficient for their own consumption, and to supply the greatest part of Texas.

Aborigines.—The Appaches cover their north-west frontier. The Lee Pawnees are a nation who rove from the Rio Grande to some distance into the province of Texas. Their former residence was on the Rio Grande, near the sea shore. They are at present divided into three bands, of 300, 350, and 100 men each. They are at war with the Tetaus and Appaches, and at peace with the Spaniards. They have fair hair, and are generally handsome, armed with bows, arrows, and lances. They pursue the wild horses, of which they take numbers, and sell them to the Spaniards.

Government and Laws.—Military and ecclesiastical power is all that is known or acknowledged in this province ; but its administration was mild under their excellent governor Cordero. The governor's civil salary is 4000 dollars per annum.

Morals and Manners.—It was evident, to the least discerning eye, that as we diverged from these parts which produced such vast quantities of the precious metals, the inhabitants became more industrious and there were fewer beggars. Thus the morals of the people of Cogquilla were less corrupt than those of Biscay or New Leon, their neighbors.

Military Force.—There are 400 dragoons maintained in this province, and stationed at Montelovez, San Rosa, Pres. Rio del Norte, San Fernandez.

Religion.—Catholic, but mild. It is in the diocese of Durango.

History.—Cogquilla had not pushed its population as far as the Rio Grande in the year 1687, as at that time La Salle established himself at the entrance of that river, it being a wilderness ; but Montelovez was established some time before this era. Of its particular history I have no knowledge.

Geography.—The province of TEXAS lies between 27° 30′ and 35° N. latitude and 98° and 104° W. longitude, bordered north by Louisiana, east by the territory of Orleans, west by Cogquilla and New Mexico, and south by New San Ander. Its greatest length from north to south may be 500 miles, and breadth from east to west 350.

Air and Climate.—One of the most delightful temperatures in the world, but, being a country covered with timber, the new emigrants are generally sickly, which may justly be attributed to putrescent vegetation, which brings on intermittent and bilious attacks, and, in some instances, malignant fevers. The justice of these remarks are proved by the observations of all the first settlers of our western frontiers, that places which, in the course of ten or fifteen years, become perfectly healthy, were, the first two or three years, quite the reverse, and generally cost them the loss of two or three members of their families.

Mines, Minerals, and Fossils.—The only one known and worked is a mine of lead.

Rivers.—The river St. Antonio takes its source about one league to the north-east of the capital of the province (St. Antonio) and is navigable for canoes to its source, affording excellent fish, fine mill seats, and water to every part of the town. It is joined by the river Mariana from the west, which forms part of the line between Cogquilla and Texas, and then discharges itself into the Rio Guadelupe about 50 miles from the sea. At the town of St. Antonio it is about twenty yards wide, and, in some places, twelve feet in depth. The river Guadelupe takes its source about 150 miles to the north-west of St. Antonio, where we crossed it : it was a beautiful stream, of at least sixty yards in width. Its waters are transparent and navigable for canoes. After receiving the waters of the St. Antonio and St. Marco it discharges itself into the south-west end of the bay of St. Bernardo. At the crossing of this river there is a range for the horses of St. Antonio and a " guarde de caballo," with an elegant site for a town.

The river St. Marco takes its source about 100 miles north, twenty west of St. Antonio, and at the crossing of the road is thirty yards in width; a clear and navigable stream for canoes. By the road this river is only fourteen miles from the Guadelupe, into which it discharges itself.

The Red river takes its source in the province of Cogquilla in 33° N. latitude and 104° 30′ W. longitude, but bending to the east, enters the province of Texas, and, after a winding course of about 600 miles, disembogues itself into the bay of St. Bernard, in the 29° N. latitude. Where the road traverses it was at least 150 yards wide, and has a guard of dragoons stationed on its banks. Its waters are of a reddish cast, from whence it probably derived its name. This stream is navigable for boats of three or four tons burden.

The river Brassos takes its source in the province of Cogquilla in 34° N. latitude and 105° W. longitude, enters the province of Texas, and discharges itself into the gulf of Mexico in 28° 40', after a course of 750 miles. It is the largest river in the province, and, where the road crosses, is 300 yards wide and navigable for large keels. From the appearance on its banks it must rise and fall 100 feet. Its waters were red and turbid, its banks well timbered, and a rich prolific soil. Here was kept the only boat I recollect to have seen in the provinces.

The river Trinity takes its source in 34° N. latitude and 99° W. longitude, and discharges itself into Galueston's bay in 29° 30' N. latitude. By its meanders it is about 300 miles in length. Where the road crosses it is about 60 yards in width, with high, steep banks covered with timber and a rich luxuriant soil.

The rivers Nachez and Angelina are small rivers, of about 20 yards in width, and after forming a junction, discharge themselves into the Trinity.

The river Toyac is a small stream, which discharges itself into the gulf of Mexico, at the same bay with the Sabine, in about 29° 50' N. latitude and 97° W. longitude.

The Sabine river, the *present* limits between the Spanish dominions and the territories of the United States in that quarter, takes its source in about the 33° N. latitude, and enters the gulf of Mexico in 29° 50'. It may be 300 miles in length by its meanders, and at the road about 50 yards in width. Here the Spaniards keep a guard and ferry boat.

Lakes.—Some small ones near the head of the Guadelupe and some branches of Red river.

Timber, Plains, and Soil.—This province is well timbered for 100 miles from the coast, but has some small prairies interspersed through its timbered land; but take it generally, it is one of the richest and most prolific and best watered countries in North America.

Animals.—Buffalo, deer, elk, wild hogs, and wild horses, the latter of which are in such numbers as to afford supplies for all the savages who border on the province, the Spaniards, and vast droves for the other provinces. They are also sent into the United States, notwithstanding the trade is contraband.

They go in such large gangs that it is requisite to keep an advanced guard of horsemen, in order to frighten them away; for should they be suffered to come near your horses and mules which you drive with you, by their snorting, neighing, &c. they would alarm them, and frequently the domestic animals would join them and go off, notwithstanding all the exertions of the dragoons to prevent them. A gentleman told me he saw 700 beasts carried off at one time, not one of which was ever recovered. They also in the night frequently carry off the droves of travellers' horses, and even come within a few miles of St. Antonio, and take off the horses in the vicinity.

The method pursued by the Spaniards in taking them is as follows: They take a few fleet horses and proceed into the country where the wild horses are numerous. They then build a large strong enclosure, with a door which enters a smaller enclosure: from the entrance of the large pen they project wings out into the prairie a great distance, and then set up bushes, &c. to induce the horses, when pursued, to enter into these wings. After these preparations are made they keep a look out for a small drove, for, if they unfortunately should start too large a one, they either burst open the pen or fill it up with dead bodies, and the others run over them and escape; in which case the party are obliged to leave the place, as the stench arising from the putrid carcases would be insupportable; and, in addition to this, the pen would not receive others. Should they, however, succeed in driving in a few, say two or three hundred, they select the handsomest and youngest, noose them, and take them into the small enclosure, then turn out the remainder, after which, by starving, preventing them taking any repose, and continually keeping them in motion, they make them gentle by degrees, and finally break them to submit to the saddle and bridle. For this business I presume there is no nation in the world superior to the Spaniards of Texas.

Population and Chief Towns.—St. Antonio, the capital of the province, lies in 29° 50′ N. latitude and 101° W. longitude, and is situated on the head waters of the river of that name and, perhaps, contains 2,000 souls, the most of whom reside in miserable mud-wall houses, covered with thatched grass roofs. The town is laid out on a very grand plan. To the east of it, on the other side of the river, is the station of the troops.

About two, three, and four miles from St. Antonio are three missions, formerly flourishing and prosperous. Those buildings for solidity, accommodation, and even majesty, were surpassed by few that I saw in New Spain. The resident priest treated us with the greatest hospitality, and was respected and beloved by all who knew him. He made a singular observation relative to the aborigines, who had formerly formed the population of those establishments under charge of the monks. I asked him " What had become of the natives?" He replied "That it appeared to him that they could not exist under the shadow of the whites, as the nations who formed those missions had been nurtured and taken all the care of that it was possible, and put on the same footing as the Spaniards, yet, notwithstanding, they had dwindled away until the other two missions had become entirely depopulated, and the one where he resided had not then more than sufficient to perform his household labor; from this he had formed an idea that God never intended them to form one people, but that they should always remain distinct and separate."

Nacogdoches is merely a station for troops, and contains nearly 500 souls. It is situated on a small stream of the river Toyac.

The population of Texas may be estimated at 7000. These are principally Spanish, Creoles, some French, some Americans, and a few civilized Indians and half breeds.

Trade and Commerce.—This province trades with Mexico by Mont El Rey and Montelovez, for merchandise, and with New Orleans by Nachitoches; but the latter, being contraband, is liable to great damage and risks. They give, in return, specie, horses, and mules.

Agriculture.—The American emigrants are introducing some little spirit of agriculture near to Nacogdoches and the Trinity; but the oppressions and suspicions they labour under, prevents their proceeding with that spirit which is necessary to give success to the establishment of a new country.

Aborigines.—The Tancards are a nation of Indians who rove on the banks of Red river, and are 600 men strong. They follow the buffalo and wild horses, and carry on a trade with the Spaniards. They are armed with the bow, arrow, and lance. They are erratic and confined to no particular district: are a tall, handsome people, in conversation have a peculiar clucking, and express more by signs than any savages I ever visited: and in fact, language appears to have made less progress. They complained much of their situation and the treatment of the Spaniards; are extremely poor, and, except the Appaches, were the most independent Indians we encountered in the Spanish territories. They possess large droves of horses.

There are a number of other nations now nearly extinct, some of which are mentioned by Dr. Sibley, in a report he made to the

government of the United States on these subjects. A few, and
very few indeed, of those nations have been converted by the missions, and these are not in that state of vassalage in which the Indians
further to the south are held.

Government and Laws.—Perfectly military, except as to the
ecclesiastical jurisdiction.

Morals and Manners.—They being on the frontier, where buffalo and wild horses abound, and not engaged in any war with savages who are powerful, have adopted a mode of living by following
those animals, which has been productive of a more wandering disposition round the capital (St. Antonio) than in any other of the provinces. Cordero, by restricting (by edicts) the buffalo hunts to certain seasons, and obliging every man of family to cultivate so many
acres of land, has in some degree checked the spirit of hunting or
wandering life, which had been hitherto so very prevalent, and has
endeavored to introduce, by his example and precepts, a general urbanity and suavity of manners, which rendered St. Antonio one of the most agreeable places that we met with in the provinces.

Military Force.—There was in Texas at the time I came
through 988 men, from the actual returns of the troops which I
have seen, five hundred men of whom were from St. Ander and
New Leon, under the command of governor Herrara. The disposition of those troops are as follows : 388 at St. Antonio, 400 at the
cantonment of ————, on the Trinity, 100 at the Trinity, and
100 at Nacogdoches. The militia (a rabble) are made somewhat
respectable by a few American riflemen who are incorporated
amongst them and are about 300 men, including bow and arrow
men.

Religion.—Catholic, but much relaxed.

History.—To me unknown, except what can be extracted from
various authors on that subject.

General Remarks on New Spain.—To become acquainted with
all the civil and political institutes of a country, it requires a perfect
knowledge of the language, a free ingress to the archives, and a residence of some years : even then we can scarcely distinguish between the statute laws and common law, derived from custom, morals, and habits. Under those circumstances it cannot be expected
that I shall be able to say much on the subject, as I possessed none
of the above advantages. I will, however, offer a few observations.
To a stranger it is impossible to define the limits of the military
and ecclesiastical jurisdictions, in every affair which relates to the

citizens, and in fact with the soldiery, the force of superstition is such that I am doubtful whether they would generally obey one of their officers in a direct violation of the injunction of their religious professions. The audiences of Mexico and Guadalaxara were formed, no doubt, as a check on the immense power of the viceroy. The number of members composing each is to me unknown, but they are formed of the viceroy, as president, with two votes, generals, and bishops. To their jurisdictions the appeals from the judgment of the intendants and all subordinate officers may be made in civil cases ; but the military and ecclesiastical decisions are distinct : yet notwithstanding all this semblance of justice, should an individual dare to make the appeal and not succeed in establishing the justice of his claim to redress, he is certainly ruined. Where justice is so little attended to, when opposed to power and wealth, as in the Spanish provinces, the appeal is a desperate remedy. This tribunal or legislative body enacts all the laws for the general regulations of their divisions of the kingdom.

The captain generalcy of the internal provinces appeared to me to be much more despotic, for the laws or regulations were issued in the form of an order merely, without any kind of a preamble whatsoever, except sometimes he would say, " By order of the king ;" and such was the style of governors of provinces.

Morals, Manners, &c.—For hospitality, generosity, and sobriety the people of New Spain exceed any nation perhaps on the globe ; but in national energy, patriotism, enterprise of character, or independence of soul, they are perhaps the most deficient : yet there are men who have displayed bravery to a surprising degree, and the Europeans who are there cherish with delight the idea of their gallant ancestry.

Their women have black eyes and hair, fine teeth, and are generally brunettes. I met but one exception to this rule at Chihuahua of a fair lady, and she, by way of distinction, was called " the girl with light hair." They are all inclining a little to enbonpoint ; but none (or few) are elegant figures. Their dress generally is short jackets and petticoats and high heeled shoes, without any head dress. Over the whole dress they have a silk wrapper, which they always wear, and, when in the presence of men, affect to bring it over their faces, but from under which you frequently see peeping a large sparkling black eye. As we approached the Atlantic and our frontiers, we saw several ladies who wore the gowns of our countrywomen, which they conceived to be much more elegant than their ancient costume. The lower class of the men are generally dressed in broad brimmed hats, short coats, large waistcoats, and small clothes always open at the knees (owing, as I supose, to the greater freedom it gives to the limbs on horseback), a kind of leather boot or wrapper, bound round the leg (somewhat in the manner of our frontier-men's leggings), and gartered on. The boot is of a soft, pliable leather, but not colored. In the eastern provinces the dragoons wear, over this wrapper or boot, a sort of jack-boot made of sole-leather, to which are fastened the spurs, by a rivet, the gaffs of which are sometimes near an inch in length ; but the spurs of the gentlemen and officers, although clumsy to our ideas, are frequently ornamented with raised silver work on the shoulders, and the strap embroidered with silver and gold thread. They are always ready to mount their horses, on which the inhabitants of the internal provinces spend nearly half the day. This description will apply generally to the dress of all the men of the provinces for the lower class ; but in their cities, amongt the more fashionable, they dress after the European or United States modes, with not more variation than we see in our cities from one six months to another.

Both men and women have remarkably fine hair, and pride themselves in the display of it. Their amusements are music, singing, dancing, and gambling. The latter is strictly prohibited, but the prohibition is not much attended to. The dance of ———— is danced by one man and two women, who beat time to the music, which is soft and voluptuous, but sometimes changing to a lively, gay air. The dancers exhibit the motions of the soul, by gestures of the body, snapping the fingers, and sometimes meeting in a *stretched embrace*. The fandango is danced to various figures and numbers.

The minuet is still danced by the superior class only. The music made use of is the guitar, violin, and singers, who, in the first described dance, accompany the music with their hands and voices, having always some words adapted to the music.

Their games are cards, billiards, horse racing, and cock fighting, the first and last of which are carried to the most extravagant lengths, losing and winning immense sums. The present commandant general is very severe with his officers in these respects, frequently sending them to some frontier post, in confinement for months, for no other fault than having lost large sums at play. At every town of consequence is a public walk, where the ladies and gentlemen meet and sing songs, which are always on the subject of love or the social board. The females have fine voices, and sing in French, Italian, and Spanish, the whole company joining in the chorus.

In their houses the ladies play the guitar, and generally accompany it with their voices. They either sit down on the carpet cross legged, or loll on a sofa. To sit upright in a chair appeared to put them to great inconvenience, and, although the better class would sometimes do it on our first introduction, they soon took the liberty of following their old habits. In their eating and drinking they are remarkably temperate. Early in the morning you receive a dish of chocolate and a cake, at twelve you dine on several dishes of meat, fowls, and fish, after which you have a variety of confections, and, indeed, an elegant desert; then drink a few glasses of wine, sing a few songs, and retire to take the *siesta*, or afternoon's nap, which is taken by rich and poor. About two o'clock the windows and doors are all closed, the streets deserted, and the stillness of midnight reigns throughout. About four o'clock they rise, wash and dress, and prepare for the dissipation of the night. About eleven o'clock some refreshments are offered, but few take any, except a little wine and water and candied sugar.

The government has multiplied the difficulties of Europeans intermarrying with the Creoles or Metifs to such a degree that it is difficult for such a marriage to take place. An officer, wishing to marry a lady (not from Europe) is obliged to acquire certificates of the purity of her descent 200 years back, and transmit it to the court, when the licence will be returned; but should she be the daughter of a man of the rank of captain, or upwards, this nicety vanishes, as rank purifies the blood of the descendants.

The general subjects of conversation among the men are women, money, and horses, which appear to be the only objects, in their estimation, worthy of consideration, uniting the female sex with their money and their beasts, and, from having treated them too much after the manner of the latter, they have eradicated from their breasts every sentiment of virtue or ambition, either to pursue the acquirements which would make them amiable companions, instructive mothers, or respectable members of society. Their whole souls, with a few exceptions, like the Turkish ladies, being taken up in music, dress, and the little blandishments of voluptuous dissipation. Finding that the men only regard them as objects of gratification to the sensual passions, they have lost every idea of that feast of reason and flow of soul, which arise from the intercourse of two refined and virtuous minds.

The beggars of the city of Mexico are estimated at 60,000 souls: what must be the number through the whole kingdom? and what reason can it be owing to that, in a country superior to any in the world for riches in gold and silver, producing all the necessaries of life and most of its luxuries, that there should be such vast proportion of the inhabitants in want of bread or clothing. It can only be accounted for by the tyranny of the government and the luxuries of the rich. The government striving, by all the restrictions possible to be invented, without absolutely driving the people to desperation to keep Spanish America dependent on Europe.

Trade, Commerce, Manufactures, and Revenue.—The trade and commerce of New Spain is carried on with Europe and the United States by the port of Vera Cruz solely, and the East Indies and South America generally by Acapulco, and, even at these ports, under such restriction, as to productions, manufactures, and time, as to render it of little consequence to the general prosperity of the country. Were all the numerous bays and harbors of the gulfs of Mexico and California opened to the trade of the world, and a general licence given to the cultivation of all the productions which the country is capable of, with freedom of exportation and importation, with proper duties on foreign goods, the country would immediately become rich and powerful, a proper stimulus would be held out to the poor to labor, when certain of finding a quick and ready sale for the productions of their plantations or manufactories. The country abounds in iron ore, yet all the iron and steel, and articles of manufactures, are obliged to be brought from Europe, the manufacturing or working of iron being strictly prohibited : this occasions the necessary articles of husbandry, arms, and tools to be enormously high and is a great check to agriculture, improvements in manufactures, and military skill. The works of the Mexicans, in gold, silver, and painting, shew them naturally to have a genius which, with cultivation and improvement, might rival the greatest masters of either ancient or modern times. Their dispositions and habits are peculiarly calculated for sedentary employments, and I have no doubt, if proper establishments were made, they would soon rival, if not surpass, the most extensive woollen, cotton, or silk manufactures of Europe, their climate being proper to raise the finest cotton in the world and their sheep possessing all the fineness of wool for which they are so celebrated in Spain. These circumstances, together with the immense quantities of the raw materials which they have on hand, wool selling for a mere trifle, and in fact, they scarcely take the half from the fleece of the sheep, for the coarse manufactures of the country and to make beds.

I cannot presume to state the revenues of the country from official documents, but the following statements I have had from so respectable a source, and they are so confirmed by my own observations, that I think much reliance may be placed on their correctness. The mint coins, per annum, at least 50,000,000 dollars in silver and 14,000,000 dollars in gold, the one-fifth of which (the duty) is equal to 12,800,000. The duties on foreign goods and the amount paid by the purchasers of monopolies, may be estimated at 4,000,000 dollars, which, with the duty on gold and silver, makes the annual revenue 16,800,000. The civil list of the kingdom is 580,000, the military 7,189,200 : these together amount to 7,760,200, which deducted from the gross revenue of 16,700,000, leaves a clear revenue for the king (from his Mexican dominions) of 9,030,800. The money paid for the support of the clergy is not included in this estimate, as they receive their revenue through its own proper channel. The best paid officers under the government cost the king nothing in a direct line, yet the oppressive manner in which they pay themselves and impoverish the people, would render it better policy to abolish their impositions and pay them out of the public treasury by a direct salary.

RETURN OF MILITARY FORCE IN NEW SPAIN.

Provinces and places.	Disciplined and regular European troops.			Regular troops of the country.			Militia with regular field offic. and under pay.			Probable Armed citizens.	
	Cavalry.	Artillery.	Infantry.	Cavalry.	Artillery.	Infantry.	Cavalry.	Artillery.	Infantry.	Fire arms.	Bows, arrows, and lances
Xalapa Ina. Vera Cruz,	..	200	2000	2000	..	..	3000	..	1000	..	..
Vera Cruz and sea ports,	..	800	2000	..	..	..	600	..	2000	..	..
Mexico,	1000	..	..	..	..	1000	3400	1000	..	..	..
Different provinces and viceroyalty,	..	..	..	100	..	..	..	..	..	15000	8000
New Mexico,	..	..	..	1100	..	..	..	..	..	1000	4000
Biscay,	..	..	..	900	..	..	..	..	..	5000	8000
Senora,	..	..	..	100	..	200	..	..	..	5000	8000
Sinaloa,	..	..	..	400	..	..	..	..	..	3000	6000
Cogquilla,	..	..	..	488	..	..	..	..	..	1000	2000
Texas,	..	..	..	..	..	..	..	..	..	500	1000
Total	1000	1000	4000	5088	..	1200	7000	1000	3000	30500	109000

	Cavalry.	Artillery.	Infantry.
European	1000	1000	4000
Regular troops Mex.	5088	.	1200
Trained militia,	7000	1000	3000
Total	13088	2000	8200

Cavalry, 13088
Artillery, 2000
Infantry, 8200

Total 23288 disciplined and effective force.

30500 undisciplined militia.
109000 bow, arrow, and lance men.

162788 total force.

The European troops are some of the choicest regiments from Spain, consequently we may put them on the supposition that they are well disciplined, and officered by men of honor and science.

The regular troops of the kingdom who are in the vice royalty, acting from the stimulant of ambition and envy, are supposed to be equal to their brethren from Europe. The militia, with the regular officers, are likewise good troops, but are not held in so high estimation as the other corps. Those three corps, forming a body of 23,288 men, may be called the regular force of the kingdom, as the militia of 139,500 would, in my estimation, be of no more consequence against the regular troops of any civilized power than the ancient aborigines of the country were against the army of Cortes.

The particular observations which follow must be considered as applying to the troops of the internal provinces, unless it is stated to the contrary.

The appearance of the Spanish troops is certainly (at a distance) a la militaire ; their lances are fixed to the side of the saddle under the left thigh and slant about five feet above the horse. On the right the carabine is slung in a case to the front of the saddle (or pommel) crosswise, the breech to the right hand, and on each side of the saddle, behind the rider, is a pistol : below the breech of the carabine is slung the *shield* which is made of sole leather three doubled, sewed together with thongs with a band on the inside to slip the left arm through ; those of the privates are round, and are about two feet in diameter. The officers and non-commissioned officers have their shields oval, bending on both sides, in order to permit the arrow to glance, and they have in general the arms of Spain with Don Carlos IV. gilt on the outside, with various other devices, which add much to the elegance of their appearance on horseback, but are only calculated to be of service against savages who have no fire-arms. The dragoons of the vice royalty do not make use of the lance or shield, but are armed, equipped, and clothed after the modern manner, as also the dragoons of the eastern provinces. When they recently expected to be opposed to the American troops they were deprived of their lance and shield, and received the straight cutlass in their stead.

Their dress is a short blue coat, with red cape and cuffs, without facings, leather or blue cotton velvet small clothes and waistcoat, the small clothes always open at the knees, the wrapping boot with the jack boot, and permanent spur over it, a broad brimmed, high crowned wool hat, with a ribband round it of various colors, generally received as a present from some female, which they wear as a badge of the favor of the fair sex and a mark of their gallantry.

Their horses are small and slender limbed, but very active and are capable of enduring great fatigue. The equipments of the horses are, to our idea, awkward ; but I believe them superior to the English, and they have the advantage over us as to the skill of the rider, as well as in the quality of the beast. Their bridles have a strong curb, which gives so great a mechanical force to the bridle that I believe it almost practicable with it to break the jaw of the horse. The saddle is made after the Persian mode, with a high projecting pommel (or, as anciently termed, bow) and is likewise raised behind : this is merely the tree : it is then covered by two or three covers of carved leather and embroidered workmanship, some with gold and silver in a very superb manner. The stirrups are of wood closed in front, carved generally into the figure of a lion's head, or that of some other beast, are very heavy, and to us present a very clumsy appearance. The horseman, seated on his horse, has a small bag tied behind him, his blankets either under him, or laying with his cloak between his body and the bow, which makes him at his ease. Thus mounted it is impossible for the most vicious horse ever to dismount them. They will catch another horse with a noose and hair rope, when both are running nearly full speed, with which they will soon choak down the beast of which they are in pursuit : in short, they are probably the most expert horsemen in the world.

At each post is a store, called the king's, where it was the original intention of the government that the soldiers should be supplied with provisions, clothing, arms, &c. at a cheap rate ; but, it being a post generally given to some young officer to make his fortune, they are subject to great impositions. When a dragoon joins the service he receives from the king five horses and two mules, and this number he is always obliged to keep good from his own pocket ; but, when he is discharged, the horses and mules receive the discharged mark and become his private property. They engage for five or ten years, at the option of the soldier, but in the bounty there is a very material difference. It is extremely easy to keep up their corps, as a private dragoon considers himself upon an equality with most of the citizens, and infinitely superior to the lower class, and it is not unfrequently that you see men of considerable fortune marrying the daughters of sergeants and corporals.

The pay of the troops of New Spain varies with the locality, but may be averaged, in the internal provinces, as follows :

RANK.	Amount of pay per annum. *Dollars.*	REMARKS.
Colonel,	4,500	With this pay they find their own clothes, provisions, arms, accoutrements, &c. after the first equipments.
Lieutenant Colonel,	4,000	
Major,	3,000	
Captain,	2,400	
First Lieutenant,	1,500	
Second Lieutenant,	1,000	
Ensign,	800	
Sergeant,	350	
Corporal,	300	
Private,	288	

Corporal punishment is contrary to the Spanish ordinances. They punish by imprisonment, putting in the stocks, and death. As a remarkable instance of the discipline and regularity of conduct of those provincial troops, although marching with them and doing duty as it were for nearly four months, I never saw a man receive a blow or put under confinement for one hour. How impossible would it be to regulate the turbulent dispositions of the Americans with such treatment! In making the foregoing remark I do not include officers, for I saw more rigorous treatment exercised towards some of them, than ever was practised in our army.

The discipline of their troops is very different from ours: as to tactics or military manœuvres, they are not held in much estimation, for, during the whole of the time I was in the country, I never saw a corps of troops exercising as dragoons, but frequently marching by platoons, sections, &c. in garrison, where they serve as infantry, with their carabines. In these manœuvres they were very deficient. On a march a detachment of cavalry generally encamp in a circle. They relieve their guards at night, and as soon as they halt the new guard is formed on foot with their carabines, and then marched before the commandant's tent, where the commanding officer of the guard invokes the holy virgin three times : the commanding officer replies, "It is well." They then retire and mount their horses, and are told off, some to act as "guard of the horses," as cavalry, others as guard of the camp, as infantry. The old guards are then paraded and relieved, and the new sentinels take post. Their sentinels are singing half their time, and it is no uncommon thing for them to quit their post to come to the fire, go for water, &c. in fact, after the officer is in bed, frequently the whole guard comes in, yet I never knew any man punished for those breaches of military duty. Their mode of attack is by squadrons, on the different flanks of their enemies, but without regularity or concert, shouting, hallooing, and firing their carabines, after which, if they think themselves equal to the enemy, they charge with a pistol and then a lance. From my observation on their discipline I have no hesitation in declaring that I would not be afraid to march over a plain, with 500 infantry and a proportionate allowance of horse-artillery of the United States army, in the presence of 5000 of these dragoons ; yet I do not presume to say that an army with that inferiority of numbers would do to oppose them, for they would cut off your supplies, and harrass your march and camp, night and day, to such a degree as to oblige you in the end to surrender to them without ever having come to action. If, however, the event depended on one single engagement, it would eventuate with glory to the American arms. The conclusion must not be drawn that I consider they are deficient in physical firmness more than other nations, for we see the savages, 500 of whom on a plain fly before fifty bayonets, on other occasions brave danger and death in its most horrid shapes with an undaunted fortitude never surpassed by the most disciplined and hardy veterans. It arises solely from the want of discipline and confidence in each other, as is always the case with undisciplined corps, unless stimulated by the godlike sentiment of love of country, of which these poor fellows know little. The travelling food of the dragoons in New Mexico consists of a very excellent species of wheat biscuit and shaved meat, well dried, with a vast quantity of red pepper, of which they make bouilli and then pour it on their broken biscuit, when it becomes soft and excellent eating.

Farther south they use large quantities of parched corn-meal and sugar (as practised by our hunters) each dragoon having a small bag. In short, they live, when on command, on an allowance which our troops would conceive little better than starving, never, except at night, attempting to eat any thing like a meal, but bite a piece of biscuit, or drink some parched meal and sugar with water during the day.

From the physical, as well as moral properties of the inhabitants of New Spain, I do believe they are capable of being made the best troops in the world, possessing sobriety, enterprise, great physical force, docility, and a conception equally quick and penetrating.

The mode of promotion in the internal provinces is singular, but probably productive of good effects. Should a vacancy of first lieutenant offer in a company, the captain commanding nominates, with the senior second lieutenant (who by seniority would fill the vacancy) two other lieutenants to the general, giving his comments on all three. The general selects two for a nomination to the court, from whom is selected the fortunate candidate, whose commission is made out and forwarded ; and, as the letters of nomination are always kept a secret, it is impossible for the young officers to say who is to blame should they be disappointed, and the fortunate one is in a direct way to thank the king only for the ultimate decision, and thus with superior grades to the colonel.

The king of Spain's ordinances for the government of his army are generally founded on justice and a high sense of honor. I could not get a set from any of the officers to take it to my quarters, consequently my observations on them were extremely cursory. They provide that no old soldier shall ever be discharged the service, unless for infamous crimes. When a man has served with reputation for 15 years and continues, his pay is augmented ; 20 years, he receives another augmentation ; 27 years, he receives the brevet rank and pay of an ensign, and 32, a lieutenant, &c. Those circumstances are a great stimulant, although not one in a thousand arrive at the third period, when they are permitted to retire from the service with full pay and emoluments. All sons of captains, or of grades superior, are entitled to enter the king's schools as cadets, at the age of twelve years.

The property of any officer or soldier, who is killed on the field of battle or dies of his wounds, is not liable to be taken for debt, and is secured, as well as the king's pension, to the relatives of the deceased.

Courts martial, for the trial of a commissioned officer, must be formed of general officers; but this clause subjects the officers of the provinces to a great species of tyranny, for the commanding general has taken upon himself to punish for all offences not capital, consequently according to his own judgment and prejudices, from which there is only an appeal to the king, and difficult is it indeed for the complaints of a subaltern to reach his majesty through the numerous crowd of sycophants who surround him, one half of whom are probably in league with his oppressor: it likewise deprives an officer of the most sacred of all rights, the being tried by his peers; for, should he be sent to Mexico or Europe for trial, it is possible he cannot take half the testimony which is' necessary to complete his justification.

There is another principle defined by the ordinances, which has often been the cause of disputes in the service of the United States :—viz. The commandant of a post (in the Spanish service), if barely a captain, receives no orders from a general, should one arrive at his post, unless that general should be superior in authority to the person who posted him, for, says the ordinance, he is responsible to the king alone for his post. That principle, according to my ideas, is very injurious to any country which adopts it; for example, we will say that a post of great importance, containing immense military stores, is likely to fall into the hands of the enemy; an officer superior to the commandant receives the information, and repairs to the post and orders him immediately to evacuate it. The commandant, feeling himself only responsible to the authority who placed him in that position, refuses to obey, and the magazines and place are lost !!! The principle is also subversive of the very root of military subordination and discipline, where an inferior should *in all cases* obey a superior, who *only* should be responsible for the effect arising from the execution of his orders. It will readily be believed that, in my thus advocating *implicit* obedience to the orders of a superior, that I do not suppose the *highest improbabilities* or *impossibilities*, such as an order to turn your arms against the *constituted authority* of *your country*, or to be the ensign of his *tyranny* or the *pander* of his vices : those are cases where a man's reason must alone direct him, and are not, nor cannot be subject to any human rule whatever.

Religion.—Its forms is a subject with which I am very imperfectly acquainted, but having made some enquiries and observations on the religion of the country, I will freely communicate them,

fearful at the same time that I lay myself open to the severe criti-
cisms of persons who have, in any degree, applied themselves to the
study of theology or the ritual of the catholic church.

The kingdom of New Spain, is divided into four archbishop-
ricks, viz : Mexico, Guadalaxara, Durango, and St. Louis Potosi ;
under them again are the sub-bishopricks—Deacons, Curates, &c.
each of whom are subject and accountable to their immediate chief
for the districts committed to their charge, and the whole is again
subject to the ordinances of the high court of inquisition held at the
capital of Mexico ; from whence is fulminated the edicts of their
censure against the heresies, and impious doctrines of the modern philosophy, both as to politics and religion ; and I am credibly
informed, that the influence of that tribunal, is greater in his Catholic majesty's Mexican dominions, than in any Catholic country
in Europe, or perhaps in the world.   A few years since, they con-
demned a man to the flames, for asserting and maintaining some
doctrine which they deemed heretical ; and a Jew who was imprudent enough to take the image of Christ on the cross, and put it
under the sill of his door, saying privately he would " make the
dogs walk over their God."   They likewise examine and condemn
to the flames all books of a modern sentiment, either as to religion
or politics, and excommunicate any one in whose hands they may
be found.   I recollect to have seen a decree of theirs published in
the Mexican Gazettes, condemning a number of books, " as here-
" tical and contrary to the sacred principles of the holy Catholic
" church, and the peace and durability of the government of his
" Chatholic majesty."   Amongst which were mentioned " Helve-
tius" on man, J. J. Rousseau's works, Voltaire's, Mirabeau's and
a number of others of that description, and even at so great a distance as Chihuahua; an officer dared not take " Pope's Essay on
Man," to his quarters, but used to come to mine to read it.

The salaries of the arch-bishops are superior to any officers in
the kingdom.   The bishops of Mexico, being estimated at $150,000
per annum, when the vice roy's is $80,000, and $50,000 allowed
for his table, falling short of the bishop $20,000.

Those incomes are raised entirely from the people who pay
no tax to the king, but give one tenth of their yearly income to the
clergy ; besides the fees of confessions, bulls, burials, baptisms,
marriages, and a thousand impositions, which the corruptions of
priestscraft has introduced, and has been kept up by their superstition and ignorance.   Notwithstanding all this, the inferior clergy,
who do all the slavery of the office, are liberal and well informed

men ; and I scarcely saw one, who was not in favor of a change of government. They are generally creoles by birth, and always kept in subordinate grades, without the least shadow of a probability of rising to the superior dignities of the church, this has soured their minds to such a degree, that I am confident in asserting, that they will lead the van whenever the standard of independence is raised in that country.

Politics.—It has often been a subject of discussion with politicians, in what manner a mother country should treat her distant and powerful colonies, in order to retain them the longest in their subjection ; for the history of all nations and all ages, have proved that no community of people separated from another by an immense ocean, feeling their power, strength, and independence, will remain long subject to the mother country, purely from the ties of consanguinity and similarity of habits, manners, and religion. Society itself having arisen from the mutual wants, fears, and imbecility of the infancy of human institutions, a large body of that society will remain no longer subject to another branch at the immense distance of 1000 leagues, than until they feel their maturity, and capability of providing for their own wants and their own defence. Therefore we may draw a conclusion than no political course of conduct, whatever will eventually prevent the separation ; but there is a line of conduct which certainly must retard it in a great measure, and prudence would dictate to the mother country, the policy of giving way, without a struggle to an event, beyond her power to prevent.

The two great examples of English and Spanish America, are before our eyes. England gave us free liberty to pursue the dictates of our own judgment with respect to trade, education, and manners, by which means we increased in power, learning, and wealth, with a rapidity unknown in the annals of the world ; and at the first attempt to infringe the rights which we had hitherto enjoyed, asserted that claim which nature and the locality of our situation gave us a right to demand, and power to defend. Had Great Britain yielded to the storm with grace and dignity, she would have secured our gratitude, ancient prejudices and affections in her favor; on the contrary, by a long and arduous conflict, the murder of thousands of our citizens, the destruction of the country, the profanation of our altars, and the violation of every right, divine and human, she implanted in the breast of the Americans, an antipathy, approaching nearly to horror, a desire of revenge almost hereditary, and destroyed the bonds of brotherhood, which might have subsisted between the two countries, which will take ages of just conduct from her to the United States to eradicate. Spain pursued a different line of conduct towards her Mexican dominions, which were settled by Europeans sixty years previous to any part of the United States, and might be termed a conquered kingdom, rather than the settlement of a savage country. This country she has therefore bound up in all the ligatures of restrictions, monopolies, prohibitions, seclusions, and superstition; and has so carefully secluded all light from bursting in on their ignorance, that they have vegetated like the acorn in the forest, until the towering branches have broke through the darkness of the wild which surrounded them, and let in the light of heaven. The approximation of the United States, with the gigantic strides of French ambition, have began to rouse up their dormant qualities, and to call into action the powers of their minds, on the subject of their political situation.

An instance of their disposition for independence, has been exhibited in their feeble attempts at a revolution on the 15th January 1624, under the vice royalty of Don Diego Carrello Galves. The insurrection on the 8th of June 1692; and more recently in 1797, under the count de Galves, when they proclaimed him king of Mexico in the streets of the capital; and 130,000 souls were heard proclaiming, " Long live Galves, king of Mexico." It was then only for *him* to have *will'd it*, and the kingdom of Mexico was lost to Charles the 4th for ever. But prefering his loyalty to his ambition, he rode out attended by his guards to the mob, with sword in hand, crying out " Long live his Catholic majesty Charles the 4th," and threatening to put to instant death with his own hand, any person who refused immediately to retire to their houses. This dispersed the people. In another quarter of the kingdom, an immense number had also collected and proclaimed him king. He sent 10,000 men against them, dispersed them, and had four beheaded. Those firm measures saved the country at that period, and for which he received the greatest honors from the court of Spain; but was poisoned a short time after, fulfilling the maxim, " that it is dangerous to serve a jealous tyrant;" for they always conceive that the same power who still'd the ocean's rage, can by his will raise the storm into all the majesty of overwhelming fury. Thus by taking his life it relieved them from the dread of his influence with the Mexicans.

England would naturally have been the power they would have looked up to, in order to form an alliance to secure their independence; but the insatiable avarice and hauteur exhibited by the

English in their late descents at La Plate, with the disgrace of their arms, has turned their views from that nation.

They therefore have turned their eyes towards the United States, as brethren of the same soil, in their vicinity, and who has within her power ample resources of arms, ammunition, and even men to assist in securing their independence, and who in that event secures to herself the almost exclusive trade of the richest country in the world for centuries, and to be her carriers as long as the two nations exist ; for Mexico, like China, will never become a nation of mariners, but receive the ships of all the world into her ports, and give her bullion in exchange for the productions of their different countries,—when, what would not be the advantages the United States would reap from the event! Our numerous vessels would fill every port, and from our vicinity enable us to carry off at least nine-tenths of her commerce : even on the coast of the Pacific no European nation could vie with us :—also, there would be a brisk inland trade carried on with the S. P. via Red river, and having a free entrance into all their ports, we would become their factors, agents, guardians, and, in short, tutelar genius, as she fears, but hates France and all French men and measures. It therefore remains for the government of the United States to decide, whether, if Bonaparte should seize on the crown of Spain, they would hold out a helping hand, to emancipate another portion of the western hemisphere from the bonds of European tyranny and oppression, or by a different policy, suffer 6,000,000 of people to become, in the hands of French intrigue, enterprise and tactics, a scourge on our south-western boundaries, which would oblige us to keep a large and respectable military force, and continually lay us liable to a war on the weakest and most vulnerable part of our frontiers.

Twenty thousand auxiliaries from the United States, under good officers, joined to the *independents* of the country, are at any time sufficient to create and effect the revolution. These troops can be raised and officered in the United States, but paid and supplied at the expense of Mexico. It would be requisite that, not only the general commanding, but that every officer, down to the youngest ensign, should be impressed with the necessity of supporting a strict discipline, to prevent marauding, which should, in some instances, be punished with *death*, in order to evince to the citizens that you come as their friends and protectors, not as their plunderers and tyrants :—also, the most sacred regard should be paid not to injure the institutions of their religion ; thereby shewing them we had a proper respect to all things in any way connected with the worship of the Deity, at the same time we permitted every man to adore him agreeably to the dictates of his own judgment.

The details requisite for the equipment, organization, &c. of the corps, so as to be adapted to the locality of the country and the nature of the service, could be easily formed, but would be impertinent here.

Should an army of Americans ever march into the country, and be guided and governed by these maxims, they will only have to march from province to province in triumph, and be hailed by the united voices of grateful millions as their deliverers and saviours, whilst our national character would be resounded to the most distant nations of the earth.

Z. M. PIKE,
Capt. 1st U. S. regt. infantry.

Washington, 12*th April*, 1808.

EXPLANATORY TABLE

OF

NAMES OF PLACES, PERSONS, AND THINGS

MADE USE OF IN THIS VOLUME.

———————

ENGLISH.	FRENCH.	INDIAN.
NATURAL Meadow.	Prairie.	
Buffalo river.	Riviere au Bœuf.	
Salt river.	Riviere au Sel.	Oahahah.
River of Means.	Riviere de Moyen.	
Iówa river.	Riviere de Ayoua.	
Stony, or Rock river.	Riviere des Rochers.	
Turkey river.	Riviere au Dindon.	
Dog's meadow.	Prairie des Chiens.	
		Ouiscousing.
Raven river.	Riviere de Corbeau.	
Yellow river.	Riviere Jaune.	
Root river.	Riviere aux Racines.	
River of Embarrassments.	Riviere d'Embarras.	
Clear Water river.	Riviere l'Eau Clair.	
River of the Prairie of Cross.	Riviere de la Prairie de Crosse.	
Chipeway river.	Riviere Sauteaux.	Ouchipewa Sippi.
The Mountain which soaks in the Water.	La Montaigne qui trempe dans l'Eau.	
River of do.	Riviere de do.	
Sandy Point.	Point de Sable.	
The Barn.	La Grange.	
Cannon River.	Riviere au Canon.	
River St. Peters.	Riviere St. Pierre.	
Falls of St Anthony.	Shute de St. Antoine.	
Rum river.	Prairie l'Eau de Vie.	
Leaf river.	Riviere aux Feuilles.	
Sauk river.	Riviere aux Saukes.	
Big Falls.	Grand rapid.	
Lower Red Cedar lake.	Le Bas Lac du Cedre Rouge.	
Raven island.	Isle de Corbeau.	
Pine river.	Riviere au Pin.	
Leech lake.	Lac Sang Sue.	

ENGLISH.	FRENCH.	INDIAN.
Sandy lake.	Lac de Sable.	
Pike river.	Riviere du Brochet.	
Bottom of the lake.	Fond du Lac.	
Swan river.	Riviere a Cigue.	
Falls of Packegamaw.	Petite Shute.	Packegamaw.
Upper Red Cedar lake.	Le Haut Lac de Cedre Rouge.	
Red lake.	Lac Rouge.	
Green bay.	La Baye Verde.	
St. Ignatius.	St. Ignace.	
Oak Point.	Point au Chene.	
		Meno Cockien.
The Turn.	La Detour.	
Island of the Turn.	Isle du Detour.	
Burnt island.	Isle Brule.	
Potowatomies island.	Isle des Poux.	
Little Streight.	Petit Detroit.	
Port of the Dead.	Port des Morts.	
Vermillion island.	Isle Vermillon.	
Red river.	Riviere Rouge.	
Stinking rapid.	Puant Rapid.	
Wolf river.	Riviere des Loups.	
Hillock of the dead.	Butte des Morts.	
		Lac Puckway.
Muddy lake.	Lac Vaseux.	

Z. M. PIKE.

[No. 3.]

Chihuahua, 20th April, 1807.

MY DEAR GENERAL,

Never did I sit down to address you with a heart so oppressed with anxiety and mortification ; but knowing the uncertainty which must exist as to the fate of myself and party, I conceive it proper to attempt a communication, although I think it extremely uncertain, owing to the difficulty of the route, if it should ever come to hand, or at least, previous to my arrival at the territories of the United States, owing to various circumstances which are not to be communicated in a letter. I was detained in the mountains of Mexico until the month of January, and in February found myself with eight of my party *only*, on the head branches of the Rio del

Norte, which I then conceived to be the sources of the Red river, our information making the latter extend the whole distance between the former and the Arkansaw, although its sources are some hundred miles below either of the others.

Here I was encountered by two officers and 100 men, who bore orders from the governor of New Mexico, to cause me and my party to march to the capital of said province; but his request was in the most polite style, and in fact, the commanding officer assured me there was not the *least constraint*, but that his excellency desired a conference, and that I then should be conducted by the most direct route, to the navigable part of the Red river, from whence I could immediately descend to Nachitoches. Although dubious of the *faith* of the invitation, and in a situation from whence I could have defended myself as long as my provision lasted, or until I might probably have escaped in the night, yet knowing the pacific intentions of our government, and the particular instructions of my general, as to my conduct in case of a rencounter with a body of Spanish troops, I conceived it most proper to comply with the demand and repair to Santa Fe; and, as the balance of my party who remained in the mountains, were, many of them, invalids, and not in a situation to be able to return, I conceived it most proper to leave orders for them to follow, accompanied by an escort of Spanish troops left for that purpose.

On my arrival at Santa Fe, his excellency governor Allencaster informed me it was necessary that I should immediately march to Chihuahua, province of Biscay, in order to present myself to his excellency the commandant-general N. Salcedo, for further orders. This being so different from what I had been taught to expect, that I demanded of governor Allencaster, in a written communication, to know if I was to consider myself and party as prisoners of war? He replied in the negative. We marched on the following day, and arrived at this place on the 2d instant, from whence, I am informed by the general, I shall march, on the arrival of the remainder of my party, for Nachitoches.

I must here acknowledge myself and party under infinite obligations to the friendship and politeness of all the Spanish officers, and in a particular manner to the commandant-general of those provinces.

Should the politics of our country make it necessary to augment the army previous to my arrival, I hope the general will approve of my aspiring to a considerable promotion in the new corps. Should the line of demarcation be amicably adjusted between the

United States and Spain, I hope to obtain the appointment of one of the commissioners, as I make bold to assert that, with respect to the arrangements necessary, and a knowledge of the country through which the line must pass, I am better instructed than any other officer of my age in our service ; and, if joined to a colleague of profound astronomical knowledge, we could surmount every difficulty.   I likewise beg leave to suggest to your excellency that I conceive the information I hold of considerable consequence in the determination of the line of limits, and that (if not already determined) I can throw considerable light on the subject.

I hope your excellency will be pleased to forward orders for me to Nachitoches, informing me if am to descend to *Orleans* or proceed to the federal city, and, if the latter, permitting me to pass by Louisiana, in order to visit and arrange the affairs of my family, to whom I beg the favor of my general to communicate the certainty of the existence of myself and Dr. Robinson, who begs to be sincerely remembered to you.

The general will pardon the requests I have made of him, knowing the confidence of my heart, in the paternal and soldierly esteem which he has manifested for him, who has the honor to be,

with every sentiment of esteem,

respect, and high consideration,

dear general,

your obedient humble servant,

(Signed)   Z. M. PIKE.
His excellency gen. Wilkinson.

N. B. Please to present my respectful compliments to your lady, and the doctor's ; and mine to James, who, I hope, has long ere this arrived in safety.

(Signed)   P.

[No. 4.]

New Orleans, May 20th, 1807.

DEAR SIR,

After having counted you among the dead, I was most agreeably surprised to find, by a letter from general Salcedo, received a few days since, that you were in his possession, and that he proposed sending you, with your party, to our frontier post.   I lament that you should lose your papers, but shall rely much on your memory, and although it was unfortunate that you should have headed Red river, and missed the object of your enterprise, yet I promise myself that the route over which you have passed will afford some interesting scenes, as well to the statesman as the philosopher. You will hear of the scenes in which I have been engaged, and may be informed that the traitors whose infamous designs against the constitution and government of our country I have detected, exposed, and destroyed, are vainly attempting to explain their own conduct by inculpating me; and, among other devices, they have asserted that your's and lieutenant Wilkinson's enterprise was a premeditated co-operation with Burr. Being on the wing for Richmond, in Virginia, to confront the arch traitor and his host of advocates, I have not leisure to commune with you as amply as I could desire; let it then suffice to you for me to say, that of the information you have acquired, and the observations you have made, you must be cautious, extremely cautious how you breathe a word, because the publicity may excite a spirit of adventure adverse to the interests of our government, or injurious to the maturation of those plans, which may be hereafter found necessary and justifiable by the government.

I leave colonel Cushing in command of the district, with plenary powers, and have informed him that you have leave to repair to St. Louis, by the most direct route, the moment you have communicated to me in *duplicate* the result of your travels, voluntary and involuntary, in relation to clime, country, population, arts, agriculture, routes, distances, and military defence. The president will be impatient to have whatever you have acquired, and to the detailed account a sketch must be added, and the original and duplicate addressed to me at the city of Washington, with the least possible delay. You may make up your report at Natchitoches, and proceed from thence to the Wascheta, and from thence to the Arkansaw, or you may descend to Fort Adams, and proceed thence to St. Louis, by the most convenient route. Colonel Cushing, whom I leave in command of the district, has my orders in your favor, and will give you every indulgence; but as an expedition is now in motion up the Arkansaw, to explore it to its source and further north-west, it is highly important you should, either in person, or by two or three confidential men, send forward to the Arkansaw every information which you may deem essential to the success of the enterprise. A Mr. Freemen, under the chief direction of Mr. Dunbar of Natchez, has the control of this operation. The escort, which consists of 55 select non-commissioned officers and privates, is commanded by lieutenant Wilkinson, seconded by lieutenant T. A. Smith. This detachment, with two boats suitably equipped, will reach Natchez in eight or ten days from the present, and will proceed with all possible dispatch. You will address your communications to lieutenant Wilkinson, who, after many hardships and difficulties, reached this place about the first of March. He has finished a pretty good traverse of the river, and his journal is interesting. I think the present party will winter near the Arkansaw Osages, about 600 miles by the river from the Mississippi. The president mentioned you and your explorations to the source of the *Great* river, in his address to congress, in handsome terms, and I am convinced he has a proper sense of your merits, and will do you ample justice. I offer you leave to go immediately to your family, because I apprehend it will be most desirable; yet, if you possess in your information aught which you may desire to communicate in person, you are at liberty to proceed, by the shortest route, to the seat of government, near which you will find me, *if alive*, three or four months hence.

I pray you to attend particularly to the injunctions of this hasty letter, and to believe me, whilst I am your general,

Your friend,

(Signed)   JAMES WILKINSON.
Captain Pike, U. S. army.

[No. 5.]

Nachitoches, 5th July, 1807.

DEAR GENERAL,

Once more I address you from the land of freedom and under the banners of our country. Your esteemed favor of the 20th May now lies before me, in which I recognise the sentiments of my general and friend, and will endeavor, as far as my limited abilities permit, to do justice to the spirit of your instructions.

I must premise to your excellency that my letter of the 20th April, dated at Chihuahua, went through a perusal by general Salcedo, previous to his forwarding it.

That letter stated the mode of my being brought into Santa Fe, and I will now state to your excellency the proceeding on the subject of my papers. I will omit the hauteur of the reception given me by governor Allencaster, for a more particular communication, which changed afterwards to extreme politeness. Being under no restrictions previous to arriving at Santa Fe, I had secreted all my papers which I conceived necessary to preserve, leaving my book of charts, my orders, and such others as to induce the governor to know me in my proper character, and to prevent his suspicions being excited to a stricter enquiry.

On examining my commission, orders, &c. he told me to remove my trunk to my own quarters, and that on the morrow he would converse with me on the subject. I had caused the men to secrete my papers about their bodies, conceiving it safer than in the baggage ; but in the evening, finding the ladies of Santa Fe were treating them to wine, &c. I was apprehensive their intemperance might discover the secret, and took them from all but one (who had my journal in full) who could not be found, and put them in my trunk, conceiving that the inspection was over ; but next morning an officer, with two men, waited on me and informed me he had come for me to visit the governor, and brought these two men to take up my trunk. I immediately perceived I was outgeneraled. On my arrival at the governor's house, his excellency demanded if I had the key. My reply was in the affirmative ; when he observed " it is well ;" my trunk would be a sacred deposit in the charge of the officer, who would escort me to Chihuahua, for which place, after dinner, I marched, under the escort of lieutenant *Don Facundo Malgares*, and 65 men, whose character I beg leave to introduce to the attention of your excellency as an European possessing all the high sense of honor which formerly so evidently distinguished his nation, as the commandant of the 600 troops who made the expedition to the *Pawnees*, as an officer of distinguished merit, who in his mode of living fully justified the pomp and style of his actions, outshines many of their governors of provinces, and whom in my future reports I shall have frequent occasion to quote. He observed to me, " The governor informs me, sir, your trunk is under restrictions, but your word of honor as a soldier that no papers shall be taken out, and you have free ingress, as usual." I gave it, and I presume it is scarcely necessary to add it was religiously adhered to.

On our arrival at Chihuahua the general demanded my trunk, and on its being opened and the papers laid on the table, he took them in hand one by one and demanded what was the purport of each, which *truth* obliged me to declare ; and had I been disposed to have equivocated, ensign Walker, of his Catholic majesty's service, who stood present and assisted in the examination, could have immediately detected the fraud ; also his excellency understands sufficient of the English language to discover the general purport of any paper.

After going throug them in this manner and separating them into two piles, he observed to me, " You will leave those papers for my inspection, and in the mean while, in concert with ensign Walker (who will give the Spanish translation) you will give me a detailed account of your route, views, destination, &c. and during that time I will examine the papers now before me." To this I complied, flattering myself that it was his intention to return me my papers, by his demanding a sketch ; also, so great was my confidence in the all-protecting *name* of my *country*, I conceived it was a greater step than the general would venture to take, to seize on the papers. But when I had finished the proposed sketch and presented it, and found a still further delay, I addressed the general on the subject, when, after a few days, some were returned but I was officially informed that " the remaining papers were seized on, but would be kept in the secret cabinet of that captain generalship, until the pleasure of his Catholic majesty was known," - at the same time presenting me with a certificate specifying the number and contents of those detained, and added that they were assorted by my *own hand, and voluntarily*. This assertion was so contrary to truth, honor, or the line of conduct a general should have pursued with a young gentleman, that I took the liberty of telling one of the officers who signed said certificate that it was incorrect. But as serjeant Meek was still in the rear, with nearly all my baggage, I took care to give him orders that none of said baggage should be opened, except by force, which will evince that, although I preferred acting like a gentleman to obliging general Salcedo to resort to rough treatment, yet that it was not a volunteer surrender of my papers. But the general will please to recollect that my journals were saved at Santa Fe, which were continued and are entire to this post ; a fortunate circumstance of the doctor's having copied my courses and distances through all the route (except an excursion we made to the source of the river La Platte) unto the Spanish territories, preserved them. These will enable me to exhibit a correct chart of the route, although not so minutely as the one seized on, which was plotted daily by the eye and angular observations. Thus my only essential papers lost were my astronomical observations, meteorological tables, and a book containing remarks on minerals, plants, &c. with the manners, population, customs, &c. of the savages ; but the result of the former were in part communicated, and probably my journal may supply part of the balance, and our memories will make the loss of the latter of but little consequence. While in the Spanish territories I was forbid the use of pen and paper, notwithstanding which I kept a journal, made meteorological observations, took courses and distances, from the time I entered their country until my arrival at this place, all of which I brought safe off in the men's guns (where I finally secreted my papers) without detection.

From our unremitting attention day and night, the immense territory they led us through, the long time we were in their country, I have been able to collect (I make bold to assert) a correct account of their military force, regular and irregular ; also, important and interesting information on geographical situations, political sentiments, and dispositions of the people of every class, manners, arts, resources, riches, revenues, value and productions of their mines, situation, &c. &c. also, with the annual revenues paid Bonaparte, and had we possessed as great a knowledge of the Spanish language when we entered the territories as when we left them, our information would have been nearly as complete as I could have wished it, if sent expressly for the purpose of acquiring it, by the open authority of his majesty. But the French language was greatly beneficial, in which my communications were sometimes made. By the serjeant, who is still in the rear and never suffered to join me, as general Salcedo conceived he would probably procure some information from him, which he could not if immediately under my orders, I expect many other communications of importance from many individuals, who promised to forward them by him. But I presume the general has found himself in an error, as I perceive by a letter from him to governor Cordero, the serjeant killed one of his men, in consequence of some improper conduct, and the general accuses him of great intractibility, as he is pleased to term it. From the foregoing statement your excellency will observe that I yet possess immense matter, the result of one year's travel, in a country desert and populated, which have *both* been long the subject of curiosity to the philosopher, the anxious desires of the miser, and the waking thoughts and sleeping dreams of the man of *ambition* and the *aspiring* soul, and in our present critical situation, I do conceive, immensely important, and which opens a scene for the *generosity* and *aggrandisement* of our country, with a wide and splendid field for harvests of honor for individuals. But my papers are in a mutilated state, from the absolute necessity I was under to write on small pieces in the Spanish country ; also, from being injured in the gun barrels, some of which I filed three times off to take out the papers. These circumstances would make it necessary, in the first place, to take a rough copy as they stand ; then it will be necessary to assort the matter, as military, political, moral, trade, clime, soil, &c. all now form an undigested mass : then, sir, the combining each, the plotting, &c. would take up a time of considerable extent for one man ; and to make duplicates after they were in order could not be done in three months. The general may recollect it was nearly that period before my reports were completed last year, although assisted by Mr. Nau and the serjeant-major, and sometimes by lieutenants Wilkinson and Graham. Also, with respect to the Spanish country, I must know the extent of the objects in view, in order to embrace those points in my reports ; and further, my dear sir, my health is by no means the most perfect, my eyes extremely weak ; that it is almost impossible for me to continue for one hour with the pen in my hand, and by that time have a considerable pain in my breast. From those circumstances my general will perceive the almost *impracticability* of my complying with the contents of his letter as to duplicate reports from this place ; but I shall immediately commence the business of arranging and digesting my papers, and will proceed with the labour with every perseverance my situation will permit of until the arrival of my serjeant and the balance of the party (should they not retard more than 20 days) when I shall proceed immediately to St. Louis, and from thence through Kentucky, Virginia, &c. to the federal city, making no unnecessary delay, and all the whole of the route prosecuting my business at every leisure moment. When at Washington I flatter myself with your assistance and advice. As I propose taking courses, distances, &c. from thence to St. Louis, it will be making the tour of the greatest part of Louisiana, crossing the main rivers at different points, when I am certain with the survey of the Missouri by captains Lewis and Clark, my own of the Mississippi, lieutenant Wilkinson's of the lower Arkansaw (which river I surveyed to its source), and Mr. Dunbar's of Red river, can be formed the completest survey of Louisiana ever yet taken.

The instruments I had with me I wish the general to inform me in what light they stood, as the most of them were ruined in the mountains by the falling of the horses from precipices, &c. and I left an order at Chihuahua for the serjeant to sell them at a certain price, as the addition of a land carriage of 500 leagues would not add to their benefit. Baroney, if alive, is with my serjeant, and has proved a noble fellow in his line, and I beg liberty to recommend him to some appointment near the Kans, should any offer. I must further add the following anecdote of my men, in whose breasts lay the whole secret of my papers, and whom I frequently, when in the Spanish territories, was obliged to punish severals for outrages committed when in a state of intoxication, yet never did one offer, or show a disposition to discover it. It is certain they knew *instant death* would follow ; but still their fidelity to their trust is remarkable. I have charged them as to communications, and shall dispose of them in such a manner as not to put it in their power to give things much publicity. Dr. Robinson has accompanied me the whole route, is still with me, and of whom I take a pleasure in acknowledging I have received important services, as my companion in dangers and hardships, counsellor in difficulties, and to whose chymical, botanical, and mineralogical knowledge the expedition was greatly indebted : in short, sir, he is a young gentleman of talents, honor, and perseverance, possessing, in my humble opinion, a military turn of mind, and would, I believe, in case of an augmentation of the army, enter, if he could obtain a rank above a subaltern. I hope the general will be pleased to have my copies *forwarded* by lieutenant Wilkinson, so that I can command the use of them at Washington ; also, all my letters written him in the expedition, as they contain information I wish to refer to, and the copies were seized. Dr. Sibley has informed me the expedition up the Arkansaw is suspended, which supercedes the necessity of my sending the express ordered.

I congratulate the general on the safe arrival of lieutenant Wilkinson, and am sorry to hear of the difficulties he encountered. I have been obliged to draw money of the Spanish government, which I have to pay to their ambassador at Washington. I supported those of my men with me all the time in the Spanish country, separated from my baggage, and never permitted to have it join me, presented to the commandant-general in a blanket cappot : I was under the necessity of going into very considerable expense to support what I not only considered my own honor, but the dignity of our army. This, where a captain's pay is 2400 dollars per annum, was a ruinous thing to my finances ; but I hope it may be taken into due consideration.

After making myself pretty perfect in the French language, I have obtained such a knowledge of the Spanish as to make me confident in asserting, in three or four years I will with ease make myself master of the latter, Italian, and Portuguese, sufficient to read all, and speak and write the Spanish. The doctor has even exceeded me in that point. I mention this to the general, as I know the interest he takes in the improvement of his military protege.

We had heard in the Spanish dominions of the convulsions of the western country, originating in Mr. Burr's plans, and that you were implicated ; sometimes that you was arrested, sometimes superceded, &c. Those reports (although I never gave credit to them) gave me great unhappiness, as I conceived that the shafts of calumny were aiming at your fame and honor, in a foreign country, where they had hitherto stood high, and were revered and respected by every class. At St. Antonio colonel Cordero informed me of the truth of the statement, which took a load from my breast and made me comparatively happy, and I hope ere long will the villany be unmasked and malignity and slander hide their heads. The before mentioned gentleman sent you by me a box of Spanish chocolate, which I shall forward to colonel Cushing. Governor Herrara said the *maliciousness* of the world was such as to forbid his writing, but begged to be sincerely remembered to you. A letter addressed to me Cincinnatti, Ohio, may possibly reach me on my route, when I hope to receive the approbation of my conduct. Many letters written to me, addressed to this place, have been secreted or destroyed : possibly the general can give me a hint on the subject.

Those ideas have made a deep impression on my mind, and did not an *all ruling passion* sway me irresistibly to the profession of *arms* and the *paths* of military *glory*, I would long since have resigned my sword for the rural cot, where peace, health, and content would at least be our inmates, should not our *brows* be crowned with laurel.

I must now conclude, as this letter has far exceeded the bounds proposed when commenced ; but the effusions of my heart are such on its contents, that I could not limit them to a more contracted space. Excuse my scrawl, as I am entirely out of practice, but believe me to be,

dear general,

with high respect and esteem,

your obedient, servant,

(Signed)   Z. M. PIKE, captain.
General Wilkinson.

[No. 6.]

The committee of the house of representatives of the congress of the United States, to whom was referred the resolution to inquire whether any, and if any, what compensation ought to be made to captain Zebulon M. Pike, and his companions, for their services in exploring the Mississippi river, in their late expedition to the sources of the Osage, Arkansaw and La Platte rivers, and in their tour through New Spain :

REPORT....

That it appears by the documents accompanying this report, that the objects of each of the exploring expeditions, together with the instructions for executing them, were communicated to, and approved by the president of the United States; that the conduct of captain Pike, in each of the expeditions, also met with the approbation of the president, and that the information obtained and communicated to the executive on the subjects of his instructions, and particularly in relation to the source of the Mississippi and the natives in that quarter, and the country generally, as well on the Upper Mississippi as that between the Arkansaw, and the Missouri, and on the borders of the latter extensive river to its source, and the country adjacent, is highly interesting in a political, geographical and historical view ; and that although no special encouragement was given to the individuals who performed these laborious and dangerous expeditions, yet it was but reasonable for them, should they fortunately succeed in the objects, to expect some regard from government ; that the zeal, perseverance, and intelligence of captain Pike, as commander, has been meritorious, and the conduct of the individuals generally who composed the parties respectively, has been faithful, and the exertions arduous. The committee therefore are of opinion that compensation ought to be made by law to captain Pike and his companions.

DOCUMENTS.

War Department, December 7, 1808.

Sir,

I herewith inclose copies of the instructions to lieutenant Pike, for the government of his conduct on the two exploring expeditions alluded to in your letter ; and likewise lists of the names of the men composing those parties. You will perceive that the instructions were given by general Wilkinson; the object however of each party, together with the instructions, were communicated to, and approved by the president of the United States.

Although no special encouragement was given to the individuals, who performed these laborious and dangerous expeditions, yet it was but reasonable for them, should they fortunately succeed in their objects, to expect a liberal reward from the government; and as there can be no reasonable doubt of the zeal, perseverance, and intelligence of the commander, or of the faithful conduct and arduous exertions of the individuals generally, composing the respective parties, it may, I trust, be presumed, that no objection will be opposed to a reasonable compensation for such meritorious services.

I am very respectfully, sir,

Your obedient, servant,

H. DEARBORN.

Hon. J. Montgomery, chairman, &c.

———

(COPY.)

Head Quarters, St. Louis, July 30, 1805.

SIR,

Having completed your equipments, you are to proceed up the Mississippi with all possible diligence, taking the following instructions for your general government, which are to yield to your discretion in all cases of exigency.

You will please to take the course of the river, and calculate distances by time, noting rivers, creeks, highlands, prairies, islands, rapids, shoals, mines, quarries, timber, water, soil, Indian villages and settlements, in a diary, to comprehend reflections on the winds and weather.

It is interesting to government to be informed of the population and residence of the several Indian nations, of the quantity and species of skins and furs they barter per annum, and their relative price to goods; of the tracts of country on which they generally make their hunts, and the people with whom they trade.

You will be pleased to examine strictly for an intermediate point, between this place and the Prairie des Chiens, suitable for a military post, and also on the Ouiscousing, near its mouth, for a

24

similar establishment, and will obtain the consent of the Indians for their erection, informing them that they are intended to increase their trade, and ameliorate their condition.

You will proceed to ascend the main branch of the river until you reach the source of it, or the season may forbid your further progress without endangering your return, before the waters are frozen up.

You will endeavor to ascertain the latitude of the most remarkable places in your route, with the extent of the navigation and the direction of the different rivers which fall into the Mississippi, and you will not fail to procure specimens of whatever you may find curious, in the mineral, vegetable, or animal kingdoms, to be rendered at this place.

In your course you are to spare no pains to conciliate the Indians and to attach them to the United States, and you may invite the *great chiefs* of such *distant nations* as have *not been at this place*, to pay me a visit.

Your own good sense will regulate the consumption of your provisions, and direct the distribution of the trifling presents which you may carry with you, particularly your flags.

I wish you a speedy, pleasant, and safe tour, and am, sir, with sentiments of respect and esteem,

Your obedient servant,

(Signed)   JAMES WILKINSON.

P. S. In addition to the preceding orders, you will be pleased to obtain permission from the Indians who claim the ground, for the erection of military posts and trading houses, at the mouth of the river St. Pierre, the falls of St. Anthony, and every other critical point which may fall under your observation ; these permissions to be granted in formal conferences, regularly recorded, and the ground marked off.   J. W.*

Lieutenant Z M. Pike, 1st regt. infantry.

—————

War Department, February 24, 1808.

SIR,

In answer to your letter of the 22d instant, I can with pleasure observe, that although the two exploring expeditions you have performed, were not previously ordered by the president of the

* For general Wilkinson's further instructions, see Part II. page 107.

United States, there were frequent communications on the subject of each, between general Wilkinson and this department; of which the president of the United States was, from time to time, acquainted; and it will be no more than what justice requires, to say, that your conduct, in each of those expeditions, met the approbation of the president; and that the information you obtained and communicated to the executive, in relation to the source of the Mississippi and the natives in that quarter, and the country generally, as well on the Upper Mississippi, as that between the Arkansaw and the Missouri, and on the borders of the latter extensive river to its source and the country adjacent, has been considered highly interesting, in a political, geographical, and historical view And you may rest assured, that your services are held in high estimation by the president of the United States; and if any opinion of my own can afford you any satisfaction, I very frankly declare that I consider the public much indebted to you for the enterprising, persevering and judicious manner, in which you have performed them.

I am, very respectfully, sir,

Your obedient servant,

H. DEARBORN.

Captain Zebulon M. Pike.

RETURN

OF PERSONS EMPLOYED ON A TOUR OF DISCOVERY AND EXPLORA-
TION TO THE SOURCE OF THE MISSISSIPPI, IN THE YEARS 1805
AND 1806.

Lieutenant Z. M. PIKE,
Interpreter PIERRE ROSSEAU,
Serjeant   HENRY KENNERMAN,
Corporals { WILLIAM E. MEEK,
          { SAMUEL BRADLEY,

PRIVATES.

Jeremiah Jackson,	Hugh Menaugh,
John Boley,	Alexander Roy,
John Brown,	John Sparks,
Jacob Carter,	Patrick Smith,
Thomas Dougherty,	Freegift Stoute,

William Gorden,	Peter Brauden,
Solomon Huddleston,	David Owings,
John Mountjoy,	David Whelply.
Theodore Miller,	

This party left St. Louis the 9th of August, 1805, but had been detached for that duty from the 1st of July. They returned the 30th of April, 1806; from which time until the 15th July, I was preparing for the second expedition to the westward, which consisted of the following persons: to wit,

Captain   Z. M. PIKE,
Lieut.   JAMES B. WILKINSON,*
Doctor   JOHN H. ROBINSON,
Serj'ts   { JOSEPH BALLENGER,*
        { WILLIAM E. MEEK,†
Corporal JEREMIAH JACKSON,†

PRIVATES.

John Boley,*	Theodore Miller,†
Henry Kennerman,	Hugh Menaugh,
Samuel Bradley,*	John Mountjoy,†
John Brown,	Alexander Roy,
Jacob Carter,†	John Sparks,†
Thomas Dougherty,†	Patrick Smith,†
William Gorden,	Freegift Stoute,
Solomon Huddleston,*	John Wilson,*

Interpreter, BARONEY VASQUEZ.†

   * Those thus marked descended the Arkansaw river, and arrived at New Orleans some time about the   of February, 1807.
   † Those thus marked are still detained in New Spain.
   The balance arrived at the Nachitoches, on or about the 1st of July, 1807. But it may probably be better to leave the whole time undefined, to be regulated by the honorable secretary of war.

                             Z. M. PIKE, major.

[No. 7.]

THE father being informed that I had some astronomical instruments with me, expressed a desire to see them : all that 1 had here was my sextant and a large glass which magnified considerably, calculated for the day or night, the remainder of my instruments being with my serjeant and party. On examining the sextant and shewing him the effect of it in the reflection of the sun— he appeared more surprised, as well as hundreds who surrounded us, at the effect of the instrument, than any nation of savages I was ever among, and here an idea struck me as extraordinary, how a man who appeared to be perfect master of the antient languages, a botanist, mineralogist, and chemist, should be so ignorant of the powers of reflection and the first principles of mathematics ; but my friend explained that enigma, by informing me of the care the Spanish government took to prevent any branch of science from being made a pursuit, which would have a tendency to extend the views of the subjects of the provinces to the geography of their country, or any other subject which would bring to view a comparison of their local advantages and situations with other countries.

[No. 8.]

LETTER TO GOVERNOR ALLENCASTER.

Santa Fe, 3d March, 1807.

SIR,

ON the arrival of your troops at my encampment, last month, under the command of lieutenant Don Ignacio Saltelo and Mr. Bartholemew ; they informed me, that your excellency had directed them to assure me, that I should be escorted through your dominions to the source of Red river, as our being on the frontiers of your province gave cause to suspicion. I conceived it more proper to comply with the request, and repair to Santa Fe, in order to explain to your excellency any circumstance which might appear extraordinary, but on my arrival here, I am informed by your excellency, that it is necessary, that myself and troops pass by Chihuahua in the province of Biscay, more than two hundred leagues out of my route. I have demanded of your excellency to know if we are to be considered as prisoners of war. You inform me, you do not consider us in that light. Not to embarrass your excellency with many demands; I only request to receive it from under your hands, in what manner I am to consider myself, and the orders for my passing into the country; also whether the expense of the voyage is to be considered as defrayed by the government of Spain or the United States. Excuse my language, as I am not much accustomed to writing in French, but your excellency having no person who understands English, obliges me to attempt the language.

I am, sir, &c.

(Signed)   Z. M. PIKE.

[No. 9.]

TRANSLATION.

THE first lieutenant of the Anglo American troops, of the name of Z. Montgomery Pike, with the party of soldiers under his command, having been met with the troops under my orders, at four days journey from the seat of government, in this province, which is under my charge, he was required personally to appear, which he voluntarily did, and complying with the orders of the commanding general of these internal provinces; I bid the said lieutenant proceed on his march, with his party equipped with horses, provisions and equipage, under the charge of an officer and sixty men of our troops, with orders to introduce him to the said commanding general in the town of Chihuahua.

I permitted said party to carry their arms and ammunition; actuated by proper consideration, and in order to grant said anglo American's petition. I certify the foregoing contents to be accurate.

Santa Fe, March 3d, 1807.

(Signed)   JOACHIN RL. ALLENCASTER.

[No. 10.]

LETTER TO GOVERNOR ALLENCASTER.

St. Fernandez, 7th March, 1807.

SIR,

ON my arrival at this village, and meeting with Dr. Robinson, he informed me that he acknowledged to lieutenant Malgares to belong to my party. As this acknowledgment in fact, only interested himself, I am constrained to explain to your excellency, my reasons for having denied his connexion with me. He marched from St. Louis with my detachment, as a volunteer, (after having with much pain and solicitation obtained permission from the general for that purpose :) on our arrival on the Rio del Norte, (then supposed Red river) he left the party in order to come to Santa Fe, with a view of obtaining information as to trade, and collect some debts due to persons in the Illinois. On my being informed of his embarrassments, I conceived it would be adding to them, to acknowledge his having accompanied a military party on to the frontiers of the province, and conceived myself bound in honor and friendship to conceal it ; but his scorning any longer the disguise he had assumed, has left me at liberty to make this acknowledgment to your excellency, which I hope will sufficiently exculpate me in the opinion of every man of honor, and of the world, for having denied a fact, when I conceived the safety of a friend, in a foreign country, was concerned in the event. The above statement will be corroborated by general Wilkinson, and he will be reclaimed by the United States as a citizen, agreeably to our treaties with Spain, regulating the intercourse, commerce, &c. between the two nations. I felt disposed to enter into an expostulation with your excellency, as to the deception practiced on me by the officers who came out with your invitation to enter the province, but will omit it, and only request that my serjeant and party may be ordered to follow with all possible dispatch, as he has all my astronomical instruments and clothing, except those I now wear. I have found lieutenant Malgares to be what you stated him, a gentleman and a soldier, and I sincerely wish the fortune of war, may one day, enable me to shew the gentlemen of the Spanish army, with whom I have had the honor of forming an acquaintance, with what gratitude I appreciate their friendship and politeness, and none more highly than your excellency.

With sincere, &c.

(Signed)   Z. M. PIKE.

[No. 11.]

LETTER TO HIS EXCELLENCY GENERAL SALCEDO.

Chihuahua, 6th April, 1806.

SIR,

HAVING been for near the space of a year, absent from my country, and the probability of its yet being two or three months before I arrive in the territory of the United States; the necessity of passing through some hundred leagues of foreign territory, with the distressed situation of my troops, has induced me to apply to your excellency for a necessary supply of money. Any arrangement which may be conceived proper for the remuneration, I will cheerfully adopt, either to pay it to the Spanish consul at New Orleans, or the embassador of his catholic majesty at Washington.

The sum which I conceive will answer the present purposes of myself and troops is 1000 dollars, for which I will give such vouchers as your excellency may conceive proper.

I have the honor to assure your excellency,

of my high respect, and

to be your obedient servant,

(Signed)   Z. M. PIKE.

[No. 12.]

TRANSLATION.

ACCEDING to the solicitation you have made in your letter of yesterday, that from the royal treasury of this place, there should be delivered you one thousand dollars, (which you say are necessary for the accomodation of the troops of the United States of America, which you have under your charge) or whatsoever other sum you choose to demand; and the government of the said United States shall refund the said sum to the Senor Marquis de Cassa Yrujo. I have directed the formula for you to sign of four corresponding and quadruplicate receipts.

God preserve you many years,

(Signed)   NIMESIO SALCEDO.

Chihuahua, 7th April, 1807.

For the 1st lieut. Montgomery Pike.

Translated from the original, by Z. M. Pike, captain.

[No. 13.]

Sketch of an expedition made from St. Louis, to explore the internal parts of Louisiana, by order of his excellency, general James Wilkinson.

I EMBARKED at Belle Fontaine, on the Missouri, (near its confluence with the Mississippi) with a command of one lieutenant, one doctor, a volunteer, two serjeants, one corporal, seventeen privates, and one interpreter; having under my charge, eight or ten Osage chiefs, who had recently returned from a visit to the city of Washington, together with about 40 men, women and children, of the same nation, redeemed from captivity from another Indian nation; and two Pawnees who had likewise been to the city of Washington.

We ascended the Missouri river to the river of the Osage, up which we ascended to the Osage towns, and arrived on or about the 18th of August, and delivered to their nation in safety their chiefs, women and children, with speeches to the nation.

Here I remained making astronomical observations, and preparing for my march by land until the 1st of September, when we took our departure for the Pawnee republic, accompanied by some Osage chiefs, who were deputed by their nation to form a treaty of peace and amity with the nation of the Kans (with whom they were then at war) under the auspices of the United States. I arrived at the Pawnee republic about the 25th of said month, where I caused to be held a conference between the Osage and Kans chiefs, and mediated a peace for the two nations. After having held councils with the Pawnees, made astronomical observations, &c. I marched from the said village on the 7th of October, and arrived at the Arkansaw on the 11th of the said month, where we remained until the 28th, preparing canoes, &c. for lieutenant Wilkinson, who descended the said river, with one serjeant, six men, and two Osage Indians. During my stay at said river, I likewise made astronomical observations. On the said day I marched with the remainder of the party up the Arkansaw, and nothing occurred worthy of note, until about the middle of November, when we met a party of Pawnees, of 60 warriors, who were returning from an expedition against the Kayaways: at first our conference was of the most friendly nature, and I made them some small presents, but they commencing to steal and plunder whatever they could with impunity, we were finally

obliged to take to our arms, and were on the point of coming to hostilities, when the Pawnees retired, and we pursued our march. We
arrived where the Arkansaw enters the mountains, on the 4th or 5th
December, where we remained until the 9th, searching for the route
across the mountains, when we marched by a trace which we discovered, leaving the main Arkansaw to our left; and much to our
astonishment! arrived about the middle of said month on a water
of the Missouri, which I ascertained to be the river *Platte;* on
which we discovered signs of immense numbers of Indians : here
we remained a few days searching for those Indians, in hopes to obtain from them information as to a route to cross the mountains to
the west, but not discovering any, we crossed a large chain by a
practicable route, and fell on a large branch of water which I then
conceived to be the head of the Red river. Here we remained a few
days to recruit our horses and ourselves, when I ordered the party
to proceed down said river, and I with two men ascended it to its
source, where I made some observations. I then returned and
overtook the party, when we continued to descend said stream, until
the perpendicularity of the rocks and other difficulties had rendered
it impossible to proceed any further with horses, several of which
had already been killed by falling from the rocks, &c.

I then caused sleds to be constructed, and soldiers to draw the
baggage on the ice, and ordered a few men to endeavour to conduct
the horses by a more eligible route out of the mountains; at the
extremity of which, we all arrived by the 9th of January, and found
that we had descended the main branch of the Arkansaw, conceiving
it to be the Red river, and was now at the same point I left on the
9th ult.

My remaining horses being in a situation not to allow me to
hope for any further assistance from them, unless permitted further
to recover : as this would have engrossed a long time, I determined
to leave some men with the horses and part of the baggage, and
proceed with the remainder and the articles absolutely necessary on
foot. On the 14th January, having constructed a small place for
my men and baggage who remained, we marched, proceeding
up a western branch of the Arkansaw, which appeared to lead in a
direct route through the mountains. On the 20th of said month,
being obliged to cross a prairie of some leagues in breadth, late in
the evening, (many of the soldiers having their feet wet) had it not
in our power to make fire until eight or nine o'clock at night. We
were so unfortunate as to ascertain that nine of the party were frozen. The ensuing day discovering that they were not able all to

march, we remained a few days to lay in provisions, when I left two soldiers and four loads of our baggage, and proceeded on our march ; but on the third day, finding another of my men not able to march, was obliged to leave him encamped, but previously furnished him with sufficient provision. We then crossed another chain of mountains, and on the 1st February arrived on the waters of the Rio del Norte, (which I then conceived to be the Red river) as some maps which I hold, portrayed the source of the Red river to lie between those of the Arkansaw and Rio del Norte. I then proceeded to choose a station where there was sufficient wood to form canoes or rafts, in order to descend the supposed river to Natchitoches.

Having in many instances experienced the insolence and presuming dispositions of the Indians, when in superior numbers, I conceived it proper to throw up a small work for the protection of ourselves and baggage, until we should be prepared to descend the river.

Four or five days after, I dispatched five of my men to return to those I left in the mountains, and bring them on if capable of marching ; if not, to supply them with provision and bring on the baggage. Dr. Robinson, who had hitherto accompanied me as a volunteer, having some pecuniary demands in the province of New Mexico, conceived that this would be the nearest point from which he could go in and probably return, previous to my being prepared to descend the river : left me on the 7th February with that view.

A few days after, hunting with one of my men, I discovered two men on horseback. I would have avoided them agreeably to my orders, but finding they continued to pursue us, I conceived it most proper to endeavour to bring them to a conference ; which, with great difficulty I effected, as they appeared to be apprehensive my intentions were hostile towards them. I conducted them to my camp, and informed them of my intention to descend the river, and made them some small presents : had they then informed me of my being on the Rio del Norte, I should have immediately retired ; but they having executed their commission, returned the following day on the immediate route to the settlements. The following day the party I had detached for the men whom I had been compelled to leave in the mountains, returned with *one* only, and all the baggage, the other two not being able to come on. I then immediately dispatched my serjeant and one man, to order and conduct on the men, horses and baggage left on the Arkansaw by a route which I conceived practicable. On the 24th or 25th of February, in the morning, two Frenchmen arrived at my camp, and informed me that an officer and fifty men of his catholic majesty's troops had marched from Santa Fe, in order to protect me from the Utahs, (who had exhibited a disposition to attack me) and would probably be at my camp in two or three days. In the course of two or three hours, I was informed by a sentinel whom I always kept on a hill, of the approach of a party of strangers, and in a short period there arrived two officers and 100 men, at a small distance from the camp; the lieutenant commandant having entered my works by my invitation, informed me, that the governor of New Mexico had been informed of my situation, and understanding I was bound for Red river, offered me any assistance which lay in his power to accomodate me. I replied that I stood in no need of assistance; that I could descend the river with craft, which I proposed constructing. He then informed me I was on the Rio del Norte, (which astonished me extremely) and that the source of the Red river was eight days march below Santa Fe; and that the governor being informed that I had missed my route, offered me mules, horses, &c. to conduct me to the Red river, and wished to see me at his seat of government. I told him that if the whole of my party were here, I would not hesitate to pay my respects to his excellency with one or two men. He then assured me that there was not the least constraint; that I could go in before or after the arrival of my party, as my inclication dictated; that if I went in now, he would leave an Utah interpreter and one man, with the men of my party I chose to leave, in order to conduct on the serjeant and party when they arrived. I finally concluded it would be more consistent with the good understanding which existed between the government of the United States and his catholic majesty, to proceed to Santa Fe, and give to governor Allencaster an explanation of my being on his frontiers. We then marched for his camp, about 12 miles distant, leaving the interpreter, one Spanish soldier, a corporal and one private of my detachment, with orders for the conduct of my serjeant when he should arrive.

The next day I was much surprised to find the lieutenant and all the regular troops, except 10, were about to remain, and that the militia officer was to conduct me to Santa Fe; the lieutenant giving as a reason, the particular orders to see *all* my party in safety at the capital. We arrived at the said town in four or five days, where I was received at first in a manner very different from what I had been taught to expect from the proffers of the lieutenant in the name of the governor. The arms of my men being taken possession of by the guard the first night of my arrival, without my knowledge, and being likewise informed that Dr. Robinson was a prisoner at some leagues distance ; they induced me to believe that a rupture had taken place between Spain and the United States, and to address a letter to the governor, demanding if I was to consider myself and party as prisoners of war ; and if the expense arising from the detention of myself and party was to be defrayed by the United States or his catholic majesty.   To this his excellency gave me a very polite verbal answer, assuring me that I was by no means to consider myself as a prisoner ; that the arms of my men were taken unknown to him, and should be immediately restored, but that it was necessary I should march immediately to join lieutenant Malgares and party, who were waiting for me at the village of St. Fernandez, in order to conduct me to Chihuahua, to be presented to the commandant general with my papers for an explanation.   On my arriving at said village, I addressed a letter to the governor, informing him that Dr. Robinson had accompanied my party as a volunteer, which I had not acknowledged at Santa Fe, as I was apprehensive that his coming on to the frontiers of the province with a military party, in case of a rupture between the two governments, might place him in a critical situation.

The lieutenant only further observes, that he has not entered into the particulars of the hardships undergone, as that, enduring thirst and famine for three or four days, at different periods ; marching over ruggid mountains, through snows three and four feet deep ; their bodies exposed to every inclemency of the weather, for want of clothes, carrying at the same time, packs of 60 or 70 pounds burthen ; in short, every hardship which a savage life in its greatest state of barbarity is exposed to, are circumstances only calculated to excite humanity, and not give explanation as to the general chain of events connected with the voyage.   He therefore refers his excellency to the commander in chief of the United States army for an explanation of the general intent and nature of the expedition, and to his notes, astronomical observations and charts for the courses, situation, &c. of the different points and rivers alluded to in the foregoing sketch.

[No. 14.]

Chihuahua, 14*th April*, 1807.

SIR,

ON my marching from Santa Fe, governor Allencaster informed me that my papers would be considered as a sacred depot until my arrival at this place, when your excellency would examine and take them into consideration.

When they were examined and taken possession of, I explained without disguise the nature and contents of *each*, conceiving that *those* only which had any relation to the object of my expedition could be interesting, and that merely a copy of the chart and translation of the official papers would be taken. You must be conscious, sir, that it was in my power to have secreted or destroyed every trace of my voyage and plans previous to my arrival at Chihuahua, but resting satisfied that no rupture had taken place between his catholic majesty and the States I have the honor to serve, which would be a justification for the seizure of my papers; I prefered leaving them in *statu quo*, to using duplicity, which in some degree always implicates the character of a military man.

Admitting the country which I explored to be contested between the two governments, each naturally wishing to gain some information as to its geographical situation, in order that they may form correct ideas as to what would be their mutual interests, founded on justice and the honor and the dignity of the nation in forming the line of demarcation. This was the view of the United States government in the expedition which I had the honor to command, and the loss of the geographical sketches taken, might be the occasion of a suspension of the final line of limits, and consequently the delay of an amicable adjustment of the now existing differences between the two governments.

Your excellency may not have an intention of detaining my papers, which I had only began to suppose from your returning part by lieutenant Walker, in which case you will please to excuse this intrusion; but I will add, that if you have it in view to detain the papers, I request you will be pleased to examine them with particular care, and you will find that there are letters from general Wilkinson, as well as his son to me, also from the latter to his father and mother, and others which are by no means of a political nature, or at least not relative to the relations exiting between the government of Spain and the United States, and therefore can by no means be interesting to your excellency. The book which contains my charts also contains part of the blotters of a voyage to the source of the Mississippi, which I presume cannot be interesting to the Spanish government.

But to conclude, I have only to request of your excellency to know if it is your intention to detain my papers now in your possession ; if so, that you may cause me to be furnished (or suffer me to take) a copy of them, and that I may receive a certificate from under your hand, of the number, nature, &c. of the said papers, and the reasons for their seizure and detention, in order that my government may be enabled to make the proper application to the Spanish court for an explanation. My reason for applying to your excellency so early on this subject, is that on the arrival of my men, who are still in the rear, I might be prepared to march in a short period of time, (for under the present aspect of affairs) I feel conscious that I am as anxious to arrive on the territories of the United States, as your excellency must be for me to quit the dominions of his catholic majesty.

In all events, I hope you will believe me to be with the highest sentiments of personal respect,

Your most obedient servant,

(Signed)   Z. M. PIKE.

His excellency, brigadier general Don Nimesio Salcedo, commanding-general of the interior province of the kingdom of New Spain.

[No. 15.]

TRANSLATION.

OF the papers connected with the expedition, which by orders of the United States government, you have made from the St. Louis of the Illinois, unto the settlements of New Mexico, and which you yourself * separated from those which you brought here and put into my hands the day you arrived in this town. There has been formed an inventory and certificate respecting each of them accompanying it to you, and deposited in the office, the 17th current, for the purpose

* See my account of the seizure of my papers, April 1st, 1807.

therein expressed; the judgment on which remains for the decision of the king, my lord, and shall be reported in the secret archives of this captain generalcy; and meditating that you have indicated in your summons official to this government, the greatest desire to arrive at the territories of the United States, have resolved that you prepare to continue your voyage in two or three days; in consequence of which, the arrangements necessary shall be made, such as you, with the people of your expedition have experienced until your arrival at this place.

God preserve you many years,

(Signed)   NIMESIO SALCEDO.

Chihuahua, 23d April, 1807.

   1st Lieutenant of Infantry, Montgomery Pike.

   Translated from the original, by Z. M. Pike, captain.

[No. 16.]

TRANSLATION.

   INVENTORY of papers which the lieutenant of infantry of the United States of America, Montgomery Pike, in the superior government, and commandant general of the internal provinces of New Spain, as belonging to a voyage which he executed from St. Louis up the Illinois to the population of New Mexico, to visit the Indian nations, and reconnoitre the country and intermediate rivers, as it appears his expedition was undertaken by provision of the government of the said United States and the orders of general Wilkinson.

No. 1. Letter from general Wilkinson to Pike, dated 24th June, 1806.

    2. Another from the same to Pike, 18th July, 1806.

    3. Another from the same to the same officer, 19th July, 1806.

    4. Another from the same to Pike, dated 6th August, 1806.

    5. Letter from lieutenant Wilkinson to his father, 27th October, 1806.

    6. Another from the same to the same, 28th October, 1806.

    7. Letter from Pike to general Wilkinson, 22d July, 1806.

    8. Letter from lieutenant Wilkinson to lieutenant Pike, 26th October, 1806.

9. Proclamation of general Wilkinson, prohibiting any citizen of the United States trading with the Indian nations without his permission, or that of the government, dated 10th July, 1805.

10. A letter from Charles Junot, agent for the Indians, to general Wilkinson, dated 10th July, 1806.

11. Notes of lieutenant Pike on the voyage from New Mexico, to Chihuahua, of four pages.

12. A rough manuscript of the Missouri and Osage rivers.

13. Letter from sergeant Ballenger to general Wilkinson, without date.

14. Letter from lieutenant Wilkinson to Pike, without date.

15. A certificate in the French language of a certain Baptist Lamie, found among those nations, and specifying his motive for being there.

16. A bundle of papers in the French language, which contained notes on the harangues and manifestoes which lieutenant Pike had delivered to the Indian nations.

17. A passport of lieutenant Pike to the Indian Winapicane, a captain of the little Osage.

18. A small draught or map of the country which is situated between the Mississippi and Santa Fe, with a description of that town, and of having met with three thousand Camanches.

19. A book 8vo, manuscript, which contains the diary of lieutenant Pike, from January, 1807, to the 2d March of the same year, when he arrived at Santa Fe, in 75 pages.

20. A book 4to. manuscript, in paste-board, with copies of letters to the secretary of war and general Wilkinson, and various observations relative to the commission of the lieutenant, in 67 pages.

21. A manuscript book in folio, containing different plans of countries, &c. with a diary with Rhumbs distances, and worked observations and meteorological tables, which arose from a revisal of the voyage, by the said lieutenant Pike, in 40 pages.

Don Franciso Valasco, first officer of the secretaries of the commandant generalship of the internal provinces of New Spain, and Juan Pedro Walker Alferez, of the company of horse of the royal presidio of Janos.

We certify that the lieutenant of American infantry, Montgomery Pike, when presented to the commandant general of the be-

26

fore mentioned provinces, Don Nimesio Salcedo, likewise produced a small trunk which he brought with him,* and that in the presence of the undersigned, opened himself, and took out different books and papers, when having separated with his own hands, under our cognizance, all that appeared to be, or that he said was private, or had no connection with the voyage ; delivered the remainder to the demand of the commandant general, which were solely those comprehended in the foregoing inventory which we have formed, and for the verification of which we have signed these presents at Chihuahua, the 8th of April, 1807.

(Signed)   FRANCISO VALASCO.

JUAN PEDRO WALKER.

Translated from the original, by Z. M. Pike, captain.

[No. 17.]

Chihuahua, April 4th, 1807.

SIR,

I HOPE your excellency may not attribute it to presumption, or a disposition to intrude when I address you on a subject foreign from my official duties, and on which I can only speak as an individual. but I should feel myself wanting in humanity, and that attention which every man owes to his fellow creatures in distress should I remain silent ; and more especially when those who are compatriots and some former companions, now in a strange country, languishing out their days, far from their friends and relations, without scarcely a dawn of hope remaining of ever again being blest with the view of their native homes. It it scarcely necessary to add that I allude to the unfortunate companions of Nolan, who having entered the territories of his catholic majesty in a clandestine manner, equally in violation of the treaties between the two governments, the laws of the United States and those of Spain, could not be reclaimed or noticed by their country ; yet from every information I have received on the subject, the men of the party were innocent, believing that Nolan had passports from the Spanish governor to carry on the traffic of horses. I pretend not to justify the many irregularities of their conduct since in the Spanish dominions, but hope that it may

* The want of candor exhibited in the certificate is manifest, and was an imbecile attempt to shew that all my actions were voluntary, and that in the delivery of my papers there was no degree of constraint.

be viewed with an eye of clemency, as they are most of them ve ry illiterate, and possessing scarcely any part of an education.

David Fero was formerly a subaltern in a company of infantry of the United States, commanded by my father at the time I served as a volunteer, but left the service (as I have been informed) owing to some irregularities of conduct; his having been once my companion entitles him at the present to my particular attention; yet I will here mention to your excellency a circumstance which may appear if known in an unfavorable light, viz. About 15 days past I was informed Fero was in town, and that he desired to see me. I was extremely mortified at receiving the information, as I conceived he must have left his post in a clandestine manner, yet I could not find in my heart to refuse the interview, which I gave, but determined at the same time to inform you of the circumstance, conceiving that you could not look on it as a matter of much criminality.

But to conclude, I have to beg of your excellency, if in your power, and consistent with the line of conduct you conceive proper to pursue, to inform me if any thing can be done towards restoring these poor fellows to their liberty, friends and country, and in a particular manner I intercede for Fero.

If it is out of the power of the general to grant them leave to return to the United States, I beg to know if there is any objection to my taking out letters to their fathers, wives &c. I should not have addressed this letter to the general, had I not conceived the fate of those men alluded to was at his disposal, as he had suffered one of them to join the service of his catholic majesty; nor neither do I request the honor of any other than a verbal reply, as I write in the character of an individual, and not as an officer of the United States.

> I am, sir,
> With high consideration,
> Your humble, obedient servant,
> Z. M. PIKE.

(Signed)

His excellency, general Nimesio Salcedo.

[No. 18.]

Natchitoches, 20*th August*, 1807.

SIR,

PREVIOUS to my departure from Chihuahua, we had entered so fully into the subject of the seizure of my papers, that I should

never have made another appeal, until I made one through our government to the ambassador of his catholic majesty, had I not received orders to that effect ; it not being known at the time those
instructions were given, that the propriety of the seizure had been
contested between your excellency and myself.   But, as you have
now had time fully to re-consider the business, it may not appear in
the same light that it did when I had the honor to address you before.   Your excellency may be induced to conceive that the measure of seizing my notes, plans, meteorological and astronomical observations, &c, for parts of the Mississippi, Missouri, Osage, Kans
and Arkansaw rivers ; waters acknowledged by the Spanish government to be within the known territories of the United States, may
not be justifiable.   Whatever may be your opinion on those subjects
I am at an entire loss to conceive, how, and upon what principle you
could involve in that seizure, letters from individuals to individuals,
the contents of which could in no wise be interesting to the Spanish
government.

I have therefore once more to appeal to your excellency, with
a hope that the time you have had for deliberation may induce you
to conceive it proper, and but an act of justice to deliver up the papers seized at Chihuahua; and hope your excellency will have the
goodness to address them to me in a packet, to the care of the commanding officer of this place.

If the continuation of an amicable understanding between the
two nations is an object of estimation in the mind of your excellency,
the final demarcation of limits must be considered as the first great
step to be taken towards its accomplishment ; and to enable my government to form a correct idea on that subject, it was requisite
they should be *well* acquainted with the geographical situation of the
heads of the Arkansaw and Red rivers, the former part of which I
had accomplished, and could with all ease have carried the remaining part of that object into execution, (after discovering my mistake
of the Rio del Norte for the Red river) had I been permitted by the
governor of New Mexico, instead of which I was hurried through
the country to Chihuahua, without having time given for the absent
part of my party and baggage to join me, by which means I was
obliged to appear in a garb and manner entirely incompatible with
the rank I have the honor to hold, and in some degree an indignity
to the country whose commission I bear.   And to add to my mortification, was then deprived of the information I had obtained at the
risque of our lives and the suffering of unknown miseries.   The information contained in my notes were not only of a geographical na-

ture, but also such as would enable the executive of the United States to take some steps to ameliorate the barbarous state of various savage tribes whom I visited; and I may be permitted to add, would have added in some small degree to the acquirement of science, which is for the general benefit of mankind.

When I left Chihuahua, I was informed my sergeant and party were detained near the place, in order that they *should not* be permitted to join me. That by a separate examination they might be intimidated to make a declaration to justify the conduct observed towards us. This I am conscious must have failed, but am at an entire loss to conceive why they should have been detained until this time, when your excellency assured me they should follow immediately. Their detention has been of considerable private injury to myself, and an insult to my government.

When I marched from Chihuahua, your excellency officially informed me that every thing was prepared for my transport to our lines, but was much surprized to have to pay for the hire of horses, &c. demanded of me at the first place where we changed our escorts; as I neither conceived it just that I should pay for an involuntary tour I had taken through your territories, neither was I prepared to do it; but as your officers were responsible, and gave their receipts for the transport, and from the orders received by captain Viana at Nacogdoches, I was obliged to hire beasts to take me to Natchitoches, although an escort of your troops were furnished.

I here, with the greatest pleasure embrace the opportunity of acknowledging the polite treatment I received from your officers in general on my route ; but in a particular manner to colonels Cordero Herrara ; to captains Barelo and Viana, with lieutenant Malgares ; to all of whom it would be my greatest pleasure to have it in my power to return the compliment.

Will your excellency do me the honor to present my high respects to your lady, and my compliments to Mr. Truxillo and father Rocus.

I am, sir,

With the most profound consideration,

Your obedient servant,

(Signed)   Z. M. PIKE, captain.

His excellency governor Salcedo.

[No. 19.]

EXCELLENT SIR,

ON the 16th of February last, John Robinson appeared before the governor of New Mexico, saying that he was a Frenchman, inhabitant of St. Louis, which place he left on the 15th June last year, with the view of going to the country of the Pananas to make recoveries; that having received information that his debtors had directed their steps to said province, he had concluded to follow them, in company with 15 other persons, who went for the purpose of hunting on the rivers of Arcs, Arkansaw and Colorado; (Red river) that in the neighbouring mountains the two last of his company had left him, for which reason he saw himself under the necessity of proceeding to the Yutas Indians, to whom he exposed his situation, and who accordingly agreed to conduct him.

On the 25th of the same month of February, at the distance of 4 days march from the town of Santa Fe, and 9 leagues west of its settlement, at the place called the Ojocaliente, (Hot Spring) near the confluence of Rio Grande del Norte, (Great North river) and that known under the name River de los Conejos, (of Rabbits) a detachment of the garrison of said province of New Mexico, met Montgomery Pike, first lieutenant of the infantry of the United States, with eight men of the said infantry; who on being given to understand that he must be conducted to said town, consented to accompany them. It was then settled that two of his men should remain on the spot with half of his catholic majesty's detachment, to wait for six others who had not yet arrived, and he proceeded to the governor's, to whom he declared, that his being in that neighbourhood was owing solely to his having been lost, and having mistaken the Rio del Norte for the Colorado. But this officer in compliance with the orders of this, his superior officer, forwarded the said first lieutenant with the six men of the American army, and the above mentioned John Robinson to this capital.

They arrived here on the 2d instant, and said officer on being presented to me, laid before me in the same manner as he had done to the governor of Santa Fe, the papers relative to his mission; the correspondence he had carried on with your excellency since it commenced, with his journals and note books.

Your excellency is not ignorant of the repeated representations made by the king's minister in the United States, and by the marquis of Cassa Calva while he was in Louisiana, summoning the

American government to carry into effect any projects of extending its expeditions into territories unquestionably belonging to his majesty ; you must therefore, without any further observations or remarks on my part, be satisfied, that the documents contain evident, unequivocal proofs, that an offence of magnitude has been committed against his majesty, and that every individual of this party ought to have been considered as prisoners on the very spot, notwithstanding such substantial and well grounded motives that would have warranted such a measure. Wishing to give the widest latitude to the subsisting system of harmony and good understanding, and above all, finally persuaded that your excellency will take such steps as your judgment may suggest, as best calculated to prevent any bad consequences on the occasion, I have concluded to keep in this general government, all the papers presented by lieutenant Pike, and to give him and his men full liberty to return to your excellency, after having treated them with attention, and offered them every assistance they stood in need of.

I am without reserve, and beyond expression, your most obedient, humble, and respectful and faithful servant, and prayeth God may preserve your excellency many years.

    (Signed)   SALCEDO.

Chihuahua, 8th April, 1807.

    General James Wilkinson.

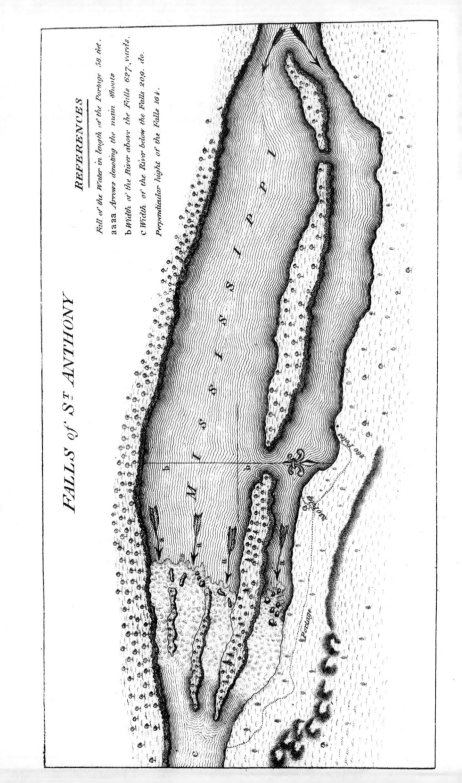

FALLS of St. ANTHONY

REFERENCES

Fall of the Water in length of the Portage 58 feet.
aaaa Arrows denoting the main Shoots
b Width of the River above the Falls 627 yards.
c Width of the River below the Falls 209. do.
Perpendicular hight of the Falls 16½.

MISSISSIPPI